PENGUIN BOOKS

SHAKESPEARE'S LANGUAGE

'A quite brilliant book ... *Shakespeare's Language* is the fruit of much study and of even more individual thought and feeling. In a better world there would be queues for it outside the bookshops and its author would be offered a seat in the House of Lords' Robert Nye, *Scotsman*

'An inspiring work' Tom Paulin, *Observer*, Books of the Year

'A beautiful and valuable book in the great tradition of Coleridge and Empson ... Sir Frank Kermode now occupies a position once held by Sir William Empson as the acutest interpreter of linguistic complications in the great scenes of Shakespeare'
Declan Kiberd, *Irish Times*

'A magnificent book, the honey of a lifetime's visits to the Shakespearean garden ... What a pleasure it is to read a critic so learned, so rammed with scholarship, who at the same time endeavours to read Shakespeare as a writer, fallible like any other'
James Wood, *Guardian*

'Frank Kermode is undoubtedly the greatest literary scholar of his generation ... The book is full of marvels ... dripping with unostentatious scholarship' Colin MacCabe, *Independent*

'Refreshing and informative, profoundly studious and at the same time bearing the happy mark of Professor Kermode's accessible style'
Muriel Spark, *Sunday Telegraph*, Books of the Year

'Such a scholarly book that it made me wish I had sat at the feet of its author and studied English with him'
Joan Bakewell, *New Statesman*, Books of the Year

'A stunning book ... that both critic and layman will enjoy'
Katie Donovan, *Irish Times*

'Kermode scrutinizes the poetry with an authority you would expect and with a vivacity and passion which is exhilarating'
Melvyn Bragg, *Independent*, Books of the Year

'"*Hamlet* is literature's greatest bazaar," says Kermode. It is a wonderful image, and appropriate to this book, through which one can wander at will, picking up this and that, brushing shoulders with strangers and friends, one's attention drawn both to unexpected treasures and to familiar joys, dazzled by the vigour and the life on show'
Richard Eyre, *Literary Review*

'Elegantly re-assert[s] the essential place of the Pleasure Principle, in reading as in writing, something most recent academic criticism has lost sight of' A. S. Byatt, *Independent*, Books of the Year

'A rich and stimulating discussion of how the Bard evolved from a dramatic poet into a dramatist ... blazing with insight and erudition'
Elizabeth Buchan, *Daily Telegraph*

ABOUT THE AUTHOR

Frank Kermode was born in 1919 and educated at Douglas High School and Liverpool University. From 1974 to 1982 he was King Edward VII Professor of English Literature at Cambridge University. He is an Honorary Fellow of King's College, Cambridge, and holds honorary doctorates from Chicago, Liverpool, Newcastle, Yale, Wesleyan, Sewanee and Amsterdam universities. He is a Fellow of the British Academy and of the Royal Society of Literature, an Honorary Member of the American Academy of Arts and Sciences and of the American Academy of Arts and Letters, and an Officier de l'Ordre des Arts et des Sciences. He was knighted in 1991. Professor Kermode's publications include *Romantic Image*, *The Sense of an Ending*, *Puzzles and Epiphanies*, *Continuities*, *Shakespeare*, *Spenser*, *Donne*, *The Classic*, *The Genesis of Secrecy*, *Essays on Fiction 1971–82*, *Forms of Attention*, *History and Value*, *An Appetite for Poetry*, *The Uses of Error*, *Shakespeare's Language* (Penguin, 2000), *Pleasing Myself* (Penguin, 2001) and an autobiography, *Not Entitled*. He has also edited *He Knew He was Right* and *The Way We Live Now* by Anthony Trollope, and *The Figure in the Carpet and Other Stories* by Henry James for Penguin Classics.

FRANK KERMODE

SHAKESPEARE'S LANGUAGE

PENGUIN BOOKS

PENGUIN BOOKS

Published by the Penguin Group
Penguin Books Ltd, 80 Strand, London WC2R 0RL, England
Penguin Putnam Inc., 375 Hudson Street, New York, New York 10014, USA
Penguin Books Australia Ltd, 250 Camberwell Road, Camberwell, Victoria 3124, Australia
Penguin Books Canada Ltd, 10 Alcorn Avenue, Toronto, Ontario, Canada M4V 3B2
Penguin Books India (P) Ltd, 11 Community Centre, Panchsheel Park, New Delhi – 110 017, India
Penguin Books (NZ) Ltd, Cnr Rosedale and Airborne Roads, Albany, Auckland, New Zealand
Penguin Books (South Africa) (Pty) Ltd, 24 Sturdee Avenue, Rosebank 2196, South Africa

Penguin Books Ltd, Registered Offices: 80 Strand, London WC2R 0RL, England

www.penguin.com

First published in the USA by Farrar, Straus and Giroux 2000
First published in Great Britain by Allen Lane The Penguin Press 2000
Published in Penguin Books 2001
021

Printed in England by Clays Ltd, St Ives plc

ISBN-13: 978–0–14–028592–5

www.greenpenguin.co.uk

Penguin Books is committed to a sustainable future for our business, our readers and our planet. This book is made from Forest Stewardship Council™ certified paper.

TO URSULA OWEN

AND ANTHONY HOLDEN

PREFACE

This book is addressed to a non-professional audience with an interest in Shakespeare that has not, I believe, been well served by modern critics, who on the whole seem to have little time for his language; they tend to talk past it in technicalities or down to it in arcanely expressed platitudes. Every other aspect of Shakespeare is studied almost to death, but the fact that he was a poet has somehow dropped out of consideration. Of course I do not mean that all modern writing on Shakespeare is rubbish; there has been plenty of high-class scholarship, here for the most part ignored. Anybody who wants to know in detail about the life of Shakespeare, the construction, location, and personnel of Elizabethan theatres, or contemporary methods of acting, will need more specialized studies. I have confined my attention as far as possible to my stated subject, without offering yet another general introduction to the plays.

My concern is for the most part with Shakespeare's dramatic verse. He was an accomplished non-dramatic poet, but his eminence depends on his work for the theatre and is emphasized by what has long been accepted as his superiority to the other dramatic poets of the time, though among them were theatre poets of high distinction, such as Marlowe, Middleton, Webster, and Jonson.

Such laudatory estimates are commonplace, and can be dismissed as hollow echoes of an obsolete and detested idolatry. But whatever else this book may be, it is not idolatrous; it shuns that ancient error as coldly as it avoids its modern counterparts. There are modern attitudes to Shakespeare I particularly dislike: the worst of them maintains that the reputation of Shakespeare is fraudulent, the result of an eighteenth-century nationalist or imperialist plot. A related notion, almost equally presumptuous, is that to make sense of Shakespeare we need first to see the plays as involved in the political discourse of his day to a degree that has only now become intelligible. These and other ways of taking Shakespeare down a peg seem, when you examine them, to be interesting only as evidence of a recurring need to find something different to say, and to say it on topics that happen to interest the writer more than Shakespeare's words, which are, as I say, only rarely invoked. The tone of these novelties is remarkably self-confident. The critics need to value their own opinion above that of many predecessors whose qualifications they might not in general wish to dispute. They have to treat as victims of imperialistic brainwashing Johnson, Keats, and Coleridge, to name only three. Of course if you can rubbish Shakespeare you can also rubbish these and comparable authorities; respect for them is merely another instance of our acceptance of unexamined bourgeois valuations. But in the end you can't get rid of Shakespeare without abolishing the very notion of literature.

On the other hand, the various forms of idolatry against which doctrines of this sort are over-reactions must also be deplored. There is no reason why we should not find passages and even plays that are routine and relatively uninteresting; a man who wrote so much, and sometimes in a hurry, might well, to borrow a phrase of Dryden's, have some flats among his elevations. In short, this book is by one who believes in the greatness of Shakespeare without what Dr. Johnson called "superstitious veneration," always remaining "on this side idolatry," like Ben Jonson.

Indeed, Jonson seems in this respect to have been the most balanced of Shakespearians. When he said that Shakespeare "wanted art" he meant the laboriously excogitated craft he himself developed, something we can admire in his work but do not look for in Shakespeare's. When he complained that Shakespeare "flowed with that facility that sometime it was necessary he should be stopped," adding that "his wit was in his own power, would the rule of it had been so too," we might want to vary his terms a little, but we understand him. Jonson read and thought a lot about poetry, ancient and modern. He believed it called for what we would call genius, even for a sort of divine madness, but also for hard labour. By proclaiming that Shakespeare was "not for an age, but for all time" he was crediting his friend with a high degree of genius, and he thought poets who had it were very rare: "only kings and poets," he remarks, as usual quoting an ancient author, "are not born every year." He himself preferred and practised poetry that showed the "labour of the file." Jonson knew that Shakespeare worked for his effects, that he had "Art," and that he learned from experience: "For a good poet's made as well as born."*

No modern critic can aspire to the authority of Jonson, but it should be possible to avoid both idolatry and counter-idolatry, always remembering the inevitable blemishes and also remembering that a true acquaintance with Shakespeare is as necessary to our culture as an understanding, however partial, of the greatness of Mozart or of Cézanne. All these artists are, admittedly, dead white males, and that, for some, is enough to discredit in advance arguments in their favour. Then there are those who refuse to value one text over another, a play by Shakespeare over an ephemeral contemporary pamphlet, or to see reason to offer the one a different form of attention from that accorded the other. The question of intrinsic or attributed value is admittedly a difficult one, but it vanishes when the object of concern is merely the interaction of all contemporary discourse in a context of political oppression and resistance. As I believe in the value of Shakespeare and, without ignoring historical issues, regard the plays as being about more than such issues, I shall not pay much attention to what are nevertheless the prevailing modes of Shakespeare criticism.

I have said something about almost all the plays. The years 1599–1600 seem roughly the time at which Shakespeare, already the author of several masterpieces, moved up to a new level of achievement and difficulty. There was a turning point, I think, and I associate it with *Hamlet* and with the poem "The Phoenix and Turtle." At about the same time, Shakespeare's company moved into the Globe Theatre. *Julius Caesar* was performed there, and *Hamlet* was written about then. So the second part of the book deals mostly with Globe plays, each of which gets a chapter to itself, except for *All's Well That Ends Well,* bundled in, for what I take to be good reasons, with *Measure for Measure,* and the two collaborative plays *Henry VIII* and *Two Noble Kinsmen.* Plays earlier than 1600 are in Part I. Dates can be uncertain, and some might want *Twelfth*

*Jonson's remarks on Shakespeare, and his general views on poetry, are in his *Timber, or Discoveries,* in Ian Donaldson, ed., *Ben Jonson* (1985), pp. 539–40, 584–85.

Night to be in Part II, but in my view it does very well where it is. The text used throughout is that of *The Riverside Shakespeare* (2nd edition, 1997), but I have omitted the square brackets used in that edition to indicate alterations to the copy-text. Now and again I have had to use some technical language when writing about texts, so I have added an appendix explaining the terms.

CONTENTS

SHAKESPEARE'S LANGUAGE

INTRODUCTION

Although a large proportion of Shakespeare's verse was spoken in the theatre, a fact that accounts for much that affected its extraordinary development, I am not, or not primarily, interested in purely theatrical matters, though I must occasionally have something to say about them. I am aware that I am writing against the current, since for many years now we have been urged to think of Shakespeare as above all a professional man of the theatre who was required to be a poet because in his time plays were mostly written in verse. In the early years of the twentieth century there was a sensible reaction against an old idea that Shakespeare was somehow too big to be thought of as submitting to theatrical limitations, that *King Lear* was too great for the stage, and so on. The reaction was necessary and beneficial. That he was essentially a man of the theatre and that he became a great master of dramatic forms intimately related to the playhouses of his time are facts that cannot be contested. He was not only a playwright but an actor, not only an actor but probably what we now call a director, and certainly a shareholder in his company. He must have spent a large proportion of his adult life in the Globe and other theatres, and it is therefore a scholarly imperative as well as a matter of general interest that we should have some idea of how things were done there, by promoters, actors, and directors (whoever they were), all of them constantly motivated by their obligation to please the audiences of the day. Generations of scholars have answered the challenge, and a lot is now known about the companies and audiences, about prompt books and parts, about acting styles and conventions, about contemporary fashions and contemporary censorship, even about which actors played what roles. The physical structure of theatres is better understood than it was fifty years ago. There is a Shakespearian archaeology. Not surprisingly, modern Globe theatres have been erected, and not only in Southwark. There is a perfectly decent one in Tokyo.

As a consequence of all this knowledge it has become a commonplace that only in performance can the sense of Shakespeare's plays be fully apprehended. It is also maintained on high authority that every production must "mine" something new from the text: "The life of a theatre," says the distinguished English director Richard Eyre, "should always be in the present tense." This is true, and the work of a modern director must always be to fuse the horizons of past and present; to read well and faithfully is always to read anew, but without introducing distortion. Eyre adds, "The life of the plays is in the language, not alongside it, or underneath it. Feelings and thoughts are released at the moment of speech. An Elizabethan audience would have responded to the pulse, the rhythms, the shapes, sounds, and above all meanings, within the consistent ten-syllable, five-stress lines of blank verse. They were an audience who *listened.*"*

"The life of the plays is in the language." Yet the language can admittedly be difficult, even baffling. This is obviously so for audiences coming in four hundred years after the event, but it must often have been true also of the original audiences, less because the language itself was unfamiliar (though much more so to us) than because of the strange and original uses an individual writer might put it to. It is true that the audience, many of them oral rather than literate, were trained, as we are not, to listen to long, structured discourses, and must have been rather good at it, with better memories and more patience than we can boast. If you could follow a sermon by John Donne, which might mean standing in St. Paul's Churchyard and concentrating intensely for at least a couple of hours, you might not consider even *Coriolanus* impossibly strenuous. And although Donne wasn't talking down to them, much of his language was familiar to his congregation.

We also need to remember how quickly the language of quite ordinary people grows strange, recedes into the past, along with other social practices

**Utopia and Other Places* (1993), p. 176.

and assumptions taken for granted in one age yet hard for a later age to understand. If you read or watch a Jacobean city comedy, say, for instance, Middleton's masterly play *A Chaste Maid in Cheapside,* you soon discover that for all the manifest life of the dialogue and the characters you are an outsider, missing jokes and implications—as perhaps, in the course of a generation or two, the allusions and jokes in the dialogue of modern soap operas will baffle the student and have to be looked up in a commentary. But the first audience could presumably follow most of it with ease and pleasure and without the effort it imposes on us. It is true that now and again Shakespeare uses a word neither the original nor the modern audience had ever heard before, which yet remains intelligible to both, as when Goneril (*King Lear,* I.iv.249) advises her father "A little to disquantity" his train. The dictionary records no earlier use of this word, and it did not catch on, but to the modern ear it has a disturbingly bureaucratic ring, rather like the euphemisms produced by government departments, and it must have surely struck the first audience also as a cold and official-sounding word for a daughter to use in conversation with her father.

But this coincidence of response must be thought unusual, and we have more often to deal with dramatic language that was almost certainly difficult even to the audiences for whose pleasure it was originally written. So we need to ask what "following" entails. It is simply inconceivable that anybody at the Globe, even those described by Shakespeare's contemporary, the critic Gabriel Harvey, as "the wiser sort," could have followed every sentence of *Coriolanus.* Members of an audience cannot stop the actors and puzzle over some difficult expression, as they can when reading the play. The action sweeps you past the crux, which is at once forgotten because you need to keep up with what is being said, not lose the plot by meditating on what has passed. Following the story, understanding the tensions between characters, is not quite the same thing as following all or even most of the meanings. Even modern editors, surrounded by dictionaries and practised in the language of the period, cannot quite do that, as almost any Shakespeare edition shows. There are passages, especially in some of the later plays, which continue to defeat learned ingenuity. Dr. Johnson, who liked Shakespeare best when he was writing simply, would struggle awhile with such passages and then give up trying, as he alleged Shakespeare to have done. ("It is incident to him to be now and then entangled with an unwieldy sentiment, which he cannot well express, and will not reject; he struggles with it for a while, and if it continues stubborn, comprises it in words such as occur, and leaves it to be disentangled by those who have more leisure to bestow upon it."*)

This is well expressed, but we, in our time, are unwilling to cut the knot so roughly. We are far from sharing Johnson's distaste for Shakespeare's more rugged and complicated passages; we have lived through a long period when much of the most favoured contemporary poetry has been defiantly obscure; so we are stimulated rather than put off by this. We tend not to discard what seems obscure but to find out something about it; we want to know not what is just going on in a general way but what the words mean, to understand the life of them.

As for the original audiences, Volumnia in *Coriolanus* remarks that

Action is eloquence, and the eyes of th' ignorant
More learned than the ears . . .

(III.ii.76–77)

and contemporary testimony exists to the effect that an onlooker, out of earshot, could still get the drift of a play, just by watching the gestures of the performers. But this kind of acting, which in any case had probably undergone severe modification before *Coriolanus* was first performed early in the reign of James I, was more demonstrative than we would care for; it may have helped the original audiences to keep up with what was going on, but it would simply make us giggle. Anyway, it does not help at all with the more complicated bits, which are beyond the reach of the most refined code of gesture, though it is vital to what came, around 1600, to be called "personation" rather than playing.

Personation, as Andrew Gurr explains,† meant something grander than mere playing or even acting; it related to a fuller representation of characters, sometimes of characters whose thoughts can plausibly be represented as rugged, involved, even obscure. Perhaps Volumnia was referring to oratory, closer to the old-fashioned playing that was aimed at a large popular audience. But in Shakespeare's plays, especially after about 1600, the life of the

**Johnson on Shakespeare,* ed. A. Sherbo (1968), p. 73.

†*The Shakespearean Stage, 1574–1642,* 3rd ed. (1992), pp. 99–100. The *Oxford English Dictionary* cites John Florio (1598) and John Marston (1602) as the earliest usage, and other citations suggest that the derivative forms of the word originated at about the same time.

piece, of the whole business of personation, is in large part not in the gesture but in the linguistic detail; we want to understand as much of this as we can. We don't want just to hang on to the general sense as if we were watching an opera in Czech.

The increasing obscurity of Shakespeare's language may be shown by the simple operation of contrasting the first of his tragedies, *Titus Andronicus,* with what is probably the last, *Coriolanus. Titus* immediately strikes one as much more "literary" than *Coriolanus,* which is as good an example as any of a work calling for intellectual virtuosity in hearers and even in readers. Here is a speech from *Titus;* it may be compared with the speech of Aufidius in *Coriolanus* (IV.vii), quoted below. Marcus comes upon his niece Lavinia, who has been raped and had her hands cut off and her tongue cut out:

Who is this? my niece, that flies away so fast?
Cousin, a word; where is your husband?
If I do dream, would all my wealth would wake me!
If I do wake, some planet strike me down,
That I may slumber an eternal sleep!
Speak, gentle niece: what stern ungentle hands
Hath lopp'd and hew'd, and made thy body bare
Of her two branches, those sweet ornaments
Whose circling shadows kings have sought to sleep in,
And might not gain so great a happiness
As half thy love? Why dost not speak to me?
Alas, a crimson river of warm blood,
Like to a bubbling fountain stirr'd with wind,
Doth rise and fall between thy rosed lips,
Coming and going with thy honey breath.
But sure some Tereus hath deflow'red thee,
And lest thou shouldst detect him, cut thy tongue.
Ah, now thou turn'st away thy face for shame!
And notwithstanding all this loss of blood,
As from a conduit with three issuing spouts,
Yet do thy cheeks look red as Titan's face
Blushing to be encount'red with a cloud.
Shall I speak for thee? shall I say 'tis so?
O that I knew thy heart, and knew the beast,

That I might rail at him to ease my mind!
Sorrow concealed, like an oven stopp'd,
Doth burn the heart to cinders where it is.
Fair Philomela, why, she but lost her tongue,
And in a tedious sampler sew'd her mind;
But, lovely niece, that mean is cut from thee.
A craftier Tereus, cousin, hast thou met,
And he hath cut those pretty fingers off
That could have better sew'd than Philomel.
O, had the monster seen those lily hands
Tremble like aspen leaves upon a lute,
And made the silken strings delight to kiss them,
He would not then have touch'd them for his life!
Or had he heard the heavenly harmony
Which that sweet tongue hath made,
He would have dropp'd his knife, and fell asleep,
As Cerberus at the Thracian poet's feet.
Come let us go, and make thy father blind,
For such a sight will blind a father's eye.
One hour's storm will drown the fragrant meads,
What will whole months of tears thy father's eyes?
Do not draw back, for we will mourn with thee.
O, could our mourning ease thy misery!

(II.iv.11–57)

The first audience would have had a very good idea of what Marcus is up to here. He is making poetry about the extraordinary appearance of Lavinia, and making it exactly as he would if he were in a non-dramatic poem. To a modern director the scene is something of an embarrassment: Marcus, instead of doing something about Lavinia, who, as his account of the matter confirms, is in real danger of bleeding to death, makes a speech lasting a good three minutes. Confronted with an obvious need to act, at first he wishes he could be planet-struck into sleep (as it happens, Shakespeare used a similar figure in *Coriolanus,* but with an entirely different force*). There is a neat

*II.ii.113: "And with a sudden reinforcement struck / Corioles like a planet." And compare *The Winter's Tale* (I.ii.201–4): "It is a bawdy planet, that will strike / Where 'tis predominant; and 'tis powerful—think it— / From east, west, north, south. Be it concluded, / No barricado for a belly." Here the planet is a compressed metaphor for female unchastity.

play on the antithesis gentle-ungentle. Marcus compares Lavinia to a lopped tree, and the blood pouring from her mouth to a crimson river. Since it pours also from her hands, she is likened to a garden ornament, a conduit with three spouts. Her breath, despite all the blood, is still described as "honey," as if this were an immutable Homeric epithet. Her cheeks are compared to the setting sun.

Marcus, a well-educated Roman in the hands of a well-educated English poet, aptly adduces a Senecan tag or proverb about unspoken grief stopping the heart. He is quick to see as apposite the story of the rape of Philomel by Tereus, which happens to be the myth on which the plot of the play is based (as the text often reminds us). But Tereus only tore out Philomel's tongue, leaving her the option of revealing her assailant's identity in a piece of sewing. The new rapist has taken notice of this and outdone him by cutting off his victim's hands as well. Marcus remembers Lavinia's voice and the sight of her hands playing on a lute, not omitting a reference to the music with which Orpheus charmed Cerberus in the underworld. We are not to think it absurd that he expresses a wish he could ease his mind by giving the culprit a good scolding. He leaves us in no doubt that he commands the means to explain why he finds the whole scene very upsetting, and even thinks of blinding Lavinia's father to spare him the same sight.

We should find this verse ridiculous, but insofar as it belongs in a theatre, that theatre is very different from the theatre of *Hamlet* or *Macbeth* or *Coriolanus,* and the task of the poet very differently conceived. We must not look here for plausible action, not even for plausible inaction or silent horror. In Peter Brook's memorable production of 1955, the speech was entirely cut; Marcus wasn't even on stage when Lavinia (Vivien Leigh) entered with red ribbons streaming from her wrists and mouth. That was a way of preserving the horror without the language that in the time of the early Shakespeare seemed a good way of representing it, a poet's way, but now embarrassing. Trevor Nunn, in 1972, cut twenty-nine lines from Marcus's speech, leaving us with neither one thing nor the other, but one really needs to choose, all or nothing; Deborah Warner, in her 1988 version, restored the whole speech.

The latest Arden editor, from whom I borrow the stage history above, is a keen advocate of the merits of *Titus Andronicus,* and he defends Marcus's speech by claiming to find in it an acceptable modern psychology. Marcus has to learn to confront suffering. "The working through of bad dream into clear sight is formalized in Marcus' elaborate verbal patterns; only after writing out the process in this way could Shakespeare repeat and vary it in the simple, direct, unbearable language of the end of *Lear:* 'Look there, look there!'... And a lyrical speech is needed because it is only when an appropriately inappropriate language has been found that the sheer contrast between its beauty and Lavinia's degradation begins to express what she has undergone and lost."* But this interpretation is surely as misguided as it is honourable. It may be true that the kind of thing we find in *Titus* was a preparation, something a poet at thirty might think right, given the sort of piece he was writing—a drama affected by the example of Seneca and, even more so, by the example of Ovid, who was the source of the Philomel/ Lavinia plot, as of much else in Shakespeare. *Titus* is probably his most learned play, and poets needed to be learned. But playwrights needed another kind of erudition than that appropriate to non-dramatic poetry. There was obviously an overlap of skills, but theirs was a different craft. It soon became apparent that the trade of the dramatic poet was different and increasingly remote from the conventional, bookish rhetorical display. Not that rhetoric was abjured, merely that it was powerfully adapted to a different task and greatly changed in the process. Of course prentice work in a more formal rhetoric could be thought as a useful, perhaps at the time an essential, preparation.

Throughout this scene Lavinia is perforce silent, and the only way of dealing with her silence was to give Marcus a very long speech. "Shall I speak for thee?" he asks. And he does. There was (as yet) no alternative. Shakespeare later found other ways of dealing with silence, not least in the characters of Virgilia in *Coriolanus* and Hermione in *The Winter's Tale.* Indeed, an increasing interest in silence might be thought to mark a general development away from rhetorical explicitness and towards a language that does not try to give everything away.

It is safe to say that at the time he wrote *Titus Andronicus* he simply lacked the means to do, or even to envisage, what he achieved later, and his treatment of silences is an illustration of this. Impossible on the printed page (in the sense that a blank space can stand in no relation to the absence of speech in a context of talk), silence can be a feature of oral rhetoric, and was proverbially valuable. "In plentiful speech there is always something to be censured," says a proverb. Loquacity was deplored, but held to be quite different from eloquence, which was praised, though perhaps not in women, where it

***Titus Andronicus,* ed. Jonathan Bate (Arden edition, 1995), pp. 62–63.

could be a sign of unchastity.* And silence itself could be eloquent. When nothing is said, runs another proverb, silence speaks. That silence could make a contribution to eloquence, that in the theatre you didn't have to lay everything out with the utmost explicitness and could treat silence itself as requiring many words (as in that speech of Marcus), was evidently a discovery Shakespeare made in the course of time.

The point is most powerfully illustrated in *King Lear* V.ii, when Edgar goes off to fight, leaving his father, Gloucester, on the empty stage while the battle proceeds in the distance. Gloucester says nothing at all. How long this silence continues depends on the director's skill or nerve. I first understood how amazingly bold this little scene was when I saw Peter Brook's 1962 production; Gloucester, horribly blinded, sat sniffing the air for an intolerably long time, in a silence only emphasized by the distant noise of battle. The silence ends when Edgar returns, defeated, and takes his father away: "Men must endure / Their going hence even as their coming hither, / Ripeness is all. Come on" (V.ii.9–11). Eleven lines, and a silence probably much longer than the speeches—a silence at the very heart of Shakespeare and not available to the author of *Titus Andronicus*. Lavinia, like Philomel, lost her tongue, but her silence must be volubly represented by the words of Marcus.

Coriolanus has Virgilia, described by her husband as "My gracious silence" (II.i.175); she speaks when she must, but is still silent by comparison with the sheer *noise* of the play, the military din of her husband and the language of the virago Volumnia; their kinds of eloquence are related to violent action as Virgilia's is to peace. Coriolanus himself professes to prefer deeds, which speak without voice, to words; what finally drives him into exile is his inability to tolerate the voices of the plebs, "The multitudinous tongue" (III.i.156), and what brings on his death is a wounding word: "Boy!" (V.vi.100–16). It forces him to scold (105) like his mother.

In *The Winter's Tale* Hermione, though happily talkative in the opening scenes, remains silent for sixteen years, in contrast to Paulina, who is "Of boundless tongue" (II.iii.92) and "bold of speech" (V.i.218). In the great final scene, when Paulina unveils the supposed statue of Hermione, Leontes is struck dumb. "I like your silence, it the more shows off / Your wonder; but yet speak," says Paulina (V.iii.21–22). Now there are competing silences on

*A remark of the female humanist Isotta Nogarolas, reported in A. Grafton and L. Jardine, *From Humanism to the Humanities* (1986), pp. 37–40.

the stage. Hermione continues hers; Leontes is struck dumb; Perdita speaks only to explain why she is kneeling. Leontes begins to contemplate the mouth of the statue: "What fine chisel / Could ever yet cut breath?" (78–79). Breath is silent but carries the possibility of speech. Hermione moves and embraces him. "Let her speak too," says Camillo (112). "It appears she lives, / Though yet she speak not," says Paulina (117–18), who has taken on the role of presenter for a sort of numinous climactic dumb-show. And at last Hermione speaks, breaking the long silence.

Such essentially dramatic silences are impossible in earlier drama that depends wholly on florid speech. Much has come to depend on everything not being said, and this is essential to the later Shakespearian development of character. At such moments silence and speech are complementary. We recall that the soliloquy, brought to perfection in *Hamlet,* is speech in silence, the speech of silence. An understanding of that fact was important to the dramatist, especially if he has been a non-dramatic poet who cannot offer a blank page but must always be talking, like Marcus in *Titus* or indeed Lucrece in *The Rape of Lucrece.*

Transformations from early work, where labour and practice have not yet made the necessary technical discoveries, might after all be expected in drama as well as in other arts—in music, for instance. We do not need to cite such exceptional instances as Beethoven, marked by the contrast between the first quartets and the last; musicologists chart this contrast confidently, deploring what they think is the momentary regression of Opus 74 to the manner of Opus 18 before progress towards the last quartets is resumed. They don't deny a relation between early and late, but they affirm an unpredictable profundity in those final works and might not object to its being represented as gesturing towards silence. The scholar Maynard Solomon suggests that certain youthful and ephemeral music of Mozart's—mostly serenades and divertimentos written between 1772 and 1776 for Salzburg entertainments (and possibly given only a single performance)—can be seen as early, undeveloped preparations, in themselves not particularly significant, for some highly original achievements of the composer's maturity.* The point can be made with specific examples. Susanna's fourth-act aria in *Le Nozze di Figaro, "Deh vieni, non tardar,"* is dramatically unusual for two reasons: the serenader is a woman and she is involved in a complicated,

**Mozart: A Life* (1995), pp. 122–23.

vengeful intrigue. The aria is high, pure, operatic Mozart, exquisite in itself yet actively involved in the ironic complexities of the denouement of an unusually contorted comic plot—thus an entirely theatrical piece, yet it might not have been possible without the precedent of that more or less routine Salzburg "social" music. The young Mozart wrote serenades in accordance with requirements quite other than those of the opera house. The pizzicato-accompanied melody, a familiar device reminding listeners of a strummed guitar or mandoline, perhaps not without a tone of irony even in Salzburg, became, as an element in the opera, music of which the apparent simplicity formed part of an extremely complex piece of lyric theatre. Considered simply as a serenade, Susanna's song may be the most perfect ever written, but we hear it in the midst of other, inexhaustibly varied, music, and at the climax of the tangled plot *("Eccoci della crisi al grande istante"),* subject to all manner of ironies, ethical, psychological, and political. We are not surprised to learn that Mozart made what was for him an unusual number of sketches for this aria; far from being a straightforward serenade it is a thread in a very highly wrought fabric (and in this respect a finer achievement than the serenade, with mandoline accompaniment, in *Don Giovanni*). Another illustration of the same sort: in *Così fan tutte,* Fiordiligi's enormously eloquent aria *"Come scoglio"* in Act I and her almost tragic *"Per pietà"* in Act II might well be found in an earlier *opera seria,* but they acquire quite different colours (and by no means the same colours) from their locations in this ambiguous comedy. Similarly the aria of Marcus in *Titus,* though a polished exercise, is a relatively simple matter considered as dramatic verse and compared with the complexities of *Coriolanus.*

These musical allusions are meant to suggest by analogy the comparable development in Shakespeare: his later language, and so his theatre, does not lose all contact with the eloquence of his early work, but moves deliberately in the direction of a kind of reticence that might, in relation to that speech in *Titus Andronicus,* be thought close to silence. Something of the old eloquence remains, but qualified now by its reduction to place in a context altogether more complex and ambiguous.

What happened in the fifteen years or so between *Titus* and *Coriolanus* is the main subject of this book. There were great changes in both dramatist and audience. Shakespeare became, between 1594 and 1608, a different sort of poet; as in the study of all artists, connections between early and late remain detectable, but the manner and purpose of his activities are transformed. Keeping the speech of Marcus in *Titus* in mind, let us look at one of roughly equal length from *Coriolanus*.

The exiled Coriolanus has formed a union with his former enemy Aufidius. They are marching triumphantly on Rome. Aufidius feels some anxiety, some mistrust of his Roman ally. He meditates:

All places yield to him ere he sits down,
And the nobility of Rome are his.
The senators and patricians love him too;
The tribunes are no soldiers, and their people
Will be as rash in the repeal, as hasty
To expel him thence. I think he'll be to Rome
As is the aspray to the fish, who takes it
By sovereignty of nature. First he was
A noble servant to them, but he could not
Carry his honors even. Whether 'twas pride,
Which out of daily fortune ever taints
The happy man; whether defect of judgment,
To fail in the disposing of those chances
Which he was lord of; or whether nature,
Not to be other than one thing, not moving
From th' casque to th' cushion, but commanding peace
Even with the same austerity and garb
As he controll'd the war; but one of these
(As he hath spices of them all, not all,
For I dare so far free him) made him fear'd,
So hated, and so banish'd; but he has a merit
To choke it in the utt'rance. So our virtues
Lie in th' interpretation of the time,
And power, unto itself most commendable,
Hath not a tomb so evident as a chair
T' extol what it hath done.

(IV.vii.28–53)

I shall discuss the language of *Coriolanus* in due course—its extraordinarily forced expressions, its obscurity of syntax and vocabulary, its contrasts of prose and harsh verse, its interweavings of the domestic and the military. For the moment we are concerned with this single example. Coleridge thought this speech "beautiful in itself" but called it "the least explicable from the mood and full intention of the speaker of any in the whole works of Shakespeare"—an obscure remark, but it's a comfort to know that even Coleridge had trouble following it, and also that despite its obscurity he thought it beautiful. He seems to be measuring it against some privileged prior knowledge of Aufidius's "mood and full intention," but we cannot tell how he came by this knowledge, which we lack. Aufidius is contemplating Coriolanus in a way that is remotely like that in which Marcus contemplates Lavinia. But he is deliberate, speculative, not painting a picture for the audience but trying to make clearer to himself just how mixed his feelings are, how difficult he finds it to take a determined position on the standing of his ally, who has been a bitter rival in the past and may be a rival again. Throughout the speech there is a blend of respect, even affection, and envy. He thinks Coriolanus will easily take Rome, and puzzles over the circumstances that led to the exiling of such a superman, asking why he could not "carry his honors even." He introduces some general considerations concerning the nature and risks of power. One knows roughly what he is brooding about, and in that sense we can, despite Coleridge's opinion, follow him. But the speech is very inward, the very opposite of Marcus's, which is intended to lay Lavinia's plight before the audience with all the colours of rhetoric. There is no rhetorical code that covers the brooding, the starts and stops of thought which are features of Aufidius's meditation. And it is certainly, ominously, obscure.

The simile of the osprey and the fish, a conventional bestiary illustration, is tersely adequate in its assertion of natural superiority; the oxymoron "noble servant" illustrates with precision the dilemma of Coriolanus. There follows a series of tentative explanations: "whether . . . whether . . . or whether": pride attendant on continuous success; inability to act in peace with the same assurance as in war—but note the strange synecdoches of "casque" and "cushion" (battlefield and senate house, represented by the military helmet and the cushion used by senators); and the hendiadys of "austerity and garb." Hendiadys is a way of making a single idea strange by splitting an expression in two, so that it calls for explanation as a minute and often rather sinister metaphor—a trick of which Shakespeare was for a time exceptionally fond and which he played most often in *Hamlet.** Most remarkable, and even

*See below, pp. 101–3.

more remote from the rhetoric of his early plays, is the device here used to simulate the movement of thought, the worrying over a perhaps insoluble problem by a mind animated by love and envy, a working out that takes precedence over clarity of exposition:

> but one of these
> (As he hath spices of them all, not all,
> For I dare so far free him) made him fear'd,
> So hated, and so banish'd; but he has a merit
> To choke it in the utt'rance.

One or other explanation must be right; in fact, Coriolanus has a touch of all these defects—no, not all, that is going too far; yet only one is needed to explain his fate; and even so one finds it hard to say so, his virtues being so great.

That is roughly what these lines mean, if one takes the antecedent of "it" in the last line to be the chief of the faults mentioned; if the antecedent is "merit," then Dr. Johnson's explanation that the merit is choked by his boasting about it is the right one. Philip Brockbank, the Arden editor, is hesitantly willing to admit that Johnson's reading points to a valuable ambiguity.* This seems to me unlikely, but the point is that given this new way of representing turbulent thinking, so different from plainly formulated thought, set out clearly and reinforced by elaborately illustrative and copious comparisons, obscurities will inevitably plague commentators as well as audiences. It is a new rhetoric, substantially established about the time of *Hamlet* and highly developed by the time of *Coriolanus* and the Romances. Sometimes it takes the poet beyond the limits of reason and intelligibility.

What should be said about this transformation? That it occurred, substantially, in the course of the greatest decade of English drama; that it happened in the writing of Shakespeare and in the ears of an audience he had, as it were, trained to receive it. We register the pace of the speech, its sudden turns, its backtrackings, its metaphors flashing before us and disappearing before we can consider them. This is new: the representation of excited, anxious thought; the weighing of confused possibilities and dubious motives; the proposing of a theory or explanation followed at once by its abandonment or

***Coriolanus,* ed. Philip Brockbank (Arden edition, 1976), p. 274.

qualification, as in the meditation of a person under stress to whom all that he is considering can be a prelude to vital choices, emotional and political.

It may be said that the gradual toughening up of the language, accompanied by a new freedom of metaphor and allusion and a rougher handling of the pentameter, is a well-known feature of Shakespeare's later work. That is so. But *Coriolanus* also illustrates another, subtler change, from the simpler expressiveness of the early plays to an almost self-indulgent, obsessive passion for particular words, their chimings and interchimings, their repetition. Of this, I shall have more to say later.

At some point, perhaps at school, perhaps during the "lost years"—the years when his movements remain obscure, though some now believe he worked as a schoolmaster in Lancashire—Shakespeare decided that he was to be a poet, at a time when poetry was, much more than it is now, thought of as a craft to be learned. There are many biographical conjectures as to how the young Shakespeare came to be involved in the London theatre, and it is usually assumed that he began work as a dramatic poet, then temporarily abandoned this career when the theatres were closed during the long period of plague in 1592–93, and turned his hand to other kinds of verse. But it seems at least as reasonable to suggest that he arrived in London intending to make his way as a poet not of the theatre but of the page. His first appearances in print were non-dramatic poems. *Venus and Adonis* (1593) and *The Rape of Lucrece* (1594) are indeed the only publications in which he ever seems to have taken a direct interest. He had found another source of income, patronage, which was perhaps more rewarding though not so easy to come by as work in the theatre, and he wrote accordingly, in the manner in which he had perhaps always hoped to work. At first, lacking a patron, he might, like many of his contemporaries, have managed to make ends meet by writing or collaborating in the writing of plays. It was roughly the equivalent of the modern practice by which young novelists write reviews to keep body and soul together while writing their books.

Shakespeare's early dramatic work was usually done in collaboration with other writers. It is not mere conjecture that he was a collaborator; the only example we have of a Shakespeare manuscript is his contribution, dating from some years after he first wrote for the stage, to the multiple-author play *Sir Thomas More* in the mid-1590s. It is at least probable that he collaborated in other plays, for instance in *Henry VI, Titus Andronicus, Edward III, The Two Noble Kinsmen, Henry VIII, Pericles,* the lost *Cardenio, Timon of Athens,* and, some say, *Macbeth.* The conditions would probably have been different for the later plays; for example, the collaborations with John Fletcher toward the end of Shakespeare's career would hardly have needed to be done under the Grub Street conditions that probably dictated the circumstances of his contributions to the earlier plays. Working with Fletcher, in a sense Shakespeare's theatrical heir, should have been easier and less destructive of individuality than the earlier collaborations, where the writers worked to complete their allocated share of a prearranged scenario.

There was a time when the imputation that the great poet was not the sole author of all the works in his canon was stubbornly rejected. But such a response is a side effect of the kind of idolatry that we need to forswear. There is little doubt that many plays in the canon are pretty well exclusively Shakespeare's, but even with those, one needs to allow for interference in the theatre.* The matter is less important than it is sometimes made to appear. Some now prefer to see works of art as the product not of a particular writer but rather of particular historical milieux, with specific technical and social constraints, merely "discourses" among all the other discourses current at the time. Without sharing that view, one can still argue that when we speak of Shakespeare (outside the restrictions of formal biography) we are talking about the plays and the poems, not directly about a man, though a man certainly wrote the verse; there is what Wallace Stevens called a "presiding personality," and it cannot be wicked or stupid to make occasional allusion to his presence.

Perhaps 1593 was the year when Shakespeare thought he could free himself from the drudgery of the theatre; he could even have welcomed the opportunity offered him by the long intermission of the plague. *Venus and Adonis,* an erotic poem in the fashionable manner, was a notable success, reaching its twelfth edition in 1636; and *Lucrece* also sold well. Calculated to please the educated taste of the time, these are works of a poet for whom the

*The question of collaboration is judiciously considered in "The Canon and Chronology of Shakespeare's Plays," in Stanley Wells and Gary Taylor, eds., *William Shakespeare: A Textual Companion* (1987), pp. 72 ff. The authors of this commentary on the *Oxford Shakespeare* note that something like half the plays composed for public theatres during Shakespeare's writing life were collaborative, and in plays written for the entrepreneur Philip Henslowe the proportion is two-thirds. If Shakespeare never, or only rarely, collaborated, he was almost alone among his peers.

rules of poetic composition were substantially the rules of rhetoric. One could still learn to be a poet; there was a craft to be studied. As Ben Jonson quite conventionally remarked in his *Discoveries,* "a poem . . . is the *work* of the poet, the end and fruit of his labour and study" (my emphasis). The poet required not only natural wit *(ingenium)* but exercise *(exercitatio)* and reading *(lectio)* "so to master the matter and style as to show he knows how to handle, place or dispose [the history or argument of the poem] with elegancy."*

You could train yourself to poetry, granted the initial gift of *ingenium,* and the first part of the training you endured at the grammar school, where you studied the *trivium* of grammar, rhetoric, and logic. This grammar-school equipment was applied, by Shakespeare's contemporaries, to the making of plays. John Lyly, some ten years senior to Shakespeare, is famous for what seem to us his rhetorical excesses. The classical authors of Greece and Rome, the "ancients," gave the best models for this "artificial" way of writing, and they were frequently invoked by poets, now dramatists, whose education was founded on them and on prescribed ancient texts and exercises in logic and rhetoric. Few now doubt that at Stratford Grammar School the poet spoke Latin and performed these exercises.†

Devotion to, or dependence on, the arts of non-dramatic poetry produces effects in Shakespeare's early plays that would seem strange in *Hamlet* or its successors, which on the whole, though not invariably, show more concern with the kind of art that conceals art. Consider, for example, the highly valued rhetorical device of repetition, which was given systematic treatment in the textbooks. It could occur at different language levels: thus alliteration is repetition at the level of letters; more extensive and varied effects are to be got from the repetition of whole words, and more again from phrases.‡ Anaphora is the repetition of a word at the beginning of a sequence of sentences or phrases; repetition at the end of them is called epistrophe. To repeat the first words at the end of the sentence or phrase is epanalepsis, and so forth. Textbook examples are

**Timber, or Discoveries,* in Ian Donaldson, ed., *Ben Jonson* (1985), pp. 582ff.

†There is a useful brief treatment of formal rhetorical devices in the Arden edition of *A Midsummer Night's Dream,* ed. Harold Brooks (1979), pp. xlv–xlviii. For more detail, see Brian Vickers, *Classical Rhetoric in English Poetry* (1970).

‡See Sister Miriam Joseph, *Rhetoric in Shakespeare's Time* (1947, reprint 1962), pp. 305–7, for examples from rhetoric books. J. Hoskyns in his *Directions for Speech and Style* (c. 1600) said that "in speech there is no repetition without importance" (quoted in L. Sonnino, *A Handbook to Sixteenth-Century Rhetoric* [1968], p. 157).

given from the Psalms (traditionally believed to be a thesaurus of rhetorical tropes) or Epistles: thus St. Paul's "When I was a child I spake as a child, I understood as a child, I thought as a child" (1 Cor. 13:11) was a familiar example of epistrophe.

There are some fine examples of repetition in the *Henry VI* plays. For instance:

> To carve out dials quaintly, point by point,
> Thereby to see the minutes how they run:
> How many makes the hour full complete,
> How many hours brings about the day,
> How many days will finish up the year,
> How many years a mortal man may live.
> When this is known, then to divide the times:
> So many hours must I tend my flock,
> So many hours must I take my rest,
> So many hours must I contemplate,
> So many hours must I sport myself,
> So many days my ewes have been with young,
> So many weeks ere the poor fools will ean,
> So many years ere I shall shear the fleece:
> So minutes, hours, days, months, and years,
> Pass'd over to the end they were created,
> Would bring white hairs unto a quiet grave.
>
> (*3 Henry VI,* II.v.24–40)

The distressed King, in a lull in the battle of Towton, is meditating on the life of the peasant, far exceeding his own in peace and comfort. It is a stock pastoral theme, and the speech is an artful exercise in pastoral. When it ends we have the allegorical episodes of the son who has killed his father and the father who has killed his son, emblems of civil war; and the scene ends with the arrival of the Queen and her train, defeated and in flight. It is a well and deliberately planned sequence of set pieces.

We may find this protracted exercise a welcome interlude in the fighting, and a polished rhetorical performance. There are comparable set pieces in later history plays, for example in *Henry V,* and, much later and in a different style, *Henry VIII;* but even as early as *King John* there are passages which one would never expect to find in the *Henry VI* plays, for example the passage in which the King orders Hubert de Burgh to kill the Prince:

K. JOHN. Death.
HUB. My lord?
K. JOHN. A grave.
HUB. He shall not live.
K. JOHN. Enough.

(III.iii.65–66)

This impressive division of one line into four speeches is surely a mark of change; language is here used not for elocution but for drama.

The point is that the development of the theatres and the pressure of the playwright's intelligence made it inevitable that new rhetorics or counter-rhetorics would intrude, although there would be lapses into the older manner, and instances when old and new conflicted like riptides.* In *Titus Andronicus* and in the early history plays these rules and schemes still govern the writing, even though the context is dramatic. The writing is not only more "artificial" (a compliment in the vocabulary of Elizabethan criticism) but much less obscure. I shall have more to say about these refined and occasionally excessive obscurities. They are also found in Shakespeare's late plays, but I must now go back to the beginning, or near it.

*This argument is not always accepted by Shakespearians. "Shakespeare did not begin his career writing rhetorically and artificially, and then by a steady and uninterrupted progression become more and more 'naturalistic'; instead, in certain respects, the verse in Shakespeare's middle plays is more artificially and self-consciously patterned than anything we find in the earlier work" (Wells and Taylor, p. 97). "A steady and uninterrupted progression" surely no one would claim; the demands of individual plays are various, and sometimes more formal rhetorical procedures are what the situation requires. "More artificially and self-consciously," etc. is excessive, but I feel that the difference between this opinion and my own is largely the product of the vagueness of such terms as "artificiality" and "pattern." Of course the "middle plays," whatever plays one may reasonably take this term to cover, are full of verse that could be described in this way, but they are already, for the most part, less dependent on the exhibition of such formal devices as analepsis, anaphora, anadiplosis, isocolon, and so forth. They certainly use rhetorical repetition, but they use it differently, and not primarily as a display of rhetorical resources. They have other business. And this is even truer of the later plays. There is what can be seen as "progression," although it is far from "steady and uninterrupted."

PART ONE

H*enry VI* is probably the earliest work of Shakespeare we now have. It belongs to 1590–91, a year or two earlier than *Titus Andronicus.* It seems likely that all three parts of it were the result of collaboration. No single hand had power over the whole; we know from Shakespeare's lines in the *Sir Thomas More* manuscript that another hand altered his brief contribution to that play; it can even be suggested that Shakespeare didn't trouble to look at the text into which his contribution was to be inserted.* It must have been assumed that at least there would be no wild discrepancy between the treatment given by the collaborators—perhaps Anthony Munday as the original author, with Henry Chettle, Thomas Dekker, Thomas Heywood, and Shakespeare producing "additions." Though it is difficult to argue from this manuscript survival to the whole practice of the theatre in the early 1590s, especially since the "additions" may have been made much later, it does tend to show that there was little room for adventurous writing by individual contributors.

If we examine a specimen of these plays, say *3 Henry VI,* we see at once that the traditions of rhetoric have not been forgotten.† The heat of battle cannot prevent Richard of York from expressing himself in similes:

*See John Jones, *Shakespeare at Work* (1995), p. 18.

†See the Arden edition, ed. A. S. Cairncross, pp. lxiv–lxv, for remarks on rhetorical procedures.

. . . all my followers to the eager foe
Turn back and fly, like ships before the wind,
Or lambs pursu'd by hunger-starved wolves.
. . .
With this we charg'd again; but out, alas,
We bodg'd again, as I have seen a swan
With bootless labor swim against the tide,
And spend her strength with overmatching waves.

(I.iv.3–21)

To a modern ear this seems, as a report on a military defeat, to be on the lazy or languid side, the swan particularly. It is hard not to think it absurd that in such a desperate extremity the Duke should seek out two comparisons with ships and lambs to describe the flight of his army, and even explain why the wolves were in pursuit. Likewise, the more far-fetched comparison of a swan swimming against the stream. An Elizabethan audience would not have thought these conceits useless ornaments; they were an accepted way of making one's points, of decorating, of enforcing pathos, and so on. Yet it is plain that as the stage developed its own habits of language these rhetorical devices came to seem inadequate. A new rhetoric swept away the old, which could henceforth be used only for special effects. When a little later York is offering Margaret his final view of her, he declares that she is

as opposite to every good
As the antipodes are unto us,
Or as the south to the septentrion.

(I.iv.134–36)

Strongly as he holds this opinion, and close as he is to death, he can still enforce his view by reference to the Antipodes and the seven stars of the Plough. His son Richard, remembering his father's courage in battle, says he attacked

As doth a lion in a herd of neat,
Or as a bear, encompass'd round with dogs,
Who having pinch'd a few and made them cry,
The rest stand all aloof and bark at him.

(II.i.14–17)

The animal figures do give a double impression of the father in battle: the lion ruthless with his easy victims, the bear more than equal to the dogs baiting him—an image from the bear pit, and the bear pit often served as a theatre; one more reminder to the audience that it is in a playhouse that derives from other forms of spectacle. (As late as 1613 Henslowe and the actor Edward Alleyn built the Hope Theatre precisely to alternate plays and bear-baiting.)

The lion and the bear make another appearance at II.ii.11–18, accompanied by more seemingly redundant animals. Clifford is counselling the King, Henry VI, against unnatural exhibitions of mercy:

> To whom do lions cast their gentle looks?
> Not to the beast that would usurp their den.
> Whose hand is that the forest bear doth lick?
> Not his that spoils her young before her face.
> Who scapes the lurking serpent's mortal sting?
> Not he that sets his foot upon her back.
> The smallest worm will turn, being trodden on,
> And doves will peck in safeguard of their brood.

The King congratulates Clifford on his oratory, "Inferring arguments of mighty force" (44), but he still rejects those arguments. And to call Clifford an orator is exactly right. These early plays, including of course *Titus,* are full of orations. In *3 Henry VI* the King is an orator, and so is the future Richard III, who has an enormous and important soliloquy at III.ii.124–95, in which he promotes himself as the villain-hero of the next play, *Richard III.* It is an oration crude by the standard of subtleties to come, yet it does establish character.

Queen Margaret has some terrific orations, the finest of which (V.iv.1–38) uses a sustained series of nautical images, ending with

> And what is Edward but a ruthless sea?
> What Clarence but a quicksand of deceit?
> And Richard but a ragged fatal rock?
> All these the enemies to our poor bark.
> Say you can swim, alas, 'tis but a while;
> Tread on the sand, why, there you quickly sink;

Bestride the rock, the tide will wash you off,
Or else you famish—that's a threefold death.
This speak I, lords, to let you understand,
If case some one of you would fly from us,
That there's no hop'd-for mercy with the brothers
More than with ruthless waves, with sands and rocks.

No use swimming, the sands and rocks are equally treacherous, and Edward, George, and Richard, the brothers, are the equivalent of them. It is all as elaborately structured as the great non-dramatic orations in *The Rape of Lucrece* addressed to Night, Time, and Opportunity.

Already in these early plays we see the use of stichomythia (dialogue in alternate lines) as a contrast or relief from the oratorical rhetoric. The operatic chorus of Queen Elizabeth, the Duchess of York, and Clarence's children in *Richard III,* II.ii, is splendid, but it truly belongs to this earliest phase of Shakespeare's work:

Q. ELIZ. Give me no help in lamentation,
I am not barren to bring forth complaints.
All springs reduce their currents to mine eyes,
That I being govern'd by the watery moon,
May send forth plenteous tears to drown the world!
Ah for my husband, for my dear Lord Edward!
CHIL. Ah for our father, for our dear Lord Clarence!
DUCH. Alas for both, both mine, Edward and Clarence!
Q ELIZ. What stay had I but Edward? and he's gone.
CHIL. What stay had we but Clarence? and he's gone.
DUCH. What stays had I but they? and they are gone.
Q. ELIZ. Was never widow had so dear a loss.
CHIL. Were never orphans had so dear a loss.
DUCH. Was never mother had so dear a loss.

(II.ii.66–79)

This ritual mourning wail undoubtedly has a certain power. Even the wisdom of the citizens has an archaic force, very different from that of future citizenries in *Julius Caesar* and *Coriolanus.* Everything seems to derive from a sort of shared dialect, and nobody sees any harm in making a point several times over, with some elegance of illustration:

3 CIT. When clouds are seen, wise men put on their cloaks;
When great leaves fall, then winter is at hand;
When the sun sets, who doth not look for night?
Untimely storms makes men expect a dearth.

(II.iii.32–35)

York's famous vituperative attack on Queen Margaret is no less elaborate (*3 Henry VI,* I.iv.111–49); likewise his son's account of his father in battle (II.i.11–24). The Messenger (himself a survival from classical tragedy) is allowed several heroic similes before getting round to reporting the death of York:

Environed he was with many foes,
And stood against them, as the hope of Troy
Against the Greeks that would have ent'red Troy.
But Hercules himself must yield to odds;
And many strokes, though with a little axe,
Hews down and fells the hardest-timber'd oak.

(II.i.50–55)

One simile strengthens another:

Their weapons like to lightning came and went;
Our soldiers', like the night-owl's lazy flight,
Or like an idle thresher with a flail,
Fell gently down, as if they struck their friends.

(II.i.129–32)

This is surely to make the points as one would make them in a non-dramatic poem, or possibly an oration, where the report and the pathos of the report can be enhanced by a succession of comparisons. There is no shortage of examples. (For instance, II.ii.9ff. shows a systematic simile production, this time of a kind that might have been thought to fall short of best practice; the rhetorician Puttenham, author of *The Art of English Poesie* [1589], might have judged it redundant.) Other cases of redundancy in the elaboration of simile are found in III.iii.135–40 and at the end of Richard's celebrated soliloquy, III.ii.124–95. Queen Margaret's tirade in V.iv.1–38 is an orator's working out of a detailed analogy of the current state of her affairs with the fate of an endangered ship from which desertion will not mean safety—a well-wrought oration, like that of Marcus in *Titus*. And for anaphora, the rhetorical use of repetition, there is Warwick's complaint to King Edward:

Alas, how should you govern any kingdom,
That know not how to use embassadors,
Nor how to be contented with one wife,
Nor how to use your brothers brotherly,
Nor how to study for the people's welfare,
Nor how to shroud yourself from enemies?

(IV.iii.35–40)

A skilful bout of stichomythia occurs in Edward's brisk and corrupt wooing of Lady Grey at III.ii.26ff. Here is part of it:

K. Edw. Now tell me, madam, do you love your children?
L. Grey. Ay, full as dearly as I love myself.
K. Edw. And would you not do much to do them good?
L. Grey. To do them good I would sustain some harm.
K. Edw. Then get your husband's lands, to do them good.
L. Grey. Therefore I came unto your Majesty.
K. Edw. I'll tell you how these lands are to be got.
L. Grey. So shall you bind me to your Highness' service.
K. Edw. What service wilt thou do me if I give them?
L. Grey. What you command that rests in me to do.

(36–45)

It might be thought that stichomythia was a route towards more naturalistic dialogue, but it is wholly faithful to an older rhetoric; strict or extensive use of it in Shakespeare's later plays, where the sense units habitually run past the line endings and often include half-lines, is barely imaginable. I cannot recall that Shakespeare ever used this device in quite this way again; it might have been tempting to do Richard's wooing of Lady Anne in a rather similar manner (*Richard III,* I.ii.68ff.), but that extraordinary passage is a good deal more varied; the value of the device was already, even before the story of the tetralogy was finished, becoming a thing of the past. Now we find single lines divided in three (a device of Seneca better worth imitating than some others):

Anne. Name him.
Glou. Plantagenet.

ANNE. Why, that was he.
GLOU. The self-same name, but one of better nature.
ANNE. Where is he?
GLOU. Here. *(She spits at him.)* Why dost thou spit at me?

(I.ii.142–44)

Shortly afterwards there is a volley of short lines, as if both players had advanced to the net (196–206). With the introduction of such resourceful variations we know we are in something like a modern theatre.

Richard III seems to have been a favourite with contemporary audiences, and was still called for in the next reign and the next; a performance is recorded in 1633. It is one of the oddities of the theatre of the period that a taste persisted for plays that were in obvious ways out-of-date; there was a hankering after the old ranting rhetorical style, for some raucous *Hamlet* or for early romances that must have looked quaint in the age of *The Winter's Tale* and *The Tempest* (which nevertheless owe them something, as *Figaro* owes something to the Salzburg serenades). It has even been suggested that *Macbeth* was written to provide another villain hero to replace *Richard III;* in fact, they appear to have coexisted in the same repertory, surprising though this may seem to us. It is perhaps worth noting that Kyd's *The Spanish Tragedy* (c. 1589) was refurbished by Ben Jonson about 1601 and continued to be reprinted until 1633.*

Not, of course, that *Richard III* did not deserve to survive. The famous opening soliloquy has all the wicked energy promised by the character in *3 Henry VI,* the wickedness being self-advertised, the manner serious yet undercut by ironies the audience can share in. It is the best opening passage in the canon thus far. Shakespeare was to become a virtuoso of openings, and this one may be a little crude compared with those of *Hamlet* and *Macbeth,* but it is all the same a great success. Margaret continues to curse effectively, though interrupted by Richard (another four-speech line, I.iii.234), and in I.iv Clarence has his great scene—perhaps the first in Shakespeare to deserve that accolade. Clarence has had a dream, and his report of it is studded with reminiscences of Seneca, yet they are not dead imitations but part of a new

*For the argument about Jonson's authorship of the additions to Kyd's play, see Anne Barton, *Ben Jonson, Dramatist* (1984), pp. 13–19. Jonson elsewhere disparaged the old play, defining an old-fashioned playwright as one who would swear that *Jeronimo* [*The Spanish Tragedy*] and *Andronicus* were "the best plays yet" (*Bartholomew Fair,* "The Induction").

conception. Imitation was another skill Jonson demanded of poets; here it is combined, as it must be, with *ingenium*. The effect is extraordinarily like Dante: he dreams that he is in the "kingdom of perpetual night."

> The first that there did greet my stranger soul
> Was my great father-in-law, renowned Warwick,
> Who spake aloud, "What scourge for perjury
> Can this dark monarchy afford false Clarence?"
> And so he vanish'd. Then came wand'ring by
> A shadow like an angel, with bright hair
> Dabbled in blood, and he shriek'd out aloud,
> "Clarence is come—false, fleeting, perjur'd Clarence,
> That stabb'd me in the field by Tewksbury . . ."
>
> (I.iv.48–56)

It is easy enough to see why this passage so impressed T. S. Eliot by "its use of infernal machinery." He claims that "the best of Seneca has here been absorbed into English," and contrasts the speech with one from Marlowe's *Dido* in order to demonstrate that it does something Marlowe could not do: "the phrase ["What scourge for perjury . . ."] has a concision which is almost classical, certainly Dantesque."* Steeped in Dante as he was, Eliot could not miss this echo. It is very unlikely that Shakespeare read Dante, and it is certain that he read Seneca, yet it is true that the passage sounds more like the *Inferno* than Seneca. The theatre was inducing its best writer to explore new styles—not to forget the more obvious splendours of a rhetoric apt to the first chronicle plays, but to find a more flexible syntax, to depend less on pre-existing rhetorical schemes, to do without the kind of formulaic writing that otherwise abounds in both *Richard III* and *Henry VI*.

This new note, heard in Clarence's account of his dream, has an eery, visionary quality, echoed long after in Eliot's own poetry—*trattando l'ombre come cosa salda,* treating shadows like solid things (*Purgatorio,* xxi). The work Shakespeare would do in the near future required this degree of virtuosity, of variety and concision. It is moving to reflect that in such a passage he silently affirms his place in a great tradition: the underworld encounter stems from *Odyssey* xi and *Aeneid* vi.

*"Seneca in Elizabethan Translation," in *Selected Essays* (1932), p. 124.

Rather less impressive are the occasional quasi-liturgical passages in *Richard III* which aim to generate power by formal repetitions, as in the scene where the ghosts of Richard's victims visit him in his tent at Bosworth (V.iii), each telling him, with appropriate variations, to "despair and die." ("And fall, thy edgeless sword. Despair and die! . . ." "Let fall thy lance. Despair and die!" "Thy nephews' souls bid thee despair and die!") Here the curses are interspersed with blessings on Richmond. It is all very Latin, and one is glad to find elsewhere a purely English joke:

> GLOU. So wise so young, they say do never live long.
> PRINCE. What say you, uncle?
> GLOU. I say, without characters fame lives long.
> [*Aside.*] Thus, like the formal Vice, Iniquity,
> I moralize two meanings in one word.
>
> (III.i.79–83)

Editors follow Dr. Johnson in adding "[*Aside.*]" to line 79, but this is wrong, for Prince Edward obviously has to hear what Richard deliberately mumbles. Shakespeare is imitating passages in the Mummers' Play, acted during traditional rural festivities, between the Doctor and his Boy, where a remark, not clearly heard, is impudent or insulting yet the explanation given is inoffensive—a trick revived by W. H. Auden in *Paid on Both Sides:*

> BOY. Tickle your arse with a feather, sir.
> DOC. What's that?
> BOY. Particularly nasty weather, sir.*

Editors have recorded instances of other Vice characters using this trick;† apparently the Mummers' Play was among the manifold sources of this stock character, his resemblance to which Richard is here exploiting. (There is a similar moment, when he teases Brakenbury in the first scene of the play, I.i.98–102.)

No doubt the most remarkable quality of this play is the complexity with which the character of Richard is presented; he is made something other than

**The English Auden,* ed. Edward Mendelson (1977), p. 10.
†See *Richard III,* ed. A. Hammond (1981), pp. 100–1.

the treacherous monster of the tradition begun by Sir Thomas More and in an obvious way required by the "Tudor myth," according to which he would be more simply the tyrant whom Richmond must overthrow in order to establish the Tudor dynasty. Out of the distorted materials of propaganda history there emerges the figure of the Vice, engagingly wicked; it was to emerge, much more elaborately, in the figure of Falstaff in *1 Henry IV.*

Increasing complexity in the verse of the plays matches increasing subtlety in their construction.* There are indications of the complexity of Shakespeare's mind even in *Titus,* not least in the freely invented and rhetorically effective additional scene of the fly killing (III.ii).† Such an episode, offering a rather oblique commentary on the main action, became a regular feature of the playwright's manner, and in *Richard III* one observes, in a play still committed rhetorically to the older styles, a new multifacetedness, a richer texture.

King John, another history play, of uncertain date but probably close to *Richard III,*‡ also offers a distorted view of its historical material. The reign of John did not have quite the contemporary political relevance of the story of Richmond and the establishment of the Tudor dynasty, but there did exist a favourable if mythical version of his historical role. He was represented as standing for England against the Pope and his allies, a myth consonant with Elizabethan propaganda, but in Shakespeare's play John is a defeated usurper, the true heir is murdered, and the hero, responsible for such celebrity as the play can boast, is a rather deviant character called the Bastard Faulconbridge. The characterisation of the Bastard is considerably more

*George T. Wright has some interesting reflections on the parallel between the complexities of iambic pentameter and of drama itself, indeed of the world at large: "Meter looks at least two ways: toward the sentence, with which it carries on its constant rivalry, and toward the larger world of character and character, whose relations it mirrors—ultimately to that world's structure of authority and resistance, and of inner selves and outer layers of reality (other person, family, party, state, cosmos)." *Shakespeare's Metrical Art* (1988), pp. 258–60.

†Here, as above, I assume an early date for *Titus;* opinion is divided on the question, and some critics place it after the period of plague of 1593–94, adducing resemblances to *The Rape of Lucrece,* which is certainly of that time.

‡The consensus is that the play is later than its shadow, *The Troublesome Reign of King John,* published in 1591, though some reverse the order. In 1598 *King John* was mentioned in a list of Shakespeare's plays, so if the consensus is correct, it belongs somewhere in the seven-year period 1591–98. If it was composed at the beginning, then it is contemporaneous with, among others, *Henry VI;* if at the end, *Romeo and Juliet* and *A Midsummer Night's Dream.* But no conjectured date is convincing.

advanced than any in the *Henry VI* plays or in *Titus:* he has a brisk dialect of his own that matches his sheer nerve; for example, when he repeatedly taunts Austria with the line "And hang a calve's-skin on those recreant limbs" (III.i.129, 131, 133, 199). It is he who makes the celebrated speech "This England never did nor never shall, / Lie at the proud foot of a conqueror, / But when it first did help to wound itself . . ." (V.vii.112–18). And it is he who utters the memorable reproach to Hubert de Burgh, who has agreed to blind the Prince:

> If thou didst but consent
> To this most cruel act, do but despair,
> And if thou want'st a cord, the smallest thread
> That ever spider twisted from her womb
> Will serve to strangle thee; a rush will be a beam
> To hang thee on . . .
>
> (IV.iii.125–30)

It is true that the Bastard, who rails against "commodity" while professing to cultivate it, is brave and loyal, but he is a complicated figure made up of incompatible elements, suggesting not a type but an individual. It may be too bold to suggest that with him a newly developed idea of character was introduced into Elizabethan drama, that he is the first of Shakespeare's characters to have just those gaps and inconsistencies that require one to see character as mysterious, as something to be argued about. One closes the gaps and unexplained divergencies by interpretation, as one must, though on a far larger scale, with Hamlet. It has been remarked that nobody else in Shakespeare talks as the Bastard does, and that his language "ridicules and undercuts the fustian of the play."* To say that is to make the play itself somewhat self-mocking, as if the author of *Henry VI* and *Richard III* had had enough of letting his characters talk like rhetoric books. There is something in this notion of undercutting, of presenting material that the play itself will covertly deride, fooling us into acceptance of what he himself rejects. Here, as in *Hamlet* and nowhere else before *Henry V,* Shakespeare reminds us that since we have entered a theatre, we have to take what the theatre offers. When in Act II the armies of France and England are stalled outside the city of Angiers,

*Herschel Baker, Introduction to *King John* in *The Riverside Shakespeare,* 2nd ed. (1997), p. 807.

the Bastard remarks that as the citizens "stand securely on their battlements" they look down on the scene as if they were an audience, safely observing the mock-dangerous goings-on, actors busily simulating warriors: "As in a theatre, whence they gape and point / At your industrious scenes and acts of death" (II.i.375–76). So the fake fighting and the rant are rescued as necessary to theatre, yet there remains more rant than the Bastard can wholly discount.

King John is also remembered for the intensity of the scene in which young Prince Arthur's eyes are threatened with red-hot irons (IV.i). A little later he throws himself from a tower and dies, whereupon other characters appear and, after failing for some time to notice the body, enter into a formal lamentation that could be matched in far earlier drama and seems in a different mode from the scene with Hubert. So the verse of the play, like its date, presents problems. Some passages sound almost like a parody of the old style: "O death, made proud with pure and princely beauty!" (IV.iii.35) depends on a simple, outmoded alliteration; the conjecture that the boy's body lies unburied because it is "too precious-princely for a grave" (40) has an old-style affectedness, drawing attention to its own unnaturalness. And when Salisbury protests against the King's determination to be crowned a second time—

> Therefore, to be possess'd with double pomp,
> To guard a title that was rich before,
> To gild refined gold, to paint the lily,
> To throw a perfume on the violet,
> To smooth the ice, or add another hue
> Unto the rainbow, or with taper-light
> To seek the beauteous eye of heaven to garnish,
> Is wasteful and ridiculous excess.
>
> (IV.ii.9–16)

—this looks almost like a joke, the last line commenting satirically on all the others. These self-mocked archaisms occur in a play capable of much more advanced dialogue and represent a mode of expression that, as we know by hindsight, could not survive much longer in a theatre shortly to be the site of the great tragedies. There is an inheritance, now almost extinguished, from narrative verse, suitable rather for Senecan-style recitation than for representations of subtler psychological forms of action. Early Elizabethan plays could be performed anywhere, for example in inn yards, and although this adaptability was never quite lost, the dedicated theatre encouraged writers to leave behind older ways of presentation. The interest of *King John* lies partly in that its archaisms coexist with hints of subtleties to come.

Early in the play Hubert makes the suggestion that France and England don't really need to fight, since John's niece, Blanch of Spain, could end the need to do so by marrying the Dauphin:

> That daughter there of Spain, the Lady Blanch,
> Is near to England. Look upon the years
> Of Lewis the Dolphin and that lovely maid.
> If lusty love should go in quest of beauty,
> Where should he find it fairer than in Blanch?
> If zealous love should go in search of virtue,
> Where should he find it purer than in Blanch?
> If love ambitious sought a match of birth,
> Whose veins bound richer blood than Lady Blanch?
> Such as she is, in beauty, virtue, birth,
> Is the young Dolphin every way complete:
> If not complete of, say he is not she,
> And she again wants nothing, to name want,
> If want it be not that she is not he.
>
> (II.i.423–36)

And so on, for many more lines. Perhaps the occasion excuses the extreme formality; the specious complexity of the last four lines may sound like later Shakespeare, the enigmatic and monosyllabic last line reminiscent of a great moment in *Troilus and Cressida,* but the conceit is slowly and elaborately expounded in the lines that follow, which do not sound like mature Shakespeare. The Bastard immediately ridicules the performance, but the Dolphin, the Dauphin, is quick to accept the plan and instantly expresses undying love for the lady:

> in her eye I find
> A wonder, or a wondrous miracle,
> The shadow of myself form'd in her eye,
> Which being but the shadow of your son,
> Becomes a sun and makes your son a shadow.

I do protest I never lov'd myself
Till now infixed I beheld myself
Drawn in the flattering table of her eye.

(II.i.496–503)

(Here "shadow," as often in Shakespeare, means "reflection," though it also implies the now usual sense, and "table" means the board on which a picture is painted.) The sentiment, though meant to suggest an exercise in courtly love, is dramatically absurd, and is at once deflated by the Bastard's aside:

Drawn in the flattering table of her eye!
Hang'd in the frowning wrinkle of her brow!
And quarter'd in her heart! he doth espy
Himself love's traitor. This is pity now,
That hang'd and drawn and quarter'd there should be
In such a love so vile a lout as he.

(504–9)

The beautiful Blanch is not over-enthusiastic, either. Yet there is more to be said of the passage than that it gives a cynical view of political and princely practices. It is a displaced love lyric that might be found in so different a play as *The Two Gentlemen of Verona,* and there is a certain absurdity in its intrusion into what is already an absurdly protracted proposal of dynastic marriage. The Bastard's acid commentary prevents our taking the lines as serious though stilted, and yet they reflect a theme that was of special interest to Shakespeare.

Other poets, including John Donne, made use of the conceit that lovers could see their own images in the eyes of the beloved, and others had punned on "son" and "sun," but here the two ideas are combined: the lady's eyes are so bright that he, the son, becomes a sun. He has never admired himself so much as when he sees himself as a picture drawn on the "table" of her eye. The picture is so wonderful that from being a shadow it becomes a sun, while the sitter, a son/sun because the son of the King, is reduced to mere shadow. The thought may be a bit confused, but the Bastard's is not, being a witty comment on the punishment for treason, which was to be hanged, drawn (disembowelled), and quartered. It may be noted that his speech, to complicate the irony, is presented in the six-line stanza (with a rhyme scheme ababcc) of erotic poetry, the stanza of *Venus and Adonis,* here used for a grotesque conceit. It is the only rhymed verse in the play, and can only be a sophisticated joke.

With the faded love talk of the Dauphin, which gives rise to the Bastard's comment, one might compare the scene in *The Two Gentlemen of Verona* where Proteus, finding Silvia "obdurate," begs a picture from her, while his jilted betrothed, Julia, eavesdrops:

> For since the substance of your perfect self
> Is else devoted, I am but a shadow;
> And to your shadow will I make true love.
> JUL. [*Aside.*] If 'twere a substance, you would sure deceive it,
> And make it but a shadow, as I am.
> SIL. I am very loath to be your idol, sir;
> But since your falsehood shall become you well
> To worship shadows and adore false shapes,
> Send to me in the morning . . .
>
> (IV.ii.123–31)

Here the talk, as so often in greater plays to come, is of substance and shadow: because Proteus cannot enjoy Silvia's substance he is reduced to the status of shadow (what Donne, in the "Nocturnal upon St. Lucy's Day," calls "an ordinary nothing") and will therefore have to be satisfied by making love to her shadow or image. Julia bitterly remarks that if the shadow were a substance he would certainly deceive it as he deceived her. Silvia catches the religious flavour of "devoted" (she is vowed to Valentine) and calls her portrait an idol, an image improperly worshipped, perhaps alluding to icons of the Virgin; but as it would suit Proteus to misbehave in this way, she will after all send him her picture. Now the portrait is both a shadow and a "false shape" (deceptive, like art as compared with natural substance).

This is much neater than the passage in *King John.* Perhaps its situation in a comic intrigue is more favourable than the context of the history play. There are tiresomenesses in *Two Gentlemen,* for instance in Proteus's old-fashionedly informative soliloquy: "To leave my Julia—shall I be forsworn? / To love fair Silvia—shall I be forsworn? / To wrong my friend, I shall be much forsworn," etc. (II.vi.1–43) or the pretty repetitions of "yet" (seven times in six lines at II.i.117). These tricks of dialogue are all right in their comic-romantic place, but the Proteus-Julia-Silvia exchange is slightly more serious. The cluster of ideas in it concerning substance and shadow has a widening semantical spread. Variations on the idea occur repeatedly in the *Henry VI* trilogy, in the Sonnets, in fact very generally; it was a favoured motif.* We shall shortly encounter a strange version of it in *Richard II.*

Richard II was composed some years later than *The Two Gentlemen of Verona,* and its dramatic language, in its relative modernity, provides a useful contrast to that of the older history plays. There are still passages that would not seem quite out of place in *Henry VI,* for instance the Duchess of Gloucester speaking to John of Gaunt:

> Edward's seven sons, whereof thyself art one,
> Were as seven vials of his sacred blood,
> Or seven fair branches springing from one root.
> Some of those seven are dried by nature's course,
> Some of those branches by the Destinies cut;
> But Thomas, my dear lord, my life, my Gloucester,
> One vial full of Edward's sacred blood,
> One flourishing branch of his most royal root,
> Is crack'd, and all the precious liquor spilt,
> Is hack'd down, and his summer leaves all faded,
> By envy's hand, and murder's bloody axe.
>
> (I.ii.11–21)

Here one cannot avoid the sense that the Duchess of Gloucester is performing an amiably elaborate exercise, working away at the vials and the branches, spilling, withering, and chopping at the right moments and tying all together at the end. Of course we always need to remember that in Shakespeare's time ornament was generally thought of as more integral to meaning than we are likely to think it; the notion had the authority of Aristotle.† Given that there was a conventional agreement about the place of ornament in the representation of emotion, and a conviction that the requirements of

*For a more elaborate discussion, see my *Forms of Attention* (1985), pp. 37ff.
†See Sister Miriam Joseph, *Rhetoric in Shakespeare's Time,* p. 39.

speech for virtually all purposes could be subsumed under a system of rhetorical figures and commonplaces, this kind of quite highly wrought writing might have lasted out the whole history of the Elizabethan-Jacobean theatre, and in some ways it did; as I have already observed, there were nostalgic, popular revivals of old, ornamented, rhetorical plays well into the seventeenth century. But we know that different ways of doing things soon developed, ways that involved breaking down the endlessly varied and repeated set forms in favour of a less settled representation of the movement of thought and emotion. We perceive change of this sort in *Richard II* rather more clearly than in *King John.*

John of Gaunt's famous scene (II.i.) opens with a burst of irregular and, one might think, intrusive rhyming, a trick that is at once caught by the Duke of York. The rhyming stops for Gaunt's eulogistic lament for England (31–68), a fine set piece on a theme popular at the time. The King himself is much given to rhyming, but that is because it better suits his habit of thought. Far from being simple ornament, it is part of the stylistic resource of the play. For *Richard II* has a new variety and flexibility. Take, for instance, the speech of Richard's favourite, Bushy, to the Queen:

> Each substance of a grief hath twenty shadows,
> Which shows like grief itself, but is not so;
> For sorrow's eyes, glazed with blinding tears,
> Divides one thing entire to many objects,
> Like perspectives, which rightly gaz'd upon
> Show nothing but confusion; ey'd awry
> Distinguish form; so your sweet Majesty,
> Looking awry upon your lord's departure,
> Find shapes of grief, more than himself, to wail,
> Which, look'd on as it is, is nought but shadows
> Of what it is not; then, thrice-gracious Queen,
> More than your lord's departure weep not—more is not seen,
> Or if it be, 'tis with false sorrow's eye,
> Which for things true weeps things imaginary.
>
> (II.ii.14–27)

Bushy is *thinking;* he has hit upon a difficult analogy and is working it out as cleanly as he can. The poet who wrote this speech is the poet of many difficult sonnets and, in time to come, of "The Phoenix and Turtle." He has some feeling for Bushy, who is kindly urging the Queen not to multiply her woes (she has spoken of "some unborn sorrow" that seems to threaten her [10]), and the tenor of what he says is clear enough: the substantial woe is her sorrow at the departure of Richard, and all the others are mere shadows of it. Tears of sorrow may impair the sight and make us suppose we can see several objects rather than just one, the important one, breaking its unity up into several elements. It is a neat and not obvious analogy. Developing this idea, Bushy thinks of "perspectives," meaning those anamorphic pictures (of which the most famous is probably Holbein's *The Ambassadors*) which offer a different image when viewed from the side (awry) rather than from directly in front. Later, in the seventeenth century, there were secret memorial portraits of King Charles I in which one could see nothing without the aid of a prism, a device which undistorted, as it were, the confusion before one's eyes. Indeed, "rightly" may be misleading in Bushy's speech, since the "right" view of a "perspective" of this kind is not from the front, the approach that seems to be meant here.

So Bushy, courteously developing his analogy, makes something of a muddle. The Arden editor, Peter Ure,* remarks that there were actually two kinds of perspective, only one of which could be thought to give an effect like that attributed to the Queen's tears. This is the device sometimes called a "multiplying-glass," as Webster illustrates in Flamineo's speech against jealousy in *The White Devil* (I.ii): "I have seen a pair of spectacles fashioned with such perspective art, that, lay down but one twelve pence o' the board, 'twill appear as if there were twenty, and see your wife tying her shoe, you would imagine twenty hands were taking up of your wife's clothes, and this would put you into a horrible causeless fury." This contrast of substance and shadow ("What is your substance, whereof are you made / That millions of strange shadows on you tend?" [Sonnet 53]) seems, as I have said, to be a recurring preoccupation of the poet. But if Bushy is thinking of multiplying-glasses, he seems also to be thinking of anamorphoses, and argues that the Queen has been eyeing the substance "awry," whereas his main contention is that she has wrongly viewed it "rightly."

If I myself am viewing the passage rightly, it is one of a kind not infrequently to be found in Shakespeare, where a complicated idea fails to find perfect expression—the kind of thing Dr. Johnson had in mind when he

***Richard II* (Arden edition, 1956), p. 70.

wrote the words I quoted in the Introduction. Johnson liked Shakespeare best when he was least rugged, but on the whole we, after the best part of a century of modernism, do not share this view, and are inclined to discover depth where Johnson found muddle, and in the sounding of that depth we bestow our leisure. The exciting thing about Bushy's speech is that in it we find Shakespeare struggling with a sentiment rendered stubborn by the circumstance that the speaker appears to be thinking, is doing his intellectual best to get his consolation across, and is getting slightly muddled in the process, the slight muddle being a by-product of the effort to represent intellection, or rather to *do* it. Bushy is consoling the Queen, and there were rhetorical rules for consolation, but he is not using them. We are rather a long way from the lamentations in Act I of the Duchess of Gloucester, who is much more at home in the old history-play tradition, into which Bushy's speech is almost an intrusion.

This is not the place to consider the character of Richard II except to remark that he has a special way of talking. All the Shakespeare kings (except on occasion Henry VI) profess assurance in their kingship, and some emphasise its sacredness; they are also inclined to dwell on the intolerable responsibilities and insecurities of their state. But Richard II alone has a habit of studying himself from the outside, as it were, a habit emblematised in the scene where he sends for a looking-glass (IV.i). When he smashes his reflection, his "shadow," it is as if he was destroying his substance. In a sense he is always calling for a mirror, finding in his reflection a king stripped of all his belongings (III.iii.142ff.), seeing himself as an analogue of Christ, betrayed by Judases and condemned by Pilates (IV.i.239–40), developing, in quite the old style, here beautifully appropriate, the figure of the two buckets (IV.i.184ff.).

The wonderful long soliloquy of the King in prison is truly transitional, for the occasion of such a lament resembles others in the earlier plays, until it becomes clear that something else is happening, that the elaborations of figure are not simply prefabricated and laid out neatly before us but hammered out. It begins:

> I have been studying how I may compare
> This prison where I live unto the world;
> And for because the world is populous,
> And here is not a creature but myself,
> I cannot do it; yet I'll hammer it out.

My brain I'll prove the female to my soul,
My soul the father, and these two beget
A generation of still-breeding thoughts;
And these same thoughts people this little world,
In humors like the people of this world:
For no thought is contented. The better sort,
As thoughts of things divine, are intermix'd
With scruples and do set the word itself
Against the word,
As thus: "Come, little ones," and then again,
"It is as hard to come as for a camel
To thread the postern of a small needle's eye."

(V.v.1–17)

He goes on to reflect that after all it was better to be a king than to be in his present state of penury, but that to resume his kingship, move back in time, would be to be once more unkinged by Bolingbroke, and so to be nothing. In conclusion:

Nor I, nor any man that but man is,
With nothing shall be pleas'd, till he be eas'd
With being nothing.

(39–41)

At this point, unexpectedly, there is music, but the music is faulty and gives rise to a moralising meditation on the broken time of his own life. The figuration is elaborate and also obscure:

For now hath time made me his numb'ring clock:
My thoughts are minutes, and with sighs they jar
Their watches on unto mine eyes, the outward watch,
Whereto my finger, like a dial's point,
Is pointing still, in cleansing them from tears.

(50–54)

The comparison is more extensive than this quotation shows, and is not easy to follow. His thoughts, ticking constantly, do the work of the minute hand, and his finger is like the gnomon of a sundial, always touching his eyes to cleanse them of tears. The trouble arises from the word "watch," perhaps originally meaning the state of being awake, as the clock always is; his eyes are also a kind of watch (they watch the world, perhaps also are sleepless). The *Oxford English Dictionary* quotes the passage to illustrate the sense "dial or clock-face." The now predominant sense of a pocket timepiece was available in Shakespeare's time but hardly seems relevant here, and the use of the word to denote what we think of as clocks persisted into the nineteenth century. The succession of conceits, though it sounds vaguely systematic, is surely very obscure—entangled in the semantics of "watch."

No other speech in Shakespeare much resembles this one, in which "the word" is truly set "Against the word." The tone is quietly meditative, but the arguments are hammered out. There is none of that furious thinking we associate with some of Hamlet's soliloquies, much less is there any promise of the tumult of Aufidius's thought in *Coriolanus* (IV.vii). Richard establishes an equation between thoughts in the little world of man's mind, generated by the interaction of female brain and male soul, and people in the greater world, generated in the usual way. Then he begins to describe different categories of thoughts as if they were people, all discontented. The "better" thoughts concerned with religion are troubled, when they set one word against another, by apparent contradictions in the Gospels (Matthew 19:14, 24). As it happens, the Duchess of York has just used the expression "sets the word itself against the word" (V.iii.122), and the poet may have been struck by the other sense of "word," meaning the word of God, an association that tempted him to introduce this comment on the conflict between the Gospel texts. Now he illustrates other sources of mental discontent: ambitious thoughts and stoical thoughts. These "still-breeding" thoughts are again compared to "many people"; and Richard sees himself as playing all their parts, again, even in this moment of quiet contemplation, seeing himself from the outside, as an actor who once played the king. Such is his discontent that nothing can ease it except the nothing that is death.

A comparison of this soliloquy with those Shakespeare wrote earlier (say, of Richard III) and later (of Hamlet and Macbeth) shows it to be very much in the middle. Like Bushy's consolatory speech, it has little tangles in it, signs however of high intelligence at work, signs of a language formidably changing to meet greater challenges. Shakespeare in this mood can hardly avoid being difficult; one might foretell, from this point of vantage, a hugely different style, a fuller use of a mind increasingly trained to think dramatically. The rewards are very great, though tangles must still be expected.

In the *Henry IV* plays that follow *Richard II* there is notable change. The verse is for the most part workmanlike, it carries on the chronicle, and it allows for strong representations of individual habits and affectations of speech, like those of Glendower and Hotspur. In *I Henry IV* Hotspur is given a sort of anti-poetry, a contempt for poetry as flummery and affectation:

I had rather hear a brazen canstick turn'd,
Or a dry wheel grate on the axle-tree,
And that would set my teeth nothing on edge,
Nothing so much as mincing poetry.

(III.i.129–32)

This, despite its theme, is of course poetry, written at about the same time as Donne's harsh satires, a time when harshness was valued and exploited for its rejection of the fashionable lyric modes. It is set against Glendower's more courtly style, acquired while he was learning to frame "to the harp / Many an English ditty lovely well" (121–22), and also depending on vatic or bardic affectations ("at my birth / The front of heaven was full of fiery shapes" [36–37]) and on the association of poetry with magic ("I can call spirits from the vasty deep" [52]). Hotspur's poetic resources are considerable, though different, as his account of the foppish courtier on the battlefield testifies:

neat, and trimly dress'd,
Fresh as a bridegroom, and his chin new reap'd
Show'd like a stubble-land at harvest-home.
He was perfumed like a milliner,
And 'twixt his finger and his thumb he held
A pouncet-box . . .

(I.iii.33–38)

Here the similes are terse, as if to demonstrate that extending them decoratively in the old manner was false and unreal. And again language is in the service of characterisation.

Of all the characters in the play Hotspur, the anti-poet, has the strongest lines, the most intense metaphors: "Were it good / To set the exact wealth of all our states / All at one cast? to set so rich a main / On the nice hazard of one doubtful hour?" (IV.i.45–48)—where "hazard" is both the doubtful outcome of battle and the game of dice so named, and "exact" has the sense of "total" but also of treasure exacted at cost for the conduct of war.* A "main" is a winning throw by the banker at dice (and so a loss to the gambler), but it could also mean "demesnes," or estates, and also, perhaps more significantly, a cock-fight: all these senses seem to be rather turbulently included in Hotspur's speech. He is capable of rant:

> By heaven, methinks it were an easy leap,
> To pluck bright honor from the pale-fac'd moon,
> Or dive into the bottom of the deep,
> Where fadom-line could never touch the ground,
> And pluck up drowned honor by the locks . . .
>
> (I.iii.201–5)

This passage is not helped by the simple antithesis of "bright" and "pale-fac'd," nor by the rhyme, nor by the explanation of how deep the deep is. But it is also in character, and if one calls much of the verse of the play "serviceable" it is not with an intention to diminish it. Like all chronicles, however simplified the action, there is in *I Henry IV* a great deal of historical and political talk to be recorded, business to be got through, and the verse is here well adapted to this end.

However, the principal innovation in *1 Henry IV,* of course followed up in its successor, is its greatly increased dependence on prose. According to Marvin Spevack,† 45 percent of the play is in prose, and the figure for *2 Henry IV* is 52 percent. The contrast is obvious with the *Henry VI* plays, where Parts 1 and 3 contain almost no prose and the greater frequency of prose in Part 2 (16 percent) is entirely explained by the scenes of the Jack Cade rebellion (trouble-seeking plebeians don't speak in verse). No play earlier than *1 Henry IV* has more than 32 percent prose. (*Love's Labor's Lost* is also remarkable in

*One of the fruits of education at the Stratford Grammar School was a familiarity with the original Latin senses of certain words. See Hilda M. Hulme, *Explorations in Shakespeare's Language* (1962), Chap. V, "'Latin' Reference in Shakespearean English," pp. 151–201.

†*A Complete and Systematic Concordance to the Works of Shakespeare,* 6 vols. (1968).

that of its verse lines 66 percent are rhymed, a proportion unapproached by any other play except *A Midsummer Night's Dream,* where the figure is 52 percent).

Shakespeare was now entering a period during which he was to use prose far more. *The Merry Wives of Windsor* reaches 87 percent, *Much Ado about Nothing* 42 percent, *Twelfth Night* 61 percent; these are comedies, and special reasons can be found for their attachment to prose, but it is worth noting that whereas the first tragedy, *Titus Andronicus,* has little prose (1 percent), *Hamlet* has 27 percent and *Coriolanus* 22 percent.*

These percentages are admittedly without much significance until one allows that there may be particular needs of genre or other circumstances for using prose, and it is not to be expected that the proportion of prose should steadily rise. (*The Merry Wives* has more prose than any other play, yet it is more or less contemporary with the *Henry IV* plays; it is domestic comedy as against national history.)

The plague years of 1592–93 are sometimes called a "watershed," and the Oxford editors surmise that only six plays—the *Henry VI* trilogy, *The Taming of the Shrew, Titus Andronicus,* and *Two Gentlemen of Verona*—were written before the plague enforced the closing of the theatres.† Of these plays three are "histories" and one a tragedy. There was no sharp generic distinction between histories and tragedies, so it is notable that in these early works prose was essentially a comic medium. It would be difficult to think of Launce in *The Two Gentlemen of Verona* as a verse-speaker. So there are clear enough demarcations among these early pieces. After they were written it appears that Shakespeare, now working on his long poems, had no occasion to use prose at all (*Venus and Adonis* and *The Rape of Lucrece* are of course composed entirely in stanzaic verse), and he did not resume the practice of prose until some time later; *King John* and *Richard II* have no prose at all. So its relative predominance in the *Henry IV* plays may seem to need explaining.

The explanation is, in short, Falstaff. It is noteworthy that the extravagances of Falstaff, and Prince Hal's in response, have themselves the effect of parodying older ways of dramatic writing. "The fortune of us that are the moon's men doth ebb and flow like the sea, being govern'd, as the sea is, by the moon" (I.ii.31–33) is a figure ingeniously continued, and might have been

*As reported in Wells and Taylor, *A Textual Companion,* p. 96.
†Wells and Taylor, *A Textual Companion,* p. 97.

spelled out in verse. Their dialogue is often a farcical competition in simile-making:

> FAL. 'Sblood, I am as melancholy as a gib cat or a lugg'd bear.
> PRINCE. Or an old lion, or a lover's lute.
> FAL. Yea, or the drone of a Lincolnshire bagpipe.
> PRINCE. What sayest thou to a hare, or the melancholy of Moor-ditch?
>
> (I.ii.73–78)

Here the range of comparison is wide, though mostly from animal lore—a castrated cat, a baited bear, a mangy lion—and then, with a brief switch out of the bestiary, a bagpipe; then again a hare, proverbially a melancholy animal, and "Moor-ditch," associated with melancholy because of its muddy dreariness. "Most unsavory similes," says Falstaff, accusing the Prince also of "damnable iteration."

Fertility and quickness of wit distinguish Falstaff, who is never without some allusion to his fatness, his immorality, or premonitions of his probable end. If he represents Carnival, he needs to make us collude in riot, when others will sound as absurdly witty as he is, and so his language must be riotous. And if we are not to be ashamed of our collusion, the riotous language must show quickness of mind and an allusive range we can admire or take credit for understanding. The Master of the Revels at an Inn of Court might have sought such virtuosity of Carnival language, and a court fool might have risked such jokes against the true Prince. But carnival ends, social discipline is resumed: "I know thee not, old man . . ." (*2 Henry IV,* V.v.47). Now the old man must act his age, and not behave as a young one might, were he sufficiently supplied with the kind of information necessary to the making of intelligent jokes. There is no need to stress the deep inventiveness of Falstaff's prose, at its best to be thought of as poetry. And nothing becomes him more than the Hostess's posthumous tribute to him (*Henry V,* II.iii.9–26), a linguistically more resourceful, more pathetic, and also of course funnier eulogy than any of the verse laments in the early histories.

The invention of Pistol for *2 Henry IV,* and his development in *Henry V,* seems particularly apt and ingenious, for he reflects directly on the old language, garbling or imitating Marlowe, using verse to demonstrate the difference between his intelligence and Falstaff's; his bragging and blustering need the old verse, not the new prose. This is as finely conceived an idea as the character of Shallow, with his endless senile talk about his youth, which is there to make Falstaff uneasy. The scholar John Jones has drawn attention to a small change that was made in *2 Henry IV:* where the Quarto of 1600 has Falstaff saying, "No more of that, Master Shallow" and the Folio version has "No more of that, good Master Shallow, no more of that" (III.ii.196). He attributes this and other changes in the passage to Shakespeare's revising hand, and certainly the alteration colours the scene in which it occurs: it is as if the author wished to show Falstaff, now slightly sadder, slightly more presumptuous, and slightly more anxious, trying to stop Shallow from mumbling on about the sort of episode he would prefer to forget or did not need to remember, there having been many more Jane Nightworks since that one. As Jones remarks, it is a change about which anybody is entitled to have a theory, though the theory of authorial revision is very attractive, and as one disbeliever reluctantly admits, the revised version "does sound like Falstaff."*

It is generally agreed that the Quarto was printed from Shakespeare's "foul papers," but since it is obvious that the later Folio has material not found in the Quarto, divergent explanations of these changes and additions are regularly offered. Not all scholars would allow that this particular change in the Folio was an authorial revision. The Oxford editors consider the theory that the compositor was adding words to "stretch copy," but they finally agree that the change was Shakespeare's work.† Perhaps it is in such tiny details that one may approach an understanding as to how character can be invented by using the resources of language, a study Jones's book does much to facilitate.

Of *Henry V,* a play in many respects unloveable but of cunning construction and impressive linguistic resource, I will say no more than that it provides what was needed, rhetorically, to round off the chronicles and to take us to another watershed, the opening of the Globe Theatre, with all that resulted from that move across the Thames. The plays were now being performed in a specialised, custom-built space; all that was done and said there was done and said in a large building designed for the purpose, and by actors whose craft had rapidly developed, been "reformed," in the direction approved of by Hamlet in his talk with the Players.

**Shakespeare at Work,* pp. 1–3.

†Wells and Taylor, *A Textual Companion,* p. 362.

I have hurried on to the Globe and my main interest, which is in the plays written from 1599 on, but I shall add something about pre-Globe plays other than the histories. *Titus Andronicus* is, fairly enough, the least admired of Shakespeare's tragedies, yet it has been said that in its time it might have seemed a great achievement. It was certainly popular, going into three editions, the last as late as 1611. Later it was so despised that many sought to attribute it to some other author. Modern critics have found reasons to admire it, mostly in scenes that are in a way inessential to the main bloody plot, with its rapes, amputations, and murders, not to speak of the grisly feast that provides Titus with his revenge on Tamora. The endless horrors can be justified if one thinks of them as in some way delicately orchestrated ("the horrible dance of violence has a viciously playful beauty"*), and there may be no harm in admitting a certain risibility in such scenes as the one that contains the stage direction "Enter a Messenger with two heads and a hand." Indeed, the whole play, including the wonderful wickedness of Aaron, has, despite its rhetorical refinements, the sort of appeal we associate with old Sweeney Todd–like melodramas, though the verse allows us to think of this play as contemporary with *The Rape of Lucrece.* But in the scene where the handless Lavinia looks through the small boy's books for Ovid's account of the rape of Philomela (IV.i), and in the one where Titus makes his friends fire arrows bearing letters to the gods and interrogates a clown (IV.iii)—of the tribe that will make later appearances in *Hamlet* and *Antony and Cleopatra* as well as in the comedies—we feel the framework of the horror story stretched, as *Hamlet* stretched the canvas of the old lost *Hamlet* of a dozen years earlier. The Clown scene is in prose, a better medium for jests and sometimes, as Shakespeare perhaps found out in writing this scene, for pathos. The grief of great ones may be given properly enhanced expression, not only by huge speeches, but by encounters with prose speakers whose language is marked by malapropisms, whose sympathy glances awry, since it is not offered in the right noble dialect. The effect is often to induce us to think more proportionately about the sorrows of great ones: tragedy celebrates their hugeness, but the presence of clowns is relevant because doomed heroes

*John Kerrigan, *Revenge Tragedy* (1986), p. 200. Kerrigan rightly stresses "the comic strain" in revenge plays.

or heroines may see in it a reduced, pastoral reflection of their plight, and the audience sees them, for a moment, forced to get down from their stilts. The clowns have nothing to do with greatness; they are its prose antithesis. They bring serpents or pigeons on demand, or make plebeian jokes over an open grave, demonstrating totally unheroic attitudes to the posturing of the mighty.

If we take *Titus* to be, at any rate in its final form, from about 1593 (and so contemporary with the poems), there is an interval of about three years before the next tragedy, *Romeo and Juliet.* These were possibly the most prolific four or five years of Shakespeare's prolific life. In poetry, comedy, and history, there were *The Taming of the Shrew, Love's Labor's Lost,* possibly *Two Gentlemen,* possibly *The Comedy of Errors,* as well as *King John, Richard II,* the additions to *Sir Thomas More,* and, as many now claim, all or part of *Edward III;* very likely some of the Sonnets belong to this period also. It should be added that the dating remains uncertain; the Oxford editors, not altogether confidently, place *Two Gentlemen* and *The Shrew* as early as 1590–91, contemporaneous with the *Henry VI* plays, with *Titus* coming immediately after that in 1592. After these plays only *Richard III* is dated before the plague closed the theatres in 1593. So it is not easy to judge how much influence on Shakespeare's habits of writing we should attribute to his work when the theatres were closed, most of which was of course non-dramatic. At any rate, it is more or less agreed that when the theatres reopened he continued to write histories (including *Richard II*) and comedies (including *Love's Labor's Lost*). The next tragedy, *Romeo and Juliet,* is a kind of twin to a comedy, *A Midsummer Night's Dream,* and both of them are fairly securely dated 1595.

Romeo and Juliet is a strikingly original play, although the topic of star-crossed lovers was not fresh. Shakespeare's immediate source is a poem by Arthur Brooke called *The Tragical History of Romeus and Juliet* (1562), a reading of which will enhance anybody's admiration for the skill and variety of Shakespeare's verse, as well as making obvious the ingenuity with which he dramatises the story (and, incidentally, alters its moral bearing, for Brooke strongly disapproves of the lovers). His play is a departure in tragedy, for it is not concerned with Rome and has no royalty or mighty hero; it offers a plausible representation of contemporary life in Italy, and its principal figures are two young and unimportant people. But Italy was gorgeous, and its stories were often of love and often tragic.

It is curious that the twin play, *A Midsummer Night's Dream,* opens on a threat of love-tragedy ("So quick bright things come to confusion" [I.i.149]) and includes a parodic version of the story of Pyramus and Thisbe, for *Romeo and Juliet* is also a version of that story, and in it quick bright things do come to confusion, brought on by the action of a malignant fate or a series of unhappy accidents. Comparison between the two plays offers remarkable testimony to the extent and variety of Shakespeare's powers as a poet. Each work is so planned that many styles are required. The sonnet that opens *Romeo and Juliet* introduces a scene that begins with proletarian prose, and the first blank verse is then spoken only after sixty or so lines by the upper-class Benvolio, who intervenes in the quarrel between the two Capulet servants and is challenged by the angry Capulet, Tybalt. Their brisk blank-verse dialogue eventually gives way when the Prince arrives and delivers a judicial, indeed monarchical speech of twenty-four grave blank-verse lines. Lady Montague then notices the absence of Romeo from the scene, which gives Benvolio a chance to explain why the boy is sunk in melancholy; and the new tone, appropriate to the account of a lover, is adopted by old Montague:

> Many a morning hath he there been seen,
> With tears augmenting the fresh morning's dew,
> Adding to clouds more clouds with his deep sighs . . .
>
> (131ff.)

He ends that speech with a rhymed couplet, and a few lines further on compares his son to

> the bud bit with an envious worm,
> Ere he can spread his sweet leaves to the air
> Or dedicate his beauty to the sun.
>
> (151–53)

Again he rounds off his speech with a rhymed couplet.

This is entirely different from the kind of thing I noticed in the ornamented argument about the double coronation in *King John;* it has a certain oddity, in that the speech is given to the father of the lovesick boy, from whom a more bracing response might be expected. The verse looks back to *Two Gentlemen of Verona,* but its placing, after the very different languages of the brawl and the Prince's oration, contrives a quite violent key change, which signals the entry of Romeo himself, suffering from a purely routine, conventional attack of love-melancholy that confers on him the right to rhyme and to choose fantastic conceits:

> Here's much to do with hate, but more with love.
> Why then, O brawling love! O loving hate!
> O any thing, of nothing first create!
> O heavy lightness, serious vanity,
> Misshapen chaos of well-seeming forms,
> Feather of lead, bright smoke, cold fire, sick health,
> Still-waking sleep, that is not what it is!
> This love feel I, that feel no love in this.
>
> (I.i.175–82)

Romeo has just told his friend Benvolio that he knows about the affray already, and the mixture in his mind of thoughts about fighting and love sets him off on a string of paradoxes. The notion of opposing qualities thus conjoined leads him into a fantasy of chaos, of which he then gives a fairly traditional account. (One can compare this with a later description of Chaos in *Paradise Lost,* ii.890: ". . . this wild abyss, / The womb of nature and perhaps her grave, / Of neither sea, nor shore, nor air, nor fire, / But all these in their pregnant causes mixed / Confus'dly, and which thus must ever fight . . .") Here is the very home of contraries, the material of the world before the creation, the first step between the original nothingness and the universe made by God, matter without form. In themselves the qualities mentioned would be "well-seeming," but in this chaos they are misshapen. Romeo, we may think, is a well-educated young man who has been taught about chaos, but he applies the lesson analogously to his own emotional condition. In his next speech, he displays a command of conventional imagery ultimately deriving from the Italian poet Petrarch, but he keeps up the chaotic paradoxes—"a madness most discreet, / A choking gall, and a preserving sweet" (193–94)—that is, bitter and destructive but also, like sugar, a preservative. Rhyming whenever he feels like it, the rhymes being more or less as conventional as his suffering, Romeo brings the scene to an end with an account of the unseducible Rosaline.

The play is about twelve or thirteen minutes old, and we have already heard poetry of much variety, following the prose of the opening. As yet there has been no mention of Juliet. The alternation of unrhymed and rhymed verse continues in the next scene, until interrupted by an illiterate prose servant. More rhyme, but it does not impede the progress of the plot: Romeo will go to the Capulet ball to compare Rosaline with other girls. And we are at once in the Capulet house (I.iii) and listening to a garrulous nurse telling, over and over again, a tale of Juliet's childhood, and here doing so in verse. Why so? Later on she will speak prose when she chooses. There are three participants in the dialogue, the Nurse, Lady Capulet, Juliet, and all speak verse; the nurse is not a female clown but a valued and intimate servant, so she speaks verse (for some reason set in italics in both Quartos), but a verse carefully differentiated from Juliet's brief contributions and from the more authoritative tones of Lady Capulet, whose speech recommending Paris as a husband modulates easily into the mood of the love-talk we have already heard, with an elaborately formal comparison, in rhyming couplets, of Paris to a beautiful book (I.iii.81–94). Only the entry of the distracted servant at the end of the scene returns us to prose.

The arrival of the Montague masquers at the Capulet house (I.iv) introduces the bawdy Mercutio, who joins in the quibbling but soon launches into his solo about Queen Mab. This brilliant scherzo was written at a time when, on the evidence of *A Midsummer Night's Dream,* Shakespeare was thinking of miniature fairies, wondering perhaps how to get them down to the size he wanted (fairies were normally imagined as far bigger) and here willing to consider them in a rather bawdy context. The speech is forty-two lines long, perhaps a whole sheet of manuscript, and may well be an afterthought inserted into a scene where it serves no narrative function. It is set mostly as prose in the second Quarto and the Folio, though as verse in Q1, a pirated text lacking authority. Editors argue about this problem, and nobody is quite sure what happened, but it is certainly plausible to consider that the speech was a later insertion.

Mercutio talks of dreams and illusions, of a fairy given to tormenting human beings, including lovers, but having a more general satirical aim: greedy clergymen, courtiers, soldiers. As Romeo says, he talks of "nothing" (96), and Mercutio glosses that word as "vain fantasy," which reminds us that the mood of *Romeo,* though darker in the end, is also that of the *Dream.*

It is typical of the method of this play that the scene of the party at the Capulet house should open with bustling servants, cheerful fellows with comic names, going about their plausible tasks and pursuing their own interests. It is in such prose passages—here and in other plays like, for example,

Measure for Measure and *Much Ado*—that we are given, however sketchily, a sense of social depth. The Capulet party could have been represented without the dialogue of servants. But they create the right party atmosphere, into which the Capulet family enters. Shakespeare is seeing to it that the plot moves on in language that gives it a certain social density—absent from tragedies, which great ones inhabit alone—and the social structure is reflected in the varieties of dialect. Hamlet encounters his gravedigger and Cleopatra her clown; the Porter is made to bear the whole weight of catastrophe in *Macbeth;* but *Romeo* is different in that the servants belong to non-royal families. They brawl for the family name and are visible on great family occasions. The Nurse, who brought up Juliet, is not only exasperating and venal but has her place in the story and is given a strongly written part; Peter, the Nurse's servant, is likewise essential. He is even mentioned unnecessarily, as if to show he is still around though not on stage (IV.iv.17, 19), and he has a whole sad and lively scene, with the musicians, to himself (IV.v). Even the musicians, who grumpily decline to play, are given ghostly comic existences: Simon Catling, Hugh Rebeck, James Soundpost. They, too, have their way of talking; it is the apparently inexhaustible command of dramatic dialects that makes all this possible.*

So, out of a babble of old men's chat about their ages and their corns, talk on the fringes of the main interest (though it shows that the feuding and riot is the work of youth, not age), we come directly to Romeo's rapt description of Juliet ("O, she doth teach the torches to burn bright!" [I.v.44]). He rhymes; Tybalt, identifying Romeo's Montague voice, has not the leisure to do so: "This, by his voice, should be a Montague. / Fetch me my rapier, boy" (54–55). Romeo's earlier forebodings are here confirmed: the announcement of love is followed at once by the threat of conflict; sweetness and gall (92) have already met. Tybalt's departure is followed by a dialogue between Romeo and Juliet in the form of a sonnet (93–107); the use of this form in this play is another proof of Shakespeare's originality and technical resource.

*See M. M. Mahood's fascinating *Bit Parts in Shakespeare's Plays* (1992), which treats of "numerous First, Second and Third Messengers, Citizens and Soldiers; a host of gardeners and gaolers, knights and heralds, ladies-in-waiting, murderers and mariners; the odd day-woman, haberdasher, vintner, hangman, scrivener . . . John Bates, Tom Snout, George Seacole, Simon Catling, Peter Thump, Neighbour Mugs; and four men who are all called Balthasar" (p. 1). Speaking of Peter, Mahood points out that, as a stage direction indicates, he was played by Will Kempe, the company's celebrated clown, and that the scene with the musicians might have covered the removal of Juliet's bed and its replacement by a tomb (p. 231).

The Montagues leave, and the concluding dialogue of Juliet with the Nurse shows that the world of the love sonnet is not the world of Capulet and certainly not the world of Tybalt. The Prologue to Act II, another sonnet, comments on the danger to the lovers. As the Friar will point out, "These violent delights have violent ends" (II.vi.9); it is the moral of the story as Shakespeare read it in his source. But he emphasises the delights, especially of anticipation, and anchors them firmly to sexual pleasure. Love itself is brought to earth by Mercutio's bawdy, and directly after his jokes comes the Balcony scene, admirable love-talk punctuated at first by a repetition of the name "Montague." The following scene, full of bawdy talk and involving the Nurse, is almost entirely in prose, until Romeo, arranging the tryst at Friar Laurence's cell, speaks a few lines of verse, while the Nurse sticks to prose.

Act III takes us straight to the crisis of the plot, the killing of Mercutio and of Tybalt. Thereafter all proceeds with efficiency; the most remarkable moment may be the lamentations over Juliet's dead body. With extraordinary boldness Shakespeare makes these sorrows absurd, as in the Nurse's speech:

> O woe! O woeful, woeful, woeful day!
> Most lamentable day, most woeful day
> That ever, ever, I did yet behold!
> O day, O day, O day, O hateful day!
> Never was seen so black a day as this.
> O woeful day, O woeful day!
>
> (IV.v.49–54)

Of course we know Juliet isn't dead, and we know that the Nurse is sly enough to imitate the mourning of her betters; but we also know that Juliet will shortly be truly dead and that the play is, after all, a tragedy—all reasons not to invite audience laughter at this point. It is as if the Nurse had strayed in from a production by Bottom. The absurdity of the speech is meant to upset generic expectations. It is followed by Friar Laurence's necessarily insincere exhortations:

> For though fond nature bids us all lament,
> Yet nature's tears are reason's merriment.
>
> (83–84)

He is saying that the parents should be glad to see their daughter dead, though he knows she is not, which would be a cause of greater joy. The scene ends with the badinage of Peter and the musicians, under which a note of indifference to mourning sounds, both in the song quoted ("When griping griefs the heart doth wound" [126]) and in the determination of the musicians to hang around and join the mourners for a free dinner. It is impossible not to see all this as a deliberate flaunting of expectation: to show that the world goes on, that there are degrees of involvement in mourning, that the Nurse looks after herself, and that the musicians must have their dinner—all this requires what an Elizabethan called "a sudden rash half-capriole" of wit, a moment of poetic high spirits, and a taste for the unexpected. It does not surprise as much as it might only because of all we know about the variety and resource of this dramatist's writing.

It is noteworthy that Romeo, exiled, married, and believing Juliet dead, sounds very different from his earlier self. Instead of elaborate love-conceits and the fantasies of melancholy he looks straight at the issue: "Thou knowest my lodging, get me ink and paper, / And hire post-horses; I will hence to-night," he says to his servant (V.i.25–26), and

> get thee gone,
> And hire those horses; I'll be with thee straight.
> Well, Juliet, I will lie with thee to-night.
>
> (32–33)

There are many rhetorical levels, abuses of rhetoric, and clashes of style in the play, but they are all set off by this use of the plainest possible style, itself a great rhetorical achievement.

Romeo and Juliet may be the most popular of the tragedies, though few would include it among the greatest. It is nevertheless a masterpiece, the virtuosities of the language matched by the subtlety of the plotting. The impotence of age—the old Capulets, the old Montagues—in the face of fiery youth, when the reason cannot yet master the blood, is a theme reflected in both. Old Capulet lays his plans for a sober marriage between Paris and his daughter, while she and Romeo make love in the same house. Juliet ecstatically welcomes the coming night while Tybalt lies dead in the street outside. The use of foreboding dreams, the timing of Romeo's return, and many other features demonstrate an unprecedented mastery of dramatic form. And it is worth recalling that the play was in its way experimental; the usual source of tragedy was an ancient hero or some comparably great figure. Here the story comes from a modern novella and is set in modern Verona. This innovation called for new thinking about tragic experience, now less remote from ordinary life. The play is sometimes said not to be truly tragic, that Romeo's late arrival is simply accident. But that may be an aspect of its modernity. We use the word "tragic" differently nowadays, and a change of sentiment in regard to tragedy may be sensed in *Romeo and Juliet.*

I have called *A Midsummer Night's Dream* a twin of *Romeo and Juliet,* a treatment of what is fundamentally the same story but this time in a comic mode. However, it develops interests that are very much part of its own substance. It lacks the fairly simple relation to a source that *Romeo* has, being Shakespeare's own invention, a set of variations on the theme of Pyramus and Thisbe. It is a festival comedy, for Midsummer Eve, St. John's Eve, was a festival occasion, when young people had licence to go "gadding over night to the woods, where they spend the whole night in pleasant pastimes," as the Puritan Philip Stubbes noted with disgust.* The play is about many human preoccupations, sometimes looked at in wonder (and interfered with) by the fairies—for example, about doting as opposed to loving, about love which is the work of the eye only and not of the whole mind. (The words "dote" and "dotes" occur eight times in the play, twice in the Sonnets, and nowhere else in Shakespeare more than once; the contexts are almost always amorous. "Doting" occurs twice in *Romeo and Juliet,* and in one of these places the Friar reproves Romeo "For doting, not for loving" [II.iii.82].) The eye is the procurer of doting desire, and "eye" is another important word in *A Midsummer Night's Dream.* "Eye" and "eyes" occur more often here than anywhere else; the nearest competitors are *Love's Labor's Lost* and *Romeo and Juliet.*

We are approaching the time when Shakespeare began to use a word or group of words as a central element, almost as a subject of exploration, in his verse. In this play we also find that diversity of plot can be unified by commonality of interest. *A Midsummer Night's Dream* is probably the most original in conception and the best executed of all Shakespeare's comedies to date, and the most elaborately wrought as well as the most "intellectual" since

*See C. L. Barber, *Shakespeare's Festive Comedy* (1959), pp. 21–22, 119.

Love's Labor's Lost (though, in its revised form, that play probably belongs to 1597, which gives it a chronological affinity with the *Dream*). Anne Barton thinks of the two plays, along with *Romeo and Juliet* and *Richard II,* as constituting "a natural group."* Perhaps one should drop *Richard II,* which was composed under different constraints; but there are genuine resemblances among the others. And they represent a new level of achievement.

A Midsummer Night's Dream is the most remarkable of them; among other things, it exhibits the most elaborate and successful correspondence between the main plot and the subplot. It clearly complies with William Empson's description of the subplot as having "an obvious effect in the Elizabethans of making you feel the play deals with life as a whole,"† but the purpose is not simply that. The subplot of Bottom and his actors is in a sense the main plot, since the Pyramus and Thisbe theme is there at last acted out, though farcically; and the plots are united not only by the performance of the play before the great ones but by the fairies, who give Bottom better insight into the truth of things than Theseus or his friends can provide; and who, when he has broken up the party ("Lovers, to bed, 'tis almost fairy time" [V.i.364]), invade his house to bless it and bless the offspring of his new marriage.

The opening scene is masterly, establishing not only the narrative but the thematic interest. Lysander is accused of corrupting the fantasy of Hermia (I.i.27): disorders of the fantasy or imagination are a main topic of the play. When Hermia complains that her father cannot see Lysander with her eyes, Theseus tells her she is required to subordinate her eyes to her father's judgement (56–57) or pay the penalty. Lysander and Hermia alone complain of the misfortunes of love: "So quick bright things come to confusion" (149). (The passage recalls not only *Romeo and Juliet* but also *Venus and Adonis,* 720–56.) Now "poor fancy's followers" (155) decide to elope. Helena complains of her ill fortune, for Demetrius prefers Hermia's eyes to hers. The emphasis is always on the eye as the source of love, or rather of doting: Helena "dotes, / Devoutly dotes, dotes in idolatry" (108–9), and Lysander hopes Demetrius will "dote" on Helena (225). Doting is a disordered condition of the imagination, otherwise called "love," and it originates in an eye uncontrolled by judgement. This formula is hammered home in the first scene, and the characteristic lamentations about the brevity and mortality of love are introduced like a second subject in a sonata.

*Introduction to *Love's Labor's Lost* in *The Riverside Shakespeare,* p. 208.
†*Some Versions of Pastoral* (1935), p. 27.

Helena, speaking for youth, argues that what her elders take to be doting is in fact something very fine:

> And as he [Demetrius] errs, doting on Hermia's eyes,
> So I, admiring of his qualities.
> Things base and vile, holding no quantity,
> Love can transpose to form and dignity.*
> Love looks not with the eyes but with the mind;
> And therefore is wing'd Cupid painted blind.
> Nor hath Love's mind of any judgment taste;
> Wings, and no eyes, figure unheedy haste;
> And therefore is Love said to be a child . . .
>
> (230–38)

In love the eye induces doting, not a rational, patient pleasure like that of Theseus and Hippolyta. Helena's remarks about the blind Cupid are traditional, love being irresponsible, a disease of the eye. But there is a contrary, neo-Platonic interpretation of blind Cupid, namely that love transcends even sight, the highest of the senses, and is indeed above intellect, and this idea, or something very like it, is at work in the play.

Doting produces disasters, like those of Adonis, Romeo, and Pyramus, whose story is to be enacted by the "mechanicals." Bottom and his friends appear in the second scene to give, in the best Shakespearian manner, a farcical but complicating treatment to this already established theme. Bacon, in his essay "Of Love," says it is unreasonable that a man, "made for the contemplation of heaven and all noble objects, should do nothing but kneel before a little idol, and make himself subject, though not of the mouth (as beasts are) yet of the eye, which was given him for higher purposes." The moral is simple: "Nuptial love maketh mankind; friendly love perfecteth it; but wanton love corrupteth and embaseth it." But Shakespeare is not simple. His title alludes to the licence of St. John's Eve, the right to make love in the woods, out of the control of the city, in the realm of nature and not of civil order. Puck is a natural force, and takes no account of civility and rational choice. He is a blinding Cupid, and the connection between them is made in a famous speech of Oberon's (II.i.155ff.): "I saw . . . Flying between the cold moon and the earth, / Cupid all arm'd." His shaft, aimed at the virgin Queen

*This anticipates the experience of Bottom with Titania.

Elizabeth, strikes a pansy, here called "love-in-idleness" ("idleness" carries the sense of wantonness or craziness). When the juice of this flower is applied to lovers' eyes, they will dote on whatever they see next. In instructing Puck to obtain the flower, Oberon's object is to punish Titania "And make her full of hateful fantasies" (258).

Puck wants to end what to him is the intolerable situation of a man and a girl lying apart "in humane modesty" (II.ii.57), as Hermia puts it, and he assumes that Hermia must have been churlishly rejected by Lysander: "Pretty soul, she durst not lie / Near this lack-love, this kill-courtesy" (76–77). When Lysander awakes, he sees Helena first and dotes on her, ascribing his change of love object to an increased maturity: "Reason becomes the marshal to my will, / And leads me to your eyes . . ." (120–21). In the next scene Bottom knows better: "reason and love keep little company together now-a-days" (III.i.143–44).

The love affair between Bottom and Titania alludes to the *Golden Ass* of Apuleius, in which Apuleius is turned into an ass but is restored to his true shape by the goddess Isis and initiated into her mysteries. The story was much admired and yielded many allegorical meanings in the Renaissance. There are unmistakeable though lightly suggested allusions to this body of lore in *A Midsummer Night's Dream.* It was an invention of genius to make Bottom the clue to them.

The antidote by which the lovers are all restored to "wonted sight" is "virtuous" (III.ii.367), having been expressed from "Dian's bud" (IV.i.73), which by keeping people chaste keeps them sane. So far the moral seems simple enough: the lovers have been subjected to irrational forces; in the dark they have chopped and changed, though without injury to virtue. When Puck releases them from the spell, they will awake, and "all this derision / Shall seem a dream and fruitless vision" (III.ii.370–71). Awake, they see well enough; Demetrius abjures the dotage that enslaved him to Hermia, and his love for Helena returns as "natural taste" returns to a person cured of a sickness (IV.i.174). Oberon, pitying the "dotage" of Titania, will "undo / This hateful imperfection of her eyes" (IV.i.62–63); she will wake and imagine she has undergone "the fierce vexation of a dream" (69). All now return to the civil, rational city, agreeing that their dreams were fantasies, that they have returned to health.

But the final awakening in this superbly arranged climax (as so often in Shakespeare, it occurs at the end of the fourth act) is Bottom's. Here the moral defies comfortable analysis. We leave behind the neat love-is-a-kind-of-madness pattern and are invited to think differently about it:

> I have had a most rare vision. I have had a dream, past the wit of man to say what dream it was. Man is but an ass, if he go about t' expound this dream . . . The eye of man hath not heard, the ear of man hath not seen, man's hand is not able to taste, his tongue to conceive, nor his heart to report, what my dream was.
>
> (IV.i.204–14)

This is a parody of 1 Corinthians 2:9ff.: "Eye hath not seen, nor ear heard, neither have entered into the heart of man the things which God hath prepared for them that love him."

Apuleius, after his transformation, might not speak of the initiation he underwent, but he was vouchsafed a vision of the goddess Isis. St. Paul experienced a transforming vision on the road to Damascus. Bottom has known the triple goddess, Titania, in a vision. His relation to Apuleius and St. Paul is of a different import from the others'; here blind love is the love of God or a goddess. Shakespeare knew the ancient distinction between the *phantasma* and *oneiros* or *somnium;* the first is what Brutus calls a "hideous dream" (*Julius Caesar,* II.i.65), but the second is ambiguous, enigmatic, of high religious import. Love is a means to grace as well as irrational passion, and it may be suggested that the two are not ultimately separable by the reason.

Theseus's set piece at the opening of the last act deals with the fantasies of lunatic, lover, and poet, but these are matters "which none of the princes of the world know," which must be spoken of "in a mystery" (1 Cor. 2:7). "God hath chosen the foolish things of the world to confound the wise" (1 Cor. 1:27): in a way he has chosen Bottom, not Theseus, who is mistaken about lunatics, lovers, or poets. The imagination which Theseus thinks to be out of control is the instrument of powers he does not understand. The doubts of Hippolyta (V.i.23–27) encourage one to believe that this "prince of the world" has got it wrong. The love of Bottom's bottomless vision at least complements, if it does not transcend, the rational love of Theseus. Bottom's play, absurd as it is, speaks of disasters, the disasters of Pyramus and of Romeo and Juliet, which do not cease to happen but for a moment become farcically irrelevant, on a marriage eve. "Tragical mirth . . . hot ice and wondrous strange snow" (V.i.57–59) is a good description of the effect of this play.

One of its characteristics deserves further mention, since it recurs with force in Shakespeare's later work. I mean the bursting through into the action of what seems a merely verbal trick. Here it is the insistent talk of eyes, the patterns of blindness and insight, wood and city, phantasma and vision, love vulgar and love celestial. The juices of love-in-idleness and of "Dian's bud" are there as complements to the talk of eyes and sight; Bottom's dream as the complement or opposite of the rationality of a prince of the world. Word and action go together, and the word must be closely attended to.

If this sounds too solemn a comment on so light a play, we may at this point look back to an earlier comedy, *Love's Labor's Lost,* noted for its word games, as confirmation that the language of comedy is not always frivolous. We find here a witty, teasing investigation of language, with hints, but no more than hints, of the sort of intense brooding over words that becomes so important in later plays. Language games were always a feature of Shakespeare's style, and apart from the famous verbal fireworks in *Love's Labor's Lost* there are already signs that quite serious linguistic investigations are being touched on by the repeated use, apparently casual or trivial, of certain words such as "will." "A sharp wit match'd with too blunt a will," which is Maria's characterisation of Longaville (II.i.49), may make us think of the formula "erected wit, infected will" in Sidney's *Apology,* and of the play on the sexual senses of the word "will" in the Sonnets. Maria, not content with a simple assertion, goes on: "Whose edge hath power to cut, whose will still wills / It should none spare that come within his power." The object here is obviously to force the word "will" on the hearer: this *will* is blunt but can still cut; *will* will still *will;* man is fallen and in need of special grace to control his will.

Katharine's comment on Dumaine warns us that the lighter senses of such words as "wit" and "grace" are still in play: in the same scene she says he has "wit to make an ill shape good, / And shape to win grace though he had no wit" (59–60). Here "grace" has sacrificed most of its theological flavour to its other sense, of physical beauty, but the opposition of wit and will is still in our ears. We may also remember Berowne's initial protest to the King, that "every man with his affects is born, / Not by might mast'red, but by special grace" (I.i.151–52). Here is a verbal plot or subplot about grace and desire (affects, or will), about "the huge army of the world's desires" with which the fallen will inevitably collude. The theological point is that without grace one cannot master these desires, which leads to the point that the attempt to do so merely by an effort of study is doomed. There are better ways of deserving grace than by repressive academic labour. (One such way is to live as a hermit or comfort the sick, as the young men are eventually driven to do.) So "grace," which means so many things, is never quite detached from its theological sense.

It may be said, then, that Shakespeare had a developing passion for exploring the range of particular words. Empson noted the remarkable array of ambiguities inherent in his deployment of words like "wit" and "sense." Here the word is "grace," which occurs in *Love's Labor's Lost* more often than in any other play (except, curiously enough, *Henry VIII,* where the frequency is partly explained by the number of noblemen formally addressed).

Not that the tone is always as solemn as it becomes in the closing passages of the play; there is also a movement that celebrates mirth and happiness in the world. These are the culture wars as the scholar Frances Yates has revealed them* to us: the wits versus the pedants, those who value affect against those who would repress it or will it away. At the bottom of this, lightly proposed, is a conflict between a libertine valuation of experience in the world and a monastic devotion to study, a conviction that wits may acquire grace from the active participation in the created world that pedants foolishly abjure. Yet affect is blind: even when the students have declared for love and the world, they do so to the wrong women: "We are again forsworn, in will and error" (V.ii.471). And at the end of the play the wits have to do penance and hope for grace in the future.

One ought not to make *Love's Labor's Lost* too serious, but there is, under the wit, this ground bass. "Will" is a multicoloured word in Shakespeare, and here its colours vary from the sense given it by the Articles of Religion in the Church of England's 1549 *Book of Common Prayer* ("We have no power to do good works pleasant and acceptable to God, without the *grace* of God by Christ preventing us, that we may have good *will,*" runs Article X) to the frankly sexual senses, for "will," by association, can include not only sexual desire but the genital organs themselves, identified, in some of the Sonnets, with those of the author, Will. (It may be worth adding that the word "will," which of course is not always a noun, occurs with much more than average frequency in this play.)

*In *A Study of Love's Labour's Lost* (1936).

These ripples of meaning may sometimes be mere elements of texture, dismissible as such, and not very relevant to the main business of a play. Thus in *Twelfth Night,* the very subtitle of which—*Or What You Will*—recalls the old fascination with "will," the choices of will are complicated by the date, Twelfth Night, when Carnival turns the world upside down, you do what you will, and nothing is but what is not. In this respect carnival is, like all theatre, a matter of disguise and appearances, of *impersonation,* of the attempt to discriminate what is from what is not by means of what merely appears. The meaning of the subtitle is less what do you want than who or what do you choose to be, allowing that in the general haze of illusion you probably won't achieve it: Orsini won't get Olivia; Olivia won't get Viola but only her double; Malvolio won't get Olivia and neither will Sir Andrew; the only character who winds up getting the partner he wants is Toby.

The idea of the identity plot must have had its origin in the twins, each of them wearing the disguise of the other, as it were, and the play is a splendid example of how serious language games can be played without slowing down dramatic progress. Viola is always reminding herself that she is not identical with the role she is playing, and this introduces a note of dubiety into other self-identifications. Olivia's reply to her question "Are you the lady of the house?" is "If I do not usurp myself, I am," and Viola replies, "Most certain, if you are she, you do usurp yourself; for what is yours to bestow is not yours to reserve" (I.v.184–89). The idea is that the need for women to marry and multiply is so strong that it cancels any right they may mistakenly think they have to remain single. (In the same way, the single identity of the young man is assaulted by the arguments of the early Sonnets.) The trick letter to Malvolio tells him, "Thou canst not choose but know who I am" (II.v.174), though in truth he *can* choose and chooses wrong. Feste, an expert in turning words inside out, dallying with them, falsifying them, says to Viola, "who you are, and what you would, are out of my welkin" (III.i.57–58), and she has a little soliloquy commending the wisdom of fools (60ff.). Later, when Viola-Cesario has her second interview with Olivia, she replies to Olivia's question "I prithee tell me what thou think'st of me" as follows:

VIO. That you do think you are not what you are.
OLI. If I think so, I think the same of you.

VIO. Then think you right: I am not what I am.
OLI. I would you were as I would have you be.
VIO. Would it be better, madam, than I am?
I wish it might, for now I am your fool.

(III.i.138–44)

Now all this can be seen to have a simple bearing on the plot of mistaken identity. Viola-Cesario's answer is a repetition of her first point: Olivia is not, as she believes, free to be single and reclusive and sunk in improperly protracted mourning. She wrongly takes Viola for a young man and is further mistaken in supposing her to be more than a servant (which, by another turn, she is). Viola's response is to say again that she is indeed playing a part. (We should recall, penetrating to another level of illusion, that she is a boy acting the part of a girl acting the part of a boy.) Olivia simply expresses a wish that Cesario had the power and right to woo her. But Viola-Cesario is offended at what she takes to be a slur, feeling she is being made a fool of by means appropriate to the profession of folly. (She has pointed this out in relation to the real fool, earlier in the scene. Viola admired that fool's wit, but it is a different matter when it comes from a social superior.) And there's a hint of the later language games in this insistence on the verbs "to be" and "to think."

In that passage the "little language" of *Twelfth Night* is involved in itself as well as in forwarding the plot. It is followed by Olivia's mistaken declaration of love, and later Olivia will advise Viola to "Be that thou know'st thou art" (V.i.149), though at the time she has already married Sebastian under the impression that he is Cesario; her point is that her husband is just as important socially as Orsino, but she addresses it to the wrong person. Elsewhere uncertainty about identity seems to exist more for its own sake. We have to listen for these slight distortions, sometimes comic, sometimes echoing a deeper theme. Sir Andrew's challenge to Viola begins "Youth, whatsoever thou art, thou art but a scurvy fellow" (III.iv.147), calling her genuinely ambiguous identity into question as a means of insult, intensified by the use of "thou." Malvolio in prison is tormented by Feste:

> . . . as the old hermit of Prague, that never saw pen and ink, very wittily said to a niece of King Gorboduc, "That that is is"; so I, being Master Parson, am Master Parson; for what is "that" but "that," and "is" but "is"?
>
> (IV.ii.12–16)

Malvolio is treated as a madman, a case of demonic possession, another form of doubling; as he protests, he is not mad, but in the cruel carnival jest appropriate to Twelfth Night he is nevertheless treated as a lunatic. When he complains of the cell being dark he is told it is light, but exactly in the manner of the mad paradoxist Belsey Bob in the Mummers' Plays: "it hath bay windows transparent as barricadoes, and the clerestories toward the south north are as lustrous as ebony" (IV.ii.36–38). This is the world turned upside down, when that that is is not. The hermit of Prague got it wrong: language, like reality, is turned upside down.

When Feste, encountering Sebastian, takes him to be Cesario, he says, "No, I do not know you, nor I am not sent to you by my lady, to bid you come speak with her, nor your name is not Master Cesario, nor this is not my nose neither: nothing that is so is so" (IV.i.5–9). It seems that few occasions for this kind of game are missed, and I suppose a truly marvellous listener would be prepared by all this lexical subplotting for the terms in which the twinship of Sebastian and Viola is finally understood:

> One face, one voice, one habit, and two persons,
> A natural perspective, that is and is not!
>
> (V.i.216–17)

A perspective painting is a good image of the state in which that that is is not, since it presents two different pictures depending on whether you view it from the front or from the side. The sameness of the twins is not identity; the fool may be wise if rightly viewed; Malvolio is a gentleman, but not really; Sir Andrew is a mock-knight, not a real one; there is a difference between wonder and madness, though they may be mistaken for one another (IV.iii.1ff.).

Twelfth Night represents a remarkable deepening of the plot of tricks or mistakes found in contemporary Italian analogues, and of the plot of mistaken identity treated earlier by Shakespeare in his Latinate *Comedy of Errors* (though even there he doubled up the identical twins to multiply the possibilities of doubting that what is is). *Twelfth Night,* a meditation on twins much more mature than the treatment of that relationship in the *Comedy of Errors,* is the most profound of the early comedies, and it is not surprising that it is dated about 1601, the nearest plays to it in time being *Hamlet* and *Troilus and Cressida,* more word-obsessed plays, as we shall see.

I have alluded before, and will need to do so again, to this use of what I have called the "little language," borrowing an expression of Virginia Woolf's.

Rabelais has a story about words spoken in cold weather that get frozen and later thaw, whereupon they are heard again. The story was well known, and there is a version of it in Castiglione's *The Courtier,* a work Shakespeare almost certainly knew. But I think of it as an allegory of the way in which certain words are thawed out, as it were, in the course of a play. We saw an instance of it in a play composed as early as *Love's Labor's Lost.* Later on, the thawing of words becomes a major element in Shakespeare's dramatic technique.

Twelfth Night is probably close in date to Shakespeare's poem "The Phoenix and Turtle," a remarkable work with no obvious parallel in the canon but one that tells us something about his language and interests at the turn of the century. Here there is no question of the audience being distracted; this work was meant for the page, or perhaps for reading aloud. It is meant to be studied, and it may throw a more direct light on the operation of the poet's mind than the plays he composed at this time. It is a reminder that the exploration of some of the remoter possibilities of language was essential to his poetry.

The poem surely represents a critical moment in the development of his art and is a key document in any discussion of Shakespeare as poet. Behind many of its terms there lie learned Latin distinctions:

So they loved as love in twain
Had the essence but in one,
Two distincts, division none.
Number there in love was slain.
. . .

Property was thus appalled,
That the self was not the same;
Single nature's double name
Neither two nor one was called.

Reason, in itself confounded,
Saw division grow together,
To themselves yet either neither,
Simple were so well compounded:

That it cried, "How true a twain
Seemeth this concordant one!

Love hath reason, Reason none,
If what parts, can so remain."

The notion of distinction without difference is borrowed from the theology of the Trinity, an issue considered by St. Thomas Aquinas. Number is slain because, as philosophers and mathematicians often remarked, one is no number. Distance and no space is another trinitarian figure: the three are one but not identical and operate at a distance, as it were. "Property" translates *proprium,* meaning the quality (here personified) that distinguishes a person. Property, the principle of a separate person, is appalled because of the conundrum presented by distinct yet undivided persons; and Reason is confounded because it works only by division, and here there is no division. "Either neither" is a wonderful enactment of this perplexing relation between the persons. They are neither divided nor the same, and so Reason confesses itself defeated by love.

What is truly extraordinary about the language of the poem is the resource with which scholastic terminology is Englished: "the self was not the same" makes its point by splitting the English word "selfsame" (used elsewhere by Shakespeare in twenty-eight places but only as a single word). Here it means one and two at the same time; this single word enacts the entire theme of the poem. How far this is from merely saying of lovers that they are in some conventional vague sense combined into a unity!

"The Phoenix and Turtle" offers a paradigm of Shakespeare's obsession with the idea of two-in-one, of doubles, of relations between substance and shadow. The birds are doubled in a mutual flame; they are two, but transcendently single, simple not compounded. Reflections of this scheme may be found everywhere in Shakespeare—in the mirrors and shadows of *Richard II,* in the "union in partition" of *A Midsummer Night's Dream* (III.ii.210), in the very texture of its contemporaries *Hamlet* and *Twelfth Night.* The puzzle of the relation of one to two (it interested Spenser, with his Una and Duessa) seems to have been a prime concern of Shakespeare's, and one can understand it as natural enough in a theatre poet: the theatre and the world, the Globe and the globe, the actor as shadow. In its purest form it calls forth a metaphysical lyric; pathologised, it summons *Hamlet.*

The poem, then, reflects an interest that was perhaps always there, given comic form in *Twelfth Night* and made the core of tragedy in *Hamlet.* Here it is transposed into an elegiac and almost diagrammatic mode, evidence of a deep, introspective concern with the semantics of identity that goes far beyond the recognitions familiar in comedy. That the works are of similar date lends colour, I think, to the speculation that around 1600 a new inwardness, almost independent of dramatic necessity, had come upon Shakespeare. Just as the verse changed and the vocabulary in general grew more inventive, so this habit of making the examination or exfoliation of a word or a group of words and the doublings of words become central to an entire play. This new richness belongs to the turn of the century, in comedy *(Twelfth Night),* in tragedy *(Hamlet),* and, I think crucially, in "The Phoenix and Turtle."

Nothing quite so bold as this poem is to be sought in *The Merchant of Venice, Much Ado about Nothing,* or *As You Like It,* all written, probably, between 1596 and 1599. The first of these, close in time to *A Midsummer Night's Dream,* has an entirely different kind of interest, since it considers the theme of Justice in the light of a supposed distinction between the Old and the New Law. The Old is represented by Shylock and lacks any tempering by Mercy, as opposed to the "gentle" Gentile dispensation, which embraces the idea of redemption. This is a summary account, and in its fullness the play qualifies it considerably, but it suffices to show that the play has a scheme anticipating those of the so-called problem plays, especially *Measure for Measure.* When Isabella reminds Angelo, the judge, that "all the souls that were were forfeit once, / And He that might the vantage best have took / Found out the remedy" (II.ii.73–75), she is using Portia's argument in the trial scene, where Shylock refuses to be merciful under "compulsion" (IV.i.183) and Portia replies with her famous speech about mercy:

> And earthly power doth then show likest God's
> When mercy seasons justice. Therefore, Jew,
> Though justice be thy plea, consider this,
> That in the course of justice, none of us
> Should see salvation. We do pray for mercy,
> And that same prayer doth teach us all to render
> The deeds of mercy.
>
> (IV.i.196–202)

But Shylock craves the law; refusing to accept payment of his loan, he has refused a bid for a secular redemption that would have echoed Christian doctrine. The gentle-Gentile pun is the kind of thing that disgusted Dr. Johnson, but it is at the centre of the argument; one finds single words or groups of words more and more often in this position. Johnson, with his dislike of all equivocation, would take it for a simple joke, since he considered that the pun was Shakespeare's "fatal Cleopatra for which he lost the world." But we are expected to hear it as the inmost part of the argument.

> Hie thee, gentle Jew.
> The Hebrew will turn Christian, he grows kind.
>
> (I.iii.177–78)

("Kind" has a multiple sense also, suggesting not only "generous" but "natural" as opposed to "savage.")

> If e'er the Jew her father come to heaven,
> It will be for his gentle daughter's sake.
>
> (II.iv.33–34)

Jessica is called "gentle" earlier in the same scene (19), too. One of the cross-currents in the play is to show the "gentle" Christians to be without kindness to the Jew; Antonio has no compunction about spitting on him, his daughter is applauded for robbing and abandoning him. The line "Now by my hood, a gentle, and no Jew" (II.vi.51) implies that only Christians can be "gentlemen"; to be a gentleman you have to be a Gentile man, as in the following instance:

> To leave a rich Jew's service, to become
> The follower of so poor a gentleman.
>
> (II.ii.147–48)

Jessica says she is daughter to her father's blood but not "to his manners" and, being naturally gentle, will therefore turn Christian (II.iii.19–21). The Duke says to Shylock, "We all expect a gentle answer, Jew!" (IV.i.34), bringing "gentle" and "Jew" together in a formula that bodes no good to Antonio. Even Antonio's ships are "gentle" (I.i.32), since they represent a legitimate form of investment (involving venture), whereas Shylock's are not, being a "breed for barren metal" (I.iii.134), mere usury, a misdirection of love. The Christians are loving (and they make loans without interest), whereas usury, traditionally compared to sodomy, unproductive of anything living, was thought of as opposite to loving.

So unforgiving justice is Jewish, while heavenly mercy is Christian and "gentle." There is a sense in which Shylock's famous speech "Hath not a Jew eyes? Hath not a Jew hands, organs, dimensions, senses, affections, passions . . ." (III.i.59ff.) has quite rightly been taken as a justified protest against the unswerving anti-Semitism of Venetian Christians, but by virtue of one omission it also makes their point. Shylock cannot say "Is not a Jew a Christian?" and without that qualification none of the others matters in the least to Antonio and Bassanio and Lorenzo. Being Christian is the indispensable requirement for Gentility-gentility.*

Shakespeare never lost the habit of including little scenes or parts of scenes that illustrate a necessary theme rather than advancing the plot. One such is the discussion between Shylock and Antonio about the biblical tale of Jacob and Laban (I.iii.71ff.). Antonio says he does not charge interest; Shylock replies that he does, and in doing so is following the guidance of Jacob. This ancestor managed by a trick to ensure that the lambs born to Laban's sheep should be "streak'd and pied," the arrangement having been made that all such lambs should fall to Jacob's share. This stratagem had divine approval: "And the man increased exceedingly" (Gen. 30:43). To Shylock it is a precedent for charging interest, making money breed by whatever means. But to Antonio, Jacob was making a venture, a legitimate use of capital involving risk and forces outside the investor's control. Neither of them treats the story simply as an example of trickery. Antonio's interpretation of Jacob's action was standard among medieval Christian commentators. His refutation of the Jew's version—"is your gold and silver ewes and rams?"—would have seemed cogent to an Elizabethan audience, who had been told that usury (variously defined and sometimes meaning only what went beyond a maximum level of interest) was theft and the "breed for barren metal" unnatural. Shylock the usurer is incapable of love or generosity; later he cannot distinguish his grief at the loss of his ducats from the loss of his daughter; indeed, he wishes he could see her dead so long as the ducats are safe. Antonio, on the other hand, has such love for Bassanio that he urges him

*James Shapiro, *Shakespeare and the Jews* (1996), argues that circumcision is important in the play—"the pound of flesh," until Shylock claims in the trial scene that he wants to have it from near Antonio's heart, would strongly connote the genitalia, "flesh being a biblical euphemism for penis." This is another important distinction Shylock fails to mention.

not even to think about the money he has borrowed, or the bond entered into with Shylock.

It is important that Portia is rich, but Bassanio's visit to her house at Belmont is a true venture, like Jason's for the Golden Fleece, and he is wise enough to choose the casket that says he "must give and hazard all he hath" (II.vii.9). When he does so, he wins "the fleece" (III.ii.241). It can be argued that however much Bassanio loves Portia, his main interest is in her money, and it is true that prominence is given to this motive. It is very like Shakespeare to allow the contrary argument to be shadowed in this way; A. D. Nuttall writes perceptively on this situation—the interactions and priorities of love and money, with the latter making its presence felt even in love-talk.*

Bassanio has to succeed, the other suitors must necessarily fail. Morocco assumes that Portia's worthiness must be reflected in what was agreed to be the worthiest of metals, gold, the metal that breeds best. Arragon avoids gold as the probable choice of the many, who are under the sway not of Truth but its enemy, Opinion, a false appearance of truth (Jews are slaves of opinion, Christians the servants of truth), but he chooses silver: he "assumes desert," which is quite different from trusting to the hand of God, and his reward is therefore precisely what he deserves, "a shadow's bliss" (II.ix.19ff.).

The Merchant of Venice is a good illustration of Shakespeare's increasing power to produce a text impregnated with ideas, and with words that are always under question from the language itself of the play. That is why the character of Shylock has been, immemorially, a ground for discussion and dispute. The framework of thought is clear: Justice and Mercy, Jew and gentle, venture and usury, love and its impossibility for some. It is there in "gentle-Gentile," the basic pun or equivoque, in the debate about Jacob, and in the plot at large. But the possible alternative readings are always at least in the margin.

The main action ends with Act IV, and Act V is remarkable for the way in which it reflects its light backward over the play. Lorenzo's talk in the opening scene is close to being a formal "praise of music." He begins by commending the beauty of the night, remembering other nights and the stories of Cressida, Thisbe, Dido, and Medea. These characters were all tragic, brought to disaster either by their own perfidy or by the pursuit of wicked revenge, by desertion or

**A New Mimesis* (1983), pp. 120–31. Nuttall notes, for example, that Bassanio's first mention of Portia puts money before beauty and virtue: "In Belmont is a lady richly left, / And she is fair and, fairer than that word, / Of wondrous virtues" (I.i.161–63).

misfortune. Yet Jessica jokingly aligns herself with them by repeating the incipit "In such a night..." She is also perfidious, a runaway, and (we may think if we choose) she will have bad fortune; hints of doom shadow the purity of the night. Then Lorenzo pronounces his *laus musicae:*

How sweet the moonlight sleeps upon this bank!
Here will we sit, and let the sounds of music
Creep in our ears. Soft stillness and the night
Become the touches of sweet harmony.

(V.i.54–57)

And he expounds to Jessica the doctrine of the music of the spheres, the harmony of the creation that human beings cannot hear since the Fall. Here the frivolous Lorenzo strangely acquires something of the gravity achieved by Milton when he wrote of the same subject in his ode "At a Solemn Music."

After his words we have audible, terrestrial music, introduced, as elsewhere in Shakespeare (notably at the climactic recognition scene in *Pericles*), with further explanations of its solemnity and of the link between human goodness and a love of music. (Shylock doesn't care for it: "Let no such man be trusted" [88].) Music is order, harmony in celestial as well as human relations; indeed, concord of every kind is a reflection of musical order. Harmony is related to love as discord to hatred. We are again close to the main theme: mercy and love versus justice and discord. Out of the discord of the quarrel about the rings comes, in the end, the concord of the newly married couples. Once again, to solve what is now a comic quarrel, the Christian Antonio offers redemption: "I dare be bound again, / My soul upon the forfeit" (V.i.251–52). The blend of seriousness (unending friendship) and bawdy talk (the play ends with one of Gratiano's many bawdy jokes) is, as we say, Shakespearian.

We are used to these blendings and tensions, yet we can still miss some of them, as I have surely done. Others strike one on rereading. For example, Portia and Nerissa, though apparently intimate friends, observe hierarchical convention in addressing one another: to Nerissa Portia is always "you," and to Portia Nerissa is always "thou" (as in their opening scene, I.ii). That they speak in prose suggests the informality of their relationship; that they discuss Portia's suitors one after another suggests intimacy; but the personal pronouns maintain difference of rank.

The Merchant of Venice has some passages we might now wish away—the clowning of Launcelot Gobbo is of much the same kind, though less amusing, than that of Launce in *Two Gentlemen of Verona,* in almost every other respect an inferior play. Yet *The Merchant* has unmistakeable virtuosity and individuality. That it immediately followed *A Midsummer Night's Dream* and was itself immediately followed by *1 Henry IV* is testimony to Shakespeare's versatility and comic range. To put Bottom at the centre of a play, and to follow that with a play in which Shylock holds that position, and then to invent, in the midst of a history play, the figure of Falstaff—this gives us a fair idea of genius in a writer who had still to stretch his wings to their full extent.

Of the remaining comedies written before 1600, *The Merry Wives of Windsor* is the least. Composed largely in prose, it is lively and resourceful in language and briskly efficient in construction. Falstaff has not yet lost his force, though it is diminished. Perhaps the play's greatest virtue lies in its having been a quarry for the libretto of Verdi's *Falstaff,* where the wit, being in the music, suffers less from the lapse of time.

Anne Barton makes the point that the play has a curious interest in the English language, which is variously tormented by numerous characters: Evans, the Welsh parson; Dr. Caius, the French physician, "engaged in a desperate grapple with the English tongue"; Slender, with his impoverished vocabulary; Pistol, with his incomprehensible rant; Nym, obsessed with his "humor" and frightening "English out of his wits" (II.i.139); Mistress Quickly, with her malapropisms. "Among all these characters, occupied in their several ways in hacking and misconstruing the English language ["Let them . . . hack our English" (III.i.77–78)], Falstaff stands out as a man who can make words do exactly what he wants them to do."* This last truth is somewhat belied by the failure of Falstaff's "cony-catching" letters, but the play has linguistic virtuosity and variety. In view of what lies ahead in *Othello* and *The Winter's Tale,* the representation of Ford's jealousy is interesting as an unwitting preliminary sketch—"If I find her honest . . ." (II.i.238), ". . . though she appear honest to me . . ." (II.ii.221–22).

Much Ado about Nothing, probably written in 1598, is, like the *Henry IV* plays, a work in which great energy has gone into prose. The witty talk of the

*Introduction to *The Merry Wives of Windsor* in *The Riverside Shakespeare,* p. 322.

upper classes owes something to the plays of John Lyly, the comic dialogue of Dogberry and his crew to the talents of the actor Will Kempe. The range of prose styles in the play is certainly extraordinary, but I find some of the Beatrice-Benedick flyting a little tedious. This, of all Shakespeare's comedies, is the one that best prefigures the comedies of the Restoration, and although none of England's later dramatists could match Dogberry, a dispassionate judge could hardly prefer the wit of Beatrice and Benedick to that of characters in a play by Congreve. No doubt it will be argued that Shakespeare has more humanity, more depth, a more critical attitude to the behaviour of such characters as Claudio. But the main interest of the play lies in the wit combats (as the tendency to think of it as *Beatrice and Benedick* suggests), and they are not always successful. Beatrice and Benedick announce themselves as wits, but the habit spreads to minor characters like Margaret (see III.iv), with whom the effect can be tedious. The most impressive moment in the play is the scene when Beatrice commands her lover to kill Claudio (IV.i.289); there is a certain relief involved, for they converse for a moment rather more like persons who have momentarily forgotten their reputations.

As You Like It, written a year or so later, close in time to *Julius Caesar,* is the most topical of the comedies and the one most involved in the intellectual interests of its period. There is very little plot, the movement being out of the city into the forest and back again; and the medium is again primarily prose. (By the calculation of the Oxford editors it is 52 percent as against 72 percent in *Much Ado* and 87 percent in *The Merry Wives; Twelfth Night* is 62 percent and *I Henry IV* 45 percent prose. After 1600, the percentage of prose falls very low, to about 20 or less. *Macbeth* has 7 percent, and Shakespeare's share of *Henry VIII* only 1 percent. This change is no doubt explained by the change in genres, the later works being tragedies or tragicomedies; there is an increase in the proportion of verse at the time of the late romances.)

Meanwhile, Shakespeare had lost his clown, his Dogberry, the actor Will Kempe, who left Shakespeare's company in 1599. Dogberry traces are found in later plays, but never in the same concentration. Still, Shakespeare's company, the Lord Chamberlain's Men, were lucky: Kempe was succeeded by Robert Armin; as Agnes Latham points out, Touchstone does not mangle the language and offers a more educated kind of wit.* There is no play of Shakespeare's, apart perhaps from *Love's Labor's Lost,* that requires of the reader or

**As You Like It,* Arden edition (1975), p. lii.

spectator more knowledge of Elizabethan culture and especially of its styles in literature than *As You Like It.* Pastoral poetry, commenting adversely on court and city life by offering a kind of ideal commonwealth in the country, was still in full favour and ripe for satire. Pastoral was so much the fashion that existing poems were rewritten with added pastoral trappings. And non-dramatic satire had been in vogue until it was suppressed in 1598, along with the erotic epyllion (the genre of *Venus and Adonis*), and satire survived only on the stage.

As You Like It may have been among the first plays put on by the Lord Chamberlain's Men, at the new Globe Theatre. This decisive venture had a spectacular beginning. The company found themselves unwilling to pay the ground rent when their lease of the Theatre in Shoreditch was up for renewal. Exercising a contractual right, they dismantled the theatre and carried the timbers across the Thames to Bankside, where they were used in building the Globe. Shakespeare had a share in the company and in the theatre, and would in the ordinary way be asked to write the first piece for the new house. That the result should be *As You Like It* was conceivably because of the desire of his colleagues to establish at once a difference of class from the sort of thing done at the neighbouring Rose Theatre, where the repertory was more raucously popular. Peter Thomson believes that an earlier version of the play had no Touchstone (a part designed, whether originally or in a post-Kempe revision, for Armin) and that the part of William may have been much longer and written for Will Kempe, who sold his share and left the company at this time. If this is so, the signing on of a very different kind of comic (Douglas Byng replacing George Formby) and the provision of a special role for him might mark the rejection of "ribaldry" and the beginning of an "inexorable move towards 'high' art."*

Certainly it is a very literary play. A corrupt court and an honest, chilly forest affirm the old polarity between the two, and between art and nature, action and contemplation. In the end, the forest converts Oliver to virtue and everybody returns to court and city to get on with the world's business. Meanwhile, the fashions of the court and city are paralleled and mocked by the inhabitants of the forest. Orlando is the younger son whose breeding can survive his starved education, a romantic theme familiar from Spenser—if

**Shakespeare's Professional Career* (1992), p. 134. Thomson draws on David Wiles, *Shakespeare's Clown* (1987).

born of noble (*nobile = non vile*) blood, a boy deserted in the wild will still show "sparks of gentle mind" (*Faerie Queene,* VI.v.1); so, too, with the King's abducted sons in *Cymbeline.* The virtue of the noble father persists: it does not guarantee virtue in the son but at least predisposes him towards it. Of course there can be faults attributable to nurture rather than nature, but lacking virtuous ancestry leaves one in the position of Caliban, "on whose nature / Nurture can never stick" (*Tempest,* IV.i.188–89).

Orlando as lover, carving names in tree trunks and writing poems to attach to them, plays a part common in pastoral poetry. By virtue of their natural habitat, it was often suggested, virtuous shepherds could love, whereas in cities love gave way to lust. Forest dwellers may be desperately lovelorn, like Orlando, who, at the beginning of III.ii, is given a conventionally elegant poem (1–10) that parodies the verse of many such lovers. Once more we see a city person imitating shepherds, in this instance imitation shepherds. Parody is again the mode in the rhymes that Celia finds in Orlando's papers, as Touchstone emphasizes and Rosalind confirms (III.ii.). The play contains "real" shepherds against which these artificial actions are to be understood. Corin is an example. But nothing is quite simple, and the wooing of Phebe by Silvius (III.v) would be simple parody only if Phebe did not respond to her lover's complaints by taking them literally. It is a good moment: she ridicules the notion that a woman's eyes kill, as lovers tended to say:

'Tis pretty, sure, and very probable,
That eyes, that are the frail'st and softest things,
Who shut their coward gates on atomies,
Should be called tyrants, butchers, murtherers!
Now I do frown on thee with all my heart,
And if mine eyes can wound, now let them kill thee.
Now counterfeit to swound, why, now fall down,
Or if thou canst not, O, for shame, for shame,
Lie not, to say mine eyes are murtherers!
Now show the wound mine eye hath made in thee;
Scratch thee but with a pin, and there remains
Some scar of it; lean upon a rush,
The cicatrice and capable impressure
Thy palm some moment keeps . . .

(III.v.11–24)

This refutation of Petrarchan love language is the more striking in that Phebe is also playing the Petrarchan part of the unachievable mistress; but its most interesting feature is that the spirit of rejection is allied with common sense, and common sense forcibly expressed. "Who shut their coward gates on atomies" has a strength that differentiates it from the workaday verse of most of the play; it is a thought that is not far out of the common way, yet it has a kind of physical accuracy, an appeal to the hearer such that he or she will blink or remember blinking in these circumstances, an involvement of the body that gives additional truth to the sentiment. "The cicatrice and capable impressure" is worthy of the poet using his full power, the second noun reinforcing and qualifying the first.* This is what one looks for in Shakespeare, and here, as in *Much Ado,* he for the most part avoids it, preferring to invest in the wit of prose encounters.

Phebe is complicated, a china shepherdess who talks sense (and, with Silvius, always in verse), and she hints at the many different tones of pastoral heard in this play. There is yet another in Rosalind's surprising intervention (here she has the courtesy to speak verse), when she demonstrates that Phebe's cold rejection of her suitor can be construed as no less artificial than the love plaints of Silvius. What right has Phebe to be "proud and pitiless" (III.v.40)? It befits no woman, and least of all an ordinary shepherd girl. Phebe is made to suffer for it, since she is at once in love with Rosalind, and before long, in the wretched poems she writes to Rosalind, will herself be droning on about scornful eyes (IV.iii.40ff.); Silvius continues in what now becomes a happy abjection. Since peasants, especially shepherds, were closer to some original state of virtuous life than city dwellers could be, their loves should be correspondingly simple, and should show up the different manners of the court and city. No doubt the vogue of pastoral was in part due not simply to literary fashion but to the growing sense that city and country were becoming continually more estranged, while the city sank ever deeper into vice. But one should not expect this play to draw a simple diagram to that effect.

The satirist is essentially urban, his ancestry stretching back to the satirists of corrupt imperial Rome, the subject of the terrible condemnations of Juvenal.

*Shakespeare was quite fond of the word "capable" and uses it with a range of meanings. The closest parallel to the usage here is probably *Henry VIII,* V.ii.45–47: "we are all men, / In our own natures frail, and capable / Of our flesh," meaning something like "susceptible to the weaknesses of our flesh."

The courtier Jacques is a mild Elizabethan descendant, professing a wish to "Cleanse the foul body of th' infected world" (II.vii.60) and earning Duke Senior's reproach that he sins in chiding sin; he is merely using the privilege of the satirist (sometimes represented as a satyr, a wild figure come in from the forest to whip the sins of the city) to discharge his own corruption on to the world (II.vii.64–69). Jacques produces the satirist's usual defence, that he attacks vices, not individuals; any man who claims to have been the intended target is accusing himself (70–87). Yet the Duke enjoys his talk (II.i.67), and he himself describes the courtiers as "usurpers, tyrants," for they have invaded the living space of the animals they hunt (II.i.61–63). Touchstone, a licensed fool, is also a city commentator; despising the shepherds, yet outmanoeuvred in debate by the shepherd Corin. His possibly fraudulent intentions towards Audrey echo another ancient theme, the courtier who meets and seduces a country girl.

As You Like It is, then, very much of its moment in having so much to do with the literary fashions of the day. The first quarter of an hour of the play in performance is in prose—an augury, for prose is the language of criticism. The romantic plot begins then, and people speak in verse, especially as Rosalind and Orlando fall in love. The girls chatter in prose, but when Duke Frederick banishes Rosalind verse supervenes, as if there was a distinction between mere talk and more performative words. In II.iv Rosalind, Celia, and Touchstone begin in prose; but Corin and Silvius enter talking verse, Silvius with a neat rhetorical flourish, because they are talking of pastoral love. Rosalind, also in love, echoes them; but Touchstone, though talking about his love for Jane Smile, reasserts the rights of prose, rendering prosaic the pastoral trappings of such contemporary poets as Richard Barnefield: "I remember the kissing of her batler and the cow's dugs that her pretty chopp'd hands had milk'd... We that are true lovers run into strange capers..." (II.iv.48–55). And so on, until the clown Corin enters, when he and Touchstone have a conversation (III.ii) that is a straight comic confrontation between court and country.

More could be said of the alternation of prose and verse (some of it song), which here is subtler, and easier to explain than it sometimes is. Rosalind and Celia are sisters to Beatrice, full of pretty answers, as Jaques says Orlando is (III.ii.266), and sometimes they are tedious, as when Rosalind lectures Orlando on Time and the proper appearance of a lover (III.ii) or Jaques on melancholy (IV.i), or speaks of history's failure to produce an example of a man who died for love (IV.i.89–104). It is useless to object to these protractions, for their liveliness and wit cannot be gainsaid, but many must have wished, while commending it as Christopher Sly in *The Taming of the Shrew* praises the play, that it would come to an end.

There are, however, considerable rewards in *As You Like It:* the charming quartet for Phebe, Silvius, Rosalind, and Orlando (V.ii.76ff.), which is reminiscent of passages in Lorenzo Da Ponte's libretti for Mozart, though Rosalind compares it to "the howling of Irish wolves against the moon" (109–10). The following brief scene between Touchstone and Audrey is introduced with as little ceremony as a song in a musical, and its aptness is simply that it is about "country copulatives" (V.iv.55), though it gives Rosalind time to change her clothes; the famous song is pleasant, though Touchstone instantly puts it down as "foolish," and then takes a great while to explain how to give the lie, or take it when given. There follows the masque of Hymen, like an operatic finale, and the message from the court to the effect that everybody, except possibly Jaques, is to go home. A dance, then Rosalind's Epilogue (few such epilogues have survived, and this one does its work well).

Praise for *As You Like It* needs to be qualified, because more than most of Shakespeare it has slipped over our horizon; it has too much to say about what was once intimately interesting and now is not. It calls for some rather specialised historical information and, in any case, its character and purpose place limitations on its language. Yet it is about this time that we see an extraordinary change in Shakespeare's language. *As You Like It* may well have been a play written for the Globe, and *Henry V* likewise. But in 1599 *Julius Caesar* was certainly played there and, in the following year, *Hamlet,* which truly began a new era.

PART TWO

JULIUS CAESAR

So far as is known, the first tragedy played in the new Globe Theatre was *Julius Caesar.* It is one of the few plays of which we have a contemporary report of a Globe performance. Thomas Platter of Basle happened to record in his diary that on 21 September 1599 (probably by the Continental calendar; the date would have been nine days earlier by the English count), he crossed the Thames and saw at a theatre that was obviously the Globe the tragedy of "the first emperor Julius Caesar with nearly fifteen characters very well acted." The performance ended with the customary dance or jig.

Platter notes that he went to the theatre around two o'clock, the usual time. *Julius Caesar* is one of the shorter tragedies, perhaps not much longer in performance than the "two hours' traffic of our stage" mentioned in the Prologue to *Romeo and Juliet.** This relative terseness is echoed in the economical construction of the play and in what might be called its dialect. With the experience of nine English history plays behind him, Shakespeare deftly selects

*Clearly this is not applicable to *Hamlet,* which is a great deal longer, as is *Othello.* The variations in length of the plays remains something of a puzzle. One should not take the *Romeo and Juliet* formula too literally; Andrew Gurr calls it "a bit of a fiction." The Lord Chamberlain laid it down in 1594 that plays should begin at two o'clock and end "between four and five," but plays got longer as time went on, and some were over 4,000 lines (*Hamlet,* Jonson's *Bartholomew Fair*), and even allowing for rapid delivery, they cannot have been performed in under three hours. See Andrew Gurr, *The Shakespearean Stage, 1574–1642,* 3rd ed. (1992), pp. 178–79.

and incorporates the narratives of Plutarch in North's translation, compressing, omitting, focussing, adjusting the relationships of the main characters, and occasionally adding material from other sources, or of his own invention.

For example, he seems to have invented the scene where Calpurnia is touched by the runners in the Lupercalian ritual, and the scene of the murder of the poet Cinna, mistaken for a politician, is taken from a hint in the historian Suetonius writing about a later epoch. Perhaps this little insertion was meant as an ironic denial that poets, except by unhappy chance, have anything to do with politics; yet this is an intensely political play, a fact that has a controlling influence over its language. The rule of Julius Caesar effectively marked the end of the Roman republic and the troubled beginning of the empire. The Elizabethans were in general anti-republican, believing monarchy to be the best system of government, and propaganda claimed that Elizabeth's right descended ultimately from the Emperor Constantine, who was the son of the Englishwoman Helen and the first Christian emperor. So there was, it was believed, a direct line to Rome in the period of Caesar's assassination and the accession of Octavius Caesar as Augustus.

Plutarch had republican sentiments but admitted that Rome, having at the time suffered a century of civil war, needed the firm single rule of Caesar. In the sixteenth century some thought of Caesar as a tyrant, and some, arguing against the official view that obedience was required whatever the character of the monarch, thought tyrants ought to be killed. Others, perhaps, like Brutus, believed that Caesar was not a tyrant so long as he did not accept the crown, that despite his virtually absolute power he had shown no disposition to use it absolutely. And Plutarch himself raises the issue of whether Caesar was a tyrant or "a merciful physician." What is certain is that to the first audience this was a play about a world-historical event, still politically relevant. The conspirators, after the death of Caesar, make the point clear enough:

> How many ages hence
> Shall this our lofty scene be acted over
> In states unborn and accents yet unknown!
>
> (III.i.111–13)

Cassius goes on to predict that when Caesar will be seen to "bleed in sport," the conspirators will be revered for having given their country liberty (114–18). There must be irony here; the audience, or most of them, knew better.

The main purpose of Shakespeare's brilliant and daring opening scene, whose principal characters disappear from the play immediately, is to set up an opposition between fickle public sentiment, now favoring Julius Caesar, and the higher class represented by the tribunes, who support the defeated Pompey. We are shown a vigorous reaction to Caesar's ambition and his triumphal entry into Rome, the latter not being customary when the defeated enemy was another Roman. The opening scene, like others, and notably that of *Hamlet,* tells us much about the kind of dramatic poet Shakespeare was. He may begin obliquely, as here, or enigmatically, as in *Macbeth;* but, as in his verse, he is always putting the simple sense into question. His plays contain other scenes that sometimes puzzle the reader or (if they are not cut by some director) the audience. Another example in *Julius Caesar* is the curious little conversation among Decius Brutus, Cinna, and Casca during the meeting of the conspirators (II.i.101–11). These men, about to pledge themselves to murder, quietly disagree as to which way is east and where the sun rises in March: a small puzzle in the midst of greater ones.

Elizabethan interest in the fate of Julius would be intense and also divided. Caesar was a monarch in all but name, and Shakespeare, who had written of many monarchs, stresses his human failings (deafness, pride, perhaps sterility). On the other hand, he omits material that would darken the portrait of Brutus, who, in the thought of the period, could be either a heroic tyrannicide or a republican hero. No simple political position can be detected in the play. Whatever view one took, these Romans had immediate importance as ancient imperial ancestors, and whatever side they were on, they must be supposed to have spoken with a sort of constrained dignity. The dialect of the tragedy is quite unlike that of its predecessor *Romeo and Juliet* or of its successor *Hamlet.* The characters, apart from the crowd, speak like Romans, conscious of the honour of being Romans, contemporaries, after all, of Cicero, a principal model of Renaissance style.

This is not to say that the work is absolutely free of the rhetorical obscurities we shall encounter in the later tragedies, but it is relatively so. The play begins with the good-humoured prose of the populace, which gives way at once to the florid scolding of the tribunes; the people are to weep into the Tiber till it overflows. The jokes of "naughty knaves" and the rant of the anti-Caesarian tribunes are at the two remote ends of the rhetorical scale. In the second scene we find the middle way, something close to the register of the remainder of the play: economical dialogue followed by a more expansive discussion between Brutus and Cassius. There is no attempt to generate high poetry; the tone is thoughtful, though never lacking in force:

CAS. Tell me, good Brutus, can you see your face?
BRUT. No, Cassius; for the eye sees not itself
But by reflection, by some other things.
CAS. 'Tis just,
And it is very much lamented, Brutus,
That you have no such mirrors as will turn
Your hidden worthiness into your eye,
That you might see your shadow.

(I.ii.51–58)

Cassius is beginning his campaign to recruit Brutus for his conspiracy, but he starts from a long way off, introducing this notion of the eye's inability to see itself, its dependence on reflections or shadows. As we have already seen, the idea of the reflection as the shadow of a substance was precious to Shakespeare, and it always called forth fine contemplative verse. "How soon my sorrow hath destroy'd my face," says Richard II after smashing the looking-glass. "The shadow of your sorrow hath destroy'd / The shadow of your face," replies Bolingbroke (IV.i.291–93). And Richard develops the theme:

The shadow of my sorrow! Ha, let's see.
'Tis very true, my grief lies all within,
And these external manners of laments
Are merely shadows to the unseen grief
That swells with silence in the tortur'd soul.
There lies the substance . . .

(294–99)

As Peter Ure has remarked, Bolingbroke and Richard are giving different senses to the word "shadow": to Bolingbroke the broken mirror bore only the shadow, not the substance; Richard speaks of the *darkness* cast by his sorrow, and Ure adds, "My sorrow—these external ways of lamenting—are simply shadows [= unreal images] of the grief within. Richard thus uses Bolingbroke's own quibble to prove, not, as Bolingbroke had wished to, that the image in the glass is unreal, but that Richard's lamentation reflects a real substance, just as the image in the glass, though itself unreal, as Bolingbroke claims, none the less reflects a real face. A shadow is unreal compared with the substance that it is a shadow of; this fact can be used either, as by Bolingbroke, to insist on the unreality of the shadow, or, as by Richard, to insist on the reality of the substance."* It may be that since, as Brutus remarks, "the eye sees not itself / But by reflection," all attempts to examine what Hamlet calls "that within that passes show" (I.ii.85) must be unreliable, for in the language of the time reflections are shadows, and shadows are not only areas of darkness but unreal and possibly false representations of substance.

Shakespeare again presents the insoluble difficulty of actually seeing what is "within" in *Troilus and Cressida,* when Ulysses and Achilles have the following discussion:

ULYSS. A strange fellow here
Writes me that man, however dearly ever parted
How much in having, or without or in,
Cannot make boast to have that which he hath,
Nor feels not what he owes, but by reflection;
As when his virtues, aiming upon others,
Heat them, and they retort that heat again
To the first giver.
ACHIL. This is not strange, Ulysses.
The beauty that is borne here in the face
The bearer knows not, but commends itself
To others' eyes; nor doth the eye itself,
That most pure spirit of sense, behold itself,
Not going from itself; but eye to eye opposed,
Salutes each other with each other's form;
For speculation turns not to itself,
Till it hath travell'd and is mirror'd there
Where it may see itself. This is not strange at all.
(III.iii.95–111)

Ulysses wants to make the point that honour and reputation lie not "within" but in the applause of others, a kind of reflection, to be represented either as reflected heat or as noise. The context, and the language or dialect, is very different from that of *Julius Caesar* or of *Richard II,* far more studied and

*Arden edition, pp. 141–42.

laborious, but the figure is still virtually the same, and, as we shall see, it is recurrent and must have real, not shadow, importance to the poetry. For actors are also shadows, as Macbeth remarked—"Life's but a walking shadow, a poor player, / That struts and frets his hour upon the stage, / And then is heard no more" (V.v.24–26). And the notion that the substance, the life "within," is inaccessible except by such treacherous mediation tells us something important about an author whose business it was to present character in all its inaccessibility, in language at least as opaque as necessary.

An instance of his doing that is the soliloquy of Brutus in II.i. The first act has the long temptation of Brutus by Cassius, brilliantly set against the shouts of the crowd. Cassius is mocking Caesar's weakness, remembering him in his fever whining for water: "Give me some drink, Titinius" (I.ii.127)—a savage put-down in itself, thin and querulous and the more so in that the report coincides with another shout from the mob that wants Caesar crowned. Cassius has an embittered and calculating eloquence, and his long speeches are barely punctuated by the replies of Brutus. Then we hear more of Caesar, with Casca's account of the behaviour of the rabblement, and Caesar's fit, all in blunt, rather Jonsonian prose. Cassius ends the scene with a self-satisfied soliloquy.

At once there is a storm, and the same Casca is now terrified—in verse, for he is suffering and talking about divine portents. Coleridge did not think this authentic, supposing that the part of the terrified and superstitious man was originally given to some person other than Casca. But it is just here that verse-prose contrasts can be effective, if less obvious than the contrast between Brutus's prose and Antony's verse in the funeral orations.* Cassius turns them to his own advantage; indeed, the control of the play so far and the tone of its verse are largely in his hands. But the second act opens with Brutus's soliloquy.

The context is designed to make Brutus gentle; the presence of the boy Lucius, fetching a taper and a book, telling his master the date, falling asleep at his instrument, all suggest a domestic calm at odds with the associations of the fatal day to come and with the "exhalations whizzing in the air" (II.i.44),

*Brian Vickers demonstrates the rhetorical rigour and symmetry of Brutus's speech, which was nevertheless so ineffective. Brutus speaks verse immediately before and after the oration; it seems his more natural manner. *The Artistry of Shakespeare's Prose* (1968; rev ed., 1979), pp. 241–45. Vickers reminds us that Brutus had forgotten the prime rule of rhetoric, that "a speech must be adapted to the nature of the audience." It is a rule that Shakespeare never forgot, although as the audience grew more clever he allowed himself to grow more clever also.

though the calm is uneasy. Coleridge declares that the soliloquy belies Brutus the "Stoico-Platonic tyrannicide," because it gives him no motive to kill Caesar; if Caesar remained as good a monarch as he now seemed, there was no reason to remove him. But, says Coleridge, there were many reasons to kill him: Caesar had crossed the Rubicon and entered Rome as a conqueror (as we saw in the first scene). He wants to know why Shakespeare did not "bring these things forward"; of course he did bring the triumphal entry forward, but not very far, and obliquely.*

It must be by his death; and for my part,
I know no personal cause to spurn at him,
But for the general. He would be crown'd:
How that might change his nature, there's the question.
It is the bright day that brings forth the adder,
And that craves wary walking. Crown him that,
And then I grant we put a sting in him
That at his will he may do danger with.
Th' abuse of greatness is when it disjoins
Remorse from power; and to speak truth of Caesar,
I have not known when his affections sway'd
More than his reason. But 'tis a common proof
That lowliness is young ambition's ladder,
Whereto the climber-upward turns his face;
But when he once attains the utmost round,
He then unto the ladder turns his back,
Looks in the clouds, scorning the base degrees
By which he did ascend. So Caesar may;
Then lest he may, prevent. And since the quarrel
Will bear no color for the thing he is,
Fashion it thus: that what he is, augmented,
Would run to these and these extremities;
And therefore think him as a serpent's egg,
Which, hatch'd, would as his kind grow mischievous,
And kill him in the shell.

(II.i.10–34)

*Samuel Taylor Coleridge, *Shakespearean Criticism* (2 vols., 1960), Vol. I, p. 14.

The truth is that the soliloquy, which has the appearance of being spoken by a man who has already virtually made up his mind, proves, on examination, to be more opaque than one at first supposes. "No personal cause": that is, no cause that relates to Caesar as a person rather than as an official of the state. He has not abused his power by failing to show mercy ("remorse"). He has not (as tyrants do) allowed his passions to evade the control of his reason. The sole positive reason Brutus gives for wanting Caesar dead is that "He would be crown'd" (12). It is the rite of coronation that might "change his nature."

The other reasons proposed are implausible: when men become great they kick away the ladder; but Caesar has shown no signs of doing so. Only the prospect of kingship, his desire for it, and the complicity of the mob make him dangerous. We are reminded that Brutus's ancestor and namesake helped to drive out the kings long ago; Romans were suspicious of kings. We are also obliged to reflect that ceremonies mean a lot to almost everybody concerned, not least Brutus, who wants the murder to be a sacrificial, ritual act, a demonic opposite of coronation. We remember that coronation and crowns were not mere empty shows to Shakespeare's contemporaries. He himself had dramatised coronations, and said much about crowns.* Coleridge was right to find the passage more difficult than it looked, but his explanation was wrong; he seemed to have hoped for a more explicit expression of Brutus's state of mind. But that cannot have been what Shakespeare wanted to provide.

We come to understand, as we approach the plays of the great period, that simple clarity was less and less Shakespeare's way. Even when the point seems simple, there is often a kind of aura of obscurity, enough strain on the language to tax the reader's mind. When Brutus has committed himself, and before the conspirators arrive, he suddenly says something more remarkable than the famous soliloquy:

> Since Cassius first did whet me against Caesar,
> I have not slept.
> Between the acting of a dreadful thing
> And the first motion, all the interim is

*There are about 380 uses of the word in the canon, counting plurals and verb forms; about ten per play. Admittedly about sixty of these usages occur in *3 Henry VI,* when the word stands for what the main action is all about; but *Julius Caesar* has fifteen, in a context where coronation should, historically speaking, be less important.

Like a phantasma or a hideous dream.
The Genius and the mortal instruments
Are then in council; and the state of a man,
Like to a little kingdom, suffers then
The nature of an insurrection.

(II.i.61–69)

This is wonderful writing: think of the propriety of "whet," with its hint of daggers to come, and the effectiveness of the short line that follows. The rest of the speech is worthy of Hamlet, for it generalises a local situation: Brutus moves away from his broodings over Caesar and contemplates the interim between any first intention to commit "a dreadful thing" (not specified as a killing or even as a crime) and the performance that follows; the moment of deep anxiety that comes between. A phantasma is specifically a bad or evil dream, glossed as "hideous." The second figure, the interior council, makes the character of the interim clearer: the man who has taken the decision is a microcosmic version of a state disturbed by insurrection: his spirit is beset, as in an angry cabinet meeting, by his lower powers, whose protests are perhaps founded in an apprehension of danger to themselves. The scene is one of deep disturbance, as the mortal instruments rebel against the decisions of the higher soul. That Brutus should, in his metaphor, think of the state as a kingdom is a way of relating the generalisation to the more specific theme: Rome as a potential kingdom.

A few years later, in *Macbeth,* Shakespeare was to give a full representation of this fraught interim in his treatment of all that passed between the decision to murder Duncan and the actual commission of the deed. We may now think we understand the disturbances that lie under the official calm of Brutus:

No, not an oath! If not the face of men,
The sufferance of our souls, the time's abuse—
If these be motives weak, break off betimes . . .

(114–16)

where the breaking off of the sentence enacts the breaking off it suggests and rejects. Later "the sufferance of our souls" is accidentally remembered—"such suffering souls / That welcome wrongs" (131–32), and used in a different sense, not as a confession of spiritual suffering, but as a reproach to all who hesitate to join the conspirators simply as honourable Romans, who need no oath, as a coward might.

After that speech, the characters, and the language, once again get down to business. Here again Brutus, with his desire for a bloodless murder and his trust of Antony, proves his incompetence as a leader; he lacks the cunning of Decius Brutus, whose trickery about omens will bring Caesar to the Senate, despite Calpurnia's dream. A clock strikes, and the day dawns; and now we see that the earlier conversation about the sun rising had its dramatic purpose. We are reminded repeatedly of the time, which is, as they say, of the essence. The Ides of March has come.

Portia's entrance reaffirms the excessive humanity of Brutus. She is celebrated for her stoical strength. "Dwell I but in the suburbs / Of your good pleasure?" (285–86). Whores dwell in the suburbs; she, Cato's daughter, is indignant at the thought of being so reduced. To express that sentiment thus is itself an indication of her dignity and mental power. Brutus gives in and will tell her all. Only a brief scene with a belated conspirator separates the Brutus-Portia dialogue from that between Caesar and Calpurnia; again male folly prevails, inducing Caesar to defy the "ceremonies" or omens in which he believes.

Shakespeare, as I've suggested, often uses a special kind of "lighting scene"—an episode a little aside from the main movement of the story that is meant to illustrate a particular aspect of it, like, for instance, the argument between Peter and the musicians in *Romeo and Juliet,* or the dispute between Shylock and Antonio concerning Laban's ewes in *The Merchant of Venice;* just the kind of scene an incautious director, worried about the pace of the performance, might be tempted to cut but must not. We see the conspirators gather at Caesar's house, meaning to escort him to the Senate; then there occurs the passage in which Portia, profoundly agitated, sends Lucius there, for no reason she can provide. She meets the polite but darkly ominous soothsayer, who immediately encounters Caesar and again warns him. These details intensify the very sense of interim that Brutus has defined. That interim seems to end with Caesar's death, a scene carried out with the utmost efficiency, Caesar bragging to the last. But we discover that this is a false end. Indeed, the true end of the story has to wait until Octavian stands over the body of Cleopatra in the next Roman play.

There are famous moments to come: the rival funeral orations in prose and verse (during Antony's performance even the plebeians use verse, until, moved to destructive action at the end of the scene, they return to prose: "Pluck down forms, windows, any thing" [III.ii.259]). Although Antony speaks at some length, the economy of the scene is extraordinary. It is followed by another brilliant "lighting" scene, recounting the fate of the poet Cinna, beset by prosy rioters: "Tear him for his bad verses" (III.iii.30); and then we are with Antony and Octavius in the quarrelsome and Machiavellian mood that, alternating with a sort of masculine Roman tenderness, dominates most of the last two acts of the play.

The quarrel and reconciliation between Brutus and Cassius at Philippi (IV.ii) is a famous set piece, first angry, then surprisingly sentimental; Brutus is angry with an obtrusive poet (again a sly comment on the redundancy of poets in political crises), but Lucius is again at hand to preserve the sentimental mood with broken music. An evil spirit appears to Brutus, perhaps the spirit he had wanted to free from Caesar's body without shedding blood. Before the battle comes a quick and angry parley; Brutus and Cassius know as well as we do that they are bound to lose.

Julius Caesar is a rather more enigmatic play than it looks at first sight. I think of it as a study in the first motion and the ultimate acting of a dreadful thing, worthy to be so called because of its millennial repercussions. Shakespeare had enacted regicide before, but here was one the consequences of which were greater and so permanent that they could be felt sixteen hundred years later in London, a city once within the *limes,* a city of the Roman Empire built by Caesar and his imperial successors.

The political import of Caesar's death is such that only poets, poets of something like Virgilian stature, could deal with it. Yet the two poets in this play are so unequal to the occasion that one is murdered in mistake for a politician and the other turned out when he interrupts politicians in conference. This later poet and playwright can hope to suggest to his audience the vast significance of what they are seeing, while at the same time ironically disclaiming all authority.

HAMLET

Hamlet, the play which may be said to offer the fullest exhibition of Shakespeare's powers, is a tragedy, and within that category a revenge tragedy, but of all the genres in the absurd list proffered by Polonius—"tragedy, comedy, history, pastoral, pastoral-comical, historical-pastoral, tragical-historical, tragical-comical-historical-pastoral, scene individable, or poem unlimited" (II.ii.396–400)—the one that best fits the play is the last, "poem unlimited." This expression is variously defined as meaning a play that doesn't conform to the classical unities of action, time, and place, but that would hardly distinguish *Hamlet* from many other plays of Shakespeare. The most recent Oxford editor says it means "plays not restricted as to their length, and not conforming to the neo-classical unities of time and place."* This play simply does so many different things, brings together so many styles, that no other (except possibly *Pericles,* where the unlimitedness is due to patchwork) compares with it.

If one looks, for instance, at the wonderful scene in which Polonius produces the catalogue of dramatic types mentioned above, one finds all the following: the beginning of the Rosencrantz and Guildenstern plot, the successful return of the ambassadors from Norway (diplomatic plot), Polonius's theory

**Hamlet,* ed. G. R. Hibbard (Oxford edition, 1987), p. 224.

that Hamlet is mad for love of Ophelia, Hamlet's teasing of Polonius ("You're a fishmonger . . . Have you a daughter?," etc.), the brilliantly sharp first dialogue between Hamlet and Rosencrantz and Guildenstern (some of it only in the probably revised Folio version), the arrival of the players, gossip about the successes of the London boys' companies (only in the Folio version), more teasing of Polonius when he comes in with stale news about the actors' arrival, further allusions to his daughter, Hamlet's welcome to the players and the recitation of part of an old play, the planning of *The Mousetrap,* the leading actor's tears, and, to conclude, Hamlet's soliloquy "O, what a rogue and peasant slave am I!"

The language of this scene varies from formal blank verse to the "antic" prose of Hamlet. His conversations with Rosencrantz and Guildenstern are in muscular prose, at first generous in tone, later darkened by suspicion. Hamlet's drama criticism—like the discussion about the London theatres and the advice to the actors on acting that come later—is also in prose, this time topical and critical. As with this last passage, which follows without modulation on the Nunnery scene, where Ophelia is "loosed" to Hamlet and violently rejected, a passage of enigmatic passion is followed by cool prose: "Speak the speech, I pray you, as I pronounc'd it . . ." (III.ii.1ff.). The Nunnery scene itself opens with Ophelia in verse more bland than blank, changing to impassioned prose at the moment when Hamlet asks her whether she is "honest"; his bitter and satirical reproaches are wholly unexpected, and his departure is lamented by Ophelia in probably the flattest and most formal verse of the entire play: "O, what a noble mind is here o'erthrown!" (III.i.150–61).

I have skipped through these two scenes merely to emphasise what familiarity may cause us to miss: the constantly shifting register not only of action but of language. The same limitless variation characterises the whole play. Take the opening scenes: T. S. Eliot, speaking as a playwright, remarked that the first scene is "as well constructed as that of any play ever written." Eliot believed that to use verse in the theatre one needed a medium that could be sufficiently elastic to sound like a natural utterance, not even registered as poetry by the audience. He describes the opening twenty-two lines of *Hamlet* as "built of the simplest words in the most homely idiom. Shakespeare had worked for a long time in the theatre, and written a good many plays, before reaching the point where he could write those twenty-two lines . . . No poet has begun to master dramatic verse until he can write lines which, like these in *Hamlet,* are *transparent.*"*

*"Poetry and Drama," in *On Poetry and Poets* (1957), p. 75.

This is entirely just: the false challenge by Barnardo; the short, anxious speeches; the dark, the cold; the quiet; Francisco's heartsickness (of which we don't know, and never will know, the cause: it belongs to the play rather than to this transient character); the interrupted, unobtrusive, yet somehow solemn beat of pentameters—all this is masterly. What is no less so is the obliquity of what follows. We are about to hear about the "apparition," "the dreaded sight," "this thing." The action of the play seems about to begin; this is, after all, where we expect exposition. But in fact no exposition occurs. In answer to Horatio's confident scepticism Barnardo begins his account of the "apparition." He does so in what was technically known to rhetoricians and poets as a chronography, a description of a particular time; thus he begins to talk in a way intended to be registered as poetry:

> Last night of all,
> When yond same star that's westward from the pole
> Had made his course t' illume that part of heaven
> Where now it burns, Marcellus and myself,
> The bell then beating one—
>
> (I.i.35–39)

but at this point his exercise, and the tale we have been led to expect, is interrupted by the entry of the Ghost. Rapid dialogue ensues: then Horatio addresses the Ghost in stately terms, but it departs. The chronography is redundant; the report on how the Ghost appeared "Last night of all" is nullified by its irruption into the present moment. Barnardo's speech, its beginning so carefully presented, is abruptly rendered useless as far as narrative is concerned. But since the Ghost says nothing whatever, our expectations that this *coup de théâtre* will supply the deficiency and set the plot in motion are defeated. The tension, so elaborately established, is slackened, and the talk takes a different turn. Horatio explains at some length the current political crisis: relations with Norway are bad, hence the armaments drive. Could this be the explanation for the appearance of the dead King? Possibly: and Horatio speculates again, reminding his friends that history offers parallels, for instance the dreadful portents that preceded the death of Julius Caesar.

This last speech is not in the Folio version of 1623, and may well have been cut. It has been suggested that it was a sort of advertisement for *Julius Caesar,* probably still in the Globe repertory at the time of the Quarto version of 1604–5, and not needed when it wasn't. This is bright but unlikely. So, I think, is the notion that the scene needed speeding up, which runs quite counter to the fact of the continuous and clearly deliberate reluctance of the entire scene to make narrative progress. A writer whose purpose was to keep the action moving on could have started the play with Hamlet himself on the battlements, drawn there in much the same way as the sceptical Horatio was. Instead, we, like the characters, are kept in the dark as to the reason for the Ghost's visitation, and young Hamlet is not even mentioned until line 170. Shakespeare did not use opening scenes for simple exposition—think of *Macbeth,* a little later, indeed of *Julius Caesar,* a little earlier—and this one, all atmosphere and very oblique, is one of his boldest.

Of course such considerations cannot quite rule out the possibility that the cut was made to save time; there is no guarantee that cuts always result in improvements, even if made by the author himself. And the play was very long, yet all the cuts in the Folio version together reduce the running time of the piece by only a few minutes.* And I think myself that this cut was against the spirit of the scene. We need its reference to a "precurse of fear'd events" (121), and the speech was rightly in the general, not specific, tone, making the death of old Hamlet and the safety of the Danish state seem matters of great historical moment. Once again, the speech is brought to an end by the arrival of the Ghost, now interrogated formally by Horatio, but again leaving without answer as the cock crows. Once more we have this tantalising false start.

Cockcrow now becomes a topic of conversation. Horatio explains it as a warning to "Th' extravagant and erring spirit" (154) that it is time for him to leave the upper world, and Marcellus affirms the duty of the cock as a messenger between worlds by reporting the belief that it crows all night long in the season "Wherein our Saviour's birth is celebrated" (159), when no spirits

*See above, p. 85. But although plays might last three hours and on occasion even more, it is hard to believe that the Folio text of *Hamlet* could have been performed at the Globe in the darker parts of the year. Q1 has 2,200 lines, and is indebted to the memories of actors who took part in a performance: 2,200 lines might take a little over two hours, about the length of time available in an open-air theatre in winter, without lighting, where performances began at two o'clock. Q2 has 3,800 lines. F cut 230 of these but added 70 more, so time seems not to have been the main consideration. Reasons for cuts will vary. The cut in IV.iv, which deprives the play of Hamlet's soliloquy "How all occasions do inform against me," can be explained by the puzzling inappropriateness of the speech at this moment in the action, for Hamlet claims to be in a position to carry out his revenge at a time when he is so far from being so that he is under guard and on his way to England. The cut in III.iv.72–77, 79–81, is more difficult; it is discussed below (pp. 121–24).

walk at night. It is a happy time, as the calming doublets and repetitions—the collocations of fairies and witches, "taking" and charming, "hallowed and so gracious"—seem, by the gentling of the rhythms as well as by the general sentiment, to assert:

> . . . no spirit dare stir abroad,
> The nights are wholesome, then no planets strike,
> No fairy takes, nor witch hath power to charm,
> So hallowed, and so gracious, is that time.
>
> (161–64)

Horatio then announces the coming of dawn, not straightforwardly like the conspirators in *Julius Caesar,* but with another chronography, once again in more poetic terms:

> So have I heard and do in part believe it.
> But look, the morn in russet mantle clad
> Walks o'er the dew of yon high eastward hill.
>
> (165–67)

This might be from *Romeo and Juliet,* except that the first line reminds us of Horatio's now vestigial scepticism; the shift into another kind of language might seem absurd were it not that we have been thoroughly prepared for it. It is indeed a fine instance of Eliot's point: the dramatic poet must have this range. We move without discomfort from that qualified scepticism to the grander style of the chronography, and then, equally without embarrassment, the verse returns to business: "Break we our watch up." Horatio now proposes that they should tell "young Hamlet" what has been happening (168–70). (This is the first mention of the hero, when the play has been in progress for about ten minutes.) Meanwhile, the doubling and antithetical phrases continue as an undertone: "This spirit, *dumb* to us, will *speak* to him" (171); "As *needful* in our loves, *fitting* our duty" (173).

The language of *Hamlet* continually varies in this and similar ways. It is dominated to an extent without parallel in the canon by one particular rhetorical device: it is obsessed with doubles of all kinds, and notably by its use of the figure known as hendiadys. This means, literally, one-through-two, and can be illustrated by some common expressions such as "law and order" or "house and home." These examples are offered by Chris Baldick, who very properly points out that "the status of this figure is often uncertain, since it usually cannot be established that the paired words actually express a single idea."* But one can justly apply the term to expressions of the sort common in *Hamlet.* The play has many doublings, but those which exhibit hendiadys are marked by identifiable tension or strain, as if the parts were related in some not perfectly evident way.

It would perhaps be too much to claim that a study of this device can take us to the heart of the play, a journey attempted in so many different ways over such a long time, but new ways are always needed. For example, John Kerrigan's 1996 book, *Revenge Tragedy,* a very full account of the genre to which *Hamlet* belongs, not only reminds us of Hamlet's remote ancestor Orestes but argues that Hamlet is concerned more with memory than with revenge, and shows how obstinately the theme of remembering occurs in the text of the play. My purpose in drawing attention to hendiadys is largely to show that in the rhetoric of *Hamlet* there may be a strain, virtually unnoticed, of a kind of compulsion that reflects the great and obvious topics, adultery and incest, deep preoccupations given external representation.†

These preoccupations seem to be related to a concern with questions of identity, sameness, and the union of separate selves—joined opposites, as John Carey called a similar preoccupation in Donne,‡ as in marriage and, in a pathologised form, incest. Questions of identity ("property") are, as I have explained earlier, given enigmatic treatment in "The Phoenix and Turtle," very probably written within a few months of *Hamlet,* whose language is uniquely full of doubles, antitheses, and repetitions. This way of writing was, in its essence, familiar from the English liturgy, and its remote origin is probably in the parallelisms found in the Psalms. Anyone who has known the *Book of Common Prayer* is familiar with such language: "We acknowledge and confess our manifold sins and wickednesses," or "Spare thou them, O God, which confess their faults, restore thou them that are penitent." The "them" in the parallel constructions of the latter may not be absolutely identical, but any slight discrepancy lends force to the pleas, allows the impression of covering all cases. There is a good deal of this kind of doubling in *Hamlet,*

**The Concise Oxford Dictionary of Literary Terms* (1990), p. 97.
†Here I draw on an earlier study of mine, "Cornelius and Voltemand," in *Forms of Attention* (1985), pp. 35–63.
‡*John Donne, His Life and Art* (1981), pp. 264ff.

and of hendiadys, where the meaning of the whole depends upon a kind of unnaturalness in the doubling, a sort of pathological intensification of the device. As George T. Wright* remarks, it can introduce unease and mystery into an expression.

The doubling also affects the structure of *Hamlet.* There are pairs of characters: Cornelius and Voltemand, two ambassadors who speak (together) only ten words; the indistinguishable Rosencrantz and Guildenstern. The play-within-the-play is an uneasy double of *Hamlet,* and the Dumb-show of the play-within-the-play. The role of revenger is doubled (by Laertes and by Fortinbras), and the chronographies of the opening scene (Barnardo's and Horatio's) form brackets for the whole of it. Laertes has a double departure and a double blessing from his father ("A double blessing is a double grace" [I.iii.53]—a line which doubles "double"). Compulsive duplication occurs everywhere, sometimes simple and vacuous, as with Polonius:

> And thus do we of wisdom and of reach,
> With windlasses and with assays of bias,
> By indirections find directions out;
> So by my former lecture and advice
> Shall you my son. You have me, have you not?
>
> (II.i.61–65)

So doubling is a principal characteristic of the language of *Hamlet.* Once alerted to it, and to its extreme form of hendiadys, one hears it throughout; it takes its part in a greater complex of linguistic devices, and serves more than one purpose. But of course I am not suggesting that it is the only characteristic that distinguishes this play. Much more celebrated is delay: although *Hamlet* is an extremely active, indeed feverishly energetic play, it does move forward slowly; notoriously, it is not only Hamlet but his play that delays. But in this respect also the movement of the play—or rather its variety of movements, sometimes speeding along, sometimes apparently dawdling—imitates and depends on the varying movement of the language. Indeed, the doubling in *Hamlet* can obviously be a means of slowing down the action as well as the language of the play, while all, paradoxically, remains, as it were, seething with sense and menace.

*"Hendiadys and *Hamlet,*" *P.M.L.A.,* 96, pp. 168 ff.

The first speech of Claudius is much concerned with the nature of his relation to others: "our sometimes sister, now our queen" boldly opens the question of incest, and what follows is full of paradoxes and oxymorons ("a figure of speech that combines two usually contradictory terms in a compressed paradox"*) that emphasise the conjunction of what is ordinarily disjunct; he has married his brother's wife

> as 'twere with a defeated joy,
> With an auspicious, and a dropping eye,
> With mirth in funeral, and with dirge in marriage,
> In equal scale weighing delight and dole . . .
>
> (I.ii.10–13)

"Defeated joy" is an oxymoron, unfolded by the image of the two eyes in the next line, expanded by the double contrasts of the next (mirth/dirge, funeral/marriage), and sealed by the concluding clause of the sentence "Taken to wife." These lines announce a theme to be repeated with disgusted irony by Hamlet himself, yoking funeral and marriage in his first encounter with Horatio: "the funeral bak'd-meats / Did coldly furnish forth the marriage tables" (I.ii.180–81). The King's stately announcement of the steps he means to take to remedy the present state of Denmark (now doubly dilapidated, "disjoint and out of frame" [20]) not only demonstrates his easy enjoyment of power (paralleled in his easy enjoyment of Gertrude), but also expresses his priorities. He knows Hamlet is present, and has important business with him; but instead of beginning it, he turns to Laertes and his father, Polonius, and discusses their request that the son might return to college. His consent enables Laertes to exhibit some very courtly doubling when he requests the King's "leave and favor"; his "thoughts and wishes" tend there, but he needs the King's "gracious leave and pardon" (51–56) before he can depart.

Only when Claudius has graciously consented to that appeal does he turn to Hamlet, opening the conversation with a sinister doublet: "But now, my cousin Hamlet, and my son," a remark that sums up in advance the evil doubling that is at the heart of the play and to which Hamlet, in his first line, replies with another punning doublet: "A little more than kin, and less than kind" (64–65).

*Baldick, *The Concise Oxford Dictionary,* p. 157.

And so, at last, when we have already been well attuned to the moods and styles of the piece, have partly learned the tune of the verse, we meet the hero. The pace of the action and the tune of the language have been established before we are expressly told what the action is to be. We do not get close to its ultimate cause for a remarkably long time, for as far as the plot goes, all this talk is merely delaying Hamlet's confrontation with the Ghost. As I remarked, if economy of plot had been the aim, the play might have started at that point, saving almost nine hundred lines, which take perhaps three-quarters of an hour to play.

Hamlet's own way of speaking, we now learn, is also duplicative:

Seems, madam? nay, it is, I know not "seems."
'Tis not alone my inky cloak, good mother,
Nor customary suits of solemn black,
Nor windy suspiration of forc'd breath,
No, nor the fruitful river in the eye,
Nor the dejected havior of the visage,
Together with all forms, moods, shapes of grief,
That can denote me truly. These indeed seem,
For they are actions that a man might play,
But I have that within which passes show,
These but the trappings and the suits of woe.

(I.ii.76–86)

Here we have not only the repetition of "seems," the extravagance of following the black cloak with the black suits, the extraordinary line 79, which could be rendered "Nor breathy breathing of forced breathing," and the concentrated theatrical references of "actions," "play," and "show" in lines 84–85. (The Folio text has "shows" instead of "shapes" in line 82, perhaps a revision intended to stress this little theatrical cluster, to emphasise the unparalleled deliberation with which this play attends to theatrical figures.)

We also hear Hamlet's first soliloquy well before Hamlet has understood that he is to be forced into the role of avenger, although he already hates his life because of his mother's too hasty marriage to a man he despises, his false father: "O that this too too sallied flesh would melt, / Thaw, and resolve itself into a dew!" (129–30),* in which "melt," "Thaw," and "resolve itself" are all

*F: Q2 has "sallied" for "solid," and many accept the emendation "sullied."

ways of saying the same thing. There follow "How weary, stale, flat, and unprofitable" (133) and "things rank and gross" (136). Where Q2 has "Fie on't, ah fie!" (135), F has "Fie on't! O fie, fie," as if an extra "fie" were more in tune with the rest. Little additions of this sort are fairly common in the Folio text, and Harold Jenkins, the Arden editor, whose copy-text is Q2, regards these as "playhouse interpolations" or "actors' modifications," though he allows that some may be scribal.* It would be rash to attribute them entirely to Shakespeare's hand, but if these alterations and intrusions are the result of faulty memory in performers it must still be admitted that they are very much in the spirit of the text they had studied. When Hamlet wants to make a note of the discovery "That one may smile, and smile, and be a villain!" (I.v.108) he calls, in Q2, for his memorandum book: "My tables. Meet it is I set it down." In F this becomes "My tables, / My tables." An actor entering into the spirit of the verse might well have got the hint for this repetition from earlier ones in the same speech ("table of my memory" has already been said) such as "trivial fond," "All saws of books, all forms, all pressures past," "the book and volume of my brain," "O villain, villain, smiling, damned villain!," "one may smile, and smile, and be a villain" (I.v.98–109).

The soliloquy, with its passionate expansiveness, is immediately followed by a conversation with Horatio in contrasting style. It is one of the great joys of this play, this sudden switch into a new key—sometimes from verse to prose, but here from the verse of passion to that of courteous and witty exchange (which recurs in Hamlet's questioning of Horatio, Marcellus, and Barnardo [I.ii.220–45]). Yet the theme, already established as it might be in a symphony, is still sounded, though the repetitions and antitheses are now more pointed, as in talk of the hasty wedding, the "funeral bak'd-meats" coldly furnishing forth the marriage tables. Horatio speaks of "the dead waste and middle of the night" (I.ii.198) ("waste" suggesting "waist," which suggests "middle"), of the Ghost's progress as "slow and stately" (202), and of "oppress'd and fear-surprised eyes" (203); the words of Marcellus and Barnardo describing the apparition are certified as "true and good" (210).

Now we are surely ready for the meeting of Hamlet and the Ghost, but instead of that we have a scene set in the household of Polonius (I.iii). The reason, structurally, must be that Laertes, a necessary counterpart to Hamlet as a kind of double—as student, avenger, and ultimately deadly opponent—is about to disappear from the play for hours. But that alone can hardly

**Hamlet* (Arden edition, 1982), pp. 62–64.

explain the curious nature of this scene. It is full of doublings, including instances of hendiadys: "For Hamlet, and the trifling of his favour, / Hold it a fashion and a toy in blood" (5–6).* In the sequence "Forward, not permanent, sweet, not lasting, / The perfume and suppliance of a minute— / No more" (8–10), simple antithesis gives way to hendiadys: "perfume and suppliance of a minute" means something like "a pleasant, transitory amusement," but the two nouns are interlocked; one can't remove either of them without destroying the sense. Laertes continues to give his sister doubled counsel: "thews and bulk," "no soil nor cautel," "safety and health," "voice and yielding," "act and place." "Fear it, Ophelia, fear it," "the shot and danger of desire," "the morn and liquid dew of youth" (10–41). Ophelia knows how to answer in the same dialect: "the steep and thorny way to heaven," like "a puff'd and reckless libertine" (48–49). And Polonius, on entering, takes the prize for doubling, emphasising the element of subdued farce in the whole scene. Since he has blessed Laertes before, he will do it again. All his famous advice to Laertes consists of antithetical commands: Be this, don't be that, do this, don't do that. Listen well but speak rarely, let your dress be rich, not gaudy. Then we have "rank and station," "select and generous" (73–74). His lecture to Ophelia carries on in the same vein, even venturing on what may be a zeugma, possibly a hendiadys: "As it behooves my daughter and your honor" (97). A tedious witticism calls for more repetition of the word "tender" (99–109). Hamlet's vows are likened to "sanctified and pious bonds" (or "bawds") (130). She is not to "give words or talk" to him (134).

So numerous are these doublings that it is easy to ignore them, but when they are pointed out, and the language of the play compared in this respect with the language of others, they seem to be of its very essence. The doubling devices give the verse its tune, or might perhaps be thought a sort of ground bass that sounds everywhere, sometimes faintly, and the few interruptions in it derive their power to surprise or amuse by the very absence of the now familiar tune.

When finally we arrive at the scene on the battlements which will get the plot moving, we are alerted to a change in temperature by a rapid string of synonyms, so that we are told four times in sixteen lines that it is cold: "The air bites shrowdly, it is very cold. / It is a nipping and an eager air" (I.iv.1–20).

*This is well explained by Jenkins: "a toy in blood," being a youthful erotic fancy, "continues the notion of frivolity in *trifling* and ephemerality in *fashion,* while [the] amorous connotations [of *toy*] are strengthened by *blood.*" Arden edition, p. 440.

We are also told the time, a disagreement about it doing the work that the chronographic elaborations did in the opening scene in the same location. We may expect the Ghost at one o'clock, but it is now only midnight, and there is plenty of time for talk. The Quarto stretches Hamlet's meditation on the Danish custom of heavy drinking to twenty-five lines, cut to four in the Folio; whoever made the cut was content to leave Horatio with a half-line ("Look my lord, it comes" [17 (F), 39 (Q2)]), words which in Q2 complete the half-line ("To his own scandal") that ends Hamlet's discourse. A single half-line was acceptable, since there are other partial lines in the text, and an extra one would pass without notice. In fact, the cut is quite neatly done, though it remains a question why it was thought necessary. The Oxford editor, G. R. Hibbard, is sure that it was made because the lines "slow the action down" to the irritation of the audience and, incidentally (though the author could not be expected to take this into account), dispose of the hardest crux in the text of the play: "the dram of eale / Doth all the noble substance of a doubt / To his own scandal" (I.iv.20–22).* As in some other cases of the kind, his explanation seems to me doubtful; the original speech continues the strategy of the piece, which has so far been to slow down the general action while maintaining a high level of interest and expectation in other respects—in the language particularly, but also in the establishing of family relationships before they are transformed by Hamlet's discovery of his father's murder.

And the speech *is* interesting. From the comment that heavy drinking was the custom in Denmark but that it would be more honourable to give it up than to follow it, Hamlet, in what we recognise as his usual way, generalises the point, arguing that a single fault (such as drunkenness) can blast the reputation of persons who in all other respects deserve better. He may be thought to have himself in mind, not as a drunkard of course, but perhaps as a melancholic. He is saying something obliquely about himself in the context of a generalisation about human character, which he will later do more obviously. In the course of this explanation he does not depart from the undersong of the play; we hear, for example, "The pith and marrow of our attribute," "the pales and forts of reason," east and west, breach and observance, Nature and Fortune, the general and the particular (I.iv.13–38 [Q2]).

When the Ghost arrives, Hamlet cries, "Angels and ministers of grace defend us!"—a pure doublet, since there is no plausible distinction between

***Hamlet* (Oxford edition, 1987), p. 356.

angels and ministers of grace; the expression is mere division without distinction (39 [Q2], 18 [F]). He continues with his succession of oppositional terms: "spirit of health, or goblin damn'd," "airs from heaven, or blasts from hell," "intents wicked, or charitable," "ponderous and marble jaws" (40–50 [Q2], 19–29 [F]). But the pace now changes, and the whole tone of the play is altered simply by the absence of these doubling or antithetical or paradoxical devices; we go fast forward to Hamlet's encounter with the Ghost. The Ghost, however, at once slows down the pace, partly by the aforesaid means. Indeed, he uses so many of those devices that he seems almost to be the author of them; it is as if his own equivocal position was the source of these movements of uncertainty, these claims to certainty, these linguistic balancings on the gulf between distinction and division. He walks the night, is by day confined in fires, and will be until his "foul crimes" are "burnt and purg'd away" (I.v.12–13). His tale would harrow the soul and freeze the blood, make "knotted and combined locks to part" (18). His murder was foul and unnatural; his murderer incestuous and adulterate. One can be adulterate without being incestuous, but not the other way round; whereas it may be thought that all murders are both foul and unnatural, this was especially unnatural, since it was fratricidal and undertaken for incestuous reasons. The poison courses through the "gates and alleys of the body" (arteries and veins; "gate" in the sense of a wider street), curdling the "thin and wholesome blood" to a "vile and loathsome crust" (67, 70, 72). The extraordinary line "Unhous'led, disappointed, unanel'd" (77) is an instance of repetition with difference: each adjective refers to the last rites, but distinguishes them: without the Eucharist, without absolution, without the anointing. The speech of the Ghost ends with a final chronography, once again in a "higher" poetic register: "The glow-worm shows the matin to be near, / And gins to pale his uneffectual fire" (89–90).

In Hamlet's reaction we detect that rather crazed excitement that is to be associated with his antic madness, but it is not antic here. He seizes on the Ghost's injunction to remember (hence the repeated "tables"), and now the dialogue becomes short and speedy, in contrast to the normal delaying tactic of doubling. Here the lines are so short that one could easily think of the passage as prose. Its pace gives an edge to Hamlet's fooling: "There's never a villain dwelling in all Denmark / But he's an arrant knave" (123–24), followed by the ironical talk of business and desires, opposites, of course, though all men have both. These are "wild and whirling words," as Horatio says (132), earning Hamlet's ironic apology: "I am sorry they offend you, heartily, / Yes, faith, heartily" (134–35). Then comes the rapid dialogue of the swearing scene, antic but serious, using the stage and the cellarage from whose depths the Ghost speaks as part of a wild and whirling action.

The almost comic violence of that scene is not continued in the next, where, with another shift in tone, we are again in the domestic setting of Polonius's house. Reynaldo is to spy on Laertes (the repetition in *Hamlet* of the theme of "lawful espials" has often been noted). Polonius is capable of hendiadys: "By this encompassment and drift of question" (II.i.10) is one such—a doublet of which the parts cannot be made distinct, to be glossed clumsily as meaning by casual, indirect enquiry or something of the sort. So with "The flash and outbreak of a fiery mind" (33), where the flash cannot be distinct from the outbreak, and both depend on the fire in "fiery." But for the most part his doublings and repetitions are meant to represent pompous tediousness. Like the play, Polonius says everything at least twice, and in recommending "indirections" he is again echoing the structure of the play he's in. But this is a comic commentary, drawing our attention to the very nature of the work, which is in mocking contrast to the way in which, unlike him, it achieves its business.

POL. He closes with you in this consequence:
"Good sir," or so, or "friend," or "gentleman,"
According to the phrase or the addition
Of man and country.
REY. Very good, my lord.
POL. And then, sir, does 'a this—'a does—what was I about to say?
By the mass, I was about to say something.
Where did I leave?
REY. At "closes in the consequence."
POL. At "closes in the consequence," ay, marry.
He closes thus: "I know the gentleman.
I saw him yesterday, or th' other day,
Or then, or then, with such or such, and as you say,
There was 'a gaming, there o'ertook in 's rouse,
There falling out at tennis"; or, perchance,
"I saw him enter such a house of sale,"
Videlicet, a brothel, or so forth. See you now,

Your bait of falsehood take this carp of truth,
And thus do we of wisdom and of reach,
With windlasses and with assays of bias,
By indirections find directions out;
So by my former lecture and advice
Shall you my son. You have me, have you not?

(II.i.45–65)

I have quoted this passage, which would hardly find a place in a collection of gems from *Hamlet,* because it is one of the many variations on the tune I have spoken of. It is rather more wordy in F than in Q2, so if there was a reviser he does not seem to have been looking for cuts. Here all is devised for repetition. Polonius catalogues the salutations that might be used by the informant Reynaldo may hit upon, doubles "phrase" with "addition" and "man" with "country," but then forgets what he is talking about. Reynaldo has to bring him back to the point by quoting him; whereupon Polonius repeats yet again the expression "closes in the consequence," adding "closes" and "gentleman" for good measure. Then comes "yesterday, or th' other day, / Or then, or then, with such or such . . ." and a list of the bad things that might be reported of Laertes; with a concluding flourish of falsehood-truth, wisdom-reach, "windlasses and with assays of bias," two ways of saying the same thing, which is also indicated by the "indirections" which find out "directions"; and, in the final two lines, "lecture and advice," and "You have me, have you not?" The speech is a little parodic scherzo, the tune of the play played in a farcical variation.

The apparition of Hamlet in Ophelia's chamber, described by her in the passage immediately following, is itself a doublet of his father's ghostly appearance, "As if he had been loosed out of hell / To speak of horrors" (II.i.80–81), but there is little doubling, which would here undercut the effect of Polonius's performance. The effect returns soon, however, in the persons of Rosencrantz and Guildenstern. They, being "neighbored to his youth and havior" (II.ii.12) (a possible hendiadys, "youthful temperament"), are set to spy on him, as Reynaldo on Laertes. The Queen requests them to "show us so much gentry and good will" (22) (courtesy becoming their rank), "For the supply and profit of our hope" (24). (This last line is interpreted in the Oxford edition as meaning "by supplying what is needed for the realization of our hope," as "fulfillment and furtherance" in the Cambridge edition, following the scholar George Kittredge: an instance of how dense these doublets can be.) The royal expressions of gratitude ("Thanks, Rosencrantz and gentle Guildenstern. / Thanks, Guildenstern and gentle Rosencrantz" [33–34]) are another parody, *scherzando,* of the main tune, and so is Guildenstern's reply: "Heavens make our presence and our practices / Pleasant and helpful to him!"—where "practices" has the slight flavour of the sense of "plots, deceits," and "helpful" keeps something of the sense, usual enough in Shakespeare, of "help" meaning "cure," as in "Love doth to her eyes repair, / To help him of his blindness," in the song "Who is Silvia?" (*Two Gentlemen of Verona,* IV.ii.39ff.).

The following section of this long scene reverts to the political plot, with the return of Cornelius and Voltemand from their Norwegian embassy. This pair is even less essential than Rosencrantz and Guildenstern, merely another show of doubleness; the message from Norway is delivered in sensible verse, with only a little doubling ("greetings and desires" [II.ii.60], "safety and allowance" [79]), and we can be taken back to the main plot and the testing of Hamlet's love for Ophelia. Here Polonius, exercising his rhetorical powers, doubles and troubles as never before:

> My liege, and madam, to expostulate
> What majesty should be, what duty is,
> Why day is day, night night, and time is time,
> Were nothing but to waste night, day, and time . . .
>
> (86ff.)

Hamlet teases him in prose, using his own indirections to find directions out, whereas he quickly detects Rosencrantz and Guildenstern at the same game, for after a friendly greeting he asks them directly whether they were "sent for," and can infer that they are, however unwillingly, spying on him. In this passage we have both the comparison of Denmark to a prison (added in F) and the famous speech of Hamlet: "I have of late—but wherefore I know not—lost all my mirth, forgone all custom of exercises . . ." (295–309)—altogether a long passage that might have been designed to show that prose can double poetry. It is a superbly crafted oration with the same undersong:

> this goodly frame, the earth . . . this most excellent canopy, the air, look you, this brave o'erhanging firmament, this majestical roof fretted

> with golden fire . . . a foul and pestilent congregation of vapors. What a piece of work is a man, how noble in reason, how infinite in faculties, in form and moving, how express and admirable in action, how like an angel in apprehension, how like a god! the beauty of the world; the paragon of animals . . .
>
> (298–307)

Prose continues in the discussion of the company of players, and the London theatre gossip (added in F), which brings the matter of Hamlet directly into the Globe itself, with its emblem, "Hercules and his load" (361). For the Globe is a double of the world, and the boys' company that Rosencrantz reports on had, for the moment, taken the world away from the Lord Chamberlain's Men. *Hamlet* is very much of its moment, in London, on Bankside, with a theatre of which the author was part-owner, with actors who played many parts yet did not lose their sense of their world or of the theatre as image of that world after which, by an appropriate metaphor, it was named, a shadow of its substance; shadow and substance being the opposites that were for Shakespeare, as I have argued, the source of so many fine things. It is worth remembering that even among the splendours of the great speech preceding this exchange, Hamlet is still thinking and speaking inside a theatre, for the Globe was equipped with a goodly frame, a promontory on which he spoke, and a "heavens," or overhanging firmament, spangled with stars.

Hamlet ends his interview with the spy-courtiers by mentioning that radical doublet "my uncle-father and aunt-mother" (376), which contains in little the whole charge of incest. Later (IV.iii.49–52) he will call Claudius "mother," disgusted at the idea that Claudius is of one flesh with Gertrude, as in a different sense he himself is. Here is an exquisitely horrible case of there being "division none," now characterised not by the happiness of true love but by its opposite, the disgustingness of incest. Hamlet wants his false friends to know that he is driven to such outlandish figures to express his disgust, for nothing else will meet his case; and he also wants them to know that he can sail this close to madness without being mad in other respects: "I am but mad north-north-west" (II.ii.378).

The manner of Hamlet's affectionate welcome to the players when they arrive at Elsinore, along with the lecture he later gives them on acting (III.ii.1ff.), has always seemed to me an essential and beautiful aspect of his character. The contemptuous quick-wittedness of his cruel teasing of Polonius (II.ii.387–413) is at once transformed into affectionate ribbing of the boy actor, all done with warmth, in strong, intelligent prose. When the play from which he requests an extract is praised as "well digested in the scenes" we are being asked, modestly, to reflect that this very commendation is due to the play Hamlet is himself in.

The lecture on acting is elegantly reflective, delivered by Hamlet to his own polished colleagues, determined, in their new theatre, to play for the "judicious" (III.ii.26) rather than the "unskillful"; this play, we remember, was singled out by Gabriel Harvey of Cambridge as one of Shakespeare's works that could "please the wiser sort." Hence Hamlet's plea for an end to the older rantings and gestures, the struttings and bellowings, which belong to an older idea of theatre and an earlier kind of theatrical language. An educated audience wanted what the old verse could no longer be thought to give, a mirror held up to nature, to human personality, virtuous and envious, and to the age itself, showing "the body of the time his form and pressure."

The supple colloquial prose of the passage has another purpose: to contrast violently with the speech Hamlet himself now recalls from a play written in very bombastic verse, though the bombast cannot help showing us where Shakespeare's rhetorical doubling had its origin: "this dread and black complexion" (II.ii.455), "Bak'd and impasted" (459), "a tyrannous and a damned light" (460), "wrath and fire" (461). Hamlet is describing, in the old conceited style, the murder of a king; and the 1st Player takes it on: "the whiff and wind of his fell sword" (473). This, as Jenkins has pointed out, is reminiscent of lines in Marlowe's *Dido:* "whisk'd his sword about. / And with the wind [*for* "wound"] thereof the King fell down." He offers other parallels, the closest being from *Troilus and Cressida:* "Even in the fan and wind of your fair sword" (V.iii.41).* It is noticeable that only the Shakespearian examples exemplify that most intimate form of doubling, hendiadys: one can't be left with the whiff or the fan without the wind. Several lines further on, "will and matter" is a complicated hendiadys, as the Oxford editor points out, glossing as "purposed business," which Pyrrhus is momentarily neglecting.† Hamlet's calling actors "abstract and brief chronicles of the time" (524) is a plain doubling, the nouns being the synonyms.

Hamlet's soliloquy, which ends the scene, begins with a doublet ("O, what a rogue and peasant slave am I!" [550]) and is a small wilderness of mirrors. An

*Arden edition, pp. 479–80.
†Oxford edition, p. 229.

actor comments on the power of an actor to simulate emotion, and on the difference between his own position and that of his mirror image in the play; he claims to have "the motive and the cue for passion" that the actor lacks, but he is of course equally an actor, equally in a play, as remote from the real world as the Globe is from the globe. Hamlet is explaining that the actor, in being without "a motive and a cue" for passion, is not like him; yet in passionately describing this difference, he is seeing his own image when he watches the actor, who really is holding up the mirror to him.

"What's Hecuba to him, or he to her?" asks Hamlet in Q2. "What's Hecuba to him or he to Hecuba?" is the Folio reading and, as it happens, also Q1's. Jenkins, using Q2 as the copy-text, finds that version "crisp and forceful," and claims the other editors prefer the longer version, which he thinks of as an actor's "(over-) emphasis" persisting only through "force of custom."* The Oxford edition as usual follows the Folio, finding the second "Hecuba" to be "a case of authorial revision, made to eliminate the repetition of *her* [in the next line] in the Q2 version."† However, it would be odd to get rid of one repetition by inserting another. John Jones, in my view more sensitively, finds the Folio reading "delicate and decisive and economical," since it not only gets rid of the "her . . . her" repetition but also creates a valuable because hypermetrical emphasis, "ruffling the iambic pentameter's smooth plumage."‡

This soliloquy is full of appropriate doublings or yoked opposites: he and Hecuba, "the motive and the cue," "Make mad the guilty, and appall the free," "confound-amaze," "eyes and ears," "dull and muddy-mettled," "property and most dear life,"** "pigeon-liver'd, and lack gall" (where the second term explains the first), "heaven and hell," "whore-drab," "my weakness and my melancholy." There is a climax of repetition in "Bloody, bawdy villain! / Remorseless, treacherous, lecherous, kindless villain!" This great scene ends

*Arden edition, p. 270.

†Oxford edition, p. 233.

‡*Shakespeare at Work* (1955), pp. 88–89. Jones notes also the short line "For Hecuba" (559) as characteristic of *Hamlet,* and associates it with the other habit of repetition, as in expressions like "Yes, yes" and "My tables" in I.v.104–8, where the repetition occurs in F but not in Q2. Jones remembers that A. C. Bradley in *Shakespearean Tragedy* (1904) noted that Hamlet alone has this "trick of speech, a habit of repetition" that is "intensely characteristic" (pp. 148–49; cited by Jones, p. 81).

**Here "property" means not "possessions" but the quality that distinguishes one thing (one life) from another. In "The Phoenix and Turtle" we read "Property was thus appall'd / That the self was not the same," appalled because separate selves had been brought into a state where there was no division between them. That these lines may have been in Shakespeare's mind when he was composing *Hamlet* is suggested by the use of the verb "appal" a few lines earlier.

with a couplet rhyming "thing" and "king," and we may remember that these words are paired again later in the play: "The King is a thing—/ A thing, my lord? / Of nothing" (IV.ii.28–30).

The purpose of the play-within-the-play is double: to test the Ghost and to test Claudius. But there is another testing, of Hamlet by the King. He is alarmed by Hamlet's "turbulent and dangerous lunacy" (III.i.4), which Guildenstern reduces to the oxymoron "crafty madness" (8). There follows shortly the famous soliloquy with its thematic opening "To be, or not to be" (55ff.). Already we are poised between alternatives. Be or not be? Suffer or take arms? Die, sleep, dream? Then we hear of the sufferings life entails (none of them, as it was long ago pointed out, can really be applied to Hamlet's own case; he speaks of "we" and "us," never of "I" or "me"):

> . . . the whips and scorns of time,
> Th' oppressor's wrong, the proud man's contumely,
> The pangs of despis'd love, the law's delay,
> The insolence of office, and the spurns
> That patient merit of th' unworthy takes . . .
>
> (69–73)

This soliloquy has been discussed interminably, but one thing is surely obvious: Hamlet is referring his own to a more general view of the human condition, and this is, I think, a new use for the soliloquy—ordinarily used for the conveyance of information to the audience—as a way of considering the human situation more largely. There is something of this new manner in Macbeth's "If it were done when 'tis done," which argues that *we* would commit crimes readily if *we* did not fear "the life to come." He is thinking of his own as a reflex of a more general ethical problem. So with Hamlet, who ends by remarking that considerations of this sort can inhibit "enterprises of great pith [pitch, Q2] and moment."

The Nunnery scene follows,* with its abrupt change of mood and tempo at line 102 ("Ha, ha! are you honest?") and its switch away from Ophelia to

*Hamlet's reply to Ophelia when she asks how he is reads, "I humbly thank you, well" in Q2 and "I humbly thank you, well, well, well" in F. On this and other such triplications ("Except my life, except my life, except my life"), see Jones, cited above.

Note that Ophelia and Hamlet address each other as "you" and not "thou," as might be expected between lovers, until Hamlet says "Get thee to a Nunnery." He continues with "thou" and "thee" until he shifts the attack to women in general: "I have heard of your paintings, too" (143).

women in general, especially those who cuckold their husbands. The tone would be that of contemporary satire, were it not for the note of antic desperation throughout. With Hamlet's exit it changes again, and Ophelia, in what seems to have been a tradition in her family, makes her lament in twelve lines of which only two lack rather dull doublets. The contrast with the vivid hendiadys of Claudius a few lines later—"I do doubt the hatch and the disclose / Will be some danger" (166–67)—is striking.

The following passage in which Hamlet commends the temperate virtue of Horatio has a double purpose, to make Horatio an image of stoical virtue and to enlist him as a spy. Now, says Hamlet, "I must be idle" (III.ii.90)—a useful word, meaning both unoccupied and acting foolishly. This he does while teasing Polonius (with another reminder of Julius Caesar) and shocking Ophelia; it is worth remembering that in some sources she was his mistress, and this may have suggested the lewdness of this patch of dialogue, though it is presented as banter. Ophelia certainly understands the double entendres. They are followed by fierce, wild jokes about his father's death.

The Dumb-show, a deliberate archaism, is slightly unusual in that it conforms rather closely to the plot of the play-within-the-play. Its bearing on the play-within-the-play, and on the situation in *Hamlet*, the play itself, has been voluminously debated.* We have a Chinese box, with the play-within-the-play nesting inside *Hamlet* and the Dumb-show within the play-within-the-play. (Incidentally, if the Folio reviser had been trying to shorten the play, there was an easy cut here.)

After a delay to accommodate more of Hamlet's indecencies (which recur during the performance) and an inept Prologue, the play launches itself into deliberately archaic verse, as it were recessed and remote from the language in which the main play does its work of holding up the mirror. Hamlet catches its tone with his rant about the croaking raven bellowing for revenge (actually a condensed quotation from an anonymous play on Richard III, of about 1591). After Claudius has risen and left the scene, Hamlet is so high that he sounds mad, and Horatio tries to bring him down. There follows another excited but funny passage with Rosencrantz and Guildenstern, all fast prose. Hamlet is a self-proclaimed mystery, announcing that his wit's

*For a useful account of the controversies, see Jenkins, Arden edition, pp. 501–5. The question is why King Claudius does not react to the Dumb-show as he does a little later to the play itself. And difficulties arise from the Dumb-show's being an exact double of the play-within-the-play, which is, in turn and by design, a double of the Ghost's account of how he was murdered.

diseased but scoring heavily over the sycophants with his analogy of the recorder which Guildenstern cannot play (354ff.). His teasing of Polonius is broader, less serious.

In III.iii Claudius reacts. He will send Hamlet to England:

> The terms of our estate may not endure
> Hazard so near 's as doth hourly grow
> Out of his brows.
>
> (5–7)

I quote this passage as an instance of the critical problems that the text of the play can produce. "Brows" is the reading of Q2; F substitutes "lunacies." This certainly looks like a revision, and is more instantly intelligible. It may, as Jenkins proposes, be a stopgap, supplied by somebody who remembered "dangerous lunacy," a phrase from an earlier scene in Act III (i.4), and sticks to "brows," implying something like "the danger springing out of Hamlet's head."* The Oxford editor, whose programme is to follow F wherever possible, is happy with "lunacies." My own view is that "brows" is much richer, and gives a reading no more obscure than a great many to be found in the plays that come after *Hamlet.* Claudius imagines, from Hamlet's appearance, his contracted brows; doubtless at the recent performance they reflected the tumult of the young man's mind and the probability that he has found Claudius out. Much might be deduced from the condition of the brows: "There is written in your brow, Provost, honesty" (*Measure for Measure,* IV.ii.153–54), "Speak sad brow and true maid" (*As You Like It,* III.ii.214–15), "As if you held a brow of much distraction" (*The Winter's Tale,* I.ii.149), "The angry spot doth glow on Caesar's brow" (*Julius Caesar,* I.ii.183), and many more; it was evidently a word Shakespeare favoured, for brow or brows occurs 129 times in the plays. Of course none of these considerations can be thought to decide the right reading in the present case. It is certainly possible that some hand or voice, perhaps not Shakespeare's own, thought the passage could be lightened a little by the substitution of "lunacies." However, one can be glad that the other, possibly original reading has not been lost. If the rather obvious simplification really was made, we have a shred of evidence that somebody was already beginning to worry about Shakespeare's tendency to write poetry that might baffle the crowd.

*Arden edition, pp. 512–13.

The response of Rosencrantz and Guildenstern to the King's proposal amounts to a servile parody of the main language theme of the play:

> Most holy and religious fear it is
> To keep those many many bodies safe
> That live and feed upon your Majesty.
> Ros. The single and peculiar life is bound
> With all the strength and armor of the mind
> To keep itself from noyance, but much more
> That spirit upon whose weal depends and rests
> The lives of many . . .
> . . . it is a massy wheel
> Fix'd on the summit of the highest mount,
> To whose huge spokes ten thousand lesser things
> Are mortis'd and adjoin'd, which when it falls,
> Each small annexment, petty consequence,
> Attends the boist'rous ruin.
>
> (8–22)

The sentiment is commonplace and the language blatant, though still remembering the tune: "many, many," "single and peculiar," "strength and armor," "depends and rests," "mortis'd and adjoin'd," "small annexment, petty consequence."* Claudius, a man prone to action, cuts through this linguistic fog:

*"Consequence" occurs four times in *Hamlet,* three times in II.i., when Polonius forgets what he is talking about and Reynaldo has to remind him (45, 51, 52), and in this place. (The total for all Shakespeare's plays is twenty.) This may not mean much, but compare the use of "pressure" and "pressures," III.ii.24, and I.v.100, where in each case the word is associated with the word "form." These are the only occasions on which Shakespeare used the words "pressure" or "pressures." In one case there is an unusual emphasis on what follows or ought to follow (such as might occur to a writer managing the narrative of this play) and in the other an idea vaguely related to the creation of form by pressure, as by a seal in wax. An important theme in *Hamlet* is memory, and memory can be represented as a form, perhaps fading, created by the pressure of a past emotion. It may even be a lamented absence, as when the youth in the Sonnets is reproved for his failure to breed: "thou no form of thee hast left behind" (ix.6). "Form" was a word Shakespeare often used, sometimes with the idea of its fading: "life, / which bleeds away even as a form of wax," in *King John* (V.iv.24), where it occurs often, being a play about a fading king. See also *Romeo and Juliet,* "Thy noble shape is but a form of wax" (III.iii.126). These are not unusual instances, and it is interesting that a particular word or group of words seem to associate themselves, almost unconsciously, with the idea of a particular play.

> ... we will fetters put about this fear,
> Which now goes too free-footed.
>
> (25–26)

Here there is no vagueness; "free-footed" is in Claudius's mind before he gets to "fetters." This is quick, planned language, quite unlike that of Rosencrantz.

Claudius's soliloquy, which follows, could itself be used to signal the fuller maturity of Shakespeare's dramatic verse in *Hamlet.* It sets us, and its writer, on the road that leads eventually to the tragic intensities of *Coriolanus.* Take these nine lines as a sample:

> May one be pardon'd and retain th' offense?
> In the corrupted currents of this world
> Offense's gilded hand may shove by justice,
> And oft 'tis seen the wicked prize itself
> Buys out the law, but 'tis not so above:
> There is no shuffling, there the action lies
> In his true nature, and we ourselves compell'd,
> Even to the teeth and forehead of our faults,
> To give in evidence.
>
> (III.iii.56–64)

It is hardly necessary to point out the differences between this kind of speech and that of Marcus in *Titus Andronicus,* or even that of Richard II as he considers his fate, or of Brutus meditating in the orchard. Here is a man suffering from his thought, working out his violent emotion in violent, immediate language, subjected to the pressure and slippage of bold, even anguished, metaphor. He asks, already knowing the answer, whether he can repent and yet retain the benefits of his crime. ("Retain th' offense" is very compressed; a soliloquy of this sort is distinguished by its great alterations of pace, its constrictions as well as its expatiations.) He speaks of "the corrupted currents of this world," where "currents" is vague—it can mean course of events, as in modern "current affairs," but also have a sense of flowing or even "sloping," "having an inclination to fall," as the *Oxford English Dictionary* puts it. A corrupt current could be a sewer. Claudius, a man of turbulent intelligence, does not develop the idea but instead presents an allegory so briefly sketched that it almost passes as something other than allegory: Offence, the crime, holds money in his hand and shoves by justice—pushes it aside. Then, relaxing into the literal, he puts it thus: that the gold obtained by the crime may be the bribe that ensures the offender's security. He contrasts this position with what obtains in the world "above," where "There is no shuffling, there the action lies / In his true nature" (61–62). "Shuffling" means underhand or equivocating conduct, here especially legal trickery (he moves from justice to law). The action (the prosecuting case in court) lies (is sustainable).* In that case full confession is unavoidable, "Even to the teeth and forehead of our faults"—here again are the brows, now compelled to be honest, and now associated with teeth. This line is usually taken to mean a hostile face-to-face confrontation, but that interpretation misses the point that the evidence of the accused is a total confession, so that the face, teeth, and brows will be ashamed, not defiant. In any case, the face is attributed to the "faults," which are now unconcealable shames; no mask, no helmet, no lie covers them.

Here we have the energy, the flurries of oblique association, that characterise Shakespeare at his best. The play of figures, echoing one another, the failure or refusal to follow the old course of milking similitudes, the changing depth of focus on Mercy, Justice, Offence, the colloquial roughness of "shove" and "shuffle," the persistent but not expansive legal references testify not only to a different range of metaphorical usage but to a different, dramatic manner of representing a man thinking, under the stress of guilt and fear. Only at the end of his speech does Claudius lapse into an older style: "O wretched state! O bosom black as death!" (67)—a line which serves to remind us that there was a continuing but increasingly tense relationship with the past.

Hamlet's speech "Now might I do it pat" (73ff.) has been the subject of much argument, largely concerned with the question whether Hamlet really means that he won't kill the King while the King is at prayer, because that would be to send him straight to heaven.† Here one need only note that whether Hamlet is really being so intransigently fierce or merely finding excuses, he remembers the tune: "hire and salary . . . grossly, full of bread . . . broad blown, as flush as May . . . circumstance and course of thought . . . fit and season'd . . . damn'd and black."

O.E.D. s.v.13: "Chiefly in *Law.* Of an action, charge, claim, etc. To be admissible or sustainable."
†For a summary of conflicting beliefs, see the Arden edition, pp. 513–15.

There follows the Closet scene, remarkable throughout for the pace and vehemence of the dialogue. The exchange between Hamlet and his mother at the outset remembers the old device of stichomythia and establishes at once the fury in their words, a fury that has to do with painful doublings. In these lines each character means something different by the word "father," and the difference is the emotional core of the tragedy:

> QUEEN. Hamlet, thou hast thy father much offended.
> HAM. Mother, you have my father much offended.
> QUEEN. Come, come, you answer with an idle tongue.
> HAM. Go, go, you question with a wicked tongue.
>
> (III.iv.9–12)

The parallelisms are obvious, and the terminal words and the repetitions of "father" reinforce an obvious pattern, with Hamlet's sneering imitations (idle / wicked; Come, come / Go, go). We should also note that the familial "thou" is used only in the first line. This is a serious row, and the animus could not be clearer than Hamlet makes it by calling his mother "your husband's brother's wife" (15), a painful exposition of consanguinity. Hamlet's killing of Polonius draws from Gertrude an unimpressive double ("O, what a rash and bloody deed" [27]) which, in his repetition, Hamlet reduces or corrects, saving "rash" for his characterisation of Polonius as "thou wretched, rash, intruding fool" (31). "A bloody deed," he calls it, then makes a more significant doubling, the killing of King Hamlet and Gertrude's marriage to his brother.

Thereupon begins the fight of Hamlet against his mother's enslavement to "custom"—to her sexual relationship with Claudius. He will "wring" her heart, "If damned custom have not brass'd it so / That it be proof and bulwark against sense" (37–38). This he does with an excitement that grows to a frenzy before the Ghost intervenes, but it is characteristic of this play that after the departure of the Ghost and despite his warning, Hamlet again repeats his demand that his mother not sleep with Claudius, rising once more into a sort of desperate, furious eloquence. Here again a reviser looking for cuts would see ways of getting them; and sure enough, there are some cuts in F, about eighteen lines in all. The first cut is III.iv.71–76. Hamlet has been forcing his mother to compare the portraits of his father and Claudius. It comes at the end of a truly terrific passage, appropriately full of strong antitheses, in which Hamlet links his mother's lack of discrimination—her preference for Claudius over her husband—to inordinate sexual appetite; her judgement is corrupted by it for "what judgment / Would step from this to this?" And, in Q2, he continues:

Sense sure you have,
Else could you not have motion, but sure that sense
Is apoplex'd, for madness would not err,
Nor sense to ecstasy was ne'er so thrall'd
But it reserv'd some quantity of choice
To serve in such a difference.

(71–76)

Then the texts agree about the following (note that the join is well made, "What devil was't" concluding the short line "Would step from this to this?"):

What devil was't
That thus hath cozen'd you at hoodman-blind?

The next four lines are absent from F:

Eyes without feeling, feeling without sight,
Ears without hands or eyes, smelling sans all,
Or but a sickly part of one true sense
Could not so mope.

Why these changes? The first cut passage is difficult at an initial hearing. You must have the use of your senses, since you could not otherwise move, but surely that sense is benumbed, for even insanity could not make such a mistake; sense could never be so deeply in the power of madness that it did not retain the very small power of choice required for this particular discrimination. The second cut analyses the sense into the senses: not one sense—sight, feeling, hearing, smell, or touch—would, even without the aid of the others, be so dull as not to perceive this difference.

One explanation for cuts may be that there is too much of this already; the point made in the first cut passage, and made again in the second, has already been established. The idea that Gertrude has stumbled on to Claudius as if in a game of blind-man's-buff might itself be thought to take care of the whole issue. Or it could be said that the second passage recapitulates, a little clumsily, the first. It is conceivable that Shakespeare himself made the cuts, not so much because of a need to shorten the play or because the groundlings might not follow the words as from a sense of redundancy. Yet redundancy is in the very nature of *Hamlet,* and so far from being inept, these passages, full of thought that is driven almost frantically along by emotion, are building up to a climax when the Ghost enters.

The excitement, the emphasis on sense, is of course sexual, as Hamlet makes plain in the rest of this speech. And when the Queen accepts his censure, seeing in her soul "black and grained spots," he is not appeased but takes the occasion of her confession to be yet more explicit:

> Nay, but to live
> In the rank sweat of an enseamed bed,
> Stew'd in corruption, honeying and making love
> Over the nasty sty!
>
> (91–94)

"Honeying and making love"! The first word occurs nowhere else in Shakespeare and rarely anywhere else; they are doing it with loverlike endearments in a bed soaked in sweat, in a place made filthy by their acts. Hamlet continues his raving: "A cutpurse of the empire and the rule" (another kind of hendiadys) and "A king of shreds and patches" (99, 102).

At this hysterical peak the Ghost enters: his reproaches are in the vein of his language at the outset of the play. Afterwards Hamlet returns to his admonitions, at first more calmly, then again with his obsessive "go not to my uncle's bed" (159). There are two more brief cuts, perhaps this time simply to reduce repetition (162–66, 169–72), because the power of habit over behaviour has already been stressed. On the point of leaving, having said good night, Hamlet touches once more on the sexual theme: "Let the bloat king tempt you again to bed . . ." (182ff.). But then he is calm again, speaking of his plans to visit England, and to "lug the guts" of Polonius out of his mother's bedroom.

The Folio cuts the lines in the Quarto in which Hamlet enlarges on his mistrust for Rosencrantz and Guildenstern and says he has a plot against them. This was, I think, a simple matter, for Hamlet cannot at this point have foreseen the circumstances under which he might turn the tables on his guards. There may be many reasons, as one revises, to save or to cut, some bad, some good, some obvious and some not. This one was desirable because it improved the self-consistency of the narrative.

The remainder of the play may be dealt with more summarily. The King's plot is moving forward; Hamlet is now antic, over the body of Polonius, and in Act IV, parting with the King, makes his most profound and horrible joke: "Farewell, dear mother . . . father and mother is man and wife, man and wife is one flesh—so my mother" (iii.49–52). There follows the final, strangely placed soliloquy (IV.iv.31ff.), which is not in the Folio at all. Hamlet is blaming himself for his failure to act despite his having so many opportunities to do so:

> I do not know
> Why yet I live to say, "This thing's to do,"
> Sith I have cause, and will, and strength, and means
> To do't.
>
> (IV.iv.43–46)

But of course he is on his way to England, under guard, so this soliloquy is actually spoken at the very first moment he does *not* have strength or means to do it. This may explain the cut. However, it would be a shame to lose what may be the finest of the soliloquies. It remembers the tune: "good and market of his time," "sleep and feed," "capability and godlike reason," "mass and charge," "tomb enough and continent," "delicate and tender"—these words ran together in Shakespeare's mind. (He liked the word "delicate." It sometimes suggested "tender," as in *Othello,* "her delicate tenderness" [II.i.232], and *The Tempest,* "subtle, tender and delicate temperance" [II.i.42]. He was surely remembering Isaiah 47:1, "thou shalt no more be called tender and delicate.") Some have remarked that the epithets do not suit Fortinbras very well.

The plot is moving fast, with the madness and death of Ophelia and the incursion of the furious Laertes, but it can always be held up. The tune is less audible when the verse is carrying action; the doublets return with the inessential passage about the visiting Lamord.

The plot against Hamlet is mature, but instead of a climax we have the graveyard scene: more delay inexplicable in commonsense terms. Even more extraordinary is the long scene with Osric (V.ii.81ff.). Osric wields courtly doubles ("very soft society, and great showing" [108], "the card or calendar of gentry" [109]—cut in F; somebody seems to have thought the Osric episode was too long), and Hamlet mocks him with "his semblable is his mirror," (118–19), even pointing out that "rapier and dagger," used by Osric as a doublet, is really two weapons, not one (145–46). Osric, as Hamlet remarks, has "only got the tune of the time" (189–90) and is a possessor of "fann'd and winnow'd opinions." Hereafter Hamlet, though complaining of heartsickness, is ready; heaven is ordinant. He asks Laertes's pardon, says he is afflicted with madness. At last we have the duel and the deaths; we are offered alternative responses, woe or wonder, and Horatio's promised explanation will expose accidental judgements, casual slaughters, plots and errors.

Not only Osric had the tune of the time; so had Shakespeare. *Hamlet* is literature's greatest bazaar: everything available, all warranted and trademarked. The sense that it constitutes a quantum leap in the development of English poetry and drama is widely shared. Some will say that greater achievements lay ahead, but in that case *Hamlet* was an essential preparation for them. Whatever a critic's approach, this will remain true; for example, the whole idea of dramatic character is changed for ever by this play. Claudius is wonderfully rendered, but is still a guilty tyrant and usurper; Polonius is a garrulous bore, a crafty operator and spymaster, yet a respected statesman; we may think we know the type or put together from experience a good idea of it, but no one much like Hamlet ever existed before. That is why images of Hamlet usually reflect what came after, not before him. To take him as the herald of a new age is neither idolatrous nor hyperbolical. In this new age we need not expect matters to be made easy for us. The new mastery is a mastery of the ambiguous, the unexpected, of conflicting evidence and semantic audacity. We are challenged to make sense, even mocked if we fail.

TROILUS AND CRESSIDA

We can accept *Hamlet* as the fulcrum of Shakespeare's career; its virtuosities represent a vast development of his linguistic powers. The works that followed are very different, but in their various ways equally adventurous. The recent past had seen the more rigid Globe successes of *Henry V* and *Julius Caesar;* behind lay the Sonnets, the highly original "The Phoenix and Turtle," and *Twelfth Night,* written at the end of a largely comic period, which proposed new tones, new structures, new variations on ancient themes. But styles and interests seem to have been changing, and the professional playwright who was doing much to change them needed himself to change.

The dates of *Troilus and Cressida, All's Well That Ends Well,* and *Measure for Measure* may be taken as 1602, 1603, and 1604; they bridge the gap between *Hamlet* (1600) and *Othello* (1604 in its original form). These plays have often been regarded as a group and labelled "problem plays," and the label is appropriate because the plays seem to present not only distinctively ethical problems but peculiar difficulties of a poetic kind.

One reason for thinking about them in this way is that it is good, in a time when the tradition of Shakespeare idolatry still lingers (the inerrancy that attaches itself to all books regarded as somehow sacred), to observe the playwright in compositional trouble of various sorts. These plays come immediately after the terrific élan and assurance of *Hamlet,* and seek new ways of dramatic speaking that seem to give the author much more trouble. Another related reason is that an understandable emphasis on the popular appeal of Shakespeare, and the insistence on the more theatrical aspects of the tradition, has somewhat obscured the fact that Shakespeare was a *thinker* who did his thinking in dramatic dialogue. Of course the thinking is not of the sort that might be expected of a philosopher or a divine; as Wallace Stevens mused, the probing of the philosopher is deliberate, the probing of the poet fortuitous.

This habit of serious wordplay, fortuitously occasioned by the random collisions of language and plot, becomes much more evident after *Hamlet;* one extra-dramatic testimony to it, already discussed, is the "metaphysical" poem "The Phoenix and Turtle," with its intense contemplation of language devoted to the mysteries of identity, sameness, and, in the old sense, property. Another is the rather baffling *Troilus and Cressida,* often regarded as a failure because of its apparent theatrical shortcomings, its apparent imbalances, and its cynicism. But we need to see the play for what it is, a new kind of intellectual enterprise, if we are to have much hope of dealing with its greater and sometimes even more difficult successors.

It is not at present fashionable to speak of an author's personal development, or of the realisation of an individual corpus or oeuvre, rather than of his or her historical situation, and of the part of others—collaborators and audiences—in the making of plays. But it remains true that the work of a writer changes under pressures that can be regarded as partly private as well as responsive to more public, cultural pressures. To give a simple instance, the construction of the Globe Theatre was certainly responsible for changes in Shakespeare's way of writing; but so was the experience of writing the Sonnets and "The Phoenix and Turtle," which have no dramatic context. The Sonnets, although recognisably belonging to a prevailing and fashionable genre, the sonnet sequence, are in some ways deviant from the genre and have an unmistakeable originality that is related to obscure personal motives. "The Phoenix and Turtle" was presumably commissioned for some special occasion that elicited an entirely new manner, a new kind of engagement with language. These were works from the same hand, a hand always ready to try something new.

Troilus and Cressida has a difficult text, and it is thought that there were two somewhat differing versions, one written for the Globe and another for some special audience, perhaps at one of the Inns of Court. The latter venue may have been the better suited to the play, which contains an unusual amount of disputation and involves arguments touching on issues of philosophy and even of law ("these moral laws / Of nature and of nations" [II.ii.184–85]). Opinions differ as to which came first—whether a Globe play was adapted for a special occasion or an Inns of Court play for the Globe. Contemporary opinion seems to have been uncertain where it belonged generically. The Quarto edition calls it a history and, in a second try, a tragedy, with an advertisement that commends it as comedy. In the Folio it is again described as a history but included with the tragedies. More recently it has been called a satire or a tragical satire.

There was evidently a small crisis at the printing house, and the play is omitted from the Folio's Catalogue, or Table of Contents. Jaggard, the printer, had wanted to place it after *Romeo and Juliet* and even started to print it there. But some problem with copyright seems to have forced him to stop the press at that point. Later, when it was impossible to place the play where he had originally intended, he inserted it between the last of the Histories, *Henry VIII,* and the first of the Tragedies, *Coriolanus.* In economically using the opening of the play that had already been set, Jaggard met another small difficulty: since the end of *Romeo and Juliet* occupied the recto of the leaf, the first page of the existing text of *Troilus* was on its reverse, the verso. He got over this by adding the Prologue (thirty-one lines in larger type, the better to fill the space). Whether this piece was newly written for the Folio or whether it existed in some manuscript that had come into the printer's hands since he abandoned his first attempt to print the text, it is not possible to say.

It is a strange passage, pompous ("The princes orgillous" [2]) and with epic pretensions ("Priam's six-gated city, / Dardan and Timbria, Helias, Chetas, Troien, / And Antenorides" [15–17]). It describes the Greeks, determined to recover Helen, as having only just arrived at Troy ("The fresh and yet unbruised Greeks" [14]); the war is about to begin. But the "prologue arm'd" then veers away from this point and explains that the action of the play will start not there but in the middle of the war. So the Prologue is only partly relevant to the play that follows, since it concerns itself entirely with the military situation and says nothing whatever about Troilus or Cressida.

Strange indeed; but there is much that is strange about the play as a whole. Sometimes one can be fairly sure about non-Shakespearian elements in the plays (in *Timon of Athens,* for example, or *Pericles*), but here the case is not so clear. But only if one requires that a Shakespeare text be untouched by other hands (an aspect of a tradition of idolatry) would one be much troubled by this circumstance. What we mean, or ought to mean, by "Shakespeare" is not some semidivine, inerrant individual but the corpus of plays we agree to call by his name. This point is worth repeating. The history of the plays as we have them includes a pretty rough passage through the theatre, where their survival could depend on a prompt copy that might, over time, deviate from the author's manuscript, and another rough passage through the press, at the hands of compositors of varying abilities setting somewhat messy copy and subject only to rather ineffective proofing. We have to accept puzzles and uncertainties.

Troilus and Cressida may be the most strenuous of Shakespeare's quasi-ethical fantasies. He took on the theme of the Trojan War, but there is little Homeric about his treatment—there is no Cressida in Homer, whose Briseis is merely an irrelevant literary ancestor; but she was, by Shakespeare's time, a figure with a long and somewhat equivocal history, well known from Chaucer and Henryson, whose Cressida ends as a leper, so changed that Troilus, encountering her, does not even recognise her. No doubt the contrast between the original Homeric version (accessible through various translations) and the degenerate representations of the tradition, together with a tendency to prefer Trojans, as putative ancestors of the British, to Greeks (although this aspect of the play has been much exaggerated) had something to do with Shakespeare's decision to use the story as the occasion for a rather peculiar inquest into value, honour, and truth. It is a course he follows with extraordinary intensity.

The play is unusual in that it contains two rather formal scenes of debate, one in the Greek and one in the Trojan camp. But its concern with ideas is not confined to those scenes, for the language is almost everywhere concerned with questions relating to value—to puzzles arising from the difficulty that value is differently conceived by different people. A broad distinction exists between the view that value can be intrinsic, or that it depends on some transcendental criterion, and the sceptical view that it depends wholly upon attribution, that the value of anything is the value one places upon it. By that standard the value of some pop star's discarded shirt is the price somebody, the last bidder at an auction, is prepared to pay for it. And the same can be true of objects that are generally held to be intrinsically more valuable—pearls or diamonds, for instance. Value can be manipulated; for example, the circulation of diamonds, which are plentiful in nature, can be artificially restricted. And, obviously, value can be reduced or destroyed by a change of fashion. So is value merely a matter of opinion?

"Opinion" is a complex word with a difficult history, and the reason for its being so is its contested relationship to "truth," a relationship from which it can never be extracted. The contest derives from deeply established ways of thinking about the truth of the world, and about statements concerning it, which may, or may only seem to be, true.

Troilus and Cressida, as commentators agree, dwells with exceptional concentration on these questions of opinion, truth, and value. Other plays by Shakespeare seem in a measure obsessed by the semantics of a particular word: *Othello* by "honest," *Hamlet* by "act," *Macbeth* by "time." But *Troilus,* so distinctive in other ways also, is unique in the degree to which its language is saturated by "opinion," and by the network of notions of which it is the centre.

The problem is an ancient one, and it interested some Greek thinkers. The Greek word *doxa,* a vastly complicated word, means "opinion," usually with the implication of wrong opinion, but it also, in Judaic and New Testament Greek, means "glory" or "honour." When it occurs in St. John's Gospel 5:41, the translators are uncertain whether the meaning is "I receive not honour from men" or "I do not accept the opinion of men" or "Not that I accept human praise." Three verses later the word occurs twice more, distinguishing the honour that comes from men from the honour that comes from God (5:44). *Doxa,* in the Greek of the New Testament, is the word for both. The Gloria, as Christians sing or say it, is called the Doxology; yet *doxa,* to Socrates as to the evangelist, can also mean something that must be distinguished from truth without being absolutely identified with falsehood, namely opinion.

For there is a human glory, fallible, dependent on the reports of the senses, on opinion in the lower sense, and a heavenly one, *doxa tou theou,* the glory of God. The relation between opinion and truth, *doxa* and *episteme,* had been a matter of keen interest long before the New Testament. Plato thought of *doxa* as existing somewhere between knowledge and ignorance; because it has to do with the world of sensory experience it cannot be identified with knowledge. It is concerned with appearances; indeed, the word *doxa* derives from a verb that means "to seem, to appear." Rhetoricians, says Plato, are concerned with opinion, not truth; so are juries, which have to rely on the witness of others. *Doxa* is associated with the lower parts of the soul, with sensation. Sensation cannot yield knowledge; what it yields is opinion.

Of course the word "opinion," coming from the Latin, lacks the heavenly sense of *doxa,* though personal glory, in so far as it depends on the admiration of the multitude, is a creation of Opinion, to which popular thought was often assimilated. In the English of Shakespeare's time the word was more often than not pejorative. We have lost most of that implication—"public opinion" is now regarded as a sort of ultimate tribunal, but for Shakespeare it connoted rather the fickleness of mobs. The first remark of Coriolanus when he confronts the indignant Roman populace uses the word: "What's the matter, you dissentious rogues, / That rubbing the poor itch of your opinion / Make yourselves scabs?" (I.i.164–66).

For Coriolanus, as for Milton's Jesus in *Paradise Regain'd,* "the people" is a "miscellaneous rabble" with no true apprehension of fame or glory; that is why he finds it so painful to have to solicit their "voices." Here, then, opinion is opposed to truth. In Jonson's *Hymenaei,* written within a couple of years of *Troilus and Cressida,* Opinion enters disguised as Truth: there appeared "two *Ladies,* the one representing *Truth,* the other *Opinion;* but both so alike attired, as they could by no note be distinguished." "The one expostulates the other," Truth calling Opinion an "illusive spright," and challenging her to contest the truth that marriage is more honourable than virginity. They have a long debate on this matter, considered appropriate to a wedding celebration. Truth calls Opinion "fantasticall," and Opinion gives a harsh account of the inconveniences of marriage, especially for women. The debate ends in a grand contest of their respective knightly champions, which is ended by the appearance of an angel. Truth has the last word on the gaudiness of Opinion, her costume being a reflection of her "uncertainties."

So opinion is a matter of appearances; in Samuel Daniel's *Cleopatra* she is the "Contriver of our greatest woes," and is "fed with shows."* She is dependent on what appears to the sense, and judges all things in the world "Not as they are but as they seem." "Opinion reigns without and Truth within." Iconographically she was "a blindfolded goddess with the world in her lap and a chameleon on her wrist." The *O.E.D.* has a striking quotation from 1538: "there is no difference between vice and virtue but strong opinion," which is close enough to Hamlet's "There is nothing good or bad but thinking makes it so."

Opinion could be regarded as an improper way of imposing purely conventional or customary constraints on individual behaviour, as when Donne (or whoever wrote the Seventeenth Elegy) attacked it from the naturalist

*Daniel's "closet drama" was first published in 1594, revised in 1599 and again in 1607, by which time he had apparently taken some hints from Shakespeare's *Antony and Cleopatra.*

position. Opinion upheld the disastrous notion of female honour, a false notion that had come between men and their natural desire for many and easily available sexual partners:

> The golden laws of nature are repeal'd,
> Which our first Fathers in such reverence held;
> Our liberty's revers'd, our Charter gone,
> And we're made servants to opinion,
> A monster in no certain shape attir'd . . .

Opinion was thus one of the instruments used by Custom to thwart human pleasure. It makes unnatural behaviour like chastity seem desirable, indeed obligatory. It is only thinking, wrong opinion, that makes it so. Of course this is Donne in his libertine mood, when he means to surprise or shock. Yet there is a strong naturalistic strain in the literature of the period, French as well as English (think of Iago), and it is part of a more general perception that one's general conduct is unduly controlled by custom, by what others think and teach, not from true knowledge but from its delusive shadow, opinion.

It is fair to add that some Shakespearian usages of the word are closer to the modern sense—ancestors of our "counsel's opinion" or the medical "second opinion." But Shakespeare never endows it with the honorific sense it now has in such expressions as "the bar of public opinion." For him, the pejorative sense was dominant; the opposition of opinion to truth was very firm. It had to do with appearance, not realities, with the outside not the inside, with the deceptiveness of the senses, with what is said about the worth of an object or a person rather than about intrinsic values.

Although Shakespeare's meditations on opinion are in some ways identifiable with a venerable intellectual position, we need to see how very differently the argument is presented, what becomes of its semantic situation, when it is studied in a complex verbal and theatrical context. The standard position, traceable to Plato and to the Stoics, was enjoying a revival of interest in Shakespeare's time.* The whole question is fascinatingly if rather tortuously considered by Pascal in the *Pensées* (89–93), where one conclusion is that opinion held in igno-

*See Peter Ure, "A Note on 'Opinion' in Daniel, Greville and Chapman," in *Elizabethan and Jacobean Drama,* ed. J. C. Maxwell (1974), pp. 209–20.

rance of the truth must be unsound, even if it coincides with the truth—a view anticipated by Socrates in *The Republic* (VI.506c). Opinion is not the same as ignorance, and it can look like truth, but even as it does so it can be disastrously misleading.

It may be best to think of the opposition of truth and opinion as having been well established though not precisely defined—one of those currents of thought that passes through educated minds without necessarily being associated with particular thinkers. If one were to consider the question of a person's value, one would drift naturally into matters of opinion; for value, worth, estimate, price are all dependent on opinion, and all the varying means of estimating the value of a person are similarly subjective. The honour of men is a relatively complicated matter involving reputation and valour, while the honesty of women seems in principle simpler, since it is almost the same as chastity; but from chastity we can pass to property, and also to jealousy, and the complication that unchastity in women dishonours their men.

We perhaps ought to consider more extensively the fortunes of this word "honesty," as William Empson did so ingeniously ("Why is it only in English that this romance word has come to mean telling truth?"*) in the chapters of his *The Structure of Complex Words* that culminate in the classic study of "Honest in *Othello.*" For Othello, too, is in its way a play about opinion, honesty (in many of its senses) being a matter of opinion, like "honour."

That opinion and honour are related to worth and price was to be an issue for Shakespeare in *Timon of Athens,* where the hero's very name is related to Greek words meaning "honour," "worth," "price," "estimate" (whether of the value of a jewel or of a man). The courtesan Timandra ("we'll do anything for gold") also suggests both "price" and "men" in appropriate combination. And the play is much concerned with worth, with gold and jewels, the nature of authority, the value of friendship. However, it is in *Troilus and Cressida* that we find something Shakespeare had not done before and never did quite so elaborately again. The play unusually includes a set debate on value and opinion, and another on authority (opinion, after all, is what creates the assumption that superior powers ought to be obeyed, indeed that these powers *are* superior, an assertion that the play, radically, questions). But these more formal discussions coexist with questionable allusions throughout the entire play to worth in men and in possessions.

***The Structure of Complex Words* (1951, rev. ed., 1995), p. 185, and see the tabulations on p. 204.

The value of people is almost a commercial matter. So Troilus says of Cressida:

> Her bed is India, there she lies, a *pearl*
>
> (I.i.100)

for which he is the questing *merchant.* And of Helen he says:

> Is she worth keeping? Why, she is a *pearl,*
> Whose *price* hath launch'd above a thousand ships,
> And turn'd crown'd kings to *merchants.*
>
> (II.ii.81–83)

The value of a woman is appraised in the same way as that of a jewel, even by Troilus, who is supposed to be convinced of Cressida's unique inherent worth (but he is also a slave of sense and appearance, witness his hectic sensuality). Diomedes says that Helen has *cost* more than she is worth—a Grecian life for every drop of her blood, a Trojan's "for every scruple / Of her contaminated carrion weight" (IV.i.70ff.). He is valuing her like a goldsmith and, finding her flesh corrupt, he lowers his estimate. We remember that the honour of all these soldiers is at stake in the struggle for the defence or recovery of Helen; their own chivalric reputations should be kept unspotted, despite any view they may have of the worthlessness of the cause. Paris jokingly calls Diomedes a "chapman," or dealer, who professionally dispraises the thing he desires to buy (IV.i.76). And certainly Diomedes has very little time for fine chivalric talk, as we see again from his treatment of Cressida, so remote from Troilus's exalted love-talk. Earlier Hector also had emphasized Helen's cost and said she was not worth it: "she is not *worth* what she doth *cost* / The keeping" (II.ii.51–52). These devaluations are essential to the mood and strategy of the play, as when Cressida enters the Greek camp and is valued, by Ulysses, as a "daughter of the game" (IV.v.63), a loose woman, without worth or honour.

These are only the most obvious instances of the play's obsession with worth and value. Words such as "worthy," "glory," "fame," "merit," "esteem," "estimate," "estimation," "value," "cost," "honour" are everywhere. And "opinion" occurs ten times, far more than in any other Shakespeare play. It is commonplace, as we have seen, that reputation, honour, fame, and all the rest depend on opinion. Opinion is what people say. In the matter of reputation, it is what other people say about you. One cannot have fame or glory by one's own inward knowledge; it has to come from the mouths of others, not from within. For a man to know he is famous he must look in the mirror of opinion;

his fame is to be found in the world's eyes, where he must look for it. Much is made, in *Troilus and Cressida,* of this reflective property of fame, and much is said about the uselessness of trying to establish one's value by self-assessment. Achilles, of course, does a lot of this, but so does Ajax, and so does Agamemnon. The habit of flattering self-assessment is responsible for the remarkable frequency in the play of compounds beginning with "self-": "self-assumption," "self-admission," "self-breath," "self-affected," "self-willed." They are as much part of the dialect of the play as all those Latinate forms like "persistive" (the only occurrence in all of Shakespeare), "protractive" (once), "attentive," "unrespective" (twice), "diminutive" (twice in the canon), "attributive" (only occurrence). The *O.E.D.* knows of no use of "attributive" or "persistive" or "protractive" before these. Their purpose is rhetorical or, perhaps, anti-rhetorical; for the contrast between exterior assessment and what is likely to be said by the Agamemnons and Ulysses of the world is again the contrast between appearance and truth, opinion and truth.

The reputation of great persons is indeed the theme of the remarkable passages concerning Achilles and, more grossly, Ajax. Fame depends on "broad rumour," on the words and behaviour of others. When praise and deference cease, fame ceases also. Here is another reduction of truth and value to mere opinion.

But more primary arguments are made about opinion, the sole support of glory and fame, in the Trojan debate. Hector thinks Helen must be returned to the Greeks because she lacks value; she is not worth the cost of keeping her. It is Troilus who asks the key question: "What's aught but as 'tis valued?" (II.ii.52). He has been saying that their honour is involved in keeping Helen, and that their valuation of her when they approved the expedition of Paris was high; it would now be dishonourable to reduce it. And he expressly tells Helenus that reason has nothing to do with the case; after all, reason would make one run away from the challenge of an enemy in battle. Value is attributed to other persons and objects by our voices; it is vain for Hector to say, "But value dwells not in particular will" (II.ii.53)—that value can be intrinsic to the object, a true value, achieved without regard to what valuations one may choose to make.

Troilus answers the point thus: suppose I value a woman enough to marry her, as we valued Helen enough to abduct her; it would be dishonourable of me to reject her when I grew tired of her. If she was "inestimable" then she ought to be so now, or we are dishonoured. The conversation is interrupted by the entry and the dire prophecies of Cassandra, after which Hector accuses Troilus of allowing sense to overcome reason, a course which would help to make Cassandra's prophecy of Trojan defeat come true. Troilus replies that we cannot judge the correctness of an act by looking back on it from its consequences, and Paris naturally supports him. Hector, without altering his view, now weakly gives in. He repeats that the arguments of Troilus and Paris are the products of passion, not reason; reason would see that despite "raging appetites" elsewhere, the first debt of a wife is to her husband. "Hector's opinion / Is this in way of truth," he says (II.ii.188–89).

This is an extraordinary remark; Hector gives in on the pretence of accepting the argument that the dignity of the Trojans requires them to keep Helen. Of course he had to give in; it was a difficult moment for Shakespeare, who needed to stage the argument and wanted Hector to win it, but he couldn't change history and stop the war. What is interesting is that in making the volte-face he allows this rather comic collision: his "opinion is this in way of truth." Thus the debate ends in muddle and the war goes on. Opinion is confounded with truth. Of course it is possible to have an opinion about the truth, but this does not make it true; in the end, Hector's only reason for accepting this opinion is that to let Helen go would damage their "joint and several dignities," which are of course themselves subject to opinion. Later Troilus distinguishes himself from other men by saying that they "fish with craft for great opinion" while he "with great truth" catches "mere simplicity" (IV.iv.103–4)—a self-estimate by one who has been in word and deed an upholder of opinion as the sole criterion of value.

Troilus indeed professes to be much concerned with truth. "I am as true as truth's simplicity, / And simpler than the infancy of truth" (III.ii.169–70). This obsession reflects his confusion about Cressida, about whom he holds an opinion that is far from the truth, a divergence of which we are made aware in the dialogue of Act III (iii). He has claimed that henceforth "True swains in love shall . . . / Approve their truth by Troilus" (III.ii.173–74), and Cressida has sworn that if she were ever untrue she should remain for ever the standard of falseness in women. (When Pandarus goes on to say that in future all pimps shall be called Pandars, he is, as things turned out, speaking the truth, and we are to suppose that Cressida is doing likewise.) When the lovers part, a dialogue occurs with the following features:

> CRES. And is it true that I must go from Troy?
> TRO. A hateful truth.
> . . .
> TRO. Hear me, love. Be thou but true of heart—

CRES. I true? How now? what wicked deem is this?
TRO. . . . I speak not "be thou true" as fearing thee . . .
But "be thou true" say I to fashion in
My sequent protestation: be thou true,
And I will see thee.
CRES. . . . but I'll be true.
. . .
TRO. But yet be true.
CRES. O heavens, "be true" again?
. . .
CRES. My lord, will you be true?
TRO. Who, I? Alas, it is my vice, my fault.
While others fish with craft for great opinion,
I with great truth catch mere simplicity . . .
With truth and plainness . . .
Fear not my truth: the moral of my wit
Is "plain and true". . .

(IV.iv.30–108)

Here, in the hurry and pain of parting, we find the words "true" and "truth" uttered and questioned some fifteen times. Those words, along with "truest," occur about sixty times in the play, and here, in a brief passage, we have a quarter of their occurrences. Earlier, in passages of apparently small import, we have such lines as Cressida's teasing "To say the truth, true and not true" (I.ii.97), which turns out to be a motto for her and the play; and Pandarus's "Troilus shall be such to Cressid as what envy can say worst shall be a mock for his truth, and what truth can speak truest not truer than Troilus" (III.ii.95–98), where the words are forced on us beyond plausibility or obvious dramatic necessity. This iterative device Shakespeare was henceforth to use often.

It is important to see that we are not being banged over the head with such words to make us concede that we are dealing with a quasi-philosophical theme. (Empson saw the difficulty when writing about the dog in *Timon of Athens,* rightly finding the trick less well performed there. "One would not expect it to solve the puzzles any more than *fool* does elsewhere, but it should make us feel better about them."*) There is no solving of puzzles, though there is a resemblance to the experience of being caught in a maze, a maze of

**The Structure of Complex Words,* p. 183. See below, p.187.

language. The matter of truth cannot be treated alone; it is, for example, embroiled with the idea of worth, as when Troilus tells Diomedes that he is "unworthy to be call'd [Cressida's] servant," and the Greek replies, "To her own worth / She shall be priz'd" (IV.iv.125, 133–34). The question of truth cannot be separated from that of worth or value.

In a remarkable speech about time, in the same scene as his long dialogue with Cressida, Troilus says that he and she, having bought each other, must now sell at a loss, while Time, no honest merchant, "with a robber's haste / Crams his rich thiev'ry up" (IV.iv.42–43). Even time is on the make, and is important because of the variations in value it permits: Helen at the time of the abduction, Helen after seven years of costly war. We might as well be in a marketplace.

The point is made again by Ulysses in his lecture on time to Achilles: "Time hath, my lord, a wallet at his back" (III.iii.145ff.). The past deeds of Achilles have been stuffed into that wallet; his worth is not what it was. "Those scraps are good deeds past . . . to have done is to hang / Quite out of fashion . . . Let not virtue seek / Remuneration for the thing it was." It is the argument also of Agamemnon: reputations fade, they have to be constantly reaffirmed by opinion; value is reflected from the eyes and mouths of others and is not inherent:

> Much attribute he hath, and much the reason
> Why we ascribe it to him; yet all his virtues,
> Not virtuously on his own part beheld,
> Do in our eyes begin to lose their gloss,
> Yea, like fair fruit in an unwholesome dish,
> Are like to rot untasted . . .
> That if he overhold his price so much,
> We'll none of him.
>
> (II.iii.116ff.)

Attributes (like "additions" or titles) come from the outside, are "ascribed." "Beheld" here means "retained, kept hold of," but it cannot avoid bringing into the context the sense of sight, so that the sense "observed" intrudes, with "eyes," into the next line. (Note again the commercial figure, and also the comparison: the senses are always involved, especially taste, the palate, which, with "palates" and "palating," is mentioned four times in this play, although Shakespeare uses the word only seventeen times altogether.) The beholder, hearer, taster cannot be compelled to endure what his palate rejects, yet honour and fame depend on his not making such a rejection. "Self-assumption" is not enough; one must be beheld, heard, tasted with favour by others under the sway of opinion.

Achilles (and, in parody, Ajax) claims respect for "Imagin'd worth," which is treated as a disease, his passions being at war with reason (II.iii.172–78). It is a disease of the blood, endemic among warriors as the venereal disease of Pandarus is endemic among libertine lovers. Self-glory and the madnesses of sexual desire are linked: Achilles and Pandarus alike bear the "death-tokens" (II.iii.177). The scene in which Ulysses offers Achilles a diagnosis of his illness, and of the neglect into which he has fallen, is remarkable for several reasons. Not to be respectfully *looked at,* or to be regarded only with "unplausive eyes" (III.iii.43), is fatal to fame. Achilles realises that he has become "poor of late," and in a thoughtful speech shows that he understands why: "What the declin'd is, / He shall as soon read in the eyes of others / As feel in his own fall" (III.iii.76–78), but he persists in believing he has all that he formerly had "Save these men's looks, who do methinks find out / Some thing not worth in me such rich beholding / As they have often given" (90–92). Ulysses patiently explains that what Achilles has he has only by "reflection" (99), a point seconded by Achilles: the eye cannot see itself except in a mirror. And Ulysses stresses once more the theme of reflection, this time in the form of a reverberating voice, or the sun's heat reflected from a steel gate:

> . . . no man is the lord of any thing,
> Though in and of him there be much consisting,
> Till he communicate his parts to others;
> Nor doth he of himself know them for aught,
> Till he behold them formed in th' applause
> Where th' are extended: who like an arch reverb'rate
> The voice again, or like a gate of steel,
> Fronting the sun, receives and renders back
> His figure and his heat.
>
> (115–23)

Achilles is persuaded, at least for the moment: "I see my reputation is at stake, / My fame is shrowdly gor'd" (227–28). So, in this fine passage of dialogue, the operations of opinion are examined in depth. Yet Ulysses is trying to manipulate opinion on behalf of the state, an organization dependent on it. He fails. His own sermon on degree belongs to the appearances of rhetoric, an attempt of the usually fraudulent sort that governments have habitually made to keep the people in order. It should be possible to see through this performance. There is the circularity of the argument: "Degrees in schools . . . / But by degree stand" (I.iii.104–8), and of course Ulysses's own attempt to cheat Achilles, "whom opinion crowns / The sinow and the forehand of our host" (142), shows how little he cares for routine ideas of rank and order.

The greatness of these rulers is itself a matter of opinion. Aeneas, professing to expect "most imperial looks" (224), such as would distinguish the great man from "other mortals" (224–25), pointedly fails to recognise Agamemnon; he looks no different from the others. Patroclus makes fun of the great man by mimicking him. And Thersites is often on hand to explain that fame, chivalry, and honour are only fancy names for anger, cruelty, and craftiness, as disguised by opinion; and that love is merely lust and appetite similarly disguised. The theme is recurrent in Shakespeare, as when Lear insists that you can convert the poor, bare, fork'd animal into a corrupt office-holder by dressing it in the garments of power and authority. Even clothes may be agents of opinion, as King Lear recognised: "Robes and furr'd gowns hide all" (IV.vi.165).

Troilus and Cressida ends with instances of dishonour, both military, when Achilles murders Hector, and erotic, as when Diomedes coldly and without difficulty seduces Cressida. Troilus, in V.ii, is forced to produce a theory that there must be two of her, a ghost that is true and a woman who is not; as he foretold in his speech at the Trojan debate, he finds it hard to modify his original estimate of her.

Opinion, says Thersites, may be worn "on both sides, like a leather jerkin" (III.iii.264–65), and the tone of the whole play shares this ambivalence. It is not making plain statements about honour or love or authority; it is not, save in the inconclusive Trojan debate, schematically placing opinion in opposition to truth or value. What it richly provides is a sense of these qualities as they occur in language and in action. The play is a dark one only because nobody, except for a moment Hector and the priest Helenus, can really speak against opinion. Everything ends in failure.

The great scene in Act V (ii), besides displaying Troilus as a man who can "invert th' attest of eyes and ears" (122) to see his woman as true, offers a Cressida who is a creature of appetite, to be observed in the arms of

Diomedes; a Ulysses who "cannot conjure" (125), opposing this truth to the opinion of Troilus. Thersites thinks that since the whole war is about a whore and a cuckold it is easy to see Cressida and Troilus in that light. For a moment we may feel pathos rather than mere disillusion.

It is tempting to feel with Thersites that valour is only anger plus opinion, that fair outsides, like the fine suit of armour peeled off by Hector in battle, contain nothing but rottenness within. But somewhere among the rich overtones of the play we should still be able to hear Hector's "value dwells not in particular will" (II.ii.53). And we remember that the story allowed Shakespeare no choice: Hector had to lose the argument, because, after all, Helen was not returned, and the war went on. So he loses the argument, but the words remain in the text. They may allow one to suppose the occulted presence of some transcendental sanction. And the mere existence of opinion may imply the existence of truth, even if only conjectured as the object of a kind of knowledge above that of the senses. It might be argued that the play defeats truth, being itself a rhapsody about opinion. But Hector's line has its place in the wonderful whirl of words: truth, like value, dwells not in particular will; but only when the two are simply confronted, as in Ben Jonson's masque, can truth have the last word.

MEASURE FOR MEASURE

Measure for Measure and *All's Well That Ends Well* are twins, with some unavoidable genetic resemblances but uneven luck, one being much uglier than the other. I have assumed that *All's Well* was born first, since the plot of the Substituted Bride, common to both plays, is an essential part of one and not of the other; so it seems that Shakespeare, wanting *Measure for Measure* to stop being a tragedy, borrowed the idea of the bed-trick, or Substituted Bride, from *All's Well.* I know this explanation does not meet the approval of the Oxford editors and may not sound wholly satisfactory to others, but it seems sensible to me.

It would be odd for a playwright to repeat a plotline immediately, but it is generally assumed that the plays are more or less contemporaries. The Oxford edition gives the date of *Measure for Measure* as 1603 and of *All's Well* as 1604–5, with *Othello* in between (1603–4). It is easy to agree that the part of the Clown in *All's Well* was written for Robert Armin, who joined Shakespeare's company in 1599. The Arden edition carefully surveys the evidence for dating the play after 1599 but concludes that there is none of any merit;* that which places *Measure* in 1604 is more impressive, and if that play came second we can say *All's Well* could have been written around 1602–4. All this

**Measure for Measure,* ed. G. K. Hunter (Arden edition, 1959), pp. xviii–xxv.

still leaves unsettled the question why two almost contemporaneous plays should use so much of the same plot material.*

All's Well is one of the weakest of Shakespeare's plays. Its wide and often inexplicable variations of manner have encouraged critics to believe that the version we have is a revision of an earlier play, possibly the one referred to by Francis Meres in his *Palladia Tamia* as *Love's Labour's Won;* if so, it was written earlier than 1598. But this old theory is no longer given much credit. The reasons given by the Oxford editors for believing that the play as it stands was written after *Measure for Measure* and *Troilus and Cressida* are no more persuasive. And of course the date of the piece has nothing to do with its value, except that it is rather surprising to find it among the works of a period beginning with *Hamlet* and including *Othello.*

Shakespeare was occasionally careless about detail, but each of these "twin" plays has not only an occasionally slipshod text but also more plot errors and inconsistencies than usual. Many of these are trivial, and we are made aware of them only by long and intense critical scrutiny. Some, like the mysterious shifts and tricks of the Duke in *Measure for Measure,* are more worrying and have called for heavy defensive work from critics who do not like their Shakespeare ever to be wrong or careless.

As to *All's Well,* the troublesome faults are less to do with structure than with texture. George Hunter, the editor of the Arden edition, expresses this well: "The characteristic verse of *All's Well* is laboured and complex but not rich . . . The verse is not 'thin' in the manner of a weak and uninterested writer, but contorted, ingrown, unfunctional."† He offers an excellent account of this superfluous contortion when he compares a passage from the play with a neat and uncontorted passage from *A Midsummer Night's Dream.* The point is not simply that the former (V.iii.42–55) is more difficult but that it is less conformable with minimal rhetorical requirements, too obscure for its own good: "the complexity is self-defeating . . . The amount of mental

*By Wright's hendiadys count, both *All's Well* and *Measure for Measure* belong to the period when Shakespeare was fondest of the device, though *All's Well* is low on the list: *Hamlet* 66, *Othello* 28, *Troilus* 19, *Macbeth* 18, *Measure* 16, *King Lear* 15, *All's Well* 9. That *Measure* has hendiadys almost twice as frequently as *All's Well* may be significant; *Hamlet* has one every 66 lines, *Antony and Cleopatra* every 383 lines, *Measure* every 176 lines, and *All's Well* every 330 lines. By this calculation *All's Well* could be taken as late, just before Shakespeare lost the hendiadys habit (the rates for *The Winter's Tale* and *The Tempest* are 1,538 and 1,032)—a guess in some ways confirmed by the verse of the play generally considered.

†Arden edition, p. lvi.

energy required is out of all proportion to any dramatic illumination of the context."*

This passage in Hunter's introduction is the best I have read concerning the verse of *All's Well That Ends Well.* That the play has a reasonably simple theme—the relations between birth and nobility, between virtue and fortune, and the complexities of the idea of honour, whether military or sexual—is obvious. Blending these ethical considerations with the folktale motifs of the Healing of the King, the Fulfilment of the Tasks, and the Substituted Bride, with Helena as the Clever Wench, might have created difficulties, but we know that Shakespeare was usually very good at that sort of thing and was later to write a series of what we now call Romances, all of them busy simultaneously with improbable old tales and more modern speculations, and all accepted as of high quality. What went wrong in *All's Well*?

We are confronted with a wilful obscurity, occurring often enough in the speeches of the Countess. It is interesting that George Bernard Shaw, who had a particular and in my opinion perverse admiration for this play, called the Countess "the most beautiful old woman's part ever written,"† but he must have been thinking of her candour, her manners, her liberality of sentiment, and her practical, almost Shavian attitude to marriage, rather than of the way she sometimes tended to put things.

> Think upon patience. Pray you, gentlemen,
> I have felt so many quirks of joy and grief
> That the first face of neither on the start
> Can woman me unto't.
>
> (III.ii.48–51)

Here the underlying point is clear enough: she has experienced so much joy and sorrow that a sudden announcement that there is to be more of either cannot make her weep, as women usually do on these occasions. But the third line is close to unintelligible on first hearing, and the fourth uses a nonce verb, "to woman," in a very forced manner. (The breaking off of such a sentence in mid-line was to be a regular feature of Shakespeare's verse henceforth, part of an underlying Shakespearian rhythm.) We shall find verses at least as

*Ibid., p. lvii.
†Quoted in ibid., p. xxxiv n.

harsh as these in *Coriolanus* and *The Winter's Tale,** but here they deserve Hunter's censure, for the obscurity does nothing for the Countess and merely puzzles the audience.

Editors are here more often than usual driven to paraphrase; there are so many passages at which the eye stumbles no less than the ear. Some of these passages are in prose, some in couplets, obscure as well as weak (e.g., Helena's "great floods have flown / From simple sources, and great seas have dried / When miracles have by the great'st been denied" [II.i.139–41], where "flown" is a conscripted rhyme for "shown" in the previous line, and the last line has so little interest in itself that it merely limps to its end). The King matches the Countess in complexity of expression:

> So like a courtier, contempt nor bitterness
> Were in his pride or sharpness; if they were,
> His equal had awak'd them, and his honor,
> Clock to itself, knew the true minute when
> Exception bid him speak, and at this time
> His tongue obey'd his hand.
>
> (I.ii.36–41)

The general idea is that the person being praised (Bertram's dead father) was affable to all ranks of society but knew exactly when his honour required him to take offence at an affront from somebody of equal rank. But the vagueness of "Were in," that whole phrase somehow missing the point, the unnecessarily ingrown "Clock to itself," meaning only that he knew when honour required him to act—all this strikes me as the most weary and mechanical writing of the mature Shakespeare; and these qualities could be further illustrated from speeches by the King, the Countess, and others. Even Helena, whose intentions are so single and so clear to herself, produces lines that drive commentators to despair:

> Yet in this captious and intenible sieve
> I still pour in the waters of my love
> And lack not to lose still.
>
> (I.iii.202–4)

*Harshness was an acceptable feature of Elizabethan-Jacobean poetic style, held to be particularly appropriate to satire and also, more oddly, to funeral elegies. Donne, a near-contemporary of Shakespeare, actually boasted of his harshness: "I sing not, Siren like, to tempt; for I / Am harsh" (Verse letter to Mr. Samuel Brooke, ll.9–10). The style was referred to, sometimes with disapproval, as "strong lines."

Again the general idea is plain enough, whether one takes "captious" in its modern sense or thinks it a contraction of "capacious," and understands "intenible" to mean "unemptiable." But what exactly does that last line mean? Presumably "I still [or always] have plenty more to waste in the same way." But the sense is too tersely given, especially in the midst of a figure which requires us to think of water improvidently splashed about.

However, when all this is said, the lines, even at their worst, continue to sound like Shakespeare, who does not always sound pleasing; some of them seem to be anticipating the greatest of all Shakespeare's onslaughts on the listener's quickness of understanding, in later plays such as *Coriolanus.*

That he could control this ruggedness is clear from the relative power of the verse in *Measure for Measure,* which, for about half its length, is one of the truly great plays. Here again there is a folktale plot, which other earlier writers had often treated; Shakespeare's main sources were a novella by the Italian writer Giraldo Cinthio, also a creditor for *Othello,* and a ten-act play by George Whetstone called *Promos and Cassandra.* The story even had a historical origin. It seems to have been widely liked because of its theme, the corruption of a judge. It is well enough known that the title derives from the St. Matthew Gospel 7:1–2, "Judge not, that ye be not judged. For with what judgment ye judge, ye shall be judged: and with what measure ye mete, it shall be measured to you again." It is perhaps not so well remembered that there is relevance also in the Epistle to the Romans 2:1: "Therefore thou art inexcusable, O man, whosoever thou art that judgest: for wherein thou judgest another, thou condemnest thyself; for thou that judgest doest the same things." These are texts for a homily, as it were, and the issues of justice and mercy, of human passion and the law were indeed regular items of discussion; they were treated by the great poet Spenser, quite recently dead, and even by King James I himself (with whom this play is in other ways associated).

Many attempts have been made to derive from the play an elaborate Christian allegory and, now that religion is out of fashion, a political message. In fact the programme of the play is announced in the Duke's first line: "Of government the properties to unfold . . ." (I.i.3). The properties of government, in this sense, are justice and mercy, as the Duke makes plain when he describes the powers he will delegate to Angelo: he says he has "Lent him our terror, dress'd him with our love" (I.i.19), these being the agents of justice and mercy. Angelo is told that "Mortality and mercy in Vienna / Live in thy tongue and heart" (44–45), and is urged "to enforce or qualify the laws / As to your soul seems good" (65–66).

This excellent opening (which contrasts strongly with the affected and laborious prose at the beginning of *All's Well*) not only explains the powers deputed to Angelo but introduces, by a series of figures, another theme, that of the testing of the judge. One cannot say that Shakespeare chose the name Angelo for this reason, but it becomes important that he shares his name with a coin. The English "angel" (originally the "noble") was so called because it bore an image of St. Michael slaying the dragon. It was in use until the reign of King Charles I and was the subject of much punning, as in John Donne's elegy "The Bracelet." When the Duke calls for Angelo and wonders "What figure . . . he will bear" (16) he is already deploying the idea of a coin with a stamped image: will it be angelic? In his lecture to his new deputy twenty or so lines later he recurs to the imagery of the goldsmith:

Spirits are not finely touch'd
But to fine issues; nor Nature never lends
The smallest scruple of her excellence,
But like a thrifty goddess, she determines
Herself the glory of a creditor,
Both thanks and use.

(35–40)

The idea of "touching" leads back to the goldsmith. The "scruple" is a goldsmith's measure. Loans were made by goldsmiths before banks existed; then as now the lender received thanks but also interest ("use"). We retain the word "touchstone" for metaphorical use, but the original sense was literal: to touch was "to test the fineness of gold (or silver) by rubbing it upon a touchstone" (*O.E.D.* s.v. "touch" 8a). A touchstone was a piece of stone, sometimes quartz, which left a distinctive mark on the gold or silver to be "tried." Angelo picks up the figure in lines 48–49: "Let there be some more test made of my mettle / Before so noble and so great a figure / Be stamp'd upon it," where he is also remembering that a noble was a coin.

One odd thing about the role of the Duke is that he gives different and not truly compatible reasons for his pretended departure. The first is to give somebody else the job of administering laws he has been too weak or too kind to enforce himself.

We have strict statutes and most biting laws
The needful bits and curbs to headstrong weed(s[steeds? jades?]),
Which for this fourteen years we have let slip . . .

(I.iii.19–21)

It would seem dreadful if he himself were to apply these bits and curbs, necessary though he believes them to be, so he gives the job to Angelo, "A man of stricture and firm abstinence" (I.iii.12). But he confesses a second motive: the testing of Angelo:

> Lord Angelo is precise;
> Stands at a guard with envy; scarce confesses
> That his blood flows; or that his appetite
> Is more to bread than stone: hence shall we see
> If power change purpose: what our seemers be.
>
> (I.iii.50–54)

He began the scene by professing his own immunity to sexual desire, and he picks Angelo because he seems to be a man of the same sort, or because he wants to find out whether that is so. This mixture of ultimately incompatible motives leads in the end to the spoiling of the play, but not before the testing of Angelo has produced scenes of unsurpassed dramatic tension.

The testing begins when Angelo condemns Claudio to death for fornication. The case is deliberately a hard one, of the kind that is said to make bad law, for Claudio and Julietta are partners in "a true contract" (I.ii.145). They are, in the law of the period, married, the contract being of *sponsalia de presenti,* immediately effective, and irrevocable, unlike the one, to be revealed later, of Angelo with Mariana, which was *de futuro* and, before consummation, revocable. The case is harder still in that sex between Claudio and Julietta was "most mutual" (154). A contemporary audience would take them to be married in law, though lacking the important endorsement of the church, which gave it validity in the eyes of the state.

The scene in which Claudio informs Lucio of his plight opens with Claudio's acceptance of his lot:

> Thus can the demigod, Authority,
> Make us pay down for our offense by weight
> The words of heaven: on whom it will, it will;
> On whom it will not, so; yet still 'tis just.
>
> (120–23)

He is willing to add that he has brought the trouble on himself: "Our natures do pursue, / Like rats that ravin down their proper bane, / A thirsty evil, and when we drink we die" (128–30). The idea is that when we use too much "liberty," for example in illicit sex, we resemble rats when they have taken poison. The poison works only when one returns to the ordinary, innocent, necessary habits of living (to the rats when they next drink), and the fact that we are poisoned is revealed, for instance, by Julietta's pregnancy. There is acceptance here, but also disgust that we are so made that we not only take our own "bane," contrive our own destruction, but "ravin" down that evil, as it might be under the imperious spell of lust. Shakespeare had years before created the figure of Tarquin in *The Rape of Lucrece,* and written Sonnet 129 ("Th' expense of spirit in a waste of shame") where "lust in action" is said to be

Past reason hunted, and no sooner had,
Past reason hated as a swallowed bait
On purpose laid to make the taker mad . . .

Claudio is not a simple character; later he shows a divided mind about the Duke's sagacious advice on dying. Here he talks about his relationship with Julietta as if it were a matter of destructive lust, and his fate deserved ("'tis just" [123]). (Contrast the levity of Mistress Overdone and Pompey, who inhabit the underworld of Vienna: "what has he done? / A woman. / But what's his offense? / Groping for trouts in a peculiar river" [87–90].) But almost at once Claudio asks whether the severity of the sentence is more a matter of Angelo's pride of office than of equity.

Here, as in the next scene between Friar Thomas and the Duke, we are invited, in the absence of any evidence, to doubt Angelo's mettle. Claudio's speech beginning at line 156 has the agitation Shakespeare now imparted to characters thinking under stress; it is one long sentence (sixteen lines) with many parentheses and qualifications and incomplete clauses—a performance comparable with that speech of Aufidius at the end of Act IV of *Coriolanus* or, nearer in time, Claudius's soliloquy in *Hamlet,* an exasperated meditation on a situation that must yet cannot be accepted.

It begins thus:

And the new deputy now for the Duke—
Whether it be the fault and glimpse of newness,
Or whether that the body public be
A horse whereon the governor doth ride,
Who, newly in the seat, that it may know
He can command, lets it straight feel the spur;
Whether the tyranny be in his place,

Or in his eminence that fills it up,
I stagger in . . .

Claudio anticipates the figure of horse-taming used by the Duke in the next scene ("The needful bits and curbs to headstrong jades"*), and the struggle with ambiguous feelings produces at once a *Hamlet*-like hendiadys: "the fault and glimpse of newness," which a reader or spectator must expand into something like "a display of new authority that may be seen as a fault." These alternations of compression and expansion are part of the style in which the mature Shakespeare expresses the wavering complexity of emotionally agitated thought; the imagery occurs as it occurs, from horsemanship, from rusty armour, from zodiacs as the measure of years. All this Claudio "staggers in."

He now has the idea of asking his sister Isabella to intercede with Angelo, thinking that her standing as a novice nun may help her persuade him to mercy.

I have great hope in that; for in her youth
There is a prone and speechless dialect,
Such as move men; beside, she hath prosperous art
When she will play with reason and discourse,
And well she can persuade.

(182–86)

This remarkable speech has attracted interesting comment. In a recent book, Jonathan Bate explains that William Empson's concept of ambiguity was a decidedly Cambridge invention; by getting rid of the either/or mentality that had been prevalent in literary analysis he was bringing to literary criticism a way of thinking inaugurated by Albert Einstein but familiar in the university of the physicist Paul Dirac; the young and prodigious Empson, says Bate, was "the first man to see the literature of the past through quantum theory's altered notion of reality." He is "modernism's Einstein."†

Be that as it may, I agree that we need new terms to praise the early Empson, for it is a return to the spirit of his work, wherever he got it from, that offers us our best hope of restoring and invigorating the practice of critical

*"Jades" is Hunter's emendation, in the Arden edition, of the original "weeds."
†*The Genius of Shakespeare* (1997), pp. 315–16.

analysis. Bate discusses one of Empson's examples of the Seventh Type of ambiguity, the type that occurs when "the two meanings of the word, the two values of the ambiguity, are the two opposite meanings defined by the context, so that the total effect is to show a fundamental division in the author's mind."* This type was of special importance not only because of the degree of "compaction" to be observed in the relation of the opposites but because it represents somehow the *deepest* poetry, what Empson calls, with only a little irony, "the secret places of the Muse," rather wickedly adapting some lines from Dante which show the poet and Virgil too intimately involved in the body of Satan: another type of ambiguity.

One example of the Seventh Type, cited by Bate, consists of this speech in *Measure for Measure.* Claudio, under sentence of death for fornication, agrees that his sister, the novice Isabella, might, with some hope of success, go to the deputy Angelo and plead for her brother's life (here I use the original spelling):

> for in her youth
> There is a prone and speechlesse dialect
> Such as moue men . . .
>
> (I.ii.182–84)

Dr. Johnson "could scarcely tell what signification to give the word 'prone,'" and after labouring at it for a while he suggested emending "prone" to either "pow'r" or "prompt." A modern reader may scorn these rather feeble suggestions, and even agree that this passage, far from suffering a loss of sense from that "distortion of words" which "is not uncommon in our authour,"† comes from the secret places of the Muse where distortions make poetry; that it is a wonderful piece of language, one of those that provoke the sort of attention T. S. Eliot had in mind when he spoke of the bewildering minute, the moment of dazzled recognition, from which one draws back and, having regained composure, tries to think of something to say about an experience too disconcerting to be thought of as simply pleasant. Empson found in Claudio's words an example of his "complete opposites": "This is the stainless Isabel, being spoken of by her respectful brother. *Prone* means either 'inactive

*William Empson, *Seven Types of Ambiguity* (1930, 2nd ed., 1961), p. 192.
†*Johnson on Shakespeare,* ed. A. Sherbo (1968), p. 179.

and lying flat' (in retirement or with a lover) or 'active,' 'tending to,' whether as *moving men* by her subtlety or by her purity, or as moving in herself, for pleasure or to do good. *Speechlesse* will not give away whether she is shy or sly, and *dialect* has abandoned the effort to distinguish between them. The last half-line makes its point very calmly, with an air of knowing about such cases; and, indeed, I feel very indelicate in explaining Claudio's meaning."*

Bate now develops this reading, perhaps wanting to strengthen its sexual suggestiveness. Empson, to whom the conflicting senses of "prone" (inactive/active) are the central issue, with support from subtle/pure, shy/sly, has "lying flat . . . with a lover," and he makes something of the final hint about Claudio's street wisdom; but Bate wants to do more along these lines. Mention of Isabella's "youth," it is now alleged, brings in "the heat of sexuality," while "prone" introduces the fleeting idea of Isabella lying flat on her back. But this is a mistake which Empson just avoided. "Prone" can certainly mean an extraordinary number of things, but it never means "flat on the back," as the *O.E.D.* (which, surprisingly, does not give this example) makes perfectly clear. Perhaps Bate would have been happier if Shakespeare had written "supine," a word he somehow omitted to use anywhere, though it was available in his time and clearly differentiated from "prone," as in the *O.E.D.*'s example from a book published in 1615 (". . . the position or manner of lying . . . eyther prone that is downeward, or supine that is vpward").

It is true that we might still somehow get from the lines the idea that Claudio, delicately, ambiguously, even unwillingly, entertains the notion that his sister may exercise an appeal that is partly sexual—as if, by a masculine intuition that against probability turns out to be shared by the precise Angelo, he sees that her nun's habit could be an element in her success as an advocate, the more apposite in that the Deputy might get from the encounter some sense of the strength of the temptation to which he, Claudio, had yielded; though given the young woman's religious vocation and the celebrated rigour of Angelo's life, one would not have expected either of them to fall. The action of the play will turn on Angelo's inflamed sexual reaction to Isabella, so we may read this expressly erotic consequence back into Claudio's speech, to the point where it can be overlooked that he could be thinking first of his sister simply as an advocate made the more persuasive by her feminine grace and by her nun's habit, which, though some might find it provocative,

**Seven Types of Ambiguity*, p. 202.

inevitably suggests chastity. But the sexual suggestion can't be wholly dispelled. J. W. Lever allows that "prone," "move," and, in the next line, "play" are "capable of suggesting sexual provocation," though he insists that the "overt drift" concerns psychology and rhetoric, usefully quoting from Thomas Wright's *The Passions of the Mind* (1601): "superiours may learn to coniecture the affections of their subiectes mindes, by a silent speech pronounced in their very countenances. And this point especially may be obserued in women." Lever thinks "prone" here suggests "the abject posture of submission or helplessness."*

This sense, which is surely present, and doesn't eliminate but probably reduces the flagrancy of the Empson-Bate interpretation, can more easily be admitted if we insist that whatever else it may mean, "prone" does not mean "supine." The commonsense view might be that Claudio is cheering himself up by arguing that Isabella might impress Angelo in two ways, by being submissive and silent, and, alternatively, by proving she is a good arguer, or by both, at appropriate moments. Critics are rightly required to resist such simple explanations; as Stephen Booth remarks in his edition of the Sonnets, sometimes "a reader will see the speaker's point without understanding (or knowing that he has not understood and cannot in any usual sense understand) the sentence that makes the point." He offers this valuable proposition while discussing Sonnet 16, but adds that in general "even where the lines are vaguest and most ambiguous they are usually *also* simple and obvious."†

Because this paradox is worth bearing in mind when one is engaged in discussions of the present kind, I am allowing myself to dwell at some length on one brief moment in *Measure for Measure.* It is in many ways typical of the problems that arise for readers of the mature Shakespeare. Ordinary readers and commentators have somewhat different interests, though they must at times converge if the commentators remember their duty. Here I've tried to do mine.

I don't feel that Empson, who elsewhere wrote finely about *Measure for Measure,* in this instance quite met the challenge of the lines in Claudio's speech, and I doubt if Bate has helped him much. Hilda Hulme, a scholar who applied her considerable knowledge of Elizabethan English to the language of Shakespeare's plays, remarks that an interest in the "total meaning"

**Measure for Measure* (Arden edition, 1965), p. 18n. Wright's book was reissued in 1604, approximately the date of the play.

†*Shakespeare's Sonnets* (1977), p. xii.

of units of language has been a "special distinction of recent criticism." She may have had Empson in mind, though she cites him only once (with approval, although his method, despite his reliance on the *O.E.D.,* is of course very different from hers). Unlike Dr. Johnson, who admired Shakespeare most when he was writing with "ease and simplicity," we now, she remarks, "take pleasure . . . in all the various modes of complex meaning," the more various and complex occurring naturally in rugged and difficult passages rather than in easy and simple ones. And so we convince ourselves that our response is closer to that of Shakespeare's contemporaries than to that of his editors from the eighteenth century to the early twentieth century. Hulme reminds us that Heminge and Condell, the editors of the 1623 Folio, though they boasted about Shakespeare's fluency, acknowledged that his readers would have various degrees of skill, "from the most able, to him that can but spell."* It has always seemed a great mystery of the early Jacobean years that audiences were able to take in at a hearing at least some of the sense of passages in a dozen great plays that often continue to baffle modern editors. Of course they had been taught by Shakespeare and had also listened to those long sermons dividing the word of God. And here Booth's remark is apposite: one can follow, catch the drift, without truly understanding, and even more in a play than in a sonnet, for the onward drive of the action will not permit one to linger over puzzles.

Hulme, as one would expect, has a look at Claudio's "prone," reminding the reader as she often does that Latin senses can lurk behind Shakespearian words, and citing a contemporary authority, Thomas Cooper's *Thesaurus Linguae Latinae,* on the expression *aures pronas,* for which he gives, as one of a number of instances, "*auribus pronis aliquid accipere* [to receive something with prone ears]. Tacit[us]. Willingly to hear."† This is useful because it connects "prone" with "speechless" in what we have seen to be a quite characteristic Shakespearian manner. Indeed, Empson uses, in another example of the Seventh Type of ambiguity, Donne's line "Even my oppress shoes, dumb and

*Cited in Hilda Hulme, *Explorations in Shakespeare's Language* (1962), pp. 3–4.

†The Latin sense of *pronus* is "leaning forward" and, by extension, "inclined towards," "favourable," and, mostly in post-Augustan Latin, "easy, without difficulty." Later still, it could mean "ready, willing" (so Lewis and Short). Although the word is capable of so many senses, it never seems to mean "lying face upward." One sense of the Latin that may persist in Shakespeare's usage is "willing to obey, anxious to please," though to press that might take us back into the matter of sexual ambiguities.

speechlesse were," making the splendidly accurate point that "*Dumb* and *speechlesse* have the same meaning, but their sound describes the silence and the noise, respectively . . ."* If we remember both Cooper and Wright, we can perhaps think of "prone" and "speechlesse," too, as being two ways of saying the same thing, though we are still struck by the apparent strangeness of "prone" and the oxymoron of "speechlesse dialect": could it mean making the plea by a kind of eloquence of demeanour rather than in words? In fact, "dialect" here belongs with "in her youth," and is associated accordingly with a sexual blooming rather than with eloquence. And the sexual attraction is made piquant by the girl's purity and vocation. Claudio does add that his sister is also an accomplished speaker, as indeed the sequel proves. Yet the word "beside," in the third line, goes some way to reinforcing the idea that even without speaking Isabella can persuade; it comes in as an afterthought, and so strengthens the sexual power Claudio almost unwittingly attributes to her.

The word "prone" has other senses, some of which, in defiance of the full Empsonian doctrine (though he admitted the need for exceptions) should be ruled out as irrelevant to the present case, some more readily than others. Shakespeare uses the word seven times. Among the other usages "prone to mischief," "I never saw one so prone" (meaning "ready"), "prone [willing] to labour" can be ruled out, though Sonnet 141 calls the sense of feeling "to base touches prone" and in *The Rape of Lucrece* we find "O that prone lust should stain so pure a bed!" (l. 684), where, as F. T. Prince correctly and modestly remarks in his Arden edition, one can interpret "prone" as "headstrong, impulsive," but "the meaning of 'prostrate, face downwards' enters in."† It is indeed an odd word, for it can mean "servile, submissive, cringing" and also "headstrong and impulsive," and it can qualify "lust." Even the commoner senses, surviving into our own English, may not gain admission: "easy, apt, liable, having a natural disposition to something," as in Hermione's "I am not prone to weeping, as our sex / Commonly are" (*The Winter's Tale,* II.i.108–9). We must impose some limits, or explanation gets lost in mere noise. The limits can be so drawn as to exclude much, but probably not to exclude every scintilla of sexual innuendo; and Hilda Hulme, who has a learned chapter on "The Less Decent Language of the Time," would not disapprove of this.

**Seven Types of Ambiguity,* p. 199.
†*The Poems* (Arden edition, 1960), p. 99n.

To make this discussion of the "prone" passage a little more complete we should consider the verb "move" as Claudio uses it. It is plural though its subject is singular. This discord is by no means unusual in Shakespeare.* I agree with Lever that the plural occurs by affinity with "prone and speechlesse," the verb deserting its singular subject "dialect," and so it has the effect of bringing "prone and speechlesse" into an even firmer association than their senses (some forms of proneness being understandably speechless) have already done. Whatever we make of it, we can take this speech as an example of Shakespeare at his richest, for at such times he will not settle for a single, simple sense, though he leaves one around to keep the reader or auditor quiet; and in this respect the passage is characteristic of the play itself.

Linguistic oscillation on a large scale is exemplified by Lucio's easy transitions between the language of the pub and brothel and his rather lofty and reverent address to Isabella. It is he who hails Isabella as "a thing enskied, and sainted" (I.iv.34), and who goes on to say

> Your brother and his lover have embrac'd.
> As those that feed grow full, as blossoming time
> That from the seedness the bare fallow brings
> To teeming foison, even so her plenteous womb
> Expresseth his full tilth and husbandry.
>
> (40–44)

We are not directly told whether to think of Lucio as genuinely committed to this attitude, or merely as teasing, or as misjudging his interlocutor, or as simply hypocritical, paying the usual tribute of vice to virtue. The saintly Isabella cuts sharply through his surprising celebration of the naturalness of sex and pregnancy with her curt paraphrase: "Some one with child by him?" (45). She speaks plainly: "I'll see what I can do" (84). Not an explicit word here about her horror of libertinism, and it is the libertine, ultimately the only member of the cast to be unequivocally condemned and punished, who speaks for natural sexuality and fecundity.

*In this case E. A. Abbott calls "move" "a subjunctive used indefinitely after a relative"; but this seems very strained in comparison with his other examples. *A Shakespearian Grammar* (1870, etc., §367).

Angelo is a character even more obviously divided, as he must be, since the story depends on his turning out to be a sexual predator, though apparently he is "a man whose blood / Is very snow-broth; one who never feels / The wanton stings and motions of the sense" (57–59). The two scenes in which Isabella pleads with this man for her brother's life are surely among the most splendid of Shakespeare's achievements. The reason why they are never less than totally absorbing has much to do with the nature of the conflict between their positions, but much more with the extraordinary power of their language.

At the beginning of Act II Angelo repeats, against the persuasions of Escalus, the doctrine enforced on him by the Duke: the law must be observed; to soften it unduly is to encourage crime in others. That he himself might have felt "The wanton stings and motions of the sense," as Escalus, with a certain timid cogency suggests (II.i.8ff.), meets with Angelo's firm rejection of the argument: the point is not that he had never been tempted, only that he had never fallen. Escalus, at any rate in his official capacity, finally though reluctantly accepts this argument that not to enforce the law is to encourage crime: "Pardon is still the nurse of second woe. / But yet, poor Claudio . . ." (284–85).

Before Isabella can visit Angelo, we are introduced to the comic libertines of the stews, as if to show that Vienna really did need a touch of discipline, or perhaps to mark the difference between the degree of Claudio's offence and theirs, which Angelo cannot himself be bothered to judge. Then Isabella enters, to the apparently implacable Angelo. Her plea that her brother's fault, but not he, should be condemned is weak, and it is briskly refused: "Condemn the fault and not the actor of it? / Why, every fault's condemn'd ere it be done" (II.ii.37–38). Isabella praises the justice of the law, and moves to depart. But Lucio, a libertine yet once more on what most take to be the right side of the argument, stirs her to further action: he takes Claudio at his word that Isabella can be more persuasive than this. Her plea is on behalf of Mercy, often considered the partner of Justice (as, for example, in the Sixth Book of *The Faerie Queene**). She says Mercy is more becoming to rulers than cere-

*The relations between justice and mercy, justice and equity, are an important part of Spenser's subject, and the idea that justice itself must be controlled by equity was a principle of Roman law. Spenser's Mercilla has two swords, a rusty sword of justice and a sceptre of clemency. See my *Shakespeare, Spenser, Donne: Renaissance Essays* (1970), p. 56.

mony. There is a certain conventionality in these early exchanges. When Angelo replies that she is wasting her time she makes a far more cogent plea for Mercy:

> Why, all the souls that were were forfeit once,
> And He that might the vantage best have took
> Found out the remedy. How would you be
> If He, which is the top of judgment, should
> But judge you as you are?
>
> (73–77)

But Angelo, though authorised by the Duke to be merciful as well as just, declares himself a mere agent of Law: "It is the law, not I, condemn your brother" (80). She pleads for time; he replies that the law, having slept, is now awake; had it always been so, it would have served as a deterrent. The speech in which he makes this point is very powerful, its imagery familiar to us from the soliloquy of Brutus in *Julius Caesar* (II.i).* Its looking-glass shows the future rather in the manner of the one held by the last of the kings in *Macbeth* (IV.i). But the language has its own peculiar urgency:

> The law hath not been dead, though it hath slept.
> Those many had not dar'd to do that evil
> If the first that did th' edict infringe
> Had answer'd for his deed. Now 'tis awake,
> Takes note of what is done, and like a prophet
> Looks in a glass that shows what future evils,
> Either now, or by remissness new conceiv'd,
> And so in progress to be hatch'd and born,
> Are now to have no successive degrees,
> But here they live, to end.
>
> (II.ii.90–99)

Here the function of judicial punishment is not so much to deter as to abort future crime. The tone is steady and assured. It seems that if Isabella

*"hatching." Compare also the metaphor used by Claudius in *Hamlet* (III.i.165–67):

> There's something in his soul
> O'er which his melancholy sits on brood,
> And I do doubt the hatch and the disclose
> Will be some danger.

can win this argument it will be less by her persuasiveness than by her prone and speechless dialect. She attacks the abuse of authority without denying its rights: "O, it is excellent / to have a giant's strength; but it is tyrannous / To use it like a giant" (107–9). Sounding less and less prone and speechless, she continues her eloquent attack on the abuse of authority, a theme soon to be given new poignancy in *King Lear.* She uses the idea of man's assumption of authority as an abuse of his soul: "Dress'd in a little brief authority, / Most ignorant of what he's most assur'd— / (His glassy essence) . . ." (118–20). Ignoring, despite all assurances, the source of his authority (which should also be a source of mercy), Angelo's edicts resemble the posturings of an ape more than the judgements of God. (This is a difficult passage but a famous one, and in itself evidence of power without instant intelligibility.) And she tells Angelo to examine his conscience for a "natural guiltiness" like her brother's (139).

The judge is moved for the first time: "She speaks, and 'tis / Such sense that my sense breeds with it" (141–42). (The ambiguities of the word "sense" here have been explored by Empson in *The Structure of Complex Words.*) Her sense is "common sense" (Isabella is rational and persuasive), but the judge's "sense" is the sensuality stimulated by her speechless dialect. She makes a mistake when offering, in a metaphor, to bribe him, but she recovers. Angelo is left to consider his position: "I am going that way to temptation / Where prayers cross" (158–59). (This is another obscure phrase, which the Arden editor amends to "where prayer's cross'd," though once again the obscurity makes for greater strength.) He soliloquises; her purity has corrupted him:

> Can it be
> That modesty may more betray our sense
> Than woman's lightness? Having waste ground enough,
> Shall we desire to raze the sanctuary
> And pitch our evils there?
>
> (167–71)

This is a vivid way of saying there is no shortage of whores, so that to lust after a virtuous woman is like tearing down a church to build privies on the site (with a glance at the existence of the mass public privies that added to the stench of late medieval cities). He is disgusted at his own desire, thinking it foul, though brought on by her virtue.

Only a brief scene between the disguised Duke and Julietta, where the mutuality of her relations with Claudio is again stressed, intervenes before Isabella's second interview with Angelo. It begins with another soliloquy:

When I would pray and think, I think and pray
To several subjects. Heaven hath my empty words,
Whilst my invention, hearing not my tongue,
Anchors on Isabel; heaven in my mouth,
As if I did but only chew his name,
And in my heart the strong and swelling evil
Of my conception.

(II.iv.1–6)

Like Claudius in *Hamlet,* Angelo is commenting on the contrast between heart and word, on the emptiness of prayer that does not reflect what is really going on in the mind. It is generally agreed that "heaven" in line 4 is a substitution for "God," and that it was made after the passage in 1606 of the Act to Restrain Abuses of the Players. Chewing God sounds more shocking than chewing heaven and, as the Arden editor remarks, suggests "a sacrilegious communion."

The tone of this second debate is quite different from that of the first, in which for a long stretch Angelo did not need to listen seriously to Isabella's plea, though presumably he was moved (more, probably, by the speechless dialect than the Christian argument). She again professes herself ready to accept Angelo's immediate reaffirmation of his verdict and begins to withdraw. He detains her, and repeats, in new language, a point he made earlier:

. . . fie, these filthy vices! It were as good
To pardon him that hath from nature stol'n
A man already made, as to remit
Their saucy sweetness that do coin heaven's image
In stamps that are forbid. 'Tis all as easy
Falsely to take away a life true made
As to put metal in restrained means
To make a false one.

(II.iv.42–49)

Here, in crowded language, we have the idea of fornication as murder and a telling return of the imagery of coining, using metals in forbidden ways. It is the image of God in man that is falsely stamped on a bastard. "Saucy sweetness" is a paradox; the first word, in Elizabethan usage, seems to mean primarily "presumptuous" or "insolent," but the *O.E.D.* adds that in this passage and in others (such as *Cymbeline* I.vi.51), it includes the notion of "wanton" or "lascivious." Illicit sex is wanton, presumptuous, but also "sweet"—an admission Angelo would earlier have avoided.

Isabella's protest, that on earth rules can be less strict than in heaven, is met with the question whether she, having argued for that concession, would herself yield to "such sweet uncleanness" (54). After more preliminaries he accuses her of trifling: "Your sense pursues not mine. Either you are ignorant, / Or seem so craftily" (74–75); "sense" again has a double sense, suggesting both "meaning" and "sensuality." Hereafter he is blunt: to save her brother she must "lay down the treasures of [her] body" (96). Isabella actually apologises for pleading on behalf of a vice she abhors; women, she says, are frail, and she remembers the image of coining: they are "credulous to false prints," meaning that they easily accept false impressions or stamps. When she finally understands his proposal she threatens to expose him. His reply has all the assurance of unquestionable authority: "Who will believe thee, Isabel?" (154). And now, having no further use for argument, he says he will "give [his] sensual race the rein." He issues an order: "Fit thy consent to my sharp appetite" (161), and threatens to torture Claudio if she refuses. Isabella then makes her notorious announcement: "More than our brother is our chastity" (185), a sentiment for which she has more often than not been reproved. In her support it might be said that she believed the choice was between the death of a man and the eternal damnation of a woman: "Better it were a brother died at once, / Than that a sister, by redeeming him, / Should die for ever" (106–8). One needs to feel the force of "redeeming," with the full implication that the archetypal redemption was made to ensure that sinners should live for ever, though this redemption would be nothing but a demonic inversion of the original.

This wonderfully contrived scene is quite short, the interaction between the two characters dramatically productive in the highest degree (we come a long way in ten minutes or so) and the language packed with senses. When Act III begins, Isabella has made her choice, and expects her brother to accept it. The act opens with the famous stoic consolation addressed by the Duke to Claudio. It is bleak, beautiful, assured, and counter to every feeling that the young should have life:

> Reason thus with life:
> If I do lose thee, I do lose a thing

That none but fools would keep . . .
. . . Merely, thou art death's fool,
For him thou labor'st by thy flight to shun,
And yet run'st toward him still. Thou art not noble,
For all th' accommodations that thou bear'st
Are nurs'd by baseness. Thou'rt by no means valiant,
For thou dost fear the soft and tender fork
Of a poor worm. Thy best of rest is sleep,
And that thou oft provok'st, yet grossly fear'st
Thy death, which is no more . . .
. . . Thou hast nor youth nor age,
But as it were an after-dinner's sleep,
Dreaming on both, for all thy blessed youth
Becomes as aged, and doth beg the alms
Of palsied eld; and when thou art old and rich,
Thou has neither heat, affection, limb, nor beauty,
To make thy riches pleasant . . .

(6–38)

The young man seems content with this formally constructed, if pagan oration. But Isabella's news changes that, and he makes his equally celebrated speech about the fear of death:*

Ay, but to die, and go we know not where;
To lie in cold obstruction, and to rot;
This sensible warm motion to become
A kneaded clod; and the delighted spirit
To bathe in fiery floods, or to reside
In thrilling region of thick-ribbed ice;
To be imprison'd in the viewless winds
And blown with restless violence round about
The pendant world; or to be worse than worst

*See the excellent discussion of both by Lever (Arden edition, 1965), pp. lxxxvii and 66. Lever suggests that the speeches of the Duke and Claudio make a formal pair, the first an exercise, somewhat skewed, in the traditional *ars moriendi* (art of dying) and the second a *contemplatio mortis,* a contemplation of death, equally traditional but equally skewed by its adaptation of pagan materials ultimately taken from Lucretius.

Of those that lawless and incertain thought
Imagine howling—'tis too horrible!
The weariest and most loathed worldly life
That age, ache, penury, and imprisonment
Can lay on nature is a paradise
To what we fear of death.

(III.i.117–31)

Few readers or auditors will fail to respond to the power of this passage, and it is typical of Shakespeare that there should occur, in the midst of his treatment of a topic so universal that he might have used the plainest language, words to make one stop and ask what they are doing there: "sensible," "motion," "delighted," "viewless." Sometimes this slightly estranging effect arises from differences between the sense of the words in Shakespeare's time and ours: "sensible" here is related to one meaning of "sense" in the play at large, the sensory (and sensual) equipment of the living body. One sense of "motion" is a puppet, so that there is a concealed paradox, a puppet with sense organs; another is a usage complimentary to works of art (comeliness, grace, spirit, etc.) and here applicable to life; another is animation, reflecting the joy of having a body that can be moved and controlled; yet another is, simply, emotion, another property of living beings. "Motion" is a rich way of talking about the living human body. The strangeness of the word is what makes one think around it in this way. "Delighted" strikes one as the oddest of these words, since the context makes it plain that the spirit is not, in any modern sense of the word, delighted. Can it be a nonce word, de-lighted, deprived of light? Hanmer emended it to "dilated"; Johnson, rather weakly if one may say so, to "delinquent." Finally, "viewless" is "invisible"; its force comes partly from the chime with "restless" in the next line. Editors add that to be blown around the earth in this way was considered the punishment of people who were too fond of the pleasures of the body, so the guilty Claudio might think himself qualified for that fate, like Paolo and Francesca in Dante. "Pendant" adds to the horror of the idea, the earth suspended in space as the sinners whirl around it. What is meant by "lawless and incertain thought"? One editor says the passage "is not susceptible of satisfactory explanation,"* and this may be true; thoughts of hell were "incertain" perhaps,

**Measure for Measure*, ed. J. M. Nosworthy (New Penguin edition, 1969), p. 167.

but not "lawless." The effect is still to make the familiar general sentiment a little strange, to stop the reader a moment.

It is at this point that the Duke, who has eavesdropped on the bitter conversation between brother and sister, intervenes with the lie that Angelo was only testing Isabella's virtue and was glad she turned him down. "I am confessor to Angelo, and I know this to be true" (166–67). This is the first and probably the worst of a series of lies. And he tells Claudio once more to ready himself for death, but Isabella is given the truth. All this is preparation for the great turn from tragedy to comedy, which necessitates the substitution of Mariana for Isabella in Angelo's bed, where, it is explained, she has a right to be.

Much has been written in defence of the second half of *Measure for Measure,* but it is surely a muddle. There are fine things in it, of course—more good scenes in the stews—but it tends to be prosy and incredible. In response to Escalus's rather disapproving characterisation of Angelo as "Justice" (III.ii.254), the Duke has a moral speech about the shame that should befall unjust judges. And thereafter interest, as I see it, is sacrificed to expediency: the Duke gets into one scrape after another and is slandered by Lucio, from whom, as absolute ruler, he exacts a stiff penalty; while Angelo, who proves to be a liar as well as an unworthy justice, is let off on condition he marries Mariana. Without prior consultation, Isabella, having reluctantly forgiven Angelo, is more or less told to forget her vocation and marry the Duke. (Her silence is often remarked, but there is little agreement about its significance.) The true theme of the play is tragic; as a tragicomedy it fails because the contrivances of the poet too much resemble those of the Duke. The poetry, often as fine as any in the canon, is all in the tragedy.

OTHELLO

If we are to believe the latest Arden editor, *Othello* is closer in date to *Hamlet* than we used to think, for he says it was composed in "late 1601." At any rate, there is a cluster of plays near this date, a year or two after *Hamlet* and probably close to *Twelfth Night* and *Troilus and Cressida.** Others prefer a date nearer 1604; that would twin the play with *Measure for Measure,* the plot for which derives from the collection of stories by Giraldo Cinthio. The issues are very complicated, and there is little certainty in any of the results.

The existence of two texts (the Quarto of 1622 and the Folio of 1623) creates problems different from those encountered in *Hamlet* or *King Lear* but no less difficult. They remain unlikely to be solved in such a way as to command anything approaching editorial consensus, and I do not in any case aspire to assist the editors in their enquiries, but with *Othello* as with *Hamlet* it is necessary on occasion to say where a particular reading originates and why one has chosen it. Textual scholars, loving their trade, will not agree, but critics hoping to comment on the language of the plays must think it unfortunate that the texts of three of the greatest of them should present these virtually intractable textual

**Othello,* ed. E.A.J. Honigmann (Arden edition, 1997). The date is discussed in Appendix 1, pp. 344–50, the text in Appendix 2, pp. 351–67, which summarises the arguments in Honigmann's book on the subject, *The Texts of "Othello"* (1996).

problems. Fortunately the plays remain for the most part intelligible, and susceptible to comment on their greatly varying styles.

What is extraordinary is the extent of the differences between plays written, one after another, in the first years of the new century. The style of *Othello* we may think of as having been formed while Shakespeare was reading for the task—mostly of Cinthio's novella, which he handles with notable skill and freedom, but also current books about the Mediterranean world.

Since the principal characters of the story were soldiers, the setting couldn't be other than military in character. Shakespeare had plenty of experience doing the military—the life of various kinds of soldier is amply recorded in the History plays and *All's Well,* and is not absent from *Hamlet*—but he had not hitherto attempted that almost invariant type, the foul-mouthed N.C.O. I myself have memories, happily remote, of Iago-like warrant officers, sycophantic self-seekers, the main difference being that Iago has a surprisingly educated vocabulary. At its core, however, is filth.

The first word of the play is Roderigo's "Tush," and Iago's reply begins with an oath: "'Sblood." His first word to Brabantio is "'Zounds" (85), repeated at line 107. None of these expletives is to be found in the Folio text. Honigmann counts fifty cases where the profanities of Q are deleted or modified in F, probably because the latter, dependent on a manuscript written by the scribe Ralph Crane, was produced after 1606, when the Act to Restrain the Abuses of the Players forbade the use of oaths or the name of God.* "Tush" and "pish" may sound like Rosalind's "pretty oaths that are not dangerous" (*As You Like It,* IV.i.189), but their elimination along with others more shocking makes a considerable difference to the tone of the play, and especially to the characterisation of Iago. The profanities occur not only in soldierly contexts, where they could be taken simply as appropriate to the language of the camp, but more significantly in the context of sexual disgust to which Iago's thoughts repeatedly refer themselves.

The opening scene, as always with Shakespeare carefully excogitated, never simple narrative exposition, is here worth particularly close attention. It does provide some necessary exposition but also describes an evil soldierly prank: you may think Roderigo must be half drunk to be seduced into the noisy demonstration outside Brabantio's house—as dangerous to him as it is useful to Iago. There have been critics, led by Dr. Johnson, who have wished

*On the cleaning up of F, see Honigmann, p. 352.

away the first act of the play, and indeed Boito eliminated it when writing the *Otello* libretto for Verdi. But this move, however correct Johnson might think it and however economical in terms of lyric theatre, would not be sufficient compensation for its cost.

This opening scene outside Brabantio's house, with the subsequent interruption of the wedding night of Othello and Desdemona, seems to me a version of charivari. Charivari was an old custom: if you disapproved of a match as being incongruous in some way, for instance if you deplored a disparity in age (or in colour) between bride and bridegroom, you could call your neighbours and make a disturbance outside their dwelling. The practice was at one time reflected in the clamorous reaction to eclipses, also instances of order disrupted, as Othello remembers in V.ii.99–101, "Methinks it should be now a huge eclipse / Of sun and moon, and that th' affrighted globe / Did yawn at alteration."

Iago will use the noise of the charivari, this "rough music," to his own ends. In the passage before they start making a row, while he and Roderigo are still whispering in the street, we judge the violence of his emotion by his vocabulary: if I don't hate Othello "Abhor me . . . Despise me" (I.i.6, 8), with a hint that, since he knows his own foulness, these are indeed the proper responses to him. Unlike Roderigo, he need not make himself known to Brabantio, and can use what sexual insults he pleases: "Even now, now, very now, an old black ram / Is tupping your white ewe" (88–89) is Iago's way of informing the senator that his daughter has eloped, and this voyeuristic and disgusted attitude to sex is constant in him. They are at it at this very moment! Imagine it! And the man is black, a devil: the senator's daughter is being "cover'd with a Barbary horse" (111), is "making the beast with two backs" (116). Brabantio recognises the speaker as a "profane wretch" (114), "a villain" (117), but Iago has disappeared before the senator has made ready to hurry with Roderigo to the Sagittary, there to continue the process of charivari and disturb the wedding night of Othello and Desdemona.

Iago's onslaught on Brabantio's susceptibilities is kept up by his pupil Roderigo ("the gross clasps of a lascivious Moor" [126]); but he is required to be somewhat civil, as Iago is not. One striking aspect of the scene is that there are echoes of *Hamlet*'s habitual hendiadys. As George T. Wright demonstrated, *Othello* comes second only to *Hamlet* in the frequency of its use of hendiadys, though it offers less than half as many instances;* Shakespeare's

*"Hendiadys and *Hamlet*," *P.M.L.A.* 96, pp. 168ff.

enthusiasm for the device was waning, as one can see as *Othello* proceeds. But the habit of expansive doubling continues at the outset of this new one: "as loving his own pride and purposes," "trimm'd in forms and visages of duty," "The native act and figure of my heart," "by night and negligence," "your pleasure and most wise consent," "play and trifle with your reverence," "an extravagant and wheeling stranger / Of here and every where," "flag and sign of love," "the property of youth and maidhood"—all these occur in the first 170 lines. Othello's opening speech in the next scene carries it on: "my life and being," "my unhoused free condition / Put into circumscription and confine" (I.ii.21, 26–27). Brabantio continues the habit in his protest to the Duke:

> my particular grief
> Is of so flood-gate and o'erbearing nature
> That it engluts and swallows other sorrows . . .
>
> (I.iii.55–57)

And:

> I therefore apprehend and do attach thee
> For an abuser of the world, a practicer
> Of arts inhibited and out of warrant.
>
> (I.ii.77–79)

There is another trace of the device in the senators' war council ("Neglecting an attempt of ease and gain / To wake and wage a danger profitless" [I.iii.29–30]). Later instances are Brabantio's "a judgment main'd and most imperfect" (99), "thin habits and poor likelihoods" (108), "indirect and forced courses" (111). The Duke calls the proposed expedition "stubborn and boist'rous" (228) and Othello refers, in Hamletian vein, to "the flinty and steel couch of war" (230), asking for Desdemona "such accommodation and besort / As levels with her breeding" (238–39); and, in a very strained expression, referring to his sight as "My speculative and offic'd instruments" (270). Desdemona, addressing the Senate, catches the habit in her speech proclaiming her part in the wooing: "That I did love the Moor to live with him, / My downright violence, and storm of fortunes, / May trumpet to the world" (I.iii.248–50). Here her own sense that the unconventionality of her choice amounts to a kind of social violence is emphasised by hendiadys ("My downright violence, and storm"). Later we have "quality and respect," "honesty and trust" (I.iii.282, 284), "worldy matter and direction" (299), and so on. The habit has spread to almost every character, but examples become harder to find as the play discovers and develops its own dialect, becomes less fond of semantic collision and contraction.

Hamlet can be coarsely bawdy, and seems to mean to offend Ophelia by being so, but although in future plays Shakespeare was to be capable of rendering deep sexual disgust (for example in *Troilus and Cressida, Timon of Athens,* and *The Winter's Tale,* and in one or two sonnets) Iago is probably his most disgusted and disgusting character, claiming precedence over Thersites and Apemantus by virtue of his centrality to an action of which he is indeed the sole agent. Mention of Desdemona having sex is all that is needed to make him talk dirty: Othello "hath boarded a land carract" (I.ii.50) means that he has gone aboard her, almost as an act of piracy or rape, as if any other explanation of the relationship were out of the question. The scene ends with a prose discussion between Iago and Roderigo, and here Iago offers the young man he means to push deeper into corruption an account of his beliefs and habits. Although it may suggest a similar self-hatred, this confession in no way resembles the Credo written by Boito for Verdi, which makes of Iago a gloomy nineteenth-century atheist. Yet it does offer a kind of philosophy.

Roderigo is in love with Desdemona, and Iago cannot think of love as anything but lust: the beloved object is a guinea hen, a loose or worthless woman; the lover is behaving like a baboon. Roderigo claims that it is not in his "virtue" or nature to stop being "fond," whereupon Iago delivers an extraordinary speech comparing the body to a garden, considered as a piece of coarse nature that the gardener, or human will, can amend. The fluency and power of this speech are remarkable—the persuasiveness of the analogy and the conceptual clarity of the conclusion drawn:

> If the beam of our lives had not one scale of reason to poise another of sensuality, the blood and baseness of our natures would conduct us to most prepost'rous conclusions. But we have reason to cool our raging motions, our carnal stings, our unbitted lusts . . .
>
> (I.iii.326ff.)

Iago's opening exclamation ("Virtue? a fig! 'tis in ourselves that we are thus or thus" [319]) ensures that the speech begins with the equivalent of an obscene gesture, but the argument that the will should have "power and corrigible authority" is perfectly conventional. This is good doctrine, the reason controlling the senses, the lower powers of the soul. Roderigo's admission that he cannot wield such control, his will being presumably unequal to the task, is met with another piece of advice: love "is merely a lust of the blood and a permission of the will" (334–35), which means that love is possible only because the will has abdicated its power over the senses. Iago's deception of Roderigo depends on the young man's willingness to believe that Desdemona is sexually corruptible, that he can buy her with presents, taking comfort meanwhile from the thought that the violent beginning of Desdemona's love for Othello will surely be followed by a movement of revulsion, as Iago's philosophy of lust would lead him to expect. And for good measure Othello will surely, in his turn, grow sick of Desdemona. "The food that to him now is as luscious as locusts, shall be to him shortly as acerb as the coloquintida" (347–49). The locust was a very sweet fruit, the food of John the Baptist in the wilderness; coloquintida was bitter and used as a purge. Iago can look about quite widely for his similes. The union of the lovers is a match between "an erring barbarian and a super-subtle Venetian" (355–56), a black man and a well-born Venetian lady; they had, at least among the vulgar, reputations, the black man for superior sexual powers, the Venetian lady for love affairs.

The aptness of this talk, and its lexical resourcefulness, display a mind, almost the mind of a poet, made formidable and alien by the context of corruption, a mind capable of seeming honest when honesty is called for but soured with its own baseness. Iago's baseness is more fundamental than a mere desire for revenge against Cassio and Othello; it is darker than Edmund's in *King Lear.* The whole point of the dialogue between Desdemona and Iago on the wharf at Cyprus (II.i) is to demonstrate that Iago, though apparently willing to pass the time of day with women, cannot quite manage to keep suppressed his loathing of them; he hates them for being sexed. That Cassio delights in touching them, smiling, taking their hands, and so forth makes him a man whom Iago hates less for his lieutenancy than for his sexual freedom, his ease with women:* "a most profane and liberal counsellor," he calls him (163–64); and although there is here a tinge of puritanical contempt for the libertine, Iago's next exchange with Roderigo, which

*W. H. Auden thought otherwise, arguing that Cassio is easy only with "women of his own class." "The Joker in the Pack," in *The Dyer's Hand* (1963), p. 262.

follows hard upon the rapture greeting Othello's safe arrival, again dwells on the image of Desdemona engaged in "the act of sport" (227). He knows that she is to be credited with a "delicate tenderness" (232), but he uses that knowledge only to persuade Roderigo that she will come to "disrelish and abhor" the Moor—"very nature will instruct her" to do so (233–34). Her flirting with Cassio is lechery, and after it copulation must inevitably follow: "hard at hand comes the master and main exercise, th' incorporate conclusion. Pish!" (261–63 [F]). (Othello, infected by Iago's corruption, echoes this "Pish!" in IV.i.42.)

In the course of the play this kind of talk is contrasted with the innocently excessive courtesies of Cassio, the secret rebelliousness of Emilia, and of course the honesty of Othello himself, before his fall. Cassio's language is so near the extreme of doting admiration that Iago can profess to believe that his "civil and humane seeming" is only a cover for his "salt and most hidden loose affection" (II.i.239–41). Of course his immediate intention is to gull Roderigo; the art of the play is to make his claim seem not quite implausible. Cassio's extravagances, however disinterested, may sometimes go over the top, as when he expresses his hopes that Othello will arrive safely in Cyprus, and "Make love's quick pants in Desdemona's arms" (II.i.80); here he uses a trope from erotic poetry, to be found also in Thomas Carew's poem "A Rapture": "Yet my tall pine shall in the Cyprian strait / Ride safe at anchor, and unlade her freight." Cassio has a touch of the libertine, and his relationship with Bianca is important to the plot, but he is incapable of the language of Iago; he combines a politely seductive way of talking* with a matter-of-fact attitude to sexual satisfaction, a not unusual combination.

A dialogue in Act II is carefully inserted to make plain this capital difference between Iago and Cassio. Iago says Othello has left early to be with Desdemona: "He hath not yet made wanton the night with her; and she is sport for Jove."

> CAS. She's a most exquisite lady.
> IAGO. And I'll warrant her, full of game.
> CAS. Indeed she's a most fresh and delicate creature.
> IAGO. What an eye she has! Methinks it sounds a parley to provocation.
> CAS. An inviting eye; and yet methinks right modest.

*Auden speaks of Cassio's "socialized eroticism," p. 262.

IAGO. And when she speaks, is it not an alarum to love?
CAS. She is indeed perfection.
IAGO. Well—happiness to their sheets!

(iii.18ff.)

This keenly written passage (some of which F tries to render as verse) contrives a social encounter that can only make Cassio uneasy; his position is such that despite his being the superior officer he cannot reprove Iago, only withhold assent to his slyly voyeuristic propositions and provide more courtly alternatives. When Iago invites him to drink to the health of "black Othello" (32), he tries to decline the invitation, such toasts being a courtesy he disapproves of because, as he explains, he has a weak head for drink. This is candid, but Iago seems to have known about this weakness already. Cassio makes a mistake when, having himself been addressed as "lieutenant" (13), he replies with "good Iago" (33), a patronising form of address like "honest," a word which from now on becomes central to the play. Iago resents it, for it is a word normally used of inferiors, but he makes use of it, since a reputation for good-humoured servile reliability suits his ends.* Cassio indeed loses this match, since it is as if he were explaining or defending his more delicate sexual attitudes by deriving them from his higher rank and class, a certain coarseness in these matters being exactly what one would expect of a social inferior.

Iago naturally has no use for the language of courtship; all love-making for him is merely the submission of the will to the base passions of the body. He assumes that Othello is a "lusty Moor" (II.i.295), perhaps because he is black, and the ideas of blackness and sexual potency were already twinned, or perhaps because he just assumes that all men are lusty. Othello himself has explained to the Duke that he wants Desdemona to come to Cyprus with him, "Nor to comply with heat (the young affects / In me defunct) and proper satisfaction; / But to be free and bounteous to her mind" (I.iii.264–66). (Here "affects" means "passions," "defunct" means not "dead" but "spent, a matter of the past," and "proper" means "personal" or even, in this context, "selfish."†) Othello is to him a gross and grossly privileged body, so deficient in

*See Empson's essay "Honest in *Othello*," in *The Structure of Complex Words*, pp. 218–49. The preceding chapters, "Honest Man" and "Honest Numbers" (pp. 185–217), are also relevant.

†See the discussion of "defunct" in Hulme, *Explorations in Shakespeare's Language*, pp. 153–54. I think the best of her suggestions is that it means "past danger." The sense of "proper" seems to be misunderstood by Honigmann ("in conformity with rule").

the cunning of intellect that he is easily duped. Iago doesn't seem to be particularly lustful himself; he may take that to be a source of strength, while still envying others who are.

All this we infer only from the language of the individual characters. As it happens, Iago's is least interesting when he is thinking in verse; his soliloquy at the end of II.i is unconvincing, almost an admission of confusion in the author as well as the character, a muddle of implausible motives where none was needed other than the established foulness of the man's imagination.* Even when Othello asks him to explain the reason for the brawl (II.iii.176ff.) he speaks of the peaceful merriment that preceded it as being "in terms like bride and groom / Devesting them for bed." His obsession gets uninhibited play when he later tells Othello what he experienced when sharing a bed with Cassio (III.iii.413–26)† and again expresses his obsessive interest in what people do in bed ("kiss me hard . . . laid his leg / Over my thigh"). When Boito rewrote this for Verdi (*"Era la notte, Cassio dormia"*), he had to leave this kind of thing out, as too strong for a polite late-nineteenth-century audience; Verdi supplied the feeling with eery music, giving the speech the air of an erotic dream.‡

The pivotal scene of the play is III.iii, which from the outset, with Iago's "I like not that" as Cassio withdraws, to the end, when Othello has accepted the charge against Desdémona and planned her death and Cassio's, is fewer than five hundred lines long, probably less than half an hour of stage time. It is extraordinarily bold. Desdemona aids the process, twice commending Iago's honesty, a conviction of which in the other characters is now essential to his design; at her exit Othello speaks of his love for her and the chaos that will follow if his love should ever cease. It is at exactly this point (93) that Iago goes to work, sowing doubts about Cassio. The dialogue is spare, at first

*Auden, who describes Iago as a practical joker, goes so far as to say that he ought to act brilliantly when being all the varieties of himself as presented to Othello, Cassio, Desdemona, etc., but badly in the soliloquies: "He must deliver the lines of his soliloquies in such a way that he makes nonsense of them" ("The Joker in the Pack," p. 258).

†On the importance in the play of the word "bed," which occurs more than twenty times, see R. B. Heilman, *Magic in the Web* (1956).

‡*Otello* is not only the finest of Shakespearian operas but in certain respects offers an intelligent commentary on its source. It has been remarked that Boito underlined certain passages in the play, for example Iago's description of love as "merely a lust of the blood and a permission of the will," but Verdi did not set them; I take these to indicate that Boito saw the importance of the lines but, feeling he could not use them, indicated that the music must somehow convey their sense. See James A. Hepokoski, *Otello* (1987), for a study of Boito's dealings with Shakespeare.

sounding almost like casual chat between a superior, who calls his interlocutor "thou," and a subordinate, who must use "you" but who, without ceasing to be deferential, can count on his boss's trust and on a long acquaintance:

> IAGO. My noble lord—
> OTH. What dost thou say, Iago?
> IAGO. Did Michael Cassio, when you woo'd my lady,
> Know of your love?
> OTH. He did, from first to last. Why dost thou ask?
> IAGO. But for a satisfaction of my thought,
> No further harm.
> OTH. Why of thy thought, Iago?
> IAGO. I did not think he had been acquainted with her.
> OTH. O yes, and went between us very oft.
> IAGO. Indeed!
> OTH. Indeed? ay, indeed. Discern'st thou aught in that?
> Is he not honest?
> IAGO. Honest, my lord?
> OTH. Honest? ay, honest.
> IAGO. My lord, for aught I know.
> OTH. What dost thou think?
> IAGO. Think, my lord?
> OTH. Think, my lord? By heaven, thou echo'st me,
> As if there were some monster in thy thought
> Too hideous to be shown . . .
> . . .
> If thou dost love me,
> Show me thy thought.
>
> (93–116)

In the first exchange the pentameters are broken up, giving the passage a peculiar uneasiness, which is reinforced by the triple "honest" and the triple "think," especially where two usages collide. "What didst not like?" asks Othello, seventy-five lines after Iago planted the expression. The question whether Cassio is or merely "seems" honest (unlike Iago, whom Othello accepts as honest all through) is now adroitly raised. "I dare be sworn I *think* that he is *honest.*" "I *think* so too . . . Why then I *think* Cassio's an honest man":

Nay, yet there's more in this.
I prithee speak to me as to thy thinkings,
As thou dost ruminate, and give thy worst of thoughts
The worst of words.

(130–33)

At which point Iago expresses moral indignation, again with sound doctrine, explaining that even a slave can keep his thoughts to himself, and that one may have "uncleanly apprehensions" (139) without revealing them. But Othello insists that if Iago *thinks* him wronged he should make known his "thoughts" (143–44); "By heaven, I'll know thy thoughts" (162).

Here we are only at the beginning of a storm; no high colours, no blasts of rhetoric; the words "honest" and "think," "thinking," "thoughts" have to do all the work. After a while Iago, who has spoken of his own "jealousy" (147), meaning something like "envy" or "undue curiosity," but without sexual implication, uses the word again, now with full sexual reference and direct application to Othello's case: "O, beware, my lord, of jealousy! / It is the green-ey'd monster which doth mock / The meat it feeds on" (165–67). The seventy or so lines of verse that have elapsed before there is any direct accusation of Cassio and Desdemona have brought Othello to "misery" (171). He soon asserts that he could never suffer cuckoldry, adding that Desdemona's infidelity, if it existed, could not be attributed to any weakness in himself: "For she had *eyes,* and chose me" (189). And now the insistence is on eyes: "I'll *see* before I doubt" (190) . . . "*Look* to your wife, *observe* her well with Cassio, / Wear your *eyes* thus, not jealious nor secure" (197–98) (not suspicious but not overconfident); "In Venice they do let God *see* the pranks / They dare not show their husbands" (202–3) . . . "She that so young could give out such a seeming / To seel her father's *eyes* up" (209–10) . . . "If more thou dost *perceive,* let me know more; / Set on thy wife to *observe*" (239–40). This string of words will culminate in Othello's demand for "the ocular proof . . . Make me to *see* 't" (360–64). A passage of high tension, generated by all the words that have been in play: "honest," "think," "see":

OTH. I do not *think* but Desdemona's honest.
IAGO. Long live she so! and long live you to *think* so!

(225–26)

Iago then touches on the disparity or disproportion between Othello and his Venetian wife, already become, through his assiduity, a credible cause of concern:

> IAGO. To be direct and honest is not safe.
> OTH. Nay, stay. Thou shouldst be honest.
> IAGO. I should be wise—for honesty's a fool . . .
>
> (378–82)

> I *think* my wife be honest, and *think* she is not;
> I *think* that thou art just, and *think* thou art not.
> I'll have some proof.
>
> (384–86)

"I see, sir, you are eaten up with passion . . . You would be satisfied? . . . but how? How satisfied, my lord? / Would you, the supervisor, grossly gape on? / Behold her topp'd?" (391–96) (here he uses to Othello himself the word Roderigo had used to Brabantio in the opening scene: "the gross clasps of a lascivious Moor" [126] and "Your daughter . . . hath made a gross revolt" [133–34], as well as "top," a variant of the word "tupping" in line 89).

> It were a tedious difficulty, I *think*,
> To bring them to that *prospect;* damn them then,
> If ever mortal eyes do *see* them bolster
> More than their own. What then? How then?
> What shall I say? Where's satisfaction?
> It is impossible you should *see* this,
> Were they as prime as goats, as hot as monkeys . . .
>
> (397–403)

The only "satisfaction" available is Iago's account of his night with Cassio.

It becomes clear, in this masterly dialogue, that Iago's interest in sex is to watch others doing it, or at least to think about them doing it. It was important therefore to develop these ideas of seeing, these increasingly coarse descriptions and conjectures. The tone has grown calculatedly immodest—"damn them then"—and this is achieved before the story about Cassio in bed, and before the handkerchief provides what looks like satisfactory ocular evidence. For the tactician Iago has correctly guessed Othello's reaction even to the possibility of his wife's unfaithfulness, and at first with all the hesitations proper to an honest man (and an inferior) communicating such a suspicion, he infects Othello with his own disgust. Following the uses of "honest," "think," and "see," with their derivatives, one begins to understand how compact and fierce this writing is. Even after the account of Cassio's dream, when Othello is ready to tear his wife to pieces, the honest man can admit "yet we *see* nothing done; / She may be *honest* yet" (432–33)—which is the moment to introduce the handkerchief, something which can be seen, something with which Iago can claim to have seen Cassio wiping his beard. And the scene ends with the pair swearing a joint oath of loyalty and vengeance.

Considering the scantiness, or absence, of incriminating evidence, and the completeness of Othello's collapse, it would be easy to read this scene as an allegory of demonic possession, a reading Othello himself for a moment considers but dismisses in the last scene of the play: "I look down towards his feet; but that's a fable. / If that thou be'st a devil, I cannot kill thee" (V.ii.286–87). The success of Iago is "diabolic" only in the sense that his temptation has discovered in Othello a horror of his tempter's apparent knowingness about sex. Once more the effect is got by reiteration: "honest," "think," etc. The magical force of this rhetoric is what makes the scene possible.

Soon the handkerchief, the false substitute for "ocular proof," becomes itself the means of equally terrible reiteration. Othello credits it with an occult power that has now become appropriate to the occasion. The Egyptian or gipsy who gave it to his mother "could almost read / The thoughts of people" (III.iv.57–58). It had the power of controlling his father's love for his mother; if she lost it he would loathe her. He is talking about his own love for Desdemona: "there's magic in the web of it" (69).

The ensuing dialogue with Desdemona—she lying about the handkerchief and crazily resuming her plea for Cassio, while he says almost nothing but "handkerchief"—is as brilliantly conceived as the Othello–Iago dialogue, and it is hard to imagine a dramatic poetry more minimally perfect:

> OTH. Is't lost? Is't gone? Speak, is't out o' th' way?
> DES. Heaven bless us!
> OTH. Say you?
> DES. It is not lost; but what and if it were?
> OTH. How?
> DES. I say, it is not lost.
> OTH. Fetch't, let me see't.
> DES. Why, so I can, sir, but I will not now.
> This is a trick to put me from my suit.
> Pray you let Cassio be receiv'd again.

OTH. Fetch me the handkerchief, my mind misgives.
DES. Come, come;
You'll never meet a more sufficient man.
OTH. The handkerchief!
DES. I pray talk me of Cassio.
OTH. The handkerchief!
DES. A man that all his time
Has founded his good fortunes on your love,
Shar'd dangers with you—
OTH. The handkerchief!
DES. I' faith, you are to blame.
OTH. 'Zounds!*

(III.iv.79–98)

It has often been remarked, by G. B. Shaw with derogatory intent, that *Othello* is the most operatic of Shakespeare's tragedies; think, for example, of the duet at the end of III.iii (where Verdi has the advantage of Shakespeare that he can make Iago and Otello swear their oath together instead of having to do it one at a time). This intense Shakespearian scene, too, is in its way equally musical. This kind of writing, by quasi-musical, quasi-magical means, achieves a rawness of passion, a conflict between innocently suicidal enquiry and a rage almost beyond words. Rage beyond words was not something the early Shakespeare would have even thought of aiming at. Here, as in *Hamlet,* a long experience of theatre has taught him a new way of writing poetry.

The strangest line in Desdemona's part comes in IV.iii. Othello has just grossly insulted and struck her in the presence of Lodovico, the Venetian envoy. Now he orders her to bed. Talking with Emilia, she remembers the maid Barbary and her song, but before she sings it she says, with apparent inconsequence, "This Lodovico is a proper man" (35). None of this passage (30–52) is included in Q. There must have been some good reason to exclude the Willow Song (perhaps the temporary unavailability of a boy actor who could sing), and the line about Lodovico was lost along with the song. Some modern editors, including Honigmann, give the line to Emilia, but only because it seems "out of character" for Desdemona.† Despite his treatment of

*F weakens this exit by substituting "Away" for "'Zounds."

†This is the reason why some editors transfer Miranda's excoriation of Caliban (*The Tempest,* I.ii.351–62) to Prospero. But the motive is not a good one, for it assumes that editors already know all they need to about the limits of the character.

her, she has continued submissive and loving to Othello, even when he acted out his horrible pretence that she was a whore and Emilia her bawd. After Othello's aria "Had it pleas'd heaven / To try me with affliction..." (IV.ii.47ff.) she hardly complains: "I hope my noble lord esteems me honest," and "Alas, what ignorant sin have I committed?" (65, 70). Even at her boldest, as when she insists on going to Cyprus, she has deserved Lodovico's compliment, "Truly, an obedient lady" (IV.i.248). Yet now, at a moment of intense marital distress, her thoughts wander momentarily to another man. Very shortly she listens with amazement to Emilia's avowal that she would be unfaithful to her husband if the reward was great enough. Desdemona says she would not behave so "For the whole world" (IV.iii.79). The fine speech (not in Q) in which Emilia stands up for women's right to sensual life against the restrictions imposed by tyrannical men is not the sort of thing Desdemona would ever have spoken (IV.iii.84–103). Yet she is rather taken by Lodovico, and at a very odd moment.

It is true that she can say unexpected things; she is represented as suffering a kind of loss of attention: after the horrible brothel scene when cast as "that cunning whore of Venice / That married with Othello" (IV.ii.89–90), she declares herself "half asleep" (97) and hardly understands what Emilia says next. These moments may contribute to any secret disposition in an audience to agree that it was less than seemly of this young woman, ignoring the "curled darlings of her nation," to marry a man so alien and so much older, an "extravagant and wheeling stranger" (I.i.136), a general whose social standing, though high, depends entirely upon his military rank in an embattled state. (As Auden remarks, Brabantio was happy enough to have Othello to supper and hear his tales, but that was another matter from having him as a son-in-law.*) And she is made to lie†—about the handkerchief, and about the identity of her murderer. Many of these traits may be attributed to a strain of feminism in the play, a hint of the ways in which women might

*"The Joker in the Pack," p. 263. Auden remarks that in a mercantile and warlike society like Venice there was need of foreign soldiers and also of usurers, the latter being Jews and socially unacceptable despite their utility. "No Venetian would dream of spitting on Othello as on Shylock, but a line was drawn nevertheless, and it excluded marriage to a high-born Venetian woman."

†"Lie" is another reiterated word; "lie/lies" occurs twenty-five times in the play. It provides the theme of Desdemona's talk with the Clown (III.iv), a scene which prepares us for Iago's casual and obscene punning in the horrible IV.i: "Lie— With her? / With her? On her; what you will . . . /Lie with her? lie on her? We say lie on her, when they belie her" (34–37)—at which point Othello has his fit. This device of hammering away at certain words is, as we have seen, a habit of the mature Shakespeare.

sometimes escape the regime imposed by their husbands—a little quiet talk with another woman, a venial fib or two. Yet the fact remains that there is a faint ambiguity in her character as we try to see it as a whole, and this is notoriously true also of Othello's.

There have been some celebrated criticisms of Othello's generally orotund way of speaking, which may be regarded as a sort of innocent pompousness or, if you dislike it, a self-regard that is not so innocent. It is easy enough to explain the choice for Othello of this particular mode of speech. He is meant to be a man whose sole reason for existence is command—after all, he is responsible for the security of an empire, Cyprus being a province that must be defended. The self-esteem of such a man can be rendered in the naturally hyperbolical terms of military glory. It has been observed that Londoners of the time were familiar with the idea of magnificent North African potentates. "The black, or tawny, soldier-hero was a figure in festivals long before he reached the Elizabethan stage . . . These Moorish shows were resplendent, soldierly and sensual . . . the role of the Moor in public spectacle was to enrich the public conception of power and sexual potency in the early stages of Tudor empire."*

The example of Marlowe's Tamburlaine was fairly recent, but Othello does not have his out-and-out bombast, and there is a touch of modesty and courtesy in his speech. His first line, "'Tis better as it is" (I.ii.6), is intended to promote calm in the face of Iago's pretended anger on his behalf; he has nothing to fear from Brabantio, he says, because of his services to the state. Here he claims royal birth, like a sultan in a Lord Mayor's Show; he will not boast of it except by mentioning it, but the final effect is not quite modest. When he speaks of his "demerits," the word (as in *Coriolanus,* I.i.275) means "merits." It is an odd word since it can also mean its opposite; but I think the point of it is to have Othello use a strange word rather than a familiar one—something he does on a good many other occasions. Its oddness makes it stand out against the bustling language of the messages concerning the military crisis, and his character is already pretty firmly established as calm, grandiloquent, unaware of his vulnerability, by the famous line "Keep up your bright swords, for the dew will rust them" (I.ii.59). This invulnerability is founded in a soldier's courage, and it does not, as he supposes, extend to the dangers of civilian life.

*Philip Brockbank, "The Theatre of *Othello,*" in *On Shakespeare* (1989), p. 200. Brockbank's information comes from *The Calendar of Dramatic Records in the Books of the Livery Companies of London, 1485–1640,* eds. D. J. Gordon and Jean Robertson (1954).

Arriving in the Senate House, where all the talk is practical, he utters an oration on the topic of his marriage ("Most potent, grave, and reverend signiors" [I.iii.76ff.]) and on his wooing of Desdemona, "Wherein I spoke of most disastrous chances: / Of moving accidents by flood and field, / Of hair-breadth scapes i' th' imminent deadly breach, / Of being taken by the insolent foe / And sold to slavery" (134–38)—a speech of forty-one lines celebrated for their grandeur, which is enhanced by the tinkling couplets and plain prose of the following speeches by the Duke and Brabantio. The speech is completely successful; the Duke is proud that his warrior deputy talks exactly as he would be expected to fight, superbly. And the grandeur depends partly on Othello's use of unusual words like "demerit" and "agnize" and "indign." The one word he finds no synonyms for is "honest," twice applied to Iago in this scene (284, 294) and repeatedly in later scenes. And it is the honest Iago who will, in the course of the play, reduce Othello's language as well as his honour.

Before the temptation scene it is impossible to imagine Othello using the vocabulary of Iago; indeed, he rarely uses language appropriate to prose. It is essential to the character that until he collapses he speaks grandly. Later come the anguished repetitions of "handkerchief," the questioning of the sense in which Iago uses the word "lie," the pathetic stress on "honesty," the unaccustomed *langue verte* picked up from Iago, and the vile berating of Desdemona, whom he calls a whore, which suits his action in striking her.

Othello's final speech has been much commented upon. In a famous essay T. S. Eliot noted that in his self-pitying grandeur, his boasting about his weapon and his past achievements, he stresses his claim to be serving the state but makes no mention whatever of Desdemona. "Humility is the most difficult of all virtues to achieve; nothing dies harder than the desire to think well of oneself . . . I do not believe that any writer has exposed this *bovarysme,* the human will to see things as they are not, more clearly than Shakespeare."* This view has been much attacked, but it has not lost all its force. Eliot does not support his observation by comment on the language of the speech, which has some resemblance to that of Othello's speech to the Senate at the outset. It repeats the point made in I.ii.18 about the respect he has won by "My services which I have done the signiory," but important differences arise from the fact that he cannot now allow himself to speak of "My parts, my title, and my perfect soul" (I.ii.31). Instead, he compares himself to Judas

*"Shakespeare and the Stoicism of Seneca," in *Selected Essays* (1932), pp. 131–32.

("the base Indian") who "threw a pearl away / Richer than all his tribe" (V.ii.347–48).* He claims not to be jealous except when "wrought." He cannot confess to weeping without explaining that it isn't his usual practice. And he ends with a recollection of one more notable service to the state.

We need not suppose that Shakespeare was contemptuous; only that, as his language suggests, Othello was human, the victim of long habit, and wanting, as he ended his life, to enter a plea for merciful interpretation. That he did not get it in the play, and has not always had it subsequently, merely shows how variable interpretation must be when it has to work on language as complex as that of *Othello*.

*"Judean" is the reading of F; Q (and F2) read "Indian." The arguments for and against are summarised by Honigmann in the Arden edition, p. 342.

KING LEAR

The relationships between the extant versions of *King Lear* are at present the subject of intense research and dispute, but I think it is agreed on all sides that any of the versions of the play we are accustomed to reading in the standard editions* cannot be very like any text performed in Shakespeare's time, or indeed long after that.

*The *King Lear* familiar to most of us is an amalgam of the first Quarto, Q1 (1608), and the Folio, F (1623), with some hints from the second Quarto, Q2 (1619, falsely dated 1608). Q1 is a poor text, careless, contaminated, and generally prone to error; F, partly dependent on Q1 and Q2, is also faulty. At present there is a tide of opinion in favour of the view that F, based on a theatrical document, perhaps a prompt-book, incorporates revisions from Shakespeare's hand. Q contains about 288 lines or part-lines not in F, including the whole of IV.iii; F includes 133 lines or part-lines not in Q1. These editorial problems occasionally have an effect on the responses of general readers; for example, the omission of IV.iii, the Gentleman's description of her struggle with emotion, her tears "as pearls from diamonds dropp'd" (IV.iii.22Q), can surely change our view of Cordelia. Some changes and omissions were apparently made with the object of muffling the idea that Cordelia headed a French invasion of Britain. Others have a quite marked effect on our response to other characters (Lear, Albany, the Fool, and Goneril). The grim closing lines of the play are spoken by Albany in Q and by Edgar in F.

Modern editors, whether or not they favour the theory that there are two distinct versions of the play, tend to choose the Folio as copy-text. Evans, in *The Riverside Shakespeare,* bases his text on F without subscribing to the theory. Halio (Cambridge, 1992) chooses F because he believes in it. The Oxford editors, confident that there are two distinct states, print Q1 and F separately. Anybody interested in scrutinising the differences between the two may consult the parallel texts in Michael Warren, ed., *The Complete Lear, 1608–1623* (1989), or *The Parallel King Lear, 1608, 1623* (1989), or, more accessibly, more cheaply, and by and large more persuasively, in René Weis, *King Lear: A Parallel Text Edition* (1993).

The question of the texts, briefly summarized in the footnote, is of great interest in itself, but it is only marginally relevant to the purposes of this book. Wherever it seems necessary or helpful I will mention Quarto-Folio differences, usually accepting the Folio version, though I am partial to the argument that F might actually represent an earlier form of the text than Q.*

It is curious that this play, which it is surely impossible for anybody who cares about poetry to write on without some expression of awe, should offer few of the local excitements to be found, say, in the narrower context of *Measure for Measure.* The explanation must be that the subjects of *King Lear* reflect a much more general, indeed a universal tragedy. In *King Lear* we are no longer concerned with an ethical problem that, however agonising, can be reduced to an issue of law or equity and discussed forensically. For *King Lear* is about suffering represented as a condition of the world as we inherit it or make it for ourselves. Suffering is the consequence of a human tendency to evil, as inflicted on the good by the bad; it can reduce humanity to a bestial condition, under an apparently indifferent heaven. It falls, insistently and without apparent regard for the justice they so often ask for, so often say they believe in, on the innocent; but nobody escapes. At the end the punishment or relief of death is indiscriminate. The few survivors, chastened by this knowledge, face a desolate future. The play demands that we think of its events in relation to the last judgement, the promised end itself, calling the conclusion an image of that horror (V.iii.264–65).

Apocalypse is the image of human dealings in their extremity, an image of the state to which humanity can reduce itself. We are asked to imagine the Last Days, when, under the influence of some Antichrist, human beings will behave not as a rickety civility requires but naturally; that is, they will prey upon themselves like animals, having lost the protection of social restraint, now shown to be fragile. The holy cords, however "intrinse," can be loosened by rats. Gloucester may be credulous and venal, but his murmurings about the state of the world, which do not move Edmund, reflect the mood of the play: "in cities, mutinies; in countries, discord; in palaces, treason; and the bond crack'd 'twixt son and father . . . We have seen the best of our time"

*I proposed this view, with far less documentation and far more cursory arguments, in "Disintegration Once More," British Academy Shakespeare Lecture, *Proceedings of the British Academy* (1994), pp. 84, 93–111. The authority of the Oxford editors is opposed to the idea of a common archetype for Q1 and F. But see Weis on this point.

(I.ii.107–12). The voices of the good are distorted by pain, those of the bad by the coarse excess of their wickedness.

The rhetoric of the play is accordingly more explicit, less ambiguous, except—and it is admittedly a large exception—in the apparent unreason of the Fool and Poor Tom and the ravings of the mad King, where the imaginations of folly flood into the language and give it violent local colour. These wild linguistic excursions come later; the opening scene is in cool, even bantering prose, but as always in Shakespeare, it achieves much more than mere exposition. Coleridge understood its depth; the opening conversation between Gloucester and Kent makes it plain that Lear has already arranged the "division of the kingdom" before the ceremony in which he formally announces it, which was therefore intended to be less the declaration of a secret intention ("our darker purpose" [I.i.36]) than a self-gratifying charade. Lear can already be seen as imperious and selfish; we discover that even giving his kingdom away is a selfish act. And immediately we are offered a critical view of the other main sufferer, Gloucester, and his relations with his natural son, Edmund. Gloucester treats Edmund's birth as an occasion for bawdy joking and does not explain why, unlike his legitimate brother, Edgar, he should have been so long absent or why "away he shall again" (32–33). All this has much to do not only with their characters but with the nature of the ensuing action in so far as it depends on the folly of Gloucester and the ingenious unregenerate wickedness of Edmund.*

Such economical writing is perhaps no more than should be expected of a dramatist in his prime. The ceremonial love competition that follows of course requires verse. The verse of the daughters Goneril and Regan has to be formal, manifestly insincere. Goneril is using what rhetoricians called "the topic of inexpressibility," standard fare in the eulogy of kings and emperors—"I love you more than words can wield the matter, / Dearer than eyesight . . . A love that makes breath poor, and speech unable . . ." (55–60). Regan follows with the well-established topical formula that Ernst Curtius calls "outdoing," or the "*cedat*-formula"—"let her yield": her sister has expressed Regan's sentiments quite well, "Only she comes too short" (72). Cordelia, coming third in order of praising, would have a hard task, but shuns this competition, meaning nevertheless to outdo her sisters by exposing

*See also, on this scene and on many other points, Stanley Cavell's penetrating essay "The Avoidance of Love," in *Disowning Knowledge* (1987).

their rhetorical falsity. She would prefer to be silent, but the only way to announce that intention is to speak about it, which she does.* She does not come out of the archaic and artificial contest well, defeated by the genuineness of her love, as France recognises; but she is far from passively yielding.

LEAR. . . . what can you say to draw
A third more opulent than your sisters'? Speak.
COR. Nothing, my lord.
LEAR. Nothing?
COR. Nothing.
LEAR. Nothing will come of nothing, speak again.
(85–90)

She does speak again, but virtually only to say nothing.† Here rhetorical formulae are used for a dramatic purpose. The rage of the King confirms that he cannot be temperate in the absence of ceremony; the love he seeks is the sort that can be offered in formal and subservient expressions, and he therefore rejects the love of Cordelia and of Kent. The rest of the scene is equally well contrived. The style of personal pronouns is worth attention: Lear is almost always, regally, "we," until he loses his temper with his daughter, when he uses "I." Kent is truly "unmannerly," freely addressing the King as "thou": "What wouldest thou do, old man? . . . Reserve thy state, / And in thy best consideration check / This hideous rashness" (146–51).

Lear has already given away everything except an imaginary possession: "Only we shall retain / The name, and all th' addition to a king" (135–36). The word "addition" seems to have interested Shakespeare. It can refer to "honours, prerogatives, titles"—as when, in *Othello,* Cassio, after his dis-

*Ernst Curtius, *European Literature in the Latin Middle Ages* (1953), pp. 162–66.

†This is the F reading; Q has "Nothing, my lord, / How! Nothing can come of nothing; speak again." We have either a revision in F or an omission in Q. The word "nothing" is to become a motif in the play, and so it is given heavy emphasis here and again at line 245: "Nothing. I have sworn . . ." In a rather similar way, the words "dearer than eyesight" are given in Regan's oration as an early warning of another powerful motif. It is very soon repeated in the exchange between Lear and Kent ("Out of my sight! / See better, Lear, and let me still remain / The true blank of thine eye" [157–59]). I have often noted the tendency of the mature Shakespeare to allow a word or set of words to occur almost obsessively: in this play there is an awful deliberation about the practice, though the full effect cannot of course be felt in the early scenes. A fine full-length study of repeated figures, "families of words and their functioning," in *King Lear* is R. B. Heilman, *This Great Stage* (1948, 1963). Heilman is particularly good on the imagery of eyes and sight.

grace, reacts to Iago's calling him "lieutenant" by saying he is "The worser that you give me the addition / Whose want even kills me" (IV.i.104–5). In *Lear* there is a way of looking at people as if they were simply basic human beings, naturally naked, wretches whose standing as more than that depends on their additions, without which they might be indistinguishable from Poor Tom: "unaccommodated man is no more but such a poor, bare, fork'd animal . . ." (III.iv.106–8). Not only honours but clothes are "additions": splendid in the case of Goneril and Regan, though meant for ostentation of rank rather than warmth; deemed unnecessary by Lear, who tries to take his off in the storm and at the moment of death; fraudulent in the case of corrupt judges, as we see in Lear's extraordinary tirade: "Robes and furr'd gowns hide all" (IV.vi.164). Clothes are emblems of "addition"—what is added, out of pride or wickedness, to the natural man.

Enid Welsford, in her valuable book on the Fool, found in the action of this tragedy "the great reversal of the Saturnalia." The Saturnalia was classical Rome's winter festival, remembered in the Christian Twelfth Night, when masters and servants changed places and a mock-king or boy-bishop ruled for a day over an upside-down world. Here Lear, stripped of additions and in his dotage, "discovers . . . what the evil have known from their cradles, that *in this world there is no poetic justice.*"* The Renaissance, like St. Paul, found much value in folly, and Erasmus, who wrote a famous book about it, also recorded the adage "Kings and fools are born, not made," which Shakespeare may have recalled when he has Lear ask, "Dost thou call me fool, boy?" and receives the reply "All thy other titles thou hast given away, that thou wast born with" (I.iv.148–50, Q only).†

Some understanding of the history and privileges of the Fool is essential to understanding *King Lear;* he is a perpetual reminder of Carnival, of the commentary on grandees allowed by custom to the humble. The Fool is both loyal and bitter; his master has reduced himself absurdly to a fool's role, and the Fool is now the source of wisdom, fantastically delineating a world turned upside down. The proper additions of the Fool include a coxcomb, and the Fool offers his to the King to take the place of a crown.

Among the additions Lear vainly wants to keep are his hundred knights,

*Enid Welsford, *The Fool: His Social and Literary History* (1935, 1968), p. 265.

†The connection with Erasmus is revealed in a lecture by Dominic Baker-Smith, "Counsel and Caprice: Seneca at the Tudor Court" (1999), p. 12.

but they are reduced to none by the savage calculations of Goneril and Regan. In the opening scene he has amused himself with calculations: how much love is due from her, how much from her, what exactly their rewards will be. He bargains with Burgundy: as a result of new calculations "her [Cordelia's] price is fallen" (I.i.197). In his turn he hears the Dutch auction conducted by his daughters: what need has he of a hundred knights, indeed of fifty, even of five-and-twenty, even, finally of one? Lear joins pathetically in the bargaining: "fifty yet doth double five and twenty, / And thou art twice her love" (II.iv.258–59). "O, reason not the need!" (264) he cries; to reduce a man to no more than what he needs, he remarks prophetically, is to make his life as "cheap as beast's" (267). For this is the moment when the storm is first heard; Lear is to find himself totally unprovided for, with shelter fit only for an animal. Now, more and more, the text begins to be full of animals—the bear, the lion, the wolf; and the King's life, without additions, is truly as cheap as a beast's.

The Gloucester plot is introduced immediately after the departure of Cordelia. First Edmund invokes nature as his goddess, a goddess who despises such human, social contrivances as primogeniture. His argument contests the legitimacy of legitimacy in a purely natural world. But there is more at stake than the ambition of the bastard. At the very outset of his scheming he and Gloucester have a perfectly motivated exchange on the subject of nothing:

> GLOU. What paper were you reading?
> EDM. Nothing, my lord.
> GLOU. No? What needed then that terrible dispatch of it into your pocket? The quality of nothing hath not such need to hide itself. Let's see. Come, if it be nothing, I shall not need spectacles.
>
> (I.ii.30–35)

Much of the poetry in the play depends on these echoes or repetitions; here "nothing" is associated with seeing, sight, and the loss of it, which Gloucester is soon to suffer. Edmund plays his trick on the foolish old man and on his brother, whose fault is "foolish honesty" (I.ii.181). The scene is followed at once by another in which we see Goneril's contempt for her father ("Old fools are babes again" [I.iii.19]) and another displaying the loyalty or foolish honesty of Kent, who is at once stripped of his additions and reduced to the status of a servant.

There are so many significant juxtapositions and encounters in the play that one might overlook the importance of Kent's assault on another servant,

Goneril's steward Oswald, who has been told to insult the King. Their relationship is brief and violent. Kent comes across Oswald again in II.ii and provokes him to fight. Prevented by Cornwall, he characterises his opponent in words that apply to all the evil persons in the play and to many in anybody's acquaintance:

> Such smiling rogues as these,
> Like rats, oft bite the holy cords a-twain
> Which are t' intrinse t' unloose . . .
>
> (73–75)

The figure is of rats biting through the complicated knots that bind together families, friends, societies; they cannot be untied and are destroyed by the evil gnawing of vermin. Shakespeare nowhere else used "intrinse," but it is a mistake to emend the word to "intrench," as some editors have done; that reading loses the idea of bonds that are visible and owe their integrity to their complexity. The lines are applied immediately to Oswald, the sycophantic evildoer, but they apply with equal force to the wicked daughters and Edmund. The basic idea lingered in Shakespeare's mind: Cleopatra asks the asp "With thy sharp teeth this knot intrinsicate / Of life at once untie" (*Antony and Cleopatra,* V.ii.304–5). Both words seem to be of Shakespeare's invention. But in the lines from *Lear* the knot intrinse or intrinsicate (perhaps, as has been suggested, a blend of "intrinsic" and "intricate") is made up of *holy* cords (the word "holy" is missing from Q1, but I guess it was present in a lost original; it carries so much of the sense of the simile).

Immediately after the scene in which Kent first accosts Oswald, another loyal dependant of the King, the Fool, makes his first entrance (I.iv.94). This is something of a crisis, for from now on the play develops a dialect of folly and madness, to be heard in counterpoint with the language of an evil that remains horribly sane. The Fool's significant first gesture is to offer his coxcomb to the King; then he sings, and the King tells him the song is "nothing"; and the pair have a dialogue on the nature of nothing (128–33). The King has divided his wit in two, like an egg cut in half, and given both sides away, leaving nothing in the middle. He is a "sheal'd peascod" (200). The Fool is insistent: "Thou hadst little wit in thy bald crown when thou gav'st thy golden one away" (162–63; note his privileged singulars, "thou" and "thy"). When Goneril insults him, Lear asks, "Does any here know me? This is not Lear. . . . Where are his eyes? . . . Who is it that can tell me who I am?" (226–230). (Here one notes a strain, only later perceptible, on the use of the word "eyes"; Lear's question is nothing one could expect: "Who am I? Where are my eyes?" is surely, on reflection, strange.) "Lear's shadow," replies the Fool: shadow, being the opposite of substance (an antithesis I have noted earlier as a favourite theme of Shakespeare's), is therefore a form of nothing.* One could compare Donne's calling a shadow "an ordinary nothing" in the "Nocturnal upon St. Lucy's Day." Lear is already thus drastically reduced.

The languages of excess and folly allow the intrusion of images and ideas that do not seem immediately relevant but are essential to the fabric of the play. After his frantic curse on Goneril, dismissed by her as "dotage" (293), Lear threatens to pluck out his eyes (301–2), and the mild Albany wonders how far his wife's "eyes may pierce" (345). The Fool asks Lear a riddle: "why one's nose stands i' th' middle on 's face?," the answer to which is "to keep one's eyes on either side 's nose, that what a man cannot smell out, he may spy into" (I.v.19–23).

Now, in Act II, comes the disastrous gathering at Gloucester's house of the daughters and their husbands, with Kent and Lear arriving later. The plot of Edmund ("Loyal and natural boy" [i.84])† against Edgar is afoot. Regan's wicked opening question to Gloucester was much admired by Coleridge: "What, did my father's godson seek your life?" (91). Here the supposed crime of Edgar is, as it were, by association exclusively attributed to Lear, his godfather. This periphrastic trick of identifying guilt by tracing kinship relations reminds one of *Hamlet:* "your husband's brother's wife" (III.iv.15) is an incriminating way of specifying the Queen his mother. Here the language of Regan, as always, characterises her as without mercy, cold and cunning. That of Lear, in reply to the Fool's tauntings, introduces his first thought and fear of madness (II.iv.56).

From this moment on, the language of *King Lear* has such force and variety that to give a convincing account of it seems close to impossible. Lear rages, and his rage is rant:

*The words "Lear's shadow" are spoken by Lear in Q and by the Fool in F.

†"Natural" here means, primarily, "dutiful to his father," but the sense of "natural = bastard" is ironically present. The idea of nature is, in *King Lear,* buffeted by ironies: invoked by Edmund as the goddess of natural sons, by Lear as the corrupter of fertility, and as a norm of conduct and temperament he is about to desert. According to Kent, "Nature disclaims" the foppish Oswald (II.ii.54–55); to Cornwall Kent's bluntness shows him to be acting a part not proper to his "nature" (98), which here means something like his servile place. More often the state of nature is what Edgar imitates when he takes "the basest and most poorest shape / That ever penury, in contempt of man, / Brought near to beast" (II.iii.7–9). Another way he expresses this aim is to say, "Edgar I nothing am" (21).

And thou, all-shaking thunder,
Strike flat the thick rotundity o' th' world!
Crack nature's moulds, all germains spill at once
That makes ingrateful man!

(III.ii.6–9)

Nature is again to take his part against his "unnatural" daughters; again the plea is for sterility, anything rather than the kind of vitality they display. The next appeal is to justice, which it was once his prerogative to dispense; now it will come, if at all, from elsewhere. It is at the disposal of the criminal, the perjured, the incestuous; the elements have become the "servile ministers" of his daughters, and the punishments fall on him, even though he is "More sinn'd against than sinning" (60). The sheer noise of Lear's speeches is a necessary prelude to his sudden turning in compassion to the Fool, and later to Poor Tom. The shouting of the King and the barbed chatter of the Fool accompany this recognition of what it is to be cold and poor, to be at the bottom level of nature. The tone changes in the lines beginning "Poor naked wretches, whereso'er you are, / That bide the pelting of this pitiless storm" (III.iv.28–29); and Lear sends the Fool before him into the hovel. There they find Poor Tom. It is superbly apt that Lear imagines Tom's troubles to have come from the ingratitude of his daughters, a punishment for his having begotten them.

Once more the theme is justice. Edgar-Tom provides a vision of unjust luxury; he has been a fine courtier,* but now, without shoes and clothes and perfume, his is an image of destitution: "here's three on 's are sophisticated. Thou art the thing itself: unaccommodated man is no more but such a poor, bare, fork'd animal as thou art" (105–8). And Lear begins to tear off his own clothes: "Off, off, you lendings! Come, unbutton here" (108–9).

This scene is in prose and yet it is poetry of the highest quality. Shakespeare had mastered the device of allowing a pattern of language to irrupt into violent dramatic action. This shedding of "additions" or "lendings" is an

*I don't know if anybody has noticed the resemblance between Tom's lines—"Let not the creaking of shoes nor the rustling of silks betray thy poor heart to woman" (94–96)—and this couplet from Donne's "Elegy IV": "I taught my silks their whistling to forbear, / Even my opprest shoes dumb and silent were." The furtive lover is given away by his perfume, and perfume is mentioned in Lear's pitying reply. The poem was written earlier than *King Lear,* but I suppose it cannot be thought very likely that Shakespeare had read it in manuscript.

instance. Another, equally extraordinary, is the tearing out of Gloucester's eyes, for which all the references to eyes and to sight and to "nothing" might have prepared us, save that the sheer violence of the act, and of all anger displayed—Cornwall's cold and Regan's sadistically excited—makes us, even four centuries later, turn our heads away from the sight.

The crazy chatter of Tom is now heard together with the lament of the newly arrived Gloucester:

> GLOU. Our flesh and blood, my lord, is grown so vild
> That it doth hate what gets it.
> EDG. Poor Tom's a-cold.
>
> (144–46)

The themes intertwine as it were musically; the cruelty of children, the unsheltered life of unaccommodated man. Gloucester himself says his wits are crazed. Lear believes that Edgar has shown himself to be a philosopher, a student of thunder, one who is so close to being the thing itself that he will understand other elemental phenomena.

The play now maintains a double movement: the craziness on the heath and the treachery of Edmund, with the cruel calculations of Cornwall, indoors. The next scene on the heath (III.vi) presents an image of mad justice in the fantasy trial of Goneril and Regan. (This wonderful scene is found only in the Quarto versions, and one can only guess why it was omitted from the Folio.) The "justicers" are a Fool (dealing with equity rather than unmitigated justice) and a Bedlam maniac ("Thou robed man of justice" [35]). "Let us deal justly," says Tom (40). Lear, now quite mad, still in his babblings, does not stray far from the obsessive language of the play: "Is there any cause in nature that make these hard hearts? [It is a philosophical question, like inquiring into the cause of thunder] ... You, sir ... I do not like the fashion of your garments" (77–80). As Lear sinks into sleep, the Fool makes his last quip and disappears from the play.

The action proceeds with another trial, this time the interrogation and punishment of Gloucester. In the midst of this obscene horror the words "justice" and of course "eyes" and "seeing" are repeated again and again, even with an echo of the Fool's earlier joke about the use of the nose to separate the eyes. The vile jellies are trampled on, and Gloucester, now an "eyeless villain," must "smell / His way to Dover" (III.vii.93–94). In the end, there are compassionate servants to bring him "flax and whites of eggs" (106) for his bleeding face; but only in Q. Whether or not this passage existed only in the Quarto, or in a lost archetype, it would seem that some hand, not willing to forgo absolute cruelty, removed it. In Peter Brook's unforgettable 1962 production, it was omitted, not on textual grounds, but because "a note of sympathy" was not wanted in this "Theatre of Cruelty."

The suitability of this play for such a theatre is well suggested in IV.i, when Edgar congratulates himself on having fallen so deep into misery that he can fall no further, at which point his eyeless father enters and Edgar understands that as long as we are capable of saying we are "at the worst" we have not yet reached that point: "the worst is not / So long as we can say, 'This is the worst'" (27–28). This might be the motto of the play, an unrelenting study in protraction; patience, which is continually recommended, is defeated by fortune, by nature, by the indifference of heaven to justice. Gloucester's famous observation "As flies to wanton boys are we to th' gods, / They kill us for their sport" (IV.i.36–37) is often contradicted by other characters, including Albany, Cordelia, and eventually Gloucester himself; but in the context it carries conviction. When father and son have met, the old countryman brings to the naked Tom "the best 'parel that I have" (49). He provides him with additions. There is something rather terrifying about the way in which, having created this nightmarish scenario, Shakespeare continues his clinical insistence on a linguistic subplot: "'Tis the time's plague, when madmen lead the blind" . . . "the best 'parel" . . . "naked fellow" . . . "Poor Tom's a-cold" . . . "Bless thy sweet eyes, they bleed" (46–54). Much of the effect of *King Lear* seems to me to arise from its own unsparing cruelty, which can sometimes seem to be an almost sadistic attitude to the spectator, an attitude enhanced by the coolness with which we are manipulated, forced to deal with a pain that does not hinder the poet from playing his terrible games.

The strongest hints that goodness can survive these trials come from Kent and, more strikingly, Albany; easily put down by his wife, Goneril, in the early scenes, Albany can now tell her she is "not worth the dust which the rude wind / Blows in [her] face" (IV.ii.30–31). This fine speech reminds us of another Shakespearian style, the one in which an initial idea makes itself more complex in its expression:

> That nature which contemns its origin
> Cannot be bordered certain in itself.

She that herself will sliver and disbranch
From her material sap, perforce must wither,
And come to deadly use.

(32–36)

The sentiment is fairly clear in the first two lines; this is another excursion into the semantics of "nature"; and the second line carries the implication that Goneril's contempt for her progenitor must be a kind of self-contempt which she will be unable to control. The remaining lines move silently to the image of the family as a tree; in destroying her father she must destroy herself, here represented as vegetation ruining itself; the "deadly use" may be the equivalent of being burned.* Goneril finds this "foolish," and Albany follows her contemptuous remark with the famous speech that ends:

If that the heavens do not their visible spirits
Send quickly down to tame these vild offenses,
It will come,
Humanity must perforce prey on itself,
Like monsters of the deep.

(46–50)

These lines are missing from the Folio and the cut is attributed by some to "authorial revision."† The cut again diminishes any confidence that evil will be overthrown, and it certainly makes a difference to the character of Albany, but he is voicing a sentiment and a mood that are found throughout the play. A little later Lear takes Cordelia to be a visible "spirit" (IV.vii.48), another bleak, insane error. Albany is soon to say that the fate of Cornwall demonstrates that there are "justicers" above (IV.ii.79), another remark that is stronger in the Folio, where the earlier pessimistic utterance is cut; but the concurrent lamentation for Gloucester's eyes (72 twice, 81, 88, 96) restores the mood of despair and horror. There is something appalling about the thought of an author who will submit his characters and his audiences to such a test.

*René Weis sees a reference to Hebrews 6:8: "But that which beareth thorns and briars is rejected, and is nigh unto cursing, whose end is to be burnt" (p. 224).

†*King Lear,* ed. Jay L. Halio (New Cambridge edition, 1992), p. 272. Halio does not print the missing lines, even in square brackets, in his main text.

IV.iii is the scene, already mentioned, that was cut from the Folio text. In IV.iv we see something of the Cordelia that is lost when the scene is excised. The lines "O dear father, / It is thy business that I go about" (23–24) inevitably recall Luke 2:49: "I must be about my Father's business." The echo is very bold, but probably without the allegorical significance sometimes attributed to it, for Lear is not God, and Cordelia could not save him, even if, absurdly, he would in that case have needed to be saved. Once again the effect is of a sort of authorial savagery; irony is too civilised a word for it.

Regan and Oswald are again at their horrible worst in IV.v ("It was great ignorance, Gloucester's eyes being out, / To let him live" [9–10]). IV.vi is probably the cruellest and paradoxically the most beautiful scene in Shakespeare. Nowadays a comparison with Samuel Beckett seems inevitable. First there is the wild moment when Edgar leads his father to the edge of an imaginary cliff top and vividly describes to the blind man the nonexistent drop beneath him. Here the energy of the verse goes into imagining the scene: the birds are below them, and "Half way down / Hangs one that gathers sampire, dreadful trade!" (14–15). Once more one feels that this trick, using great poetic resource, is cruel; the scene must look either absurd or deeply shocking. One notices that Edgar insists on the "eyes' anguish" (6), on the act of casting down one's eyes, on "the deficient sight" (23), even as he is demonstrating what it is to see. He also contrives to mention his change of "garments" (10). The obsession with additions and with vision is not peculiar to Edgar; he is serving the play as a whole. When he takes on his second role as the man who comes to the aid of Gloucester on the beach, he again stresses the vastness of the cliff face: "Do but look up. / Alack, I have no eyes" (59–60). Edgar tells his father that he has been preserved from a devil by "the clearest gods" (73), a lie in the service of filial piety, followed by a plea for patience in circumstances that will make patience less and less useful or possible.

The hopelessness of patience is at once demonstrated when Gloucester encounters the mad King. The thread of sense in Lear's ravings is his memory of kingship ("they cannot touch me for coining" [83]) and forfeited power, along with the ingratitude of his daughters. The King, accustomed to being the agent of justice, now finds he is human, and since man's life is now known to be as cheap as beast's, he concludes that crimes such as lechery should not be punished. But the great speech turns into a disgusted rejection of sexuality, stronger even than Iago's. There follows an amazing passage in which the topics of the King's mortal body, the authority of kings, justice, nature, clothes (additions), lust, eyesight, nothingness, and apocalypse are all introduced.

> GLOU. O, let me kiss that hand!
> LEAR. Let me wipe it first, it smells of mortality.
> GLOU. O ruin'd piece of nature! This great world
> Shall so wear out to nought. Dost thou know me?
> LEAR. I remember thine eyes well enough. Dost thou squiny at me?
> No, do thy worst, blind Cupid, I'll not love. Read thou this challenge; mark but the penning of it.
> GLOU. Were all thy letters suns, I could not see.
> . . .
> LEAR. Read.
> GLOU. What, with the case of eyes?
> LEAR. O ho, are you there with me? No eyes in your head, nor money in your purse? Your eyes are in a heavy case, your purse in a light, yet you see how this world goes.
> GLOU. I see it feelingly.
> LEAR. What, art mad? A man may see how this world goes with no eyes. Look with thine ears . . .
>
> (IV.vi.132–51)

Lear speaks prose and Gloucester verse. The prose is appropriate in the same way as Poor Tom's; this is "matter and impertinency mix'd, / Reason in madness!" (174–75), which also resembles in some ways the Fool's, for Lear is now, with the privilege of madness, playing a fool's role, being "The natural fool of fortune" (191). The dreadful emphasis on blindness is the prime mark of Lear's madness and the play's cruelty, but nothing could be more sanely calculated than this dialogue. At one point Lear takes over the talk, curses authority in disgusted verse, and advises Gloucester, "Get thee glass eyes, / And like a scurvy politician, seem / To see the things thou dost not" (170–72)—after which he tries to remove his boots, and does remove his "natural" crown of wildflowers and weeds; they have helped to cover the naked wretch. Offering Gloucester his eyes, Lear counsels him to be patient, for the world is so designed that endurance of sorrow is required from the moment of birth.

Gloucester, now acquainted with apparently inescapable demands for patience, is willing to call the gods "ever-gentle" (217), a view of them inconsistent with the arrival of Oswald, in search of Gloucester's "eyeless head" (227). Edgar dispatches this "post unsanctified / Of murtherous lechers" (274–75), and Gloucester ends the scene wishing he could be as mad as the King:

> Better I were distract,
> So should my thoughts be sever'd from my griefs,
> And woes by wrong imaginations lose
> The knowledge of themselves.
>
> (281–84)

This coiled sequence is characteristic of Shakespeare in this period: If I were mad, I should be unaware of my huge sorrows—that is the simple sense, but the idea grows complicated: thoughts and griefs are severed, as if one could experience griefs as griefs without being aware of them. That idea is then rephrased: "wrong imaginations" are crazy fantasies, which disable the holder of them from knowing about his woes.

When we think of Shakespeare's imagination at its most incandescent, as perhaps we do in the foregoing dialogue between Gloucester and Lear, it is well to remember that the more normal business of playwriting can also be intellectually challenging; indeed, it habitually is so in Shakespeare, from *Hamlet* on. Cruelty is always a matter of a poet's calculation, like Cornwall's or Regan's. Dr. Johnson said he could hardly bear to read *Lear* to its conclusion, and Keats spoke of having to *burn* through the "fierce dispute / Betwixt damnation and impassioned clay." Somewhere in our heads we have, as Johnson quite expressly had, a desire that some justice will prevail, that Cordelia should not be allowed "to perish in a just cause, contrary to the natural ideas of justice, to the hope of the reader, and, what is yet more strange, to the faith of the chronicles." For although several versions of Cordelia survive in chronicles and other poems, including the old *King Leir,* on which Shakespeare drew, no Cordelia except his is murdered. Johnson seems to be expressing dismay at a cruelty inflicted on him personally, and I think he is not alone in feeling like that. There is a cruelty in the writing that echoes the cruelty of the story, a terrible calculatedness that puts one in mind of Cornwall's and Regan's. Suffering has to be protracted and intensified, as it were, without end.

The Book of Job, which was so obviously in the playwright's mind, ends with Job's patience rewarded and his goods restored; Lear has no such restoration. It is in the imagery of torment proper to representations of the Last Judgement that we might find parallels;* they envisage an endlessness of torture and are often beautiful. It is the play itself that is an "image of that horror" (V.iii.264).

The King is captured and in friendly hands; the "kind gods" (IV.vii.13) appear to have relented; he sleeps and has been clothed in "fresh garments" (21). Music plays (but only in the Quarto), and in Shakespeare music is often a signal of peace and reconciliation, as in *The Merchant of Venice* and *Pericles.* Here it is meant to be restorative, and is followed by the blissful recognition scene of Lear and Cordelia. It has extraordinary beauty, resembling the recognition scene in *Pericles,* which is an exercise in that mode of a virtuosity that betokens long research. There is forgiveness and mutual benediction, and no real reason to think they are not final; but of course they are not.

In the midst of the happenings that are to bring disaster there occurs a brief scene† that is a miniature of the play's intentions. Edgar brings his father to a shelter and goes off to fight: "If ever I return to you again, / I'll bring you comfort" (V.ii.3–4). Nothing is heard except the sound of battle. Gloucester is alone and silent on the stage, using his ears as eyes, as Lear had told him to. Then Edgar returns, but with no comfort: "King Lear hath lost, he and his daughter ta'en" (6). He offers a hand, tries to drag his father away; but Gloucester has had enough: "No further, sir, a man may rot even here" (8). Edgar then speaks the famous lines "What, in ill thoughts again? Men must endure / Their going hence even as their coming hither, / Ripeness is all. Come on"—to which Gloucester replies, "And that's true too" (9–11).

Edgar uses the obvious point that his father must leave his refuge just as he arrived at it, to make a more general stoical point about death. "Ripeness is all," though much quoted, is not an unambiguous piece of wisdom; is the ripeness of time referred to, or the preparedness of the sufferer? Edgar wants to hurry away; his "Come on" may strike a note of impatience at the old man's "ill thoughts." And Gloucester, trailing off, seems to treat the observation as a mere platitude. What is certain is that he waited in the shadow of his tree for good, conclusive news and comfort and got neither. That is the way *Lear* works.

*English churches often had Doomsday paintings over the chancel arch. There is such a painting in the Guild Chapel at Stratford. For more details about such paintings, their defacement and recovery, see Mary Lascelles, "*King Lear* and Doomsday," in K. Muir and S. Wells, eds., *Aspects of King Lear* (1982), pp. 55–65.

†See above, p. 11, in my discussion of Shakespeare's silences.

The King himself, a prisoner with his daughter (V.iii), now vainly imagines a happy ending, while Cordelia imagines they have reached the worst (4), not having heard Edgar's lesson in IV.i. Lear is given the kind of fantastic poetry Shakespeare had long known the trick of: Lear's thoughts are on the court he has lost; he cannot hope to have another, but he remembers, in a gently satirical way, the customary talk of courtiers: "Who loses and who wins; who's in, who's out"—only with this addition: he and his daughter will

> take upon 's the mystery of things
> As if we were God's spies; and we'll wear out,
> In a wall'd prison, packs and sects of great ones,
> That ebb and flow by th' moon.
>
> (15–19)

Here the simplicity of the beginning ("We two alone will sing like birds in a cage") gives way to more compacted language, with its hints of a wider frame of discourse. And Lear continues with even more intellectual force and originality:

> He that parts us shall bring a brand from heaven,
> And fire us hence like foxes. Wipe thine eyes;
> The good-years shall devour them, flesh and fell
> Ere they shall make us weep!
>
> (22–25)

The biblical image of foxes attacked or flushed out by fire (Judges 15:4–5) is combined with the obscure "the good-years" ("the good" in Q), never properly explained but seemingly a disease; the relations between these items are no longer those of demented association; the King is not fully sane, but no longer raving.

The rest of the story concerns Edmund's fatal move to kill Cordelia and the King, the love lives of Regan, Goneril, and Edmund, and the fuller emergence of Albany as the man in charge. Edmund dies at his brother's hand, Edgar tells his father's story, Goneril and Regan die, and with all this going on, everybody forgets about Lear and Cordelia until it is too late. The King enters with his daughter in his arms, thinking she is dead, wondering if she still breathes. Amidst the pathos of this ending the King complains of his eyes (v.iii.280), asks for a button to be undone so that he can once more shed an addition. Within these intensities the words "see" and "look" resound, the latter four times in Lear's last ten words.

This is the craftiest as well as the most tremendous of Shakespeare's tragedies. One can imagine awestruck colleagues wondering what the author, with three great and wholly distinct tragic achievements behind him, could possibly do next. There is a finality about *Lear;* it even instructs us to think that. But another great tragedy followed, and it was in its turn very different, though possessing, like its predecessors, its own dialect.

MACBETH

Unlike the other three plays in the group traditionally regarded as Shakespeare's four greatest tragedies, *Macbeth* does not present the problems that arise from the existence of two or more texts. The only authoritative text is that of the 1623 Folio. But this simplicity does not mean that there are no difficulties. Some parts of the text (III.v, IV.i.39–43, 125–32, and the interpolated songs at III.v.33 and IV.i.43) are clearly not by Shakespeare but by Thomas Middleton, his versatile and able contemporary,* and there are some indications that the play was cut. It is a good deal shorter than the others, it contains more topical allusions, and in other ways it stands idiosyncratically on its own.

It is generally agreed that *Macbeth* was written, at any rate in something like its present form, immediately after *King Lear* and shortly before *Antony and Cleopatra,* around 1606. It contains allusions to the Gunpowder Plot and the trial of the conspirators early in 1606; there is much play on the idea of "equivocation," notorious then because Father Garnet, the Jesuit missionary who was interrogated for his part in the Catholic plot to blow up Parliament, defended the legitimacy of its use by prisoners seeking to avoid self-accusation when subjected to torture.

*The songs are also found in Middleton's play *The Witch.*

At any rate, *Macbeth* cannot be earlier than 1603, for it celebrates the reign of James I, the first Stuart King of England. The Show of Kings in Act IV illustrates the course of the royal inheritance from Banquo to James, and on into the future, and the play touches on other interests of the monarch—demonology is one, and another is his personal safety, for the Gunpowder Plot, had it succeeded, would have endangered him.* Whether it was a success in 1606—after June of that year the theatres were closed by the plague for many months—we do not know, but many believe it was performed at court during a visit of King Christian IV of Denmark, July–August 1606. The astrologer Simon Forman described a performance at the Globe in April 1611.

Looking at it from a distance, we can see that the distinctive character of the language of *Macbeth* is largely dictated by its structure. From the first suggestion of a plot on Duncan's life until his murder, the play exists in a world of nightmare doubt and decision: to kill or not to kill. As Thomas de Quincey expressed it in his superb essay "On the Knocking at the Gate in *Macbeth*," the knocking makes it known "that the reaction has commenced, the human has made its reflex upon the fiendish; the pulses of life are beginning to beat again; and the re-establishment of the goings-on of the world in which we live makes us profoundly sensible of the awful parenthesis that had suspended them."† Or one could cite Brutus's soliloquy in *Julius Caesar:*

> Between the acting of a dreadful thing
> And the first motion, all the interim is
> Like a phantasma or a hideous dream.
>
> (II.i.63–65)

The action before the murder is situated in this "interim" (Macbeth himself uses the word in I.iii.154), and the verse is designed to match the terrible and uncertain decisions that occupy it. The play as a whole is greatly preoccupied with time; the Show of Kings itself covers many generations, and there is lasting concern about lineal descendants, Macbeth fearing that whereas he

*The topicality of the play is carefully examined in A. R. Braunmuller's introduction to the New Cambridge edition (1997).

†The essay first appeared in the *London Magazine* for October 1823 and has often been reprinted.

has no prospect of dynastic successors, Banquo has—a difference underlined by the Weird Sisters. The way to succeed Duncan was to kill him; the way to prevent the succession of Banquo's heirs was to kill both Banquo and Fleance. In both cases it was necessary to consider interference with the future as the Sisters foresaw it. So, in the early part of the play, the verse is full of equivocations about the present and the future, as forecast by the gnomic sayings of the Three Sisters.

Their opening lines represent a new departure, for they tell us nothing directly about the subject of the play, speaking only of the future as perceived from the present. "When shall we three meet again? / In thunder, lightning, or in rain?" offers an apparent choice of weathers that is not a choice at all, which partly prefigures the plight of Macbeth and suggests a vain selection of some aspects of futurity at the expense of others not mentioned—fine weather, for instance. The answer to these questions is "When the hurly-burly's done, / When the battle's lost and won." Hurlies and burlies go together like thunder and lightning, won battles are also lost; so we have false antitheses, ghostly choices, an ironic parody of human powers of prediction. "Fair is foul, and foul is fair" is a paradox echoed by Macbeth in the first line he speaks (I.iii.38). In his mouth the words may be taken at face value, as referring to the bad weather on one hand and the pleasures of victory on the other; the Sisters' use of the idea is darker and more complex. Perhaps what strikes them as fair is what to others would be foul, a crown got by crime, for instance. The paradox is oracular; oracles are traditionally equivocal. *Macbeth* is a play of prophecy focussed, with great concentration, on the desire to feel the future in the instant, to be transported "beyond the ignorant present." When Macbeth asks the Sisters, "what are you?" (I.iii.47), their reply is to tell him what he *will* be. The present is the long interim between thought and act (an interim that disappears when Macbeth decides to let the firstlings of his heart become the firstlings of his hand, "To crown my thoughts with acts, be it thought and done" [IV.i.149]). The first part of the play is set in a time when there is still a gap between the thought and the deed, and its language enacts this dizzying gap.

Here, perhaps more than in any other of Shakespeare's plays, an idiosyncratic rhythm and a lexical habit establish themselves with a sort of hypnotic firmness. "Lost and won," say the Sisters at the beginning of the first scene: "What he hath lost, noble Macbeth hath won," says Duncan at the end of the second, having just before that rhymed "Macbeth" with "death." These moments of ingrown self-allusion contrast with the old-style rant of the bleeding Sergeant. The scene in which Macbeth and Banquo encounter the Sisters (I.iii) fully exhibits the new and peculiar ambiguous, doubling manner. Are these figures inhabitants of the earth or not? Men or women? Alive or not? They reply with their prophecy: he is already Glamis, will be Cawdor, will be King. Banquo answers with questions to Macbeth: why does he *fear* what seems so *fair*? Then he addresses the Sisters: "Are ye fantastical, or that indeed / Which outwardly ye show?" (53–54). Are you what you appear to be, or mere apparitions? Why do you speak to him and not to me?

> If you can look into the seeds of time,
> And say which grain will grow, and which will not,
> Speak then to me, who neither beg nor fear
> Your favors nor your hate.
>
> (58–61)

Here the rhythms reinforce the return to the original question: What can be known of the future in the present? Him/me, grow/not grow, beg/fear, favors/hate, even when they are not, as it were, necessary, part of the substance, the oppositions and alternatives sound on continually. "Lesser than Macbeth, and greater. / Not so happy, yet much happier. / Thou shalt get kings, though thou be none" (65–67). Macbeth calls the Sisters "imperfect speakers" (70), meaning that what they say is not complete enough to be understood or to satisfy him. But they vanish, leaving their imperfect speeches to be completed according to taste: "Your children shall be kings. *You* shall be king" (86). The "self-same tune" is now repetitively in our ears.

When Rosse confirms Macbeth's appointment as Thane of Cawdor, Banquo's reaction is to ask, "What, can the devil speak true?" (107). And Macbeth begins the famous sequence of allusions to borrowed or ill-fitting garments: "why do you dress me / In borrowed robes?" (108–9). Banquo repeats the figure almost immediately (144–46). Here these robes, if borrowed, must be on loan from the future, and they confirm a devil's prophecy, although the fiend as a rule "lies like truth" (V.v.43). Banquo fears that this truth has been told to do harm: "The instruments of darkness tell us truths, / Win us with honest trifles, to betray 's / In deepest consequence" (I.iii.124–26). And Macbeth, contemplating a future in which he may have to murder in order to fulfil the prophecy of kingship, speaks a long aside which now completely establishes the rhythm of the interim:

This supernatural soliciting
Cannot be ill; cannot be good. If ill,
Why hath it given me earnest of success,
Commencing in a truth? I am Thane of Cawdor.
If good, why do I yield to that suggestion
Whose horrid image doth unfix my hair
And make my seated heart knock at my ribs,
Against the use of nature? Present fears
Are less than horrible imaginings:
My thought, whose murther yet is but fantastical,
Shakes so my single state of man that function
Is smother'd in surmise, and nothing is
But what is not.

(130–42)

The tempting promise of the Sisters, here compacted in the sinister phrase "supernatural soliciting," seems good in so far as it began with a now undoubted truth; it seems bad in that the temptation to murder induces in him an unnatural fear and brings up the image of a dead king. These fears arise from something less than the horrors would be if they were actual; yet they are already actual enough to shake him terribly. He is "rapt" (142), his ordinary behaviour forgotten in thoughts of that imagined future action. "[N]othing is / But what is not"—that is, the present is no longer present, the unacted future has occupied its place. These difficult thoughts all turn on the incantatory rhythm of "Cannot be ill; cannot be good," and of "nothing is / But what is not," as indeed will much of the verse from this point on until Duncan is dead.

More than any other play, *Macbeth* dwells on this moment of crisis, a moment that seems exempt from the usual movement of time, when the future is crammed into the present. St. Augustine wrote about such a moment, the gap between desire and act. Though he was certain of the end desires, he was "at strife" with himself. The choices to be made were "all meeting together in the same juncture of time." He said to himself, "Be it done now, be it done now," but he continued to hesitate between fair and foul, crying, "How long? How long? Tomorrow and tomorrow?"* This, for

**Confessions,* VII, xii *("quamdiu, quamdiu, 'cras et cras'?").* Reading *Macbeth,* I find it hard to believe that Shakespeare did not know this work, especially Book XI.

Macbeth, as for the saint, is the moment when the soul distends itself to include past and future. Throughout the early scenes we are being prepared for the astonishingly original verse of the great soliloquy in I.vii.

Duncan, in Shakespeare though not in his Holinshed source a father-king of unquestioned benevolence, has given Macbeth more cause to revere him, but he has also revealed that his son Malcolm is his chosen heir. At this point Macbeth has a choice: he must "fall down, or else o'erleap" (I.iv.49). He decides to "let that be / Which the eye fears, when it is done, to see" (52–53): again the opposition of the done and the undone, of future deeds and present imaginings. We now encounter Lady Macbeth, reading her husband's letter about the Weird Sisters, who "referr'd me to the coming on of time" (I.v.8–9). She joins in the speculations about present and future: "Glamis thou art, and Cawdor, and shalt be / What thou art promis'd" (15–16). But she suspects his resolution:

Thou wouldst be great,
Art not without ambition, but without
The illness should attend it. What thou wouldst highly,
That wouldst thou holily; wouldst not play false,
And yet wouldst wrongly win. Thou'ldst have, great Glamis,
That which cries, "Thus thou must do," if thou have it;
And that which rather thou dost fear to do
Than wishest should be undone.

(18–25)

Here are sibilant, conspiratorial whispers, all about what it is to be wanting rather than to have the thing desired. The sneering yet somehow feverish pun "highly/holily" expresses the absurdity of wanting something great, wanting it a lot, and yet trying to get it honestly, that is, without (as the case requires) committing murder.

Lady Macbeth, in foreseeing that her husband may be deterred by fear from doing as he wishes, occupies, for the moment, the position of one who has known how to distinguish proper from improper actions but has moved on to a loftier view of these matters, transcending the question of choice between good and evil. For support in this attitude she prays for release from the compunction accepted as natural to women who bear and suckle children: she prays to be evil. Macbeth's letter has encouraged her to think of the future rewards to be had from success in this prayer; it has, she claims, transported her "beyond / This ignorant present"; she feels "The future in the instant"

(56–58). Between tonight and tomorrow Duncan must die. So powerful is the spell of time on the play that when she counsels Macbeth to give nothing away by his expression she tells him "To beguile the time," to "Look like the time," to think of "our nights and days to come" (63–69). The Macbeths, and the reader, are pinned down by an urgent poetry to a present moment that has no content or meaning save in its fantasies of the future. Only with the arrival of Duncan does the rhythm relax, and we have some of that mature Shakespearian verse that sometimes makes so much trouble for itself:

> All our service
> In every point twice done, and then done double,
> Were poor and single business to contend
> Against those honors deep and broad wherewith
> Your Majesty loads our house.
>
> (I.vi.14–18)

Lady Macbeth's arithmetical measuring of gratitude—even if multiplied by two and then again by two our service would only count as one, given your generosity—is reflected in the doublings of the verse; she goes on to repeat her sums like an accountant (25–28). On many occasions Shakespeare, needing a simple expression, cannot avoid complicating it in this way, as if by an excess of energy, but they should be distinguished from passages in which that energy is fully and properly employed; and one of the greatest of these is Macbeth's soliloquy at the beginning of I.vii:

> If it were done, when 'tis done, then 'twere well
> It were done quickly. If th' assassination
> Could trammel up the consequence, and catch
> With his surcease, success; that but this blow
> Might be the be-all and the end-all—here,
> But here, upon this bank and shoal of time,
> We'ld jump the life to come. But in these cases
> We still have judgment here, that we but teach
> Bloody instructions, which, being taught, return
> To plague th' inventor. This even-handed justice
> Commends th' ingredience of our poison'd chalice
> To our own lips. He's here in double trust:
> First, as I am his kinsman and his subject,

Strong both against the deed; then, as his host,
Who should against his murtherer shut the door,
Not bear the knife myself. Besides, this Duncan
Hath borne his faculties so meek, hath been
So clear in his great office, that his virtues
Will plead like angels, trumpet-tongu'd, against
The deep damnation of his taking-off;
And pity, like a naked new-born babe,
Striding the blast, or heaven's cherubin, hors'd
Upon the sightless couriers of the air,
Shall blow the horrid deed in every eye,
That tears shall drown the wind. I have no spur
To prick the sides of my intent, but only
Vaulting ambition, which o'erleaps itself,
And falls on th' other—

(1–28)

The passage is famous, and so are some examples of interpretative criticism it has attracted.* Like St. Augustine, Macbeth has to consider what is implied by his need to do in order to possess what is by that act done. The triple repetition of "done" gives a fairly commonplace, even proverbial saying† an intense local force. If the murder could of its own power prevent all that follows such a deed, if Duncan's death could put an end not only to him but to all that would follow it, then at this stationary moment in time he would "jump the life to come," risk consequences in another life. But paraphrase of this sort entirely misses the force of "surcease, success," a compaction of language into what has been called a "seesaw rhythm" that is the motto rhythm of the great interim. "Be-all and end-all," another such compaction, has passed into the common language, yet it seems to be Shakespeare's coinage. If only time could be made to stop at the desired moment of the future! However, to be and to end are antithetical, they can only contra-

*For example, Cleanth Brooks, "The Naked Babe and the Cloak of Manliness," in *The Well Wrought Urn* (1947). Brooks's methods are no longer in fashion, and his emphasis on the structural importance of images has often been contested, but if it is valid anywhere it is valid in relation to *Macbeth.*

†"The thing that is done is not to do"—M. P. Tilley, *A Dictionary of the Proverbs in England* (1950, s.v.). We have not yet done with these repetitions: "Things without all remedy / Should be without regard: what's done, is done" (III.ii.12); "What's done cannot be undone" (V.i.65).

dict each other; time, as Hotspur said in his dying speech, "must have a stop," though our experience of it does not. The act of murder cannot be an end;* nothing in time can, in that sense, be "done." You can't have hurly without burly, surcease does not imply the end of success (succession). No act is without success in this sense.

Macbeth has three times wished it were: if doing it were an end; if surcease cancelled success; if "be" were "end." Now a calculator like his wife, he finds a double reason not to kill the King: "He's here in double trust" (I.vii.12). But there is a third reason: Duncan's virtue, in the extolling of which Macbeth produces the extraordinary figures of the naked babe and the mounted cherubim. Finally he returns to the original idea of needing to leap over an obstacle, but now he falls. This is an extraordinary, excited mingling of disparate figures—the King's virtues blaring out like the trumpets of angels in church statuary or on maps; pity totally vulnerable but riding the wind as if propelled by the blast of trumpets, again as on a map; or angels, now vengeful, riding the winds and making the assassination known to the world. As Empson remarked, "The meanings cannot all be remembered at once, however often you read it; it remains the incantation of a murderer, dishevelled and fumbling among the powers of darkness."† And yet Macbeth has come close to a decision; it is the entrance of his wife that makes him change it.

There ensues a remarkable dialogue. Macbeth announces that he will "proceed no further in this business," adding, in a mixed metaphor, that he has "bought / Golden opinions from all sorts of people, / Which would be worn now in their newest gloss, / Not cast aside so soon" (31–35). The gold of the opinions may shine, have gloss, but the gloss suggests new clothes, and they take over the sentence. But this mixture is mild compared with what Lady Macbeth offers in reply:

> Was the hope drunk
> Wherein you dress'd yourself? Hath it slept since?

*Hilda Hulme in *Explorations in Shakespeare's Language* persuasively suggests that "trammel," in the third line of the speech, means "to bind up a corpse within a shroud" (pp. 21–22). The word is usually taken to derive from the noun "trammel," a fishing or fowling net, a hobble for a horse, or a device for hanging pots over a fire; where the first sense is preferred, the net being a figure for the catching up of "success." See Empson, *Seven Types of Ambiguity,* pp. 49–50. Hulme's proposal is apt in that a murdered body so bound up would rather vividly symbolise an end, here so much desired.

†Empson, *Seven Types of Ambiguity,* p. 50.

And wakes it now to look so green and pale
At what it did so freely? From this time
Such I account thy love. Art thou afeard
To be the same in thine own act and valor*
As thou art in desire?

(35–41)

Here the abstraction hope is called "drunk," yet it is put on like a garment; then it goes to sleep and wakes up with a hangover. Macbeth's dread of acting in accordance with his desire is translated into a sneer at sexual incapacity; "act and valor" is a hendiadys, "courageous action," but the split emphasises the slur on manhood/virility. This savage utterance spans the tenses: "Was . . . Hath it . . . wakes it now . . . what it did . . . Art thou." In reply Macbeth asserts his manhood; he had forgotten what manhood meant when he resolved on murder. She scorns his humane interpretation, his virtue (*virtus,* manliness) in lines of monosyllabic force: "When you durst do it, then you were a man; / And to be more than what you were, you would / Be so much more the man" (49–51). All this redefining of manliness leads her on to proclaim her own unwomanly resolution; she would kill her own baby (54–59). Macbeth is impressed: "Bring forth men-children only!" (72). Since time and place "adhere" (52) he will proceed with the plan, meanwhile mocking the time (wearing a false face of welcome) (81).

It would not be easy to match the imaginative intensity of this scene; its language both explains and deepens our imperfect apprehension of the characters—the speeches are, in the sense of the word Macbeth applied to the Weird Sisters, "imperfect": the words present themselves for processes of interpretation that cannot be ended. One might suppose the Macbeths to be whispering; there is a continuous sense of menace, still present in the next scene (II.i), when Banquo and Fleance enter. It is night; the stage directions insist on the need for torches and the dialogue insists on darkness. We are told it is after midnight. Banquo is afraid to sleep and dream. Macbeth apologises for the inadequacy of the entertainment provided for the King, using one of those unnecessarily involved expressions so common in Shakespeare

*Echoed by Macbeth, speaking of Banquo: "He hath a wisdom that doth guide his valor / To act in safety" (III.i.52–53), where the halves of the hendiadys ("act," "valor") are split. This marks a difference between the two men: Macbeth is accused of lacking the courage to act in accordance with his illicit desire; Banquo temperately controls his aggression.

when the point is pointless courtesy, or some other inessential: "Being unprepar'd, / Our will became the servant to defect, / Which else should free have wrought" (17–19), where the strained middle line begets the next one, to mark the opposition between "servant" and "free"; these twists are so much in Shakespeare's manner that one again senses a surplus of intellect or of rhetorical resource, as if the motor idled too fast.

Meanwhile, bad dreams and fantasies crowd in: Macbeth with his "dagger of the mind" (38) and his celebration of night, when half the world is dead, wicked dreams disturb sleep, witchcraft is at work; the horror suits the time. The murder follows immediately; the tense and nervous dialogue ("Did not you speak? When? Now. As I descended? Ay." [II.ii.16–17]) is as far from fustian as one can get; fustian returns with the announcements of the King's death. The price of murder is sleeplessness, and between lines 32 and 51 "sleep" and its derivatives echo through the dialogue, eight times in lines 32–40. Lady Macbeth scorns her husband's infirmity of purpose; if the corpse bleeds (as corpses were said to do at the approach of their killers) she will smear the blood on the faces of the drugged grooms. She even makes a sinister pun: "I'll gild the faces of the grooms withal, / For it must seem their guilt" (53–54). Macbeth is left with the horror of his bloody hands. Then the knocking begins.

The Porter scene, misunderstood by some critics, including even Coleridge, is not a mere imitation of the Hell Porter episodes in miracle plays but, as De Quincey saw, the hinge of the play. The knocking connects the scenes, connects what went before with what comes after Duncan's death. It gives scope for banter about equivocation, an idea central to the entire play; the witches equivocate, the future equivocates, the Macbeths equivocate, the language generally equivocates. The Porter jokes that drink stimulates sexual desire and impairs sexual performance, but his words have a more general application; it comes between desire and performance, the position of Macbeth in the interim time. Drink is another equivocator, but, unlike Macbeth's equivocations, it also brings on sleep. So, at this critical moment in the action, in the dark moment, disturbed only by the knocking, a central theme is persistently sounded—yet in an episode presented as grotesquely comic.

After that moment time moves stormily forward, heading into the consequences that Macbeth knew would follow and that MacDuff compares with "The great doom's image" (II.iii.78). The ironies of Macbeth's lamentation have often been noticed: when he says, "The wine of life is drawn, and the mere lees / Is left this vault to brag of" (95–96), he is speaking of his own ruined life. And we are reminded, in undertones, of what it means to be more than "a man"—to kill the grooms, to show "an unfelt sorrow" (136–37)—and also of what it is to be a true man. Banquo and the rest put on "manly readiness" (133), which means more than merely getting dressed.

Macbeth, even when arranging the feast, is preoccupied still with time; Banquo has to go away, his time calls upon him, his absence will fill up the time till supper. "Let every man be master of his time," commands Macbeth (III.i.40). New antithetical terrors declare themselves, remembering the old rhythms: "To be thus is nothing, / But to be safely thus" (47–48). The means to be so will depend on the murderers: "We are men, my liege. / Ay, in the catalogue ye go for men" (90–91), and all the talk of men and "th' worst rank of manhood" (102) that follows is ironical.

Lady Macbeth now understands that having one's desire is not enough; she reproves her husband, "what's done, is done," she insists (III.ii.12). He is tortured by his dreams, envies the peace of the dead. He has a plan. "What's to be done?" asks Lady Macbeth (44), but he will not say. He prays for night to come, "Scarf up the tender eye of pitiful day" (46). Fleance escapes the murderers and renews Macbeth's "restless ecstasy," his fear of the future, which promises much to Banquo's line but nothing to his. He is "cabin'd, cribb'd, confin'd, bound in / To saucy doubts and fears" (III.iv.23–24), the three words meaning much the same thing yet enforcing the misery of his bondage. Still absorbed by fantasies of the future, he reminds himself that the danger from Fleance will come only with time; he has "no teeth for th' present" and can be dealt with "to-morrow" (30). There follows the Banquet scene, of which I here note only Lady Macbeth's insistence that her husband's fear derogates from his manhood: "Are you a man?" (57); is he "quite unmann'd in folly?" (72). Finally Macbeth rebuts these angry sneers: "What man dare, I dare" and "I am a man again," he says, having done more than a man should dare (98, 107).

Between his wife's insults and his defence of his manhood comes the speech in which he thinks about a past time, "Ere humane statute purg'd the gentle weal" (75). "Humane" has the sense "human" with a tinge of the modern "humane," and Macbeth is thinking, rather ironically, of a lawless time in the past, when ambition was not inhibited by human laws, somewhat like the state to which he is soon to reduce Scotland. But he thinks also of a time when dead men stayed dead and there were no troublesome ghosts; to this time he cannot return, yet without doing so he cannot be "a man again." Meanwhile, in the present, his behaviour "spoils the pleasure of the time" (97), and the banqueters are dismissed. We are reminded of the time: the night is almost at odds with morning (126).* Now Macbeth regresses into primitive terrors:

> It will have blood, they say; blood will have blood.
> Stones have been known to move and trees to speak;
> Augures and understood relations have
> By maggot-pies and choughs and rooks brought forth
> The secret'st man of blood.
>
> (121–25)

Here "augures" is more immediately intelligible than "understood relations." There is a typical blend of precise and vague; the latter term must refer to occult relationships in the world, such that however secret the crime, it has repercussions in an invisible world, and these may by divination be understood and lead to detection.

In his despair Macbeth sees no way to go but forward into more crime. III.vi is a "choric" comment: Lennox and "another Lord" have seen through Macbeth's lies, compare his evil deeds with "pious Edward," the "holy king" of England (27, 30), and fear for the fate of Macduff. As Act IV begins, we have more equivocal prophecies. The Sisters summon their "masters" (IV.i.63),† who allow him no comment as they warn him of Macduff. They

*"Time" occurs forty-four times (plus "times," three times) in the play, the relative frequency being .267 percent (+ .018 percent). The comparable figure for *Hamlet* (forty-eight occurrences) is .162 percent, for *King Lear* twenty-seven, .107 percent, for *Antony and Cleopatra* thirty-three, .139 percent, for *Timon of Athens* twenty-eight, .157 percent, and for *Coriolanus* thirty-two, .120 percent. For comparison, "honest" in *Othello* occurs forty-two times (.162 percent). Figures from M. Spevack, *A Complete and Systematic Concordance to the Works of Shakespeare,* Vol. III (1968).

†This word is misunderstood by editors: Cambridge thinks them "superiors," and Arden does not comment. The term is technical and applies to the helpers of magicians, as in *The Tempest,* V.i.36–41: "you demi-puppets . . . by whose aid / Weak masters though ye be . . ." and Spenser, *The Faerie Queene,* III.viii.4: "She was wont her sprights to entertaine, / The maisters of her art." Ben Jonson in the *Masque of Queens* speaks of the witches' "little masters or martinets" (H. A. Evans, ed., *English Masques* [1906], pp. 39–40).

assure him that no man born of woman can harm him (a prophecy that is of course equivocal, for it turns out that Macduff's was a Caesarian birth—though we should also remember the earlier equivocations about manhood) and gave him the false idea that Birnam Wood cannot come to Dunsinane. "Show his eyes, and grieve his heart," cry the witches (110), and the masters produce the Show of Kings, the Banquo line, the Stuart line, stretching out "to th' crack of doom" (117).

The rest of the piece is now preordained. Macbeth forgets about "understood relations" and turns on Time, which he will frustrate by crowning his thoughts with acts, abolishing the interval between them—"be it thought and done" (149). No more struggles with conscience, with the prospect of judgement. Lady Macduff and her children die at once. Then follows the long and curious lull of IV.iii, where Macduff and Malcolm, in England, test one another, and there is more evidence of the virtues of the good King Edward. This is rather generally, and I think correctly, thought a blemish on the play, certainly its least-well-written scene. It comes nearest to the tone of the rest with Macduff's response to the news of his family's slaughter. Malcolm urges Macduff to be a man:

MAL. Dispute it like a man.
MACD. I shall do so;
But I must also feel it as a man . . .
. . .
O, I could play the woman with mine eyes . . .
. . .
if he scape,
Heaven forgive him too!
MAL. This tune goes manly.

(219–35)

The insistent enquiry into the meanings of manliness is almost as impressive as the researches into "time."

These are at once remembered: "The night is long that never finds the day" (240). But for Lady Macbeth night and day are now one: she "watches" while she sleeps. A little water has not cleared her of the deed of murder. It may be "time" to be rid of the spot of blood, the smell of blood; useless now to reproach her husband ("Fie, my lord, fie, a soldier, and afeard?" [V.i.36–37], "Look not so pale" [63]). "What's done cannot be undone" (68).

This superbly planned and written scene is her last. The rest of the play concerns the overthrow of Macbeth. At first he is still deceived by equivocation: "The spirits that know / All mortal consequences" (V.iii.4–5) have given predictions he wrongly takes to be assurances. But he is made to express his awareness of the disaster already on him: "I have liv'd long enough; my way of life / Is fall'n into the sear, the yellow leaf" (22–23), and the rewards of kingship he had sought so urgently are denied him. The Doctor cannot cure him, or his stricken land. "The time approaches" (V.iv.16). He has lost the power to feel even fear, having "supp'd full with horrors" (V.v.13). The death of the Queen leaves him unmoved:

> She should have died hereafter;
> There would have been a time for such a word.
> To-morrow, and to-morrow, and to-morrow,
> Creeps in this petty pace from day to day . . .
>
> (17–20)

It is as if he is at last confronting the mere successiveness of time, the senseless days, one after another, that end only in death, a lifeless progress, so different in spirit from the thrills of that original interim. Only now does he "begin / To doubt th' equivocation of the fiend / That lies like truth" (41–43). The last proof of it is Macduff, not of woman born: "Such a one / Am I to fear, or none" (V.vii.3–4). The news of Macduff's birth "hath cow'd my better part of man" (V.viii.18) and at last shown him that he has dealt with "juggling fiends / That palter with us in a double sense" (19–20). Even in this extremity Macduff talks of "th' time" (24) and is allowed to say "the time is free" (V.ix.21). In Malcolm's triumphant concluding speech, the word "time" occurs three times (26, 31, 39).

It is surely impossible to deny that certain words—"time," "man," "done"—and certain themes—"blood," "darkness"—are the matrices of the language of *Macbeth.* In the period of the great tragedies these matrices appear to have been fundamental to Shakespeare's procedures. One might guess they took possession of him as he did his preparatory reading. That they are thereafter used with conscious intention and skill seems equally certain. They are one aspect of the language of the plays that show deliberation—more, in some ways, than their plotting, which, however skilful, can sometimes be somewhat careless. In these echoing words and themes, these repetitions that are so unlike the formal repetitions of an earlier rhetoric, we come close to what were Shakespeare's deepest interests. We cannot assign them any limited significance. All may be said to equivocate, and on their equivocal variety we impose our limited interpretations.

ANTONY AND CLEOPATRA

Perhaps we should not trouble ourselves too much about dates and the exact order of composition of Shakespeare's plays, but it is important that *Antony and Cleopatra,* usually dated towards the end of 1606, is very close in time to *King Lear, Macbeth,* and *Timon of Athens,* with *Coriolanus* soon to follow. The composition of these plays within a span of a couple of years is astonishing, and would be so even if one left *Timon* out of account. And perhaps we should also congratulate the anonymous but marvellous boy who played Lady Macbeth, Cleopatra, and possibly also Volumnia in *Coriolanus.**

In theme, structure, and rhetoric *Antony and Cleopatra* is strikingly different from the others. It is a history play, but its principal source is Plutarch's *Life of Antonius,* treated with the same blend of fidelity and freedom we find in Shakespeare's rehandling of English historians. It treats of Roman history at its turning point, the time between the effective end of the republic and the establishment of empire. Its theme, therefore, is world history, and in its

*Andrew Gurr states that one boy continued to play women's parts till he was twenty-one, though others switched to male parts much earlier (*The Shakespearean Stage,* p. 95). Muriel Bradbrook is convinced that Cleopatra and Volumnia were played by a man (*Shakespeare: The Poet in His World* [1978], pp. 213–14).

deliberate grandeur and political scope the play keeps us continually aware of the greatness of its subject. When Octavius prophesies that "The time of universal peace is near" (IV.vi.4), he may simply mean that the period during which the Roman world was divided between him and Antony was about to end; but his auditors would recall the familiar idea of the "Augustan peace," the years when providence ensured conditions favourable to the birth of Christ and the foundation of an empire that would ultimately become the Christian empire. Of course Octavius, later Augustus, had to win; otherwise the centre of empire would have been Alexandria, and the style of empire Oriental and pagan. The defeat of Antony and Cleopatra was as necessary as the silencing of the pagan oracles, the replacement of the Roman gods by Christ.

In that sense the victory of Octavius at Actium was held to change the world. The play continually reminds us of the tremendous historical alteration produced by the ending of the war between him and Antony. A. C. Bradley calls the play "the picture of a world catastrophe," and so it is. Friendship between the two leaders would be "a hoop" to hold them "staunch from edge to edge / A' th' world" (II.ii.115–16). Menas repeatedly tells Pompey during the drinking party that by an act of murder, by killing "These three world-sharers" (II.vii.70),* he can be "lord of the whole world" (61, 62, 65). Octavia remarks that war between her husband and brother would be "As if the world should cleave" (III.iv.31), and Antony at Actium loses "half the bulk o' th' world" (III.xi.64).

Shakespeare's use of a particular word or set of words to give undercurrents of sense to the dramatic narratives is, of course, a device used in later literature—it is a feature of E. M. Forster's novels and a trick also of Virginia Woolf's. Bernard, the writer in *The Waves,* says he is tired of stories and longs "for some little language such as lovers use, broken words, inarticulate words, like the shuffling of feet upon the pavement." The "little language" may be a muttered undersong to the main tune of the narrative, as it is in *Between the Acts* and sometimes in Shakespeare, or it may blare out like a trumpet entry.

An example of the quieter mode is the use, in *Antony and Cleopatra,* of the word "become" and its derivatives; they occur seventeen times in the play (as against three times in *Lear,* six times in *Macbeth,* four times in *Timon,* nine in *Coriolanus;* "became" is the sole occurrence in *Hamlet*). What is to be made of this? The first occurrence is in the ninth line of the play: "his captain's heart /

*Cf. "The senators alone of this great world" (II.vi.9).

. . . is become the bellows and the fan / To cool a gipsy's lust" (I.i.6–10). Antony, hearing of his wife's death, reflects that "The present pleasure, / By revolution low'ring, does become / The opposite of itself" (I.ii.124–26). Cleopatra taunts Antony: "Look . . . / How this Herculean Roman does become / The carriage of his chafe" (I.iii.83–84). "Since my becomings kill me when they do not / Eye well to you" (I.iii.96–97). "Good Enobarbus, 'tis a worthy deed, / And shall become you well . . ." (II.ii.1–2). "She makes hungry / Where most she satisfies; for vildest things / Become themselves in her" (II.ii.236–38). "Near him, thy angel / Becomes a fear . . ." (II.iii.22–23). "Till I shall see you in your soldier's dress, / Which will become you both . . ." (II.iv.4–5). "Enjoy thy plainness, / It nothing ill becomes thee" (II.vi.78–79). "Observe how Antony becomes his flaw" (III.xii.34). "A good rebuke, / Which might have well becom'd the best of men, / To taunt at slackness" (III.vii.25–27). And so on.

Some of these occurrences would normally escape notice; "become" is a useful word not earnestly to be dwelt upon. Yet it has many senses, as the *O.E.D.* demonstrates. "What's become of Waring?" "The powers given us by Nature are little more than a power to become." "Nothing in his life / Became him like the leaving of it" (*Macbeth,* I.iv.7–8). "She will become thy bed" (*The Tempest,* III.ii.104). In *Antony and Cleopatra* the word is often used, as it were naturally, in these senses, but occasionally it has enough strain on it to make one pause. For example, Cleopatra's "my becomings kill me when they do not / Eye well to you" is a noun usage noted as "rare" by the *O.E.D.,* which cites only Shakespeare's Sonnet 150 ("Whence hast thou this becoming of things ill . . .") as a second example. The strain on the noun is enhanced by the peculiar use of "Eye" as a verb to mean "appear under scrutiny." This is so out of the way that I think it fails to illustrate the sense it is cited to exemplify in the dictionary (I.5a), which offers nothing else very like it.

The strangeness of Cleopatra's remark arises from its remoteness from the plain sense of the sentiment. She has just explained that the change in their situation has so disconcerted her that she hardly knows what she is saying. The speaker in the sonnet is saying that his friend has the ability to make unworthy things seem pleasant. Cleopatra calls her demeanour in general her "becomings," which, like her speech, are out of order when Antony treats her coldly, as he has just done. But the train of the words is very Shakespearian; one often, in these later plays, has the choice of pondering or passing on. "Vildest things / Become themselves in her" is a little easier, but here "become" means rather more than it usually does in this kind of context:

"make themselves becoming" or even "become becoming." There is no special difficulty in Antony's use of the word in I.ii.124, although the sentiment in which it figures is not expressed simply: in the turn of the wheel, pleasure, brought low, finds itself transformed into pain. "Thy angel / Becomes a fear" is very striking; the guardian angel becomes a shapeless, abstract menace, and the verb, with an initial stress, is very conspicuous.

"Becomes/becoming" is, then, identifiable as part of *Antony and Cleopatra*'s "little language," and even its commonplace occurrences reinforce this sense of a semantic subplot. It may nag gently at us, reminding us how much the play is concerned with "becoming": what becomes a Roman, in manners, including the manner of dying; what will become of the world when this contention is over and the entire history of Europe and Roman-Christian empire opens up. There is the question of what kind of behaviour "O'erflows the measure" (I.i.2) (like the Nile)—behaviour such as submission to a "gipsy," and endless Egyptian carousing. To stay within measure is to live as Antony once did, when he bore adversity "with patience more / Than savages could suffer" (I.iv.60–61). It is to conduct oneself with the habitual chilly reserve of Octavius, and that is becoming conduct, since it presages the morality and power of the world to come or, in the now obsolete expression, the becoming world.

The use of the word "world," however, is a different matter. The trumpets sound; attention is continually drawn to it. The same device, using "dog," is something of a failure in *Timon,* but here, with "world," it is a success because of its manifest relevance to the theme and ambitions of the play. It is sounded at once: Antony is "The triple pillar of the world transform'd / Into a strumpet's fool" (I.i.12–13). The antithetical relation between the two significant parts of the world, Rome and Egypt, is also put before us immediately, not only in Antony's negligent treatment of the messenger from Octavius but also in his language: "Let Rome in Tiber melt," he says, "Here is my space" (34–35). He chooses to be where Egypt melts into the fertilising Nile, and the point about the voluptuous flooding of Egypt is made vividly in later passages: "Melt Egypt into Nile! and kindly creatures / Turn all to serpents!" cries Cleopatra in her anger at the news that Antony has married Octavia (II.v.78–79). The Nile has serpents (Antony considers her one of them [I.v.25]), and "kindly creatures" is a contracted idea: creatures, each in its natural kind, should turn into snakes; the other sense of "kind" is also present.*

*In II.v.94–95, Cleopatra tells the messenger she would be happier if he were lying, "So half my Egypt were submerg'd and made / A cestern [lake, pond] for scal'd snakes!"

What will decide the fate of the world? The answers are multiple; there is the cowardice of Cleopatra at Actium; the weakness of Antony in fleeing with her; and "the luck of Caesar." The second scene of the play seems lighthearted but is serious in so far as it is about luck, the hope of good fortune. The word "fortune" recurs (14, 26, 33, 45, 63, 74)* and is related at once to the "o'erflowing Nile" (49–50). Antony's angel becomes a cloud; he loses to Caesar at cards and cockfighting. Fortune is leading him into "dotage"—a word pronounced in the first line of the play and taken up by Antony himself (117). This is a word now associated mostly with old age, but in Shakespeare it normally (though not in *Lear*) means "infatuation," as often in *A Midsummer Night's Dream.*

These brilliant opening scenes put all the cards on the table: Antony is still capable of a Roman thought: he would not dream of mistreating a messenger bringing unwelcome tidings (later he has one whipped, in Cleopatra's manner); and he is aware of his unbecoming conduct: "O then we bring forth weeds / When our quick winds lie still" (109–10). Here the very energy of the figure is Roman; it refers to labour, the labour of the plough; it is full of force, opposed to the relaxation of Egypt.

So the possession of the world is at risk; the politics of the piece is of universal import. The ribaldry of Enobarbus has to be stilled, and Sextus Pompeius has to be resisted. Octavius and Antony agree; Antony thinks of the fickle populace:

> Our slippery people,
> Whose love is never link'd to the deserver
> Till his deserts are past, begin to throw
> Pompey the Great and all his dignities
> Upon his son . . .
> . . .
> whose quality, going on,
> The sides o' th' world may danger.
>
> (I.ii.185–92)

One notes the freedom, the unconfined mental force of this, the conversational compression of "whose quality, going on," and the quick figure of a world with two sides—sides not in the competitive sense but in the physical, as when Leontes, in *The Winter's Tale,* says that he is like one who, having

*It is used forty-four times in the play; no other play has even half as many occurrences.

drunk, sees a spider in the cup, and "cracks his gorge, his sides, / With violent hefts" (II.i.44–45). And Octavius, also brooding on the news of Pompey's successes, is no less vigorous:

> It hath been taught us from the primal state
> That he which is was wish'd, until he were;
> And the ebb'd man, ne'er lov'd till ne'er worth love,
> Comes dear'd by being lack'd.
>
> (I.iv.41–44)*

The sentiment is the same, the imagery different, and even more energetic, with its mixed figures of tide and price. The marriage of Antony to Octavia is of course a political move. A Machiavellian sense of political reality tempers Antony's licence and is the entirety of Octavius's mentality; a lack of it causes Pompey to reject the advice of Menas to murder the triumvirs, an out-and-out Machiavellian prescription. When Ventidius declines to pursue the defeated Parthians, he tells us something new about the megalomaniac Antony: subordinates must not be threateningly famous. The temperaments, though not the ambitions, of the great men are very different, and Octavius's is the more Roman, but Antony's is Roman, too, with an Egyptian inclination. Hence the force of the comparison between them: a version of Virtue opposed to a version of Pleasure.

But these comparisons are not allowed to be simple. Dryden's version of the story of Antony and Cleopatra is called *All for Love, or The World Well Lost.* Shakespeare offers Antony his choice, the choice made by his supposed ancestor and patron, Hercules, between Virtue on its hilltop and Pleasure, with hell's bonfire at the end of the path. It is plain that Antony finally makes the wrong choice, but it is clearly the business of the play also to complicate the issue by making pleasure admirable as well as weakeningly seductive and, sometimes, in the presentation, amusing. The characters of the lovers must be aggrandised. Antony is "The demi-Atlas of this earth" (I.v.23)—Atlas, whom Hercules

*Note also the lines that follow: "This common body / Like to a vagabond flag upon the stream, / Goes to and back, lackeying the varying tide, / To rot itself with motion" (44–47). This metaphor was too compactly apt to be forgotten; Antony says of Octavia as they part: "Her tongue will not obey her heart, nor can / Her heart inform her tongue—the swan's down feather, / That stands upon the swell at the full of tide, / And neither way inclines" (III.ii.47–50), the feather remaining constant as the tide changes, unlike the "flag" of Octavius's lines.

relieved of his burden, the world—and Cleopatra, self-described as "A morsel for a monarch" (I.v.31),* is allowed, in the extraordinary last act, all the poetic excesses associated with the language of the East, the Asiatic as compared with the Attic. She is to Octavia as Pleasure is to Virtue; she is Isis and Venus (as in Enobarbus's famous passage about her barge [II.ii.206ff.], she "makes hungry / Where most she satisfies" [II.ii.236–37]). Octavia's "beauty, wisdom, modesty" (240) can offer no real competition; "I' th' East my pleasure lies" (II.iii.41). Antony is Hercules to Cleopatra's Omphale; she dresses him as a woman (II.v.22), in Roman eyes a gross effeminacy and so recognised by the Renaissance poets (Spenser, for example), who signify the loss of manhood, *virtus,* in the same way.

In the confrontations of Octavius and Antony the former occupies the high moral ground. At Pompey's party Caesar doesn't get drunk; "Be a child o' th' time," says Antony; "Possess it, I'll make answer," replies Octavius (II.vii.100–1). The division between them soon declares itself. War between them, with Octavia the ostensible occasion of it, will be "As if the world should cleave" (III.iv.31); it will be ground between "a pair of chaps" (III.v.13). But so it must be, and the noble characters grow, in their own ways, nobler. Octavius becomes shrewder, and gets rid of Lepidus. Cleopatra appears in the habiliments of Isis; Antony, though more proudly Herculean than ever, has "given his empire / Up to a whore" (III.vi.66–67) but levied "The kings o' th' earth for war" (68). There is an epic catalogue, lifted from Plutarch and not without its irony, of many kings of the earth. Antony is "the Emperor" (III.vii.20)—a term reserved for him throughout the play until the quiet, scheming entry of Octavius in the last scene, when he is greeted by the title only a moment after Cleopatra's ecstatic eulogy of Antony as a lord of universal bounty, the true emperor.

Antony's defeat in the naval battle is called his "wounded chance" (III.x.35), but luck comes into the matter only because Octavius has it all; it is against his luck that Antony, under Cleopatra's influence, made so disastrous a bet. He has "lost command" (III.xi.24). Now, he says, he must "dodge / And palter in the shifts of lowness, who / With half the bulk o' th' world play'd as

*Later on Antony, in a rage, describes her as "a morsel, cold upon / Dead Caesar's trencher" (III.xiii.116–17), and Enobarbus calls her "his Egyptian dish" (II.vi.126). These words chime with the imagery of Egyptian banqueting and appetite generally. On a favourable view Cleopatra "makes hungry / Where most she satisfies," like an exquisite dinner; on another, she is what is left on the plate when great men have dined.

I pleased, / Making and marring fortunes" (III.xi.62–65). Yet one notes the *power* of this complaint, the vigorous self-contempt of "dodge and palter," the compression of "the shifts of lowness" (the mean tricks forced on those without power), and finally the recollection of the possession of power as a power to *play,* as if at cards. In such games, we have been told, he always lost to Caesar, who has now made his fortune and marred Antony's. Antony is left to defy fortune: "Fortune knows / We scorn her most when most she offers blows" (73–74).

But Octavius is now "Lord of his [Antony's] fortunes" (III.xii.11). In that brief scene of only thirty-six lines, "fortune" or "fortunes" occurs three times. In the next, when Cleopatra is answering Caesar's messenger Thidias, we hear again of "the universal landlord" Caesar's "fortunes," and Thidias offers advice that might have come direct from Machiavelli: "Wisdom and fortune combating together, / If that the former dare but what it can, / No chance may shake it" (III.xiii.79–81). As it happens, Thidias's own luck has run out, and Antony has him whipped; another indication that his "wisdom" has been depleted.

"Authority *melts* from me," he says (90), melting being another recurrent idea in this play—the Nile, and Antony's empire. He turns on Cleopatra, and the verse here is remarkable:

ANT. Cold-hearted toward me?
CLEO. Ah, dear, if I be so,
From my cold heart let heaven engender hail,
And poison it in the source, and the first stone
Drop in my neck; as it determines, so
Dissolve my life! The next Caesarion smite,
Till by degrees the memory of my womb,
Together with my brave Egyptians all,
By the discandying of this pelleted storm,
Lie graveless, till the flies and gnats of Nile
Have buried them for prey!

(III.xiii.158–67)

Here she begins by taking up the accusation of a cold heart, imagines it as shedding poisoned hail which melts ("determines," meaning comes to an end, a remote way of saying "melts" or "dissolves," which is reserved for the next line). The destruction then becomes more general; her son—whose mention suggests "womb" and its "memory," preserved in her children—will "discandy"* or, once more, dissolve as the hailstones melt; finally the whole pride of Egypt will be consumed, no longer by the hail but by the insects of the Nile. Antony is pacified by this transcendental rant, and swears to be wildly courageous, though understanding that his "hours" are no longer "nice and lucky" (178–79). As for Octavius Caesar, he is "twenty times of better fortune" (IV.ii.3).

In IV.iii, one of those scenes used by Shakespeare that comment on rather than advance the action, like the Parthian scene (III.i), the soldiers on watch hear the ominous music that means Hercules is abandoning Antony. (In Plutarch the god is Bacchus; Shakespeare takes the moment to emphasise Antony's claim to protection from his ancestor god.) In twenty-one lines it does much, giving to the fate of Antony a quasi-mythological grandeur which henceforth infuses much of the verse. Enobarbus deserts: "O, my fortunes have / Corrupted honest men!" (IV.v.16–17). But the tones of imperial grandeur persist. Antony scores an inconclusive victory and greets Cleopatra as if she were more than human, calling her "this great fairy" (IV.viii.12), while she gives him the welcome due to a god:

> Lord of lords!
> O infinite virtue, com'st thou smiling from
> The world's great snare uncaught?
>
> (16–18)

The marvel is that in this play bombast, or what ought to be at best nickel silver, is somehow transmuted into fine gold. Given infinite virtue, unlimited manly power, Antony hardly deserves congratulations on managing, like an animal, to escape the hunter; there is a deliberate glory in the greeting, but it has a faintly ill-omened sound.

Fighting by sea again, with all the omens bad, "Antony / Is valiant, and dejected, and by starts / His fretted fortunes give him hope and fear / Of what

*"Discandying" is an eighteenth-century emendation of the Folio's "discandering." It admirably joins the sequence "determines," "dissolve," and is soon to be significantly echoed in IV.xii.22. A stream could be called "candied" if ice formed on the surface, presumably from the use of "candy" to mean a coating of sugar.

he has, and has not" (IV.xii.6–9). This is absolutely typical of the mature Shakespeare, part of the run of his mind; it sounds like *Macbeth.* The point is made by the time we have heard "hope and fear," but Shakespeare ties another knot in the concluding line, as if to make sure the sense cannot be unbound; this trick gives the reader or listener work to do, relating "what he has" to "hope," and "what he has not" to "fear."

The final battle lost ("Fortune and Antony part here" [IV.xii.19]), Antony again turns on Cleopatra. Deserted by so many of his followers, he utters a very remarkable complaint:

> All come to this? The hearts
> That spannell'd* me at heels, to whom I gave
> Their wishes, do discandy, melt their sweets
> On blossoming Caesar; and this pine is bark'd,
> That overtopp'd them all.
>
> (20–24)

Here is a strange mixture of metaphors: hearts (of course a synecdoche for "men" or, ironically, "brave men" or "friends") that followed him like dogs now melt themselves, and also melt the sweets he has given them, slavering them over Caesar, represented as a tree in blossom compared with Antony, a taller tree but doomed to die by having had its bark stripped away, with a hint of the usual attention dogs give to trees. There are few passages even in this play that whirl so dizzily from one association to another. Antony heard Cleopatra's "discandying" speech, quoted above, and echoes it in this unrelated passage some time later. Melting is his fate, and it impregnates this complaint.

And so Antony himself melts. The intellectual energy of the verse is now probably more intense than anywhere else in Shakespeare, except possibly in *Coriolanus,* yet it is never completely wild. Antony asks Eros to consider shapes seen in clouds: "That which is now a horse, even with a thought / The

*The Folio reads "pannelled," and the eighteenth-century editor Hanmer emended this to "spanieled," which suits well with the idea of spaniels fawning and slavering (see Caroline Spurgeon, *Shakespeare's Imagery and What It Tells Us* [1935], p. 195). Moreover, "spanell" was an alternative spelling of "spaniel," and it is normal enough for Shakespeare to make a verb of a noun. However, Hilda Hulme argues that the word Shakespeare wrote was correctly rendered by F, and that "panel" or "pannel" means a prostitute, a sense that survives in some dialects; so the hearts follow Antony like whores (*Explorations in Shakespeare's Language,* pp. 102–8). This explanation is worth considering, but it forfeits the dog-candy connection, and recent editors have not accepted it.

rack dislimns, and makes it indistinct / As water is in water" (IV.xiv.9–11). "Rack" is drifting cloud; "dislimns" is an essential, irreplaceably apt new word (later uses are quotations of this one, as the *O.E.D.* notes); an artist "limns" and the cloud breaking up does the opposite for the horse. Antony is dislimned like the shapes in the cloud; he "cannot hold this visible shape" (14). He adds another complaint against fortune: he has been cheated at cards by the swindler Cleopatra and the lucky Caesar.

Antony's death calls forth verse of an exalted tone peculiar to this play. "The star is fall'n. / And time is at his period," say the guards (IV.xiv.106–7). Here the note of apocalypse differs from that sounded in *Lear* ("Is this the promis'd end? Or image of that horror?") because it suggests an enormous hyperbole—here the death of one godlike man, "the greatest prince o' th' world" (IV.xv.54), is the death of the entire world.

Octavian, however, remains to rule the world, for he is "the full-fortun'd Caesar" (IV.xv.24). But his luck doesn't quite hold out, for he is thwarted by Cleopatra. She utters her astonishing, almost triumphing lament:

> The crown o' th' earth doth melt. My lord!
> O, wither'd is the garland of the war,
> The soldier's pole is fall'n. Young boys and girls
> Are level now with men; the odds is gone,
> And there is nothing left remarkable
> Beneath the visiting moon.
>
> (IV.xv.63–68)

The grandeur of Antony entitles him to be called the crown of the earth, but again this crown *melts;* he adorned the war like a victor's wreath, but the wreath is withered. "Pole" is of grandly uncertain meaning: the pole star (the guard, over Antony's not quite dead body, says "The star is fall'n" [IV.xiv.106]), possibly the tent pole that upheld the soldier's world. Each of these figures elevates Antony from ordinary humanity: he is a melting crown, a withered garland suggesting a defeated hero; a heavenly guide or a prop. The rest of the passage says that with Antony all distinction of merit or achievement dies; children are equal to grown men, the unevenness that allows a man to be great, to be an emperor, is abolished. And the conclusion drops into an extraordinary simplicity ("nothing left remarkable"), qualified only by the strange redundancy of "visiting"—though Cleopatra, resolved on suicide, will also renounce "the fleeting moon" (V.ii.240) as the woman's "planet." What is altogether striking about the speech is that it conveys a kind of keening, quite unlike the formal expressions of mourning and lamentation found in the mouths of women in the earlier history plays;* in place of rhetorical pattern one has a diversity of figure, that restless movement of intelligence that characterises the later verse of Shakespeare.

There is a contrast with Caesar's expressions of regret that follow shortly. He undercuts Cleopatra's extravagances by saying that the death of Antony should have been more portentous: "The round world / Should have shook lions into civil streets . . . The death of Antony / Is not a single doom, in the name lay / A moi'ty of the world" (V.i.15–19). His Antony was not the whole world, only half of it; his portents signify not universal collapse but a temporary interference with the civic peace of Rome and his own imperial progress. The eulogy is formal, but always attentive to the importance of victorious Caesar: "we could not stall together / In the whole world . . . my mate in empire" (39–43). He breaks off his tribute at the call of business: "Hear me, good friends—/But I will tell you at some meeter season" (48–49). And he plans to lead Cleopatra in his triumph.

She, however, has seen how she must triumph over Caesar: "'Tis paltry to be Caesar; / Not being Fortune, he's but Fortune's knave, / A minister of her will" (V.ii.2–4). She has it in her power to do the deed "Which shackles accidents and bolts up change" (6)—a wonderfully vigorous line, imprisoning chance and forcing change into a cell like a despised convict. To Caesar's messenger she is crafty enough to say she is "his fortune's vassal" (28). Seized by Romans, she tells Dolabella her dream of the Emperor, the universal hero, the god. It has been suggested that the imagery derives from the Book of Revelation and from a mythographer's description of the god Jupiter.† This is plausible, and the passage is like the vision of a god or an angel:

His face was as the heav'ns, and therein stuck
A sun and moon, which kept their course, and lighted

*See above, for example, p. 28.

†The passage from the mythographer Cartari is quoted in *Antony and Cleopatra,* ed. John Wilders (Arden edition, 1995), p. 281. Revelation 10:1–2: "And I saw another mighty angel come down from heaven, clothed with a cloud: and a rainbow was upon his head, and his face was as it were the sun and his feet as pillars of fire: And he had in his hand a little book, open: and he set his right foot upon the sea and his left foot on the earth."

The little O, th' earth.
. . .
His legs bestrid the ocean, his rear'd arm
Crested the world, his voice was propertied
As all the tuned spheres, and that to friends;
But when he meant to quail and shake the orb,
He was as rattling thunder. For his bounty,
There was no winter in't; an autumn* it was
That grew the more by reaping. His delights
Were dolphin-like, they show'd his back above
The element they liv'd in. In his livery
Walk'd crowns and crownets; realms and islands were
As plates dropp'd from his pocket.

(V.ii.79–92)

This colossal figure is credited with power over the world and then over the universe; his very voice expressed the harmony of the spheres, inaccessible to mortal ears. The rapid switch from the seasonal imagery to that of the dolphin leaping out of the sea is again typical of Shakespeare's late style—no laborious working out of the figures, instead a sort of impatience at the unexplored resources of language. Then another move, to kings and princes as servants wearing his livery, and finally a cosmic image of liberality, "realms and islands" carelessly dropped, like coins from his pocket. Cleopatra defends herself against Dolabella's gentle scepticism: this was not a mere dream; it is true that fancy or imagination produces in dreams stranger stuff than nature can contrive, but in this case we are talking about reality, about nature's masterpiece, something real and actual, not the mere shadows produced by dreaming.

With the entry of the new, actual Emperor, she reallocates the title she conferred on Antony: "Sole sir o' th' world," she calls him (120), for all the world is now his (134). The episode of Seleucus and the inventory reminds us that Cleopatra has not lost her cunning. She is trying to trick Caesar into believing that her withholding of much property signifies her intention to

*F reads "Antony." The eighteenth-century emendation is generally accepted, but there are those who defend "Antony"—see Wilders, Arden edition, p. 305. These arguments seem forced, and I take "autumn" to be correct. So, in his text, does Wilders.

live; and he wants her for his triumph. Cleopatra wins this bout. Her last hours have the kind of splendour she attributed to Antony. It is at this point that her women, Charmian and Iras, catch the tone of royal magniloquence: "Finish, good lady, the bright day is done, / And we are for the dark" (193–94). She gets the asps from the Clown and is dressed as a queen, an "eastern star," "A lass unparallel'd" (308, 316); at last she can mock "The luck of Caesar" (286). Evidence of Shakespeare's eye for a wonderful line can be found in Plutarch, where the soldier, seeing Cleopatra dead, asks, "Is that well done, Charmian?" and she answers, "Very well . . . and meet for a Princess descended from the race of so many noble kings." "She said no more, but fell down dead . . ." This becomes:

> It is well done, and fitting for a princess
> Descended of so many royal kings.
> Ah, soldier! *Charmian dies.*
>
> (326–28)

All that was needed was the substitution of the apparently pleonastic "royal" for Plutarch's mere "noble." One needs to add the notion of beautiful excess to Coleridge's famous account of the style of this play, "happy valiancy." *Antony and Cleopatra* takes the world-sharers, exposes them as they are, both ruthless politicians and one a libertine, and with controlled hyperbole elevates them to a status so grand that only an exercise of linguistic genius could prevent their seeming inflated or absurd.

TIMON OF ATHENS

There is much that is baffling about *Timon of Athens.* It is not often performed, and a strong sense of its oddity has deflected critical interest; apart from *Titus Andronicus* it is probably the least admired of Shakespeare's tragedies (though G. Wilson Knight, a powerful and idiosyncratic interpreter, thought it the most remarkable of them).

Most critics accept that it is either unfinished or the product of a collaboration, or both. I will not recapitulate the controversies, but merely say that in my belief the play survives in an unfinished state. That is the essential presupposition of what follows.* Of course one cannot rule out the possibility that Shakespeare had a collaborator, and there is evidence to support the claim that it was Thomas Middleton; but it is unfinished all the same.

Timon was included in the Folio of 1623 only when it became necessary to find a substitute for *Troilus and Cressida,* which seems to have run into copyright problems. Being much shorter, *Timon* does not fill the space

*E.A.J. Honigmann believes that Shakespeare did not always write his scenes in the order in which they appear. He argues that the middle scenes of *Timon* were "roughed out" before Shakespeare realised he had made a mistake about the value of the talent, so that I.i and part of II.ii belonged "to a later phase of composition." *Timon,* he points out, is far from unique in this respect (*The Stability of Shakespeare's Text* [1965], pp. 142–50). Although Honigmann seems not to think so, this theory surely lends force to the hypothesis of incompletion; work on the roughed-out middle scenes was never completed.

allowed for that play; even though it was padded out, there remains a gap in the pagination of the Folio. Copies survive with the original leaf having the end of *Romeo and Juliet* on one side and the beginning of *Troilus and Cressida* on the other. There is a gap between *Timon* and *Julius Caesar* which corresponds to the difference in length between the printed text of *Timon* and that of *Troilus,* which was half again as long as *Timon* when it eventually appeared between the Histories and the Tragedies. It has more than once been suggested that but for this emergency *Timon* might not have been included at all.

The date of its composition is quite uncertain; editors nowadays say 1605 or 1606, wanting it to be not too distant from *King Lear. Timon* draws on Plutarch's *Life of Antony,* which Shakespeare used more extensively in *Antony and Cleopatra* (also dated about 1606, which, if it was the year in which Shakespeare also produced *Lear* and *Macbeth,* was certainly an *annus mirabilis*). No absolutely convincing reasons can be given for any date, though no one seems to argue that the play can be other than Jacobean, that is, after 1603.

It seems to me likely that the play was sketched out in advance, and that some sections were written in a final form while others were not. Some speeches, such as that of Alcibiades to the Senators at III.v.40–58, and that of Flavius before Timon's cave at IV.iii.458–71, are obviously rough and unfinished. Apemantus's announcement of the arrival of the Poet and Painter (IV.iii.351) would presumably have been altered in any final version, since it occurs eighty-odd lines before they turn up. The intervening lines concern the visit of the Banditti and a dialogue with Flavius—a considerable diversion for which the author forgot to make allowance by deferring the stage direction. That change would clearly have been necessary in a prompt copy, and the text as we have it is unlikely ever to have been staged. Thus it was presumably set from "foul papers," that is, from a manuscript written by the author or authors, with much mislineation, with prose set as verse and verse as prose. The stage directions generally are of the kind produced by the writer rather than the prompter, and there are confusions in speech headings which would have had to be eliminated in a theatrical manuscript.

These considerations are of critical interest primarily because evidence of Shakespeare at work is rather rare, despite the survival, for example, of lines in *Love's Labor's Lost* (IV.iii.287–362, V.ii.817–22) that should presumably have been cancelled. It would be incautious to assume that the working method for this play was exactly like that for all the others; in fact, the evidence rather favours the view that *Timon* was differently conceived. Nevertheless, some conclusions may be drawn from its present condition.

The plan seems to have been something like this: an opening scene based on the *Paragone,* a scheme devised in Italy of a formalised dialogue between a poet and a painter and usually meant to emphasise the superiority of the painter in the depiction of moral qualities. This debate occupies the first ninety-four lines of the play. Timon then enters and deals with a request from an "old Athenian" before turning his attention to the painter and the poet (152) and adding his comments on their carefully written disputation. The scene then takes its course, with Timon speaking to the Jeweller and dealing with the comments of Apemantus.

The next scene offers systematically arranged exempla of Timon's excessive generosity, as when he refuses the return of his loan to Ventidius. As entertainment for his guests Timon now offers a set-piece representation of a masque and a Banquet of Sense.* More instances of foolish generosity follow.

Events turn against Timon; loans are called in; Flavius expounds his debts, expecting relief. His appeals are rejected (III.i–v) with commentary by "three Strangers." Timon, enraged, orders another banquet. (Here the subplot gets rather perfunctory attention: Alcibiades's appeal is rejected by the Senate.) The second banquet is a demonic parody of the first, a banquet of water and stones and insults.

Timon's first tirade against humanity occurs in IV.i, his second in IV.iii. Here begins a rather mechanical procession of visitors to Timon in the woods: Alcibiades and his whores, Apemantus, the bandits, Flavius the steward, the Poet and Painter (inverting the opening scene, as the second banquet inverts the first), and the desperate Senators urging him to return to Athens. The play ends with the death of Timon and the conquest of Athens by Alcibiades.

All this would have been provisionally plotted, but not all of it exists in a fully worked-out state. What is striking is the imitation of already existing poetical schemes, although the prefabricated structure does not inhibit the freedom of the texture. The *Paragone* scene is fully written in a characteristically contorted style. The Poet's account of his art in a sense belies itself:

> Our poesy is as a gum, which oozes
> From whence 'tis nourished. The fire i' th' flint
> Shows not till it be strook; our gentle flame
> Provokes itself and like the current flies
> Each bound it chases.

(I.i.21–25)

*See below, p. 236.

Johnson called this "very obscure. He seems to boast the copiousness and facility of his vein, by declaring that verses drop from a poet as gums from odoriferous trees, and that his flame kindles itself without the violence necessary to elicit sparkles from the flint. What follows next? that it, 'like a current, flies / each bound it chafes.' This may mean that it expands itself notwithstanding all obstructions; but the images in the comparison are so ill-sorted, and the effect so obscurely expressed, that I cannot but think something omitted that connected the last sentence with the former."* But in the verse of the mature Shakespeare such disconnections and collocations are common; we have seen how powerful the "ill sorted" images of Lady Macbeth could be ("Was the hope drunk / Wherein you dress'd yourself?") and sometimes ill-sortedness can occur without comparable power, as here. The sentiment that "poesy" is an almost involuntary, effortless oozing is expressed with much inappropriate effort: it is like a gum, we are told, not like a spark from a flint; it provides its own momentum like a river overflowing its banks. The "chafing" river has so little associative connection with the oozing tree that Johnson thought something must have been left out. But the conjecture is unnecessary. Only the Poet uses this kind of language; the Painter is by comparison simple. The Poet talks in this self-regardingly elaborate way because he is a Poet, and he keeps it up whether he is approving the Painter's likeness of Timon ("To th' dumbness of the gesture / One might interpret" [33–34]) or describing his own tribute to the great man:

> My free drift
> Halts not particularly, but moves itself
> In a wide sea of wax; no levell'd malice
> Infects one comma in the course I hold,
> But flies an eagle flight, bold, and forth on,
> Leaving no tract behind.
>
> (45–50)

One's intuition that this is not really meant to be clearly understood is confirmed by the Painter's rejoinder: "How shall I understand you?" (51). "Halts not particularly" is intelligible—doesn't dwell on individual aspects of the man—but the "wide sea of wax" will give anybody pause; indeed, it is

***Johnson on Shakespeare*, p. 707.

safe to say that nobody knows what it means. The usual conjecture concerns wax tablets, as used for writing in the ancient world. It strikes me as more likely that it is a very forced way of referring to the sea as "waxing," in the sense that the moon does; so this is a full sea as opposed to a "drift" capable of analysis into "particulars," a situation in which the imagination is not cramped by detail but remains free and powerful. The notion of "malice" infecting a "comma" is also difficult, but the comma is here less an orthographical device than another way of saying "a particular," a detail, the idea being that in not halting at particulars the Poet shows that his purpose is not to satirise such things, since he has grander plans in mind. But these are guesses, and the lines are clearly meant to be baffling; the contrast between poetry of this kind and the kind of poetry it purports to describe is obvious, but any benefit it confers is obtained at the expense of baffling all the auditors. In responding to the Painter's confession that he cannot understand him, the Poet spells things out more plainly: "I will unbolt to you," he says (51). What the open door reveals is an allegory, but the Painter sticks to his point that the allegorical message could be expressed in a painting "More pregnantly than words" (92).

The *Paragone* concerns relative value, and *Timon of Athens* is full throughout of talk about value, estimation, and so forth. It also concerns flattery and the corruption of art by greed. But the immediate point is that the scene is written with deliberate care, with a strength that occasionally seems muscle-bound, and with some satirical intent. (The Poet is of course a sycophant, and this shows in the way he speaks; it may be hinted that poetry more generally can be similarly accused.*) In being so fully finished, with such deliberation of manner and evident polish, the whole scene differs markedly from other passages in the play. The change is obvious in the dialogue that opens the next scene, which seems plain and flat by comparison:

> It hath pleas'd the gods to remember my father's age,
> And call him to long peace.
> He is gone happy, and has left me rich.
>
> (I.ii.2–4)

*William Empson, in a famous essay, points to "a delicate irony on the part of Shakespeare" when "the Poet describes how he has written what amounts to the play of *Timon* as a means of flattering Timon and getting money out of him." ("Timon's Dog," in *The Structure of Complex Words,* p. 180).

And the speech of Flavius, I.ii.191–204, can hardly be anything other than a rough draft. It is curious to speculate that Shakespeare might have worked in this way; other poets who began with rough, prosy versions are Ben Jonson and Yeats.

It was now necessary to get on with the action of the play, to which the *Paragone* contributes nothing directly. The verse, specially honed and complicated for the set piece, is now merely cruising. The dialogue fluctuates without apparent point from verse to prose, and has a distinctly unfinished look; it seems less interested, and is certainly less highly wrought.

It is surprising, one is almost willing to say un-Shakespearian, to use and to develop so devotedly a prefabricated scheme in quite the way the playwright did in the opening scene. Act V of *The Merchant of Venice* contains what is, as we have seen, quite close to a formal *laus musicae* (there were set ways of praising music) but more allusive, less rigid. The effect of prefabrication or rigidity is confirmed by the next set piece, the Banquet of Sense. Unlike the preceding dialogue, this episode is crafted. The masque is introduced by Cupid:

> Hail to thee, worthy Timon, and to all
> That of his bounties taste! The five best senses
> Acknowledge thee their patron, and come freely
> To gratulate thy plenteous bosom. There,
> Taste, touch, all, pleas'd from thy table rise;
> They only now come but to feast thine eyes.
>
> (I.ii.122–27)

The "topic" of the Banquet of Sense was frequently developed in painting, especially in the Netherlands, and is not unusual in the literature of the time. Ben Jonson used the scheme at least three times (*Poetaster* IV.v, *The New Inn* III.ii,* *Loves Welcome, The King and Queenes Entertainment at Bolsover*). George Chapman, admittedly a recondite poet, devoted a long

*Give me a banquet o'sense, like that of *Ovid,*
A form to take the eye; a voice, mine ear;
Pure aromatics to my scent; a soft
Smooth, dainty hand, to touch; and, for my taste,
Ambrosiac kisses to melt down the palate.

Shakespeare alludes to the theme in *Venus and Adonis* and *Antony and Cleopatra.* For the Banquet of Sense as a *topos,* see my *Shakespeare, Spenser, Donne: Renaissance Essays,* pp. 84–115.

poem to the theme. Banquets (which usually meant, in the English of the time, minor repasts, not dinners) are not in themselves deplorable, but in painting and poetry they demonstrate a sensuality which, out of the control of reason, leads to other sins. Cupid here speaks first of the lowest powers of the soul, the senses of taste and touch, the last associated with sex. The banquet represents the temptation to follow, downwards, the urgings of the senses rather than take the steep upward path of heroic virtue. There is always an implicit contrast with the heavenly banquet, the Eucharist. Shakespeare will not allow us to forget this—hence the allusions to the Last Supper: "the fellow that sits next him, now parts bread with him, pledges the breath of him in a divided draught, is the readiest man to kill him" (I.ii.46–49); "Who can call him / His friend that dips in the same dish?" (III.ii.65–66); and "It grieves me to see so many dip their meat in one man's blood" (I.ii.40–41).

In the text as we have it, not a great deal is made of this scene, though in performance, provided with music and choreography, it might be another matter. Structurally it must have seemed a good idea to balance this last banquet of the prosperous Timon (in which he administers all too fully to the sensual pleasures of his base guests) with its opposite, where the feast is a mockery, an occasion for him to reject those who had rejected him (III.vi), and the servings are of stones and lukewarm water, tasteless, colourless, odourless, with no appeal to the senses: "Uncover, dogs, and lap!" (85). Timon in his rage throws the water and the dishes in their faces, raving the while; they scramble for their caps and gowns and depart.

So there are these set pieces, the *Paragone* and the opposed banquets. Another deliberate structural device, though of a different kind, is the repeated use of the word "dog," the subject of a subtle study by William Empson. The cynic Apemantus invites the appellation "dog" because he is a snarler, but dogs also fawn; dogs flatter but also love their masters. ("Cynic" comes from the Greek for "dog.") From some of his references to them Shakespeare is thought not to have liked dogs, especially spaniels, which slaver. Timon does say to Alcibiades, "I do wish thou wert a dog, / That I might love thee something" (IV.iii.55–56), but this only implies a minimum of love that is nevertheless greater than any he can afford Alcibiades. The word occurs twenty times in this quite brief text* and is obviously meant to

*There are more allusions to dogs in *Two Gentlemen of Verona,* but that is explained by the fact that the dog Crab is quite an important character.

be hammered into our ears, with all its semantic complexities. And yet, as Empson also felt, the trick of insisting on a particular point or metaphor by much repetition doesn't seem to work in this play; one feels that these allusions are stuck in, as it were, and they do not one feel constitutive of the text, as "honest" is in *Othello.* And yet they are possible evidence of how Shakespeare sometimes went about his business.

Apemantus, the Cynic commentator, is there as soon as the action begins; he sees through everybody and knows the evil of wealth and the falseness of Timon's guests, but also, which he finds just as contemptible, Timon's own mad generosity. His role in the early scenes is to provide commentary on this crazy extravagance and on the greed and flattery of Timon's suitors. It is in the final flyting encounter in the wilderness that he comes fully into his own.

Meanwhile, Timon has been somewhat over-schematically rejected by his "trencher-friends" (III.vi.96) and by everybody else except his faithful steward; he has given his last banquet and retired to the woods. Now he begins a series of tirades of wider scope. He rages against the world at large, against all human relations, and especially the sexual, much in the manner of the mad Lear: "Destruction fang mankind!" (IV.iii.22). From feasting he descends to digging for roots, and as he does so finds gold, the "yellow slave" (34) that corrupts human society. He is now visited by various characters, either exemplary or necessary to the plot, slight as it is.

Of these hate-filled speeches, extraordinary as they are in their rhetorical violence and lexical resource, I think it can be said that they lack the force of the comparable passages in *Lear.* The old King has what in the circumstances is the blessing of true madness. A victim of foully cruel ingratitude, he has given away royal power, not merely money, and he is old. Timon's petulance is certainly on the heroic scale, but his hatred of men and women derives from a disappointment which may not seem quite grave enough to justify his condemnation of society and indeed of the planet. He comes to see himself as a mere type of hatred: "I am Misanthropos, and hate mankind" (54). Confronted by Alcibiades and his whores, he condemns first war and military honour, and then sex. As his own name remembers the Greek word for "honour" or "value," that of the whore Timandra combines the senses "worth" and "man." It was traditional that prostitution was a form of usury, the lending of bodies at interest, and as usury is sinful, this form of it brings on the punishment of sin, in the form of sexual diseases. Thus a hatred of money and a hatred of sex coalesce in Timon's diatribes, and in his showering gold on the willing whores. Alcibiades is urged to slaughter without mercy:

Put armor on thine ears and on thine eyes,
Whose proof nor yells of mothers, maids, nor babes,
Nor sight of priests in holy vestments bleeding,
Shall pierce a jot.

(124–27)

("Proof" refers to the toughness of the armour.) The whores will take all he can give, including the insults: "Paint till a horse may mire upon your face: / A pox of wrinkles!" (148–49). Timon (151–66) spells out the horrors of syphilis, urging the women to spread it. These lines have an hysterical eloquence, matched by his prayer that the earth no longer breed humans but only hideous or dangerous animals.

And so the time is ripe for the climactic slanging match with Apemantus, who begins by accusing Timon, in his role of hermit and hater of mankind, of mimicking his manners. Timon insults him back: he imitates Apemantus for want of a dog to mimic. Apemantus, now speaking verse, explains why he resents Timon's imitations and why Timon will find no flatterers in the state of nature. Here again there are echoes of *Lear:*

Call the creatures
Whose naked natures live in all the spite
Of wreakful heaven, whose bare unhoused trunks,
To the conflicting elements expos'd,
Answer mere nature; bid them flatter thee.

(227–31)

The comparable passage in *King Lear* is:

You houseless poverty . . .
Poor naked wretches, whereso'er you are,
That bide the pelting of this pitiless storm . . .

(III.iv.26ff.)

But Lear, at this moment of self-knowledge, speaks a poetry of pity for the destitute, whereas Timon rails against "mere" (pure, and in the context "unmerciful") nature and speaks for beasts, not men. Timon's talk here is as excessive as it was when he was the universal benefactor, the parody of a generous man, as Apemantus, with no intention but to be disagreeable, correctly states:

If thou didst put this sour cold habit on
To castigate thy pride, 'twere well; but thou
Dost it enforcedly. Thou'dst courtier be again,
Wert thou not beggar.

(IV.iii.239–42)

Timon, in reply, sounds like Lear again: Apemantus was never bred to power and luxury, so it is all the harder for Timon, who was. But Apemantus is right: "The middle of humanity thou never knewest, but the extremity of both ends" (300–1). The dialogue descends to prose, and then to the merest yelling: "Beast! Slave! Toad! . . . Rogue" (371–74). As Timon prepares for his death and once more curses gold, the Banditti arrive, gladly receive gold, and provoke an amazing speech on thievery as the motive power of the universe:

I'll example you with thievery:
The sun's a thief, and with his great attraction
Robs the vast sea; the moon's an arrant thief,
And her pale fire she snatches from the sun;
The sea's a thief, whose liquid surge resolves
The moon into salt tears; the earth's a thief,
That feeds and breeds by a composture stol'n
From gen'ral excrement; each thing's a thief.
The laws, your curb and whip, in their rough power
Has uncheck'd theft. Love not yourselves, away,
Rob one another.

(435–45)

This is wonderfully bitter and full of energy, though 443–45 is hard to explain until one feels the force of the nonce-word "uncheck'd": the law, which was meant to check theft, now allows it, having seen that the unchecking is done by all the forces of nature, indeed by "each thing." "Your curb and whip" is addressed to the thieves, whose profession is licensed by the lawless thievery of the entire world. The grandeur of this perverse anacreontic—a verse form in praise of love or wine, amatory or convivial—is at once "placed" as hysterical by the reaction of the bandits. They are criminals who, as they often do in Shakespeare, have a professional charm; they take the gold and say they will think about becoming honest later on.

Flavius the steward, next in the procession of visitors, provides the sole counter-example of honesty and fidelity. It is hard not to see the hero of this play as being constantly under ironic surveillance; it is the price of his high misanthropic language. Poet and Painter, having heard about the gold, now return, with revised plans for flattering Timon in his new circumstances; they are teased and driven away like dogs. The Senators, come to ask Timon to save Athens from Alcibiades, are rejected just as contemptuously. And Timon makes his last pronouncement, this time giving notice of his own death. It is as grandiose as his misanthropy:

> say to Athens,
> Timon hath made his everlasting mansion
> Upon the beached verge of the salt flood,
> Who once a day with his embossed froth
> The turbulent surge shall cover . . .
>
> (V.i.214–18)

"Embossed" here means "foaming," but it carries other senses, including, perhaps, that of rhetorical inflation and, perhaps, of an animal foaming at the mouth.* The assonance of "turbulent surge" is also very grand, and so are Timon's two epitaphs—they contradict each other in detail, and the author must have meant to strike one of them out (V.iii.3–4), but they agree in sentiment: "Here lie I, Timon, who, alive, all living men did hate" (V.iv.72).

It is usual in this connection to cite a remark of Aristotle in the *Politics* to the effect that a man without benefit of a community *(polis)* must be either a beast or a god. Timon illustrates the saying; in the city he regards himself as above its ordinary dealings, contemptuous of common sense, distributing largesse like a benevolent god; in his chosen state of nature he is not much different from the beasts with whom he compares himself. The language of the play reflects the divine aspirations of the godlike Timon, his pretensions exposed by the flattery of the artists and the cynicism of Apemantus. Timon, reduced to the condition of nature, where roots are more valuable than gold, cannot accept civility from anybody, is coarser than Apemantus, and speaks a language as ironically qualified by the context as that of the earlier scenes; he lives not in a state of nature but in a state of misanthropy, now extended to

**O.E.D.:* emboss . . . v1, 1b and 2, 3, giving contemporary examples.

include pretty well everything. What he most specifically rejects, as Aristotle might have predicted, is Athens, the *polis* that bred him. In both halves of the play Apemantus, with appropriate support, is around to comment on his self-deceit. The language of Timon's tirades against society and the universe in general is truly spectacular, but shown to be in excess of any language of just complaint.

If the play is unfinished, the reason may be that its thunder had been stolen in advance by *King Lear*. Or perhaps the scheme proposed was too rigid, too diagrammatic, almost too academic. Or possibly Shakespeare and his collaborator came to think it not only lacking in action but, at any rate in the second half, too monotonous. We cannot know how many projects were sketched by Shakespeare, with or without collaborators, and then, perhaps, developed up to a point, before being discarded. And it is not likely that we shall ever know in detail how this play got into the Folio.

CORIOLANUS

Coriolanus, the last of Shakespeare's tragedies, is his most political play—not in the sense that it alludes openly to the politics of 1607–8, its probable date, but more abstractly. It is a study in the relationships between citizens within a body politic; the relationship of crowds to leaders and leaders to led, of rich to poor. The *polis* has its troubles: dearth, external enemies, enmity between classes. The patricians have a ruthless but narrow and selfish code of honour. The people are represented by tribunes who are in their own way equally ruthless, scheming politicians. The monarchic phase of Roman history has recently ended, the kings replaced by an oligarchy tending to be oppressive, committed to warfare as the ultimate proof of valour and worth, and largely indifferent to social obligation.

Coriolanus is their great warrior, bred to believe that personal merit can be measured by the number of wounds sustained in battle, saviour of the city but inept in dealing with the commonalty, an ugly political innocent. The early years of King James I had seen popular disturbances in England, and a royal proclamation of 1607 stated that "it is a thing notorious that many of the meanest sort of people have presumed lately to assemble themselves riotously in multitudes."* The virtues and defects of aristocracy had been

*For an account of these disturbances and their possible relevance to the play, see Geoffrey Bullough, ed., *Narrative and Dramatic Sources of Shakespeare,* Vol. V (1964), pp. 455–59.

demonstrated, towards the end of Queen Elizabeth's reign, by the career of the Earl of Essex, a bold commander but a threat, ending fatally for himself, to state security. A sermon that William Barlow preached in 1601 characterised Essex as an ungoverned governor: "great natures prove either excellently good or dangerously wicked: it is spoken by Plato but applied by Plutarch unto Coriolanus, a gallant young, but a discontented Roman, who might make a fit parallel for the late Earl." But *Coriolanus* is not a veiled comment on contemporary politics. Its application is far more general: it concerns the education of an elite, the relations of power and need in a state, the tragic end of a great but exorbitant hero. Shakespeare hardly looked further than his well-thumbed Plutarch for the story, but he imposed a scheme on the material (which he adapted pretty freely) and wrote the play in a harsh, rather cold style suited to its theme of glorious war and civic strife.

Indeed, this is probably the most difficult play in the canon, and it prompts one to think again about the problems it must always have set audiences and readers. It is true that the original audiences, many of their members oral rather than literate, were, as I mentioned in the Introduction, trained to listen and must have been rather good at following. Still, one might well ask what "following" entails. In Shakespeare's plays, especially after 1600, say from *Hamlet* on, the life of the piece, the secret of personation, is in the detail, and we need to understand as much of that as we can.*

Coriolanus amply illustrates these new conditions. It has passages that continue to defeat modern editors, for example I.i.257–58, 276–78, and I.ix.45–46: "When steel grows soft as the parasite's silk, / Let him be made an overture for th' wars!" Philip Brockbank, a first-rate editor, needed a note of almost a thousand words to justify his reading of "ovator" for "overture"; whichever is right, the sense remains much too obscure for an audience to pick up in the theatre. There are many such passages in the late plays. Once in Stratford I asked a well-known actor how he would deliver some lines in *The Tempest* that still baffle commentators: "But these sweet thoughts do even refresh my labors, / Most busil'est when I do it" (III.i.14–15). He said he

*See Gurr, *The Shakespearean Stage,* pp. 99–100. Personation, says Gurr, was "a relatively new art of individual characterisation . . . distinct from the orator's display of passions, or the academic actor's portrayal of . . . character-types." It seems impossible to exaggerate the effect of this change on the resources of the playwright; a change in acting style, the developing technique of Burbage and the others, made possible a new flexibility and an increased range and depth of dramatic language.

would try to speak them *as if* he understood them perfectly. The idea was to prevent the audience from worrying about the meaning, the next best thing to making the meaning clear. Of course the actor mustn't seem to be baffled, for that would be a false note in the characterisation. The meaning is best left to editors and commentators. I myself, when editing *The Tempest,* wrote a note of about a thousand words on the passage, to nobody's great benefit.

However, there are times when obscurity is actually part of the personation, when a character is meant to be baffled and to show it. In *Cymbeline* Jachimo makes a bewildering speech to Imogen, ranting on about Posthumus's imaginary bad behaviour in Italy, where, it is claimed, he was unfaithful to Imogen. Here is the latter part of Jachimo's tirade:

> It cannot be i' th' eye: for apes and monkeys
> 'Twixt two such shes would chatter this way, and
> Contemn with mows the other; nor i' th' judgment:
> For idiots in this case of favor would
> Be wisely definite; nor i' th' appetite:
> Sluttery, to such neat excellence oppos'd,
> Should make desire vomit emptiness,
> Not so allur'd to feed.
>
> (I.vi.39–46)

The expression is so tortuous (and his subject so improbable) that Imogen cannot follow him and asks, "What is the matter, trow? . . . What, dear sir, / Thus raps you? Are you well?" (47, 50–51). We must think of Jachimo's speech as delivered at speed, an impression confirmed by the lines with weak endings ("and," "would"), the strangeness of the language about apes and monkeys, and the complexity of the last two lines: confronted with such "Sluttery" (meaning Posthumus's Italian mistress) sexual desire would strive to evacuate itself like someone vomiting on an empty stomach. The huddle of figures (apes, idiots, vomiting), the remoteness of the language from its theme, the mysterious air of disgusted excitement—considering these aspects, the response of Imogen and presumably of the audience is intelligible.

Such writing is very different from the tone of Richard II's great soliloquy (see above, p. 43) and is most striking when it is used to imitate the actual movement of thought in a character's mind. He may be studying a situation and deciding how to deal with it. Consider Brutus in the orchard (*Julius Caesar,*

II.i). He is on the brink of a terrible decision, whether to spare Caesar or to kill him; but there is not much in the lines to suggest great perturbation:

> It must be by his death; and for my part,
> I know no personal cause to spurn at him,
> But for the general. He would be crown'd:
> How that might change his nature, there's the question.
>
> (10–13)

Julius Caesar is dated 1599, just before what I take to be a sort of revolution in Shakespeare's language. When we compare this with the speech from *Coriolanus,* written eight or nine years later, that I quoted in full in the Introduction (p. 14), we see clearly the change that had come over the language of the writer who dominated this great decade of English drama; we must infer that the change had affected the understanding of the "understanders" who heard it in the theatre. They had been trained to deal with such shifts. What we feel, even before we start to unpack the language, is its pace, its sudden turns and backtrackings, its metaphors flashing before us and disappearing before we can grasp them. We recognise the representation of anxious thought, a weighing of possibilities, a weighing of Coriolanus. Aufidius proposes a theory or explanation but abandons or qualifies it almost before he has uttered it, as a person might do under the pressure of similar considerations. This kind of thing was now being done in verse for the first time. If one had to say where it was first achieved, one might say in Claudius's soliloquy in *Hamlet,* III.iii.

The gradual toughening and gnarling of language, accompanied by a new freedom and variety of metaphor and a more rugged pentameter, are well-recognised features of Shakespeare's later work. But *Coriolanus* illustrates another and less obvious change. As I have tried to show, the earlier plays do on occasion indulge a passion for particular words, their chimings and repetitions and their semantic range; *Love's Labor's Lost* is an instance. In that play, and in other comedies, there is a good deal of play with what I have called, in Virginia Woolf's expression, "little language." "The Phoenix and Turtle" is in this sense an exercise in little language. Not much later comes the intricacy of the lexical chains in *Troilus and Cressida, King Lear, Macbeth,* and *Timon of Athens.* In *Coriolanus* we have this lexical and syntactic habit in its full maturity: stubborn repetition, free association, violent ellipses; in short, a prevailing ruggedness of tone.

The opening act as a whole is long and military. It begins with a prose scene in which the plebeians rehearse an uprising, but their complaints are interrupted by the arrival of Menenius, who makes his celebrated comments about the interrelation of the parts of the body politic, allegorised as parts of the single human body (I.i.96ff.). This speech has its origin in Plutarch but is also indebted to a contemporary publication, Camden's *Remains* (1605). It is, like many Shakespearian overtures, a carefully composed thematic statement. The mutinous talk of the people is what the plot requires us to attend to, but without Menenius's speech we should not have borne in mind the larger ideological context. More important, we should not have been ready for the extraordinary network of allusions to parts of the body in later scenes.

Once upon a time the limbs revolted against the belly because it seemed to do no work. Menenius, a jovial character, very loveable in his dealings with his peers, is trying to act as a go-between, though privately he detests the plebs. He explains the essential service done by the belly for the mutinous members (he calls the leading citizen "the great toe of this assembly" [155]). At the simplest level of plot this scene, despite its ostensible good humour, alerts us to the state of affairs between patricians and plebs; until the entrance of Coriolanus the tone is almost bantering. Menenius's leisurely lines—one of the few seemingly leisurely passages in the play—quietly establish a kind of lexical grid. "The great toe of this assembly" is a joke, but it introduces language that is later no joke at all, when anger commands the scene and we are bombarded with body parts: breasts, hearts, palates, teeth, belly, and bosom, above all mouths and tongues and what issue from them, voices.

Voice, in the English of the time, was the word for "vote." Shakespeare never uses the word "vote," and it would have suited his purposes much less well, for "voice" relates the suffrage of the people to their disgusting bodies. When Coriolanus is forced to solicit the voices of the people by showing them his wounds he is reluctantly electioneering, and the bribe he offers is the most precious commodity of his caste, wounds sustained in battle. "I have wounds to show you . . . Your good voice, sir . . . if it may stand with the tune of your voices . . ." (II.iii.76–86). He must offer these in return for the voices of the people who, in his strong opinion, should not have voices or votes anyway. But the "voice of occupation," that is, of the proletariat (IV.vi.97), has to be heard. It is Menenius, appalled at the news of Coriolanus's approach, who uses that expression, and he associates their voice with their garlic breath so that their votes stink of their wretched diet. Soon their voices represent their whole bodies and certainly their power. Their voices exiled Coriolanus; they "hooted" him out of the city; Cominius adds that he's afraid they will "roar him in again" (124). They will be paid for their "voices" (136); "Y' are goodly things, you voices!" (146).

All these illustrations, coming from a single scene and all depending on a bold use of synecdoche as well as on the insistent repetition of "voice" and "voices," are very deliberate. *Coriolanus* is a play about anger, but it is calmly plotted. To Coriolanus the crowd is an anonymous, diseased body made up of individual vile bodies that unfortunately can be transformed into potent voices that are capable of making intolerable demands on his honour. From his first lines he despises their vileness, while Menenius greets him as "noble," an appellation very frequently bestowed on Coriolanus; it soon becomes tinged with irony. The epithet applies only to patricians; the opposite of "noble" is "vile." "What's the matter, you dissentious rogues, / That rubbing the poor itch of your opinion / Make yourselves scabs?" (I.i.164–66). Here at the outset a plebeian political protest is represented as a bodily disease. The itch, a disease of poverty, along with stinking breath and sweat, stands for opinion, ever fallible and ever the word for ignorant popular thought.* Later the people are "measles" and "tetters." "The wiser sort" of listener would recognise this opening as a kind of thesaurus packed with meanings to be fully realised only later. Such auditors, borne on by the stream of language, would remember this beginning in order to take their bearings.

The third scene, a conversation between upper-class ladies, is there solely to shed light on the causes of Coriolanus's extraordinary, unbiddable intransigence. It has no source in Plutarch. His mother's attitude to warlike achievement, beside which, in her view, nothing else counts, is expressed in her loving talk of reputation, blood, and wounds. Her language is violent because her love for her son is so involved in his heroically violent feats of arms that only thus can it be expressed. And he is as he is to please his mother. The boy, the son of the hero, also under the rule of his grandmother, is commended for violently tearing a butterfly to pieces: "One on 's father's moods," says Volumnia contentedly; "Indeed la, 'tis a noble child," says her friend Valeria (I.iii.66–67). They speak a familial and a class dialect.† In this society

*See the discussion of opinion, pp. 130ff.

†There is a fleeting reminiscence of this episode when Cominius speaks of "boys pursuing summer butterflies" (IV.vi.94).

loss of blood in war is "physical" (curative) (I.v.18), and to look as if one had been flayed is a mark of honour (I.v.22–29, 57).* The hero's wife, Virgilia, feebly opposes her pacifism to this upper-class military boasting.

In the campaign at Corioli, Coriolanus, as usual, treats the common soldiery as a diseased body and himself behaves less like a man than a war machine. As a result of this action he acquires the name "Coriolanus"—an "addition" that will have a part to play in his death. Names, always important, are now even more so. When Coriolanus asks as a favour that a poor prisoner from Corioli who had done him some service should be freed, the request is at once granted, but Coriolanus cannot remember his name. In North's Plutarch the plea is on behalf of "an old friend and host of mine, an honest wealthy man" whom Coriolanus wishes to rescue from the fate of being sold as a slave. There is no mention in Plutarch—where this incident happens immediately before Cominius awards Titus Martius *his* new name—of Coriolanus forgetting the man's name. Here is a small piece of evidence as to the way in which Shakespeare, working closely to a source, might find interesting interconnections where there are none in the original; Plutarch is not interested in the Volscian's name or whether Coriolanus remembers or forgets it. In Shakespeare the "addition" of a name to Caius Martius involves the subtraction of a name from "a poor man." When Menenius is turned away from the Volscian camp (V.ii) the guards jeer at this confidence in the power of his name, and "name," as we shall see, becomes a central issue in the last scenes.

The tribunes are dismayed at the triumph of their enemy; Brutus (II.i.205–21) gives a wonderfully sour and animated account of Coriolanus's reception in Rome; but they know his weakness and will politically exploit it. The language of the following scene is full of the energy this play derives from its "little language," as in the speech of an "officer" whose role is simply to carry in cushions: "he hath so planted his honors in their *eyes* and his actions in their *hearts* that for their *tongues* to be silent and not confess so much were a kind of ingrateful injury," plucking "reproof and rebuke from

*One notes in the conversation of the women with Menenius (II.i.146ff.) the unquestioned equivalence of wounds with honour: "Where is he wounded? I' th' shoulder and i' th' left arm . . . seven hurts i' th' body . . . i' th' neck . . . i' th' thigh—there's nine that I know . . . twenty-five wounds upon him . . . Now it's twenty-seven." This bizarre accounting, coming from Coriolanus's mother and his friend, tells us much about the ethos of the patricians and about the education of Coriolanus, whom Plutarch described as "churlish and uncivil, and altogether unfit for any man's conversation" (where "conversation" has the broader sense of "company").

every *ear* that heard it" (II.ii.28–34). The speech of Menenius that follows has all the metrical roughness appropriate to a commendation of Coriolanus, and it suits the language of Cominius's eulogy: "He was a thing of blood, whose every motion / Was tim'd with dying cries" (109–10). Menenius can only exclaim "Worthy man!" (122).

Here begins the matter of soliciting "voices," a part that Coriolanus says he will "blush in acting" (145).* He must now wear the "gown of humility" and act the suppliant. Were his scars received only to "hire" the "breath" of plebeians? (149–150). The scenes that follow are extraordinary in the relentlessness of their use of "voice" and related words such as "tongue" and "breath." Should the citizens, they grotesquely but appositely ask themselves, put their "tongues into those wounds and speak for them" (II.iii.7)? Will they give their voices (36), their "own voices with [their] own tongues" (45)? Coriolanus hates their breath, wishes they would clean their teeth, but arrogantly "begs" their "worthy voices" (79–80) and says he will show his wounds "in private" (77).

The weight of the dialogue is always against this hero. All he needs to do to have the consulship, as a citizen temperately points out, is "to ask it kindly" (75). He need not even "counterfeit the bewitchment of some popular man" (101), for the voices are his for the asking. But they are dependent on stinking breath and stand for plebeian bodies. The words "voice" and "voices" occur forty-eight times in the play, thirty-two times in this scene; such battering of the audience is unparalleled in the canon. "Voices" remains a synecdoche for citizens, for "poor people":

> Here come moe voices.—
> Your voices? For your voices I have fought;
> Watch'd for your voices; for your voices bear
> Of wounds two dozen odd; battles thrice six
> I have seen, and heard of; for your voices have
> Done many things, some less, some more. Your voices?
>
> (125–30)

*Coriolanus again thinks of himself as playing a part. See also "You have put me now to such a part which never / I shall discharge to th' life" (III.ii.105–6); Volumnia urges him to perform it (109) and he deplores a rift between the "body's action" and the mind (122), detesting the role of the mountebank (132). Finally, there are: "Like a dull actor now / I have forgot my part, and I am out, / Even to a full disgrace" (V.iii.40–42) and "The gods look down, and this unnatural scene / They laugh at" (184–85).

The Third Citizen in his comment (166–73) uses "voices" five times. Brutus the tribune takes up the cry, adding "bodies," "hearts," and "tongues":

> Why, had your bodies
> No heart among you? Or had you tongues to cry
> Against the rectorship* of judgment?
>
> (203–5)

Coriolanus will not play the part assigned him (124). Since he can only "play / The man I am" (III.ii.15–16), he is plainly not a politician. The opening of Act III repeats the litany of tongues, mouths, teeth, and voices, taste and palate. The plebs are to him merely a disease, physically repellent, and their voices, which sum them up, equally so. It is his failure to see that nevertheless they *are* the city (III.i.198) that changes the perspective and shows him to be the diseased part of the body politic. ("He's a disease that must be cut away" [293].) The first two scenes of this act insist on this theme of disease: sores, gangrene, infection, an iteration consonant with the theme of the body politic as outlined by Menenius. Coriolanus is undone by choler (anger, one of the humours of the body, and when out of control the cause of illness and disease), and he ignores Menenius's counsel: "Put not your worthy rage into your tongue" (240). Doing exactly that, he narrowly avoids execution and is banished from the city. His responses to the sentence are celebrated. "I banish you!" (III.iii.123) and "There is a world elsewhere" (135). Under the sway of the tribunes, scorned by Coriolanus ("You being their mouths, why rule you not their teeth?" [III.i.36]), the people turn into a mob, as Coriolanus turns into a mechanism of violence.

In the last two acts "voice" yields precedence to "name," though one must remember that names are uttered by voices. With great deliberation Shakespeare states (or restates) the theme of names when Coriolanus meets Aufidius in his house at Antium:

> AUF. Whence com'st thou? What wouldst thou? Thy name?
> Why speak'st not? Speak, man: what's thy name?
> COR. If, Tullus,

*"Rectorship," otherwise not used by Shakespeare, is an out-of-the-way synonym for "rule" or "discipline." The use of nonce-words to disturb such a context—all familiar body parts, and all resounding constantly in the text—seems typical of the craft of Shakespeare's later plays.

Not yet thou know'st me, and, seeing me, dost not
Think me for the man I am, necessity
Commands me name myself.
AUF. What is thy name?
COR. A name unmusical to the Volscians' ears,
And harsh in sound to thine.
AUF. Say, what's thy name?
Thou hast a grim appearance, and thy face
Bears a command in't; though thy tackle's torn,
Thou show'st a noble vessel. What's thy name?
COR. Prepare thy brow to frown. Know'st thou me yet?
AUF. I know thee not. Thy name?
COR. My name is Caius Martius, who hath done
To thee particularly, and all the Volsces,
Great hurt and mischief; thereto witness may
My surname, Coriolanus.

(IV.v.52–68)

His friends have forsaken him and suffered him "by th' voice of slaves to be / Hoop'd out of Rome," with no possession other than that name (77–78). "Only that name remains" (73). This extraordinary passage serves, with great economy, to remind us that the entire play is named after an "addition" to the name Caius Martius, and that the loss of this name will cause his death. It is impossible to imagine more deliberate writing; the confrontation of the generals is a pivotal moment in the play, certainly, but so to draw out the moment of mutual recognition beyond the necessity of the action is to compel attention to the matter of naming. The "little language" and the necessities of plot here coincide to wonderful effect.

The generals address each other in the second person singular, suitable for conversation with inferiors and children but also between lovers, and their language hereafter stresses the quasi-amorous nature of a relationship based on heroic fights, on envy. The life of such men is so simplified by their passion for fighting, for name and fame, that joy and pride in these qualities cannot be distinguished from emotions relative to love and sex. "Our general . . . makes a mistress of him" (194–95). But Aufidius also wavers between love and treachery.

The Roman exile has brought his name to the very city where his claim to it will be most resented. Meanwhile, Rome and the tribunes celebrate a phony peace. Threatened by Coriolanus, they might like to "Unshout the noise that banish'd Martius!" (V.v.4). "Unshout" is a monstrous, spectacular nonce-word, absolutely proper to this context, given that it has the support of all those shouts, roars, and hoots, as perhaps to no other. Meeting Cominius, the exile will not answer to the name "Coriolanus," indeed he "forbade all names; / He was a kind of nothing, titleless, / Till he had forg'd himself a name a' th' fire / Of burning Rome" (V.i.12–15). His identity can be retrieved only by the fame of victory, but this time the city to be destroyed is Rome, not Corioli. He has mistaken their names as well as losing his own. He can hardly aspire to be called "Romanus."

He resolves to face his mother without proper filial respect, to behave "As if a man were author of himself, / And knew no other kin" (V.iii.36–37). But this desolation (to be titleless, nameless, kinless) is not sustainable. He gives in to "the most noble mother of the world" (V.iii.49) and to the presence of his son, who, as he is reminded, is destined "to keep your name / Living to time" (126–37). Not to yield, Volumnia tells him, would be to acquire a name "dogg'd with curses" (144), a name "To th' ensuing age abhorr'd" (148). Moreover, he would lose the important epithet "noble" (145), preferring his surname "Coriolanus" to the prayers of his mother and wife (169–71).

The hero yields to his mother and Rome is saved, but he must now deal with Aufidius, whose lethal plot is consummated simply enough by a taunt concerning names—by his calling Coriolanus merely "Martius" and saying the Roman had "whin'd and roar'd away" (V.vi.97) a Volscian victory.

> Cor. Hear'st thou, Mars?
> Auf. Name not the god, thou boy of tears!
>
> (99–100)

Martius got his original name from Mars. The insult to his name, and the insult of "boy"—a man at the beck and call of his mother—together with the sneer about whining and roaring like a plebeian, are intolerable:

> "Boy," false hound!
> If you have writ your annals true, 'tis there
> That, like an eagle in a dove-cote, I
> Flutter'd your Volscians in Corioles.
> Alone I did it. "Boy"!
>
> (112–16)

The terminally stressed "I" at the end of line 114 and the "Alone I did it" of the last line emphasise the self-regard of his claim to fame and to his surname. His enemies end the play with concessive talk of his "noble" nature, for they, too, are in this respect like him, soldiers and destroyers; the word "noble" tolls ironically through the last lines of this savage play, probably the most fiercely and ingeniously planned and expressed of all the tragedies.

The planning, like the ferocity of manner, has largely to do with words. They are so used as to ensure that in this bleak landscape no one is accorded true respect, not the generals, not the populace, not the tribunes, not the mother, not Menenius, and not Coriolanus himself, unless we mishear the undertones of such words as "noble," "fame," and "report." Like his son, who "mammocked" the butterfly, he has been reared to follow a way of life that despises mere civility. He complains that the Romans once "godded" him, but there is no middle way, and when not a god he is a beast, a fitting inhabitant of "th' city of kites and crows" (IV.v.42), until he takes a treacherous refuge with another treacherous hero, in a country which has good cause to hate him, no less for his name than for his fame.

Aufidius, in the last lines of the play, gives his murdered rival a military funeral and promises him "a noble memory" (V.vi.147–53). But the word "noble," and the words "name" and "fame," have acquired dark and changing colours from their disposition in the language of this play; and we are left to consider the mental puzzles so deliberately made to involve us in daunting ambiguities.

PERICLES

Pericles is in some ways another outsider among Shakespeare's plays; it was not included in the Folio of 1623, though it isn't altogether clear why. A quarto version appeared in 1609, and this version was incorporated in the Third Folio of 1664, along with other plays not now thought to be by Shakespeare. A short novel by George Wilkins (1608) apparently derives from the play as performed by Shakespeare's company. The date of composition is disputed; if it was written in 1607, as some say, it may be earlier than *Coriolanus*. For a long time, however, it has been grouped as a "Romance," along with *Cymbeline, The Winter's Tale,* and *The Tempest,* and there are good reasons for this arrangement.

The text of the Quarto is very bad, and it sets editors virtually insoluble problems. However, there seems to be general agreement that Shakespeare had little or no part in what are normally printed as the first two acts. As the Oxford editors remark, "By 1606–8 Shakespeare's poetic style had become so remarkably idiosyncratic that it stand out—even in a corrupt text—from that of his contemporaries, and approximately the last three-fifths of the play . . . betray clear evidence of his presence."* It is nevertheless true that the first scenes also occasionally have lines that sound like idiosyncratic

*S. Wells and G. Taylor, eds., *William Shakespeare: A Textual Companion* (1987), p. 130.

Shakespeare: "The blind mole casts / Copp'd hills towards heaven, to tell the earth is throng'd / By man's oppression, and the poor worm doth die for 't" (I.i.100–2). The scene between Pericles and the fishermen (II.i) might also be accepted as Shakespeare's, but for the most part the early acts are clumsy and perfunctory.

Recognition is a regular feature of dramatic plots, and in the course of business Shakespeare had written many recognition scenes, but the one in *Pericles* has a special importance. Aristotle treated recognition (*anagnorisis*) as that part of the plot which presented "a change from ignorance to knowledge," a change produced by what he called *peripeteia,* a reversal or turning point: the moment when the direction of the story is altered in preparation for the recognition that, "against expectation," as Aristotle puts it, brings it to an end by discovering at last its true course, hitherto concealed. The peripety may signal or occasion the downfall of a tragic hero; in comedy it may bring about an unexpected prosperity. Thus in *Oedipus Rex* the hero's belated understanding that he has killed his father, married his mother, and brought the plague to Thebes is a recognition following on a peripety, a sudden shift in the action.

Recognition is often, but not necessarily, recognition of a person or a relationship established in the past and obscured by time. Whether the term applies to the new knowledge of both the audience and the characters is a disputed point.* A familiar form of recognition occurs in fiction, and especially in romantic stories. In the *Odyssey* the recognition of Odysseus is brought on by the identification of his scar; in other stories it may be a birthmark or some token of identity. The actual scene of recognition may be very long, as in the *Aethiopica* of Heliodorus, a third-century Greek romance.†

Such ancient tales, which have much in common with later romances, were clearly of interest to contemporaries of Sidney and Spenser. Romance plots were popular at the time. Shakespeare builds the Plautine elements of *The Comedy of Errors* into a framework consisting of such a romance story.

*Modern interpretations of the terms "peripeteia" and "anagnorisis" are expounded at length and with clarity in Terence Cave, *Recognitions: A Study in Poetics* (1988), pp. 181–219.

†See Cave, pp. 16–21. For an account of other Greek romances and the continuation of their interests in later fiction, see Margaret Anne Doody, *The True Story of the Novel* (1996). *Daphnis and Chloë,* an early third-century romance by Longus, makes much use of tokens as proofs of identity. The Latin novel *Apollonius, King of Tyre,* from the fifth or sixth century, tells the story borrowed by Shakespeare for *Pericles*—the recognition is brought about by the conformity of detail between the daughter's story and her father's memory.

Two old romantic plays, *Mucedorus* and *The Rare Triumphs of Love and Fortune,* seem to have enjoyed a renewed popularity about the time of *Pericles* and Shakespeare's other romances; his company performed *Mucedorus* in 1610. It has some resemblance to *The Tempest,* and it has been argued that *The Rare Triumphs* anticipates aspects of *Cymbeline*.

The revival of these old plays may reflect a more general resurgence of interest in plays surviving from the reign of Queen Elizabeth. *Philaster,* a play by Shakespeare's younger associates Francis Beaumont and John Fletcher, is "full of echoes" of Philip Sidney's *Arcadia*—and the name "Philaster" is a version of Astrophel, "star-lover," which was Sidney's pseudonym. *Philaster* (1610) was a Blackfriars play, more or less contemporary with *Cymbeline,* which is certainly a Globe play, but was very likely performed at Blackfriars also. *Pericles* lacks the fashionable aspect of these later tragicomedies, but may still owe its existence to a new interest in Elizabethan romance and chivalry.*

The later romances are affected by a new interest in the possibilities of tragicomedy, and *Pericles* is closer than they to the form and shape of its ultimate ancient source. It is simple in its episodic structure, and one feels the whole of Shakespeare's enterprise was to see what could be made of the recognition scene, how it could be drawn out, given the greatest possible emotional force. Like its original, the story begins with incest and ends, by a kind of inversion, in the recognition of Marina by her desolate father, and their subsequent reunion with her mother, Thaisa, long supposed dead. Plots of this kind, in which the heroine is born, suffers vicissitudes of fortune, and is a mature young woman at the end, call for episodic treatment; here a Chorus, the old poet Gower, speaking a fake old-fashioned language, is used to maintain continuity. In *The Winter's Tale,* based on a modern romance story by Greene, Perdita is born at the outset and married by the end, and Shakespeare uses the bolder and in the event more subtle device of introducing Time himself to explain the passage of sixteen years.

It is agreed that in the beginning of what is usually called Act III, as Pericles on shipboard prays against the storm for the safe delivery of his child, and then laments his wife's death, the voice is certainly the voice of Shakespeare:

> A terrible child-bed hast thou had, my dear,
> No light, no fire. Th' unfriendly elements

*See Frances Yates, *Shakespeare's Last Plays* (1975).

Forgot thee utterly, nor have I time
To give thee hallow'd to thy grave, but straight
Must cast thee, scarcely coffin'd, in the ooze,
Where, for* a monument upon thy bones,
The e'er-remaining† lamps, the belching whale
And humming water must o'erwhelm thy corpse,
Lying with simple shells.

(III.i.56–64)

And he places the necessary tokens in the coffin. Here is mature Shakespearian verse, the mixture of end-stopping and overrunning, the violence of "belching," "humming," the strong concluding final line of the sentence (a favourite device), with "Lying" in sudden contrast to the activity of the sea and its inhabitants. Behind this passage there may be a recollection of Clarence's dream in *Richard III* (I.iv.9–33).

Marina is the first of the virgin paragons, the magical and nowadays virtually unplayable romance heroines. When we first encounter her, she is carrying a basket of flowers but complaining in authentic accents: "Ay me! poor maid, / Born in a tempest when my mother died, / This world to me is a lasting storm, / Whirring me from my friends" (IV.i.17–20). She is as yet unaware of the magical quality of her birth, attended by all the elements: "Thou hast as chiding a nativity / As fire, air, water, earth, and heaven can make / To herald thee from the womb" (III.i.32–34). This is virtually a divine nativity. The noun could be used as a synonym for birth in the ordinary way, but usually had a theological or astrological inflection; this is, at least, an unusual child, a child of spiritual power.

The brothel into which Marina is sold by pirates may remind us of the "low" scenes in *Measure for Measure*. She is accused of speaking "holy words to the Lord Lysimachus" (IV.vi.132–33), in this context a shocking, almost blasphemous thing to do, and has herself a speech condemning Boult's obscene trade that has much powerful indignation:‡

*"Instead of."

†Some editors read "And e'er-remaining." The idea is to attach the lamps to the monument she cannot have. The present reading would make the sun and moon the lamps presiding over her burial in the depths of the sea. If the lamps are in apposition to the whales and the water, the sense is very strained; either way, however, the effect is of real sublimity.

‡Yet Shakespeare is kind to Boult, as he had been to Pompey, also a bawd, in *Measure for Measure*. It has more than once been noticed that he reserved a special, sometimes oddly sympathetic voice for murderers, hangmen, and crooks of various kinds. One hears it in Boult's reply to Marina, here quoted.

Thou art the damned door-keeper to every
Custrel that comes inquiring for his Tib.
To the choleric fisting of every rogue
Thy ear is liable; thy food is such
As hath been belch'd on by infected lungs.

(165–69)

Her indignation summons the Shakespearian fondness for the abrupt, violent, usually monosyllabic verb: "fisting" and "belch'd" here, "dodge" and "palter" in *Antony and Cleopatra,* and many such local violences in *Coriolanus*. The reply of Boult memorably provides an instance of a different aspect of Shakespearian style: "What would you have me do? Go to the wars, would you?" (170–71). Marina's just indignation is deflated: it's dark and dirty work but somebody has to do it. And no one is so low as not to deserve credit for wit and good prose, or bad prose that makes an audience laugh, as with Dogberry and Bottom's mechanicals. It is in this world of language that the grandest, with their auras of divinity, must after all work out their missions.

The recognition scene between Marina and her father (V.i) is one of Shakespeare's most remarkable, certainly one of his most carefully composed. Marina is brought on board his ship to cure him. Her power to do so depends on her high birth, her use of music, and her association with the sea, which gave her the name Marina. She is magical, born of the sea like Venus, and in a tempest, so not "of any shores" (103). When we first see her, she is scattering flowers on the water, her mother's supposed grave. She emerges unstained from the ordeal of the brothel and goes to cure her father. He rejects her, but she persists in trying to make him speak. Eventually he does so, saying her beauty makes him think of his wife and daughter. His tone grows exalted:

Prithee, speak.
Falseness cannot come from thee, for thou lookest
Modest as Justice, and thou seemest a palace
For the crown'd Truth to dwell in.

(119–22)

Marina has the attributes of a queen, like Elizabeth in *The Faerie Queene*.

Now Pericles demands her history. She tells him her name, and that she is a king's daughter. But that does not bring about an end, nor does the reference to her royal mother and her nurse, Lychorida, or her talk of Cleon. It must seem that she has said more than enough to satisfy him, but he wants still more confirmation. Even after saying that his joy is so intense that Helicanus must strike him to restore his senses, he still wants to know her mother's name. Only when she gives him that does he bless her. He calls for fresh garments, and hears the "music of the spheres" (229). He has delayed the full recognition and been rewarded for it. Sleeping, he has a vision of Diana, in preparation for the next necessary recognition, with Thaisa.

The extraordinary quality of the scene with Marina depends on its slow-moving length, on the long-awaited union of the aged father and the wonderful daughter, and on the hints and whispers of supernatural agency: Marina's native royalty, signified by her birth from the sea, is endorsed by the music that symbolises cosmic harmony. The second recognition (with Thaisa) is perhaps a mistake, one that Shakespeare would carefully avoid in *The Winter's Tale,* where he was faced with a similar problem in reuniting Leontes with both Perdita and Hermione successively. What is sure is that his interest in the romance plot, combined with his theatrical sense, led him to this very deliberate experimentation in recognition. In *Cymbeline* there is another experiment, this time with multiple recognitions piled one on another, often to rather comical effect.

Shakespeare had written many recognition scenes in the course of his career, but it seems that they now became almost the principal reason for writing plays; and *Pericles,* with its sunderings and reunions, its suffering king and its princess of magic virtue, its interest in the sea and music, is the prototype of the romances with which his career drew to its end.

CYMBELINE

It is often and plausibly said that the acquisition of the indoor Blackfriars Theatre by the King's Men in 1609 had a more or less immediate effect on the work of their chief dramatist. Of Shakespeare's interest in the Blackfriars there is no doubt; he was a shareholder, and even bought a house in the Blackfriars precinct, right across the river from the Globe and close to where the modern Mermaid Theatre stands—a short boat trip connected the two theatres. The company must obviously have taken account of the different conditions: the new house was not, like the Globe, open to the sky; the seats were a great deal more expensive; there could be artificial lighting, subtler music (oboes, not trumpets), and possibly a quieter style of acting. And it is probable that *Cymbeline* and the later plays were performed at the Blackfriars. Yet we know for sure that *Cymbeline* and *The Winter's Tale* were also done at the Globe, where they were seen and described, probably in the spring of 1611, by the astrologer Simon Forman (who died, as he had precisely predicted, on 12 September 1613).

Cymbeline was the first of Shakespeare's plays to have a deity descend, as Jupiter does in V.iv, "sitting upon an eagle," and such spectacular contrivances could have been used at the Blackfriars in imitation of the "machines" of the court masques; but they probably could have been replicated at the Globe.* The late plays, including, almost certainly, *The Tempest*

*See Gurr, *The Shakespearean Stage,* p. 190.

(the most masque-like of them) and certainly *Henry VIII,* a collaboration with John Fletcher, were performed at the Globe, which burned down during a performance of the history play on 29 June 1613. Fletcher, Shakespeare's young successor as chief writer to the King's Men, is firmly associated with the Blackfriars, Shakespeare to a lesser degree; it does no harm to think of his plays as primarily Globe plays during the years between 1598 and 1611 or so. Of course they had often been performed elsewhere, at the Inns of Court, at the courts of Elizabeth and James, in various halls, on various tours in England and abroad. They could be adapted to any stage, certainly to that of the Blackfriars.

Cymbeline, classified by the editors of the Folio of 1623 as a tragedy, is really a tragicomic romance. Tragicomedy, according to the rules drawn up in Italy, should bring characters near to death but not kill them, presenting "the danger, not the death,"* and Shakespeare departs from this rule in despatching Cloten. To put it another way, it is a sort of history play with a romance plot mixed in. The history, or what passes for it, concerns the refusal of the ancient British to pay tribute to the Romans under duress. Having defeated the imperial forces sent to bring them into line, they decide to pay the tribute anyway. There was at the time a vogue for plays about the ancient British; Fletcher wrote one about Boadicea *(Bonduca).* The accession of King James—simultaneously James VI of Scotland and James I of England—in 1603 gave the inhabitants of both countries the right to call themselves British, and to reflect on the historical or prehistorical period when the term had last been applicable. Cymbeline is a king of vague historical record, thought to have reigned at the time of the birth of Christ.

The play reflects two somewhat opposed ideas about the Roman occupation of Britain: the proud islanders must be brave and able to defend their heritage, but the Romans must be welcomed for civilising the natives. Something of this duality is reflected in the way in which the wicked Queen and Cloten, her stupid and boorish son, stand up very nobly to the Roman ambassador Lucius (III.i).

The ancient and implausible story of the wager on Imogen's virtue is taken from Boccaccio; the pastoral tale of the King's lost sons is a familiar romance

*The authority for tragicomedy goes back to Aristotle, *Poetics* XIII. The chief Italian model was Guarini's *Il Pastor Fido,* and the form was closely associated with pastoral; hence Fletcher's *The Faithful Shepherdess* of 1608. In Guarini and Fletcher one finds the Shakespearian themes of royal birth and resurrection from death or seeming death.

theme, and is close to the story of Child Tristram in Spenser's *Faerie Queene,* Book VI.* Among other contemporary prejudices evident in the play one notes a certain tendency to dislike and disparage Italians. The Sienese Jachimo is wicked enough, though hardly a plausible contemporary of Augustus Caesar; he is as cunning in his Italian way as Posthumus is naïve in his British. The play is something of a mishmash, though one sees that it could have made a variety of appeals to its Jacobean audience.

Structurally the plan is that all the plots should come together in a multiple recognition scene in V.v. This scene is sometimes, and rightly, said to have a rather farcical effect, not perhaps altogether unintended. The King is doing honour to the heroic sons with whom he is about to be reacquainted when a doctor arrives with news of the death of his wife. He receives it with eery calm, cheering himself up at the news of his wife's death by reflecting that the doctor will himself die sooner or later:

> Who worse than a physician
> Would this report become? But I consider,
> By med'cine life may be prolong'd, yet death
> Will seize the doctor too.
>
> (27–30)

Learning of her evil deeds, he quickly extends his disapproval of his deceased wife to all women: "O most delicate fiend! / Who is't can read a woman?" (47–48).

Lucius, a polite Roman diplomat and general, arrives with Imogen, now his page. Cymbeline at once falls in love with her, as Lucius had. "His favor is familiar to me. Boy, / Thou hast look'd thyself into my grace, / And art mine own" (93–95). Here, though the neologistic "look'd thyself" does a lot of work, the moment of father-daughter recognition is as curt and hurried as the one in *Pericles* is protracted. This is father-daughter love at first sight, and it has to be got out of the way of all the recognitions to come. The pastoral heroes now identify Imogen as the boy whose funeral they had arranged. Pisanio also recognises her. He confronts Jachimo, who confesses his villainy

*Spenser's Tristram is "a Briton born, Son of a king," and a great hunter. His appearance makes it clear that he is of noble race. He is anxious to learn "the use of arms" and kills a boorish knight who bothers a lady.

at length, whereupon Posthumus reveals his presence. Imogen approaches him, but here there is a total failure of recognition: he mistakes his wife for a male page and knocks her down. Pisanio now has a chance to explain that he did not give her poison, and the druggist Cornelius tells how he substituted benign preparations for the Queen's malignant drugs. These were responsible for Imogen's long sleep, which, although harmless, caused Belarius and his boys to suppose her dead. "My boys, / There was our error," confesses Belarius (259–60).

Now Imogen and her husband at last embrace, with the most venerated lines in the play:

IMO. Why did you throw your wedded lady from you?
Think that you are upon a rock, and now
Throw me again.
POST. Hang there like fruit, my soul,
Till the tree die!

(261–63)

Here the figurative switch from wrestling to horticulture, with an agility unimpeded by the emotion of the moment, has a kind of success that is easier to applaud, or simply register as "Shakespearian," than to explain. Tennyson loved it; he called for *Cymbeline* on his deathbed, and when he dropped the copy and cracked the binding the volume is reported to have stayed open at this place.

Altogether, however, the verse of the play strikes me as over-worked. In *Coriolanus* one rarely feels that the sheer involution of some passages is beyond the necessity of its expression; here I think that feeling recurs. Indeed, the opening dialogue between "two Gentlemen" is already over the top. Its energy does not seem to be that of the Gentlemen, whose linguistic excitement can mean little to an audience; it has nothing to do with characterisation and even serves to obscure the necessary business of exposition. The Gentlemen come on merely to explain why the King is upset by his daughter's marriage and to state, with obscure hyperbole, that she has nevertheless chosen a very splendid husband:

1 GENT. ... I do not think
So fair an outward and such stuff within

Endows a man but he.
2 GENT. You speak him far.
1 GENT. I do extend him, sir, within himself,
Crush him together rather than unfold
His measure duly.

(I.i.22–27)

The struggle with the idea that in straining to praise him the Gentleman has managed to diminish rather than exaggerate Posthumus's virtues seems to be simply a waste of energy—evidence, perhaps, that there was a nervous excess of energy to be wasted. When one remembers the splendidly contrived opening passages of *Julius Caesar, Hamlet, Othello, Macbeth,* and *Coriolanus,* this scene must seem clumsy, albeit very energetic. This excess continues, for example, in Jachimo's verse in I.vi, where admittedly one can find dramatic reason for it, but even the admirable Imogen is often unnecessarily hard to understand. In *The Winter's Tale* the language is often just as difficult, but that play provides occasion for tormented obscurity in the crazed jealousy of Leontes, which is set off against the relative simplicity of the long pastoral act and the calm ecstasies of the Recognition scene. Here the tone is frantic for little evident reason. It is not prompted by the romance story. Posthumus has a right to be upset, but when he talks about it he merely rants in a manner more likely to repel than to attract sympathy; indeed, the effect is sometimes comical.

The text is riddled with inexplicable complexities. Cloten cannot always understand his mother:

QUEEN. . . . so seem as if
You were inspir'd to do those duties which
You tender to her; that you in all obey her,
Save when command to your dismission tends,
And therein you are senseless.
CLOT. Senseless? not so.

(II.iii.49–53)

Cloten catches only one word, the last, and so misses the point, which is simply that he should obey Imogen in everything except when she tells him to leave her alone; and after all "senseless," given the figurative sense in which the Queen uses it, is very strained. A further complexity arises from the fact that Cloten, fool though he is, can on occasion command a kind of eloquence that has vigour and clarity:

> For
> The contract you pretend with that base wretch,
> One bred of alms and foster'd with cold dishes,
> With scraps o' th' court, it is no contract, none;
> And though it be allow'd in meaner parties
> (Yet who than he more mean?) to knit their souls
> (On whom there is no more dependancy
> But brats and beggary) in self-figur'd knot,
> Yet you are curb'd from that enlargement by
> The consequence o' th' crown, and must not foil
> The precious note of it with a base slave,
> A hilding for a livery, a squire's cloth,
> A pantler—not so eminent.
>
> (II.iii.113–24)

Here the notion of an invalid contract is diverted, as it might be in angry conversation, by a consideration of the baseness of Posthumus. His lack of social status is rendered in a familiar Shakespearian context of disgusting food—cold scraps, leftovers from the better sort of people. Cloten then begins to concede that even poor people (even Posthumus) are allowed to marry; the nobility of "knit their souls" is swallowed up at once by the thought that such "self-figur'd knots"—marriage bonds entered into solely at the will of the impoverished parties—are of no importance, since the children that result will be paupers like their parents. Imogen, however, is a different case; she lacks that "enlargement" (freedom from constraint) that poor people and Posthumus have. Her liberty is restricted because she is the heir presumptive to the throne. She is not entitled to stain or deface the reputation of the monarch by marrying a man of low degree and employment, a wretch so far beneath her. The speech has anger and also lexical and logical force. It is curious that of all the persons of the drama such language should be given to Cloten, the stupid Prince.

The sense one has that *Cymbeline* is somehow unserious, that the author was partly at least writing to amuse himself and quick-witted auditors, is confirmed by certain jokes and puzzles in the plotting. Consider, for instance, the matter of Posthumus's handkerchief. When he is forced to leave Imogen he waves a handkerchief; Pisanio reports that he stood on the deck of the ship doing so (I.iii.11–12). The stage direction for V.i is *"Enter* POSTHUMUS *alone with a bloody handkerchief,"* which he immediately swears to keep as a reminder that he had actually wanted to have Imogen killed. It is like a covert allusion to *Othello,* another tale of jealousy and handkerchiefs.

Even odder is the little subplot of Posthumus's clothes. In II.iii Cloten and Imogen have a row, prompted by the remarks of Cloten I've already quoted. In reply Imogen tells Cloten he is so grossly inferior to her husband in nobility that he wouldn't be fit to be the "under-hangman" (130) in the kingdom of Posthumus. To stress her point she says:

> His mean'st garment,
> That ever hath but clipt his body, is dearer
> In my respect than all the hairs above thee,
> Were they all made such men.
>
> (133–36)

This insult is developed as it goes on in the usual mature Shakespearian manner; there is little reason to believe that a large army of men, one for each hair of Cloten's body, would command her respect. But Cloten, as before, does not grasp the whole sense of what is said to him, and seizes only on the insulting allusion to "His mean'st garment," repeating it four times in the course of the remaining twenty lines of the scene. We have learned from one of the Gentlemen in the opening scene that Posthumus is equally meritorious inside and out, so his meanest garment, as a sort of medium between the two, would also be too noble for Cloten. But Cloten is hurt by the remark and can think only of this reference to Posthumus's meanest garment; procuring a suit of Posthumus's clothes, he goes in pursuit of Imogen when she rushes off to Milford-Haven to find her husband with the invading Roman forces. He has a plan to kill Posthumus and ravish Imogen while wearing a suit of her husband's clothes:

> He on the ground, my speech of insultment ended on his dead body, and when my lust hath din'd (which, as I say, to vex her I will execute in the clothes that she so prais'd), to the court I'll knock her back, foot her home again.
>
> (III.v.140–44)

We are bound to wonder why the clothes of the incomparable Posthumus fit Cloten exactly. ("How fit his garments serve me!" he says. "The lines of my body are as well drawn as his; no less young, more strong, not beneath him in fortunes . . ." [IV.i.2ff.].) But he has the bad luck to run across one of the royal boys, Guiderius, who kills him and cuts off his head. Before he does that, Guiderius takes the opportunity of commenting contemptuously on Cloten's (Posthumus's) clothes (IV.ii.81–84). When Imogen awakes from her drugged sleep and discovers Cloten's corpse, she at once identifies it as that of Posthumus, judging by the clothes and the physique of the dead man. (And when she learns that her husband has believed the slander of Jachimo, she describes herself as "stale, a garment out of fashion" [III.iv.51].) Lastly, when Posthumus comes on the scene waving his bloody handkerchief, he announces that he will shed his Italian clothes and dress as a British peasant (V.i.1–24).

This device of the garments is somewhat akin to the repetition of words relating to eyes and sight in *Lear,* which infest the language and then break forth into the action when Gloucester's eyes are put out. But here the effect is of a trick, played in the hope, perhaps, that the wiser sort would find it amusing. The similarity of physique between the two men, such that a wife could not distinguish them if their heads were off, is repeatedly drawn to our attention. Long ago I saw a production at Stratford which tried to disarm the joke by making the clothes of Posthumus absurdly too big for Cloten, but that runs against the very explicit text. The whole garment-body plot is perhaps rather meant to be puzzled over than reasonably accounted for—a little theatrical poser set for a new kind of audience that was likely to enjoy it, like a conceited poem. One would not have tempted the audience who turned up for *Titus Andronicus* with teasers of this sort.

It may well be, as others have suggested, that the scenes of Belarius and the royal children are also not without ironical inflections. The helter-skelter recognitions may also be tongue-in-cheek. Yet certainly at other moments in the play it can be said with confidence that nobody is joking; one of them is the fine speech of Sicilius after the vision of Jupiter:

> He came in thunder, his celestial breath
> Was sulphurous to smell; the holy eagle
> Stoop'd, as to foot us. His ascension is
> More sweet than our blest fields.
>
> (V.iv.114–17)

Here again, as in many such rapt passages, the figuration is surprisingly rapid and unexpected: the smell of the thunder stroke represented as the breath of the god; the menacing swoop of the divine eagle; the word "holy" attracting the word "ascension," of which the first association is probably Christian and liturgical; and the strangeness of "our blest fields," with the suggestion that the fields of heaven are no more blessed than ours, however Elysian they may be.

In such moments, and in the scene of Posthumus's dialogue with his gaolers, we know we are on home ground. The clearing up of the political crisis and the reunions of Cymbeline and his sons and daughter, of his daughter and her husband, are rattled off as if in a demonstration of dramaturgical virtuosity. *Cymbeline* may have set out to please an audience thought, by the dramatist as well as by itself, to be cleverer than the one at the Globe, ready to applaud in-jokes and tricks and sophisticated parody of older, simpler romance plays. If that is so, *The Winter's Tale*—very likely another Blackfriars/Globe play, with its romance plot, its much longer, much more developed pastoral episode—represents a return to a certain seriousness.

THE WINTER'S TALE

The plot of this play belongs to the traditions of romance and tragicomedy, and because we have direct access to its source we can see that much thought went into its devising. Shakespeare based the play on a prose novella, *Pandosto: The Triumph of Time,* written by his old enemy Robert Greene, but he made some significant changes. *Pandosto* was a popular book, first published in 1588 and often reprinted. It is modelled on Greek romance, and Shakespeare underlines the connection by giving the characters new Greek names (Pandosto becomes Leontes, Bellaria Hermione, and so on). He gives Greene's rogue the name Autolycus, in mythology the son of Hermes, under one aspect the god of thieves. There are no originals in Greene for Paulina and Antigonus.

In Greene's story the reunion of Perdita with Leontes ends badly, and Hermione is not restored to life. (Oddly enough, Simon Forman's quite detailed record of a performance at the Globe in May 1611 makes no mention of the Statue scene, but Forman was not a reliable reporter.) Greene allows the jealousy of Pandosto rather more justification than Shakespeare seems to give Leontes. (As Geoffrey Bullough remarks, Greene showed Leontes's suspicions growing, but Shakespeare was "interested, not in the origins of jealousy . . . but in its effects. Leontes' jealousy, like Lear's division of his kingdom, is a postulate which we must accept."*) Hermione's baby is cast away in an open boat, a fate reserved by Shakespeare for Miranda in *The Tempest;* Leontes is persuaded of his error by the oracle. The pastoral material of Act IV has a slightly different flavour, for Greene's Prince is reluctant to become a shepherd in order to win Perdita's love, whereas Florizel is not. The young lovers take ship and are driven by a storm (not by their choice or on the advice of Camillo) to the coast of Bohemia (Shakespeare turns Sicily and Bohemia around). Leontes imprisons Florizel and lusts after Perdita. Ambassadors from Polixenes request the freeing of Florizel and the execution of Perdita, and Leontes agrees to do as he is asked; but the shepherd who had found Perdita as a baby is able with his tokens to convince Leontes of her identity. The marriage of the Prince and Princess reconciles the kingdoms, but Leontes takes his own life.

These and other minor differences tend to show that here, as before, Shakespeare's main interest in pastoral tragicomedy lay in the scenes of recognition, specifically in the mutual recognition of persons parted for a generation, and most of all of fathers and daughters.

Greene describes the growing up of the lost Princess, but Shakespeare, here as in *Pericles,* needs a great gap in time before Perdita is sixteen, marriageable, and capable of the actions which lead to her being reunited with her parents. (Another stock theme, the apparent difference in rank between her and her lover, becomes important in the pastoral episode, with bearings on the outcome.) Since the convention of tragicomedy was that no principal character must be allowed to die, it was necessary to include Paulina's improbable sequestration of Hermione for the same length of time. Paulina, though strongly characterised, is, technically, a character invented to bring on (however tardily) the catastrophe.

The long concealment of Hermione is very audacious, and it has often been remarked that in no other play of Shakespeare's is information of this importance kept from the audience. Indeed, the concealment of vital elements of the story is foreign to the conventions of the Elizabethan-Jacobean

*Geoffrey Bullough, ed., *Narrative and Dramatic Sources of Shakespeare,* Vol. 8 (1975), p. 137. "He considered with himself that Egistus [Polixenes] was a man, and must needes love: that his wife was a woman, and therefore subject unto love, and that where fancy forced, friendship was of no force. These and such doubtfull thoughtes a long time smoothering in his stomacke beganne at last to kindle in his minde a secret mistrust, which increased by suspition, grewe at last to be a flaming Jealousie, that so tormented him as he could take no rest" (159).

stage generally. Obviously the recognition was of the highest importance, and in the design of the play all the elements must serve it. Another practical problem in dramaturgy was that the story actually contained two distinct Recognition scenes: Perdita's with her father, Hermione's with both Leontes and Perdita. Having encountered a similar difficulty in *Pericles,* Shakespeare now sought a better solution: with the same boldness that enabled him to make Time a principal character, he transformed the Perdita recognition into a mere report by anonymous though lively gentlemen (V.ii), which allowed him to concentrate intensely on the second recognition, the Statue scene. If, as some have conjectured (partly because Forman did not report that scene), there was an earlier version of the play in which Hermione was not saved from death and was, as it were, resurrected at the end, one supposes that a Perdita scene would have borne all the emotional weight of recognition, like the comparable scene between Marina and Pericles in the earlier play. But *The Winter's Tale* shifts the emphasis, and the scene of Hermione's return to life is the focus of the entire play. The conclusion remains a matter of reunion between generations, but now it is no longer of father and daughter alone.

In May 1999 a Russian company visited London with a highly professional and deeply considered production of *The Winter's Tale.* Time, at first apparently an old peasant with a broom, uselessly, everlastingly, brushing down the stage, was, at the end of Act III, suddenly transformed into a pretty young girl. The long, often frivolous pastoral in Act IV obviously made the director uneasy and was heavily cut. This was a fault, because it forfeited the contrast of innocence and gaiety with the dark sexuality of the opening scenes. But the director's imagination was obviously much affected by the Statue scene, in which the mood, for him, was less of joy than of a sort of awed dismay. At its end Hermione, Leontes, and Perdita were formed in an unmoving group, themselves a multiple statue. Their reunion had involved something like mutual, enlightened fear. Then Time led on to the stage the dead boy, Mamillius, who had disappeared from the play long before. He knelt a moment before his mother and father, and then Time took him by the hand and led him away.

Despite its apparent infidelity to the text, this version of the scene was extraordinarily affecting and, perhaps, rightly considered, not false but true to the spirit of Shakespeare, who worked hard to induce a sort of religious awe in this scene. The return to life of Hermione seems not a theatrical trick but an epiphany, such that those who experienced it might well seem silent, aghast. At any rate, that was the effect conveyed by that final tableau, Leontes and his family still and silent as Mamillius once again was taken from them.

The statue is described in advance by Paulina as excelling whatever "hand of man hath done" (V.iii.17): "prepare / To see the life as lively mock'd as ever / Still sleep mock'd death" (18–20). It was commonplace to point out the resemblance of sleep to death, and also to speak of painting as surpassing or mocking the reality it portrayed, but here the commonplaces are intertwined: the relation of "still sleep" to death is made parallel to the relation between the work of art and its subject, as if death were the reality and art the fiction that transcends it. As Hermione is supposed by all save Paulina to have been long dead, the statue, when she reveals it, will represent death as a still sleep represents it, yet also be the transcendent fiction. Only when the statue moves do we discover that, as Polixenes explained to Perdita, art is itself an agent of nature (IV.iv.88–97).

Leontes wants to call the statue Hermione, saying that its remaining silent is appropriate: "thou art she / In thy not chiding; for she was as tender / As infancy and grace" (V.iii.25–27). Here is a transition from the silence of the stone to the good nature of Hermione and then, quickly, to the more surprising comparison of the calm of the woman to the tenderness of a child ("infancy and grace" may be an instance of hendiadys: "childlike grace," or the like). It is the measured pace and certainty of such speeches, their easy movement from one unexpectedly apt figure to another, that marks Shakespeare's late style at its most beautifully assured. It can go on without a break to the comment that this representation of Hermione is more aged than the real woman had been; but here, too, Paulina's reply is a compliment to the artist, who let go by some sixteen years, as it were mocking the life, outdoing nature.

Leontes dwells on the life of the statue but supposes it false:

O, thus she stood,
Even with such life of majesty (warm life,
As now it coldly stands), when first I woo'd her!
I am asham'd; does not the stone rebuke me
For being more stone than it? O royal piece,
There's magic in thy majesty, which has
My evils conjur'd to remembrance, and
From thy admiring daughter took the spirits,
Standing like stone with thee.

(34–42)

Already the intellectual pressure of the verse of the scene is great. The contrast between "majesty (warm life)" and "coldly stands" brings up the fearful ambiguity of the situation, the poise between nature and art, sleep and death, warmth and cold; the stone is supposed to be cold, yet it stands for the Queen's warm life. It comes to Leontes that it is he who is as cold as the stone, the reason being another attribute of the statue, its majesty (mentioned twice), which has magic force and which has called up to him memories as magicians conjure up devils. Then, with wonderful unexpectedness (the transition being a weak-ending "and"), he makes us look at Perdita, a girl full of vital life but now "Standing like stone with thee"—a mock statue, nature mocking art, but also a figure of adoration. From what Camillo and Polixenes and Paulina say, we infer that Leontes is weeping. He will not have the curtain drawn, and slowly the statue moves out of art into life: "Would you not deem it breath'd? and that those veins / Did verily bear blood? . . . we are mock'd with art" (64–68).*

In one sense Paulina is like Prospero in *The Tempest,* running a show, a scene of magic straight from some old romance. It is the calm intensity of the verse that makes it something else. "There is an air comes from her. What fine chisel / Could ever yet cut breath?" (78–79) is, to my mind, one of the most miraculous moments in Shakespeare. The slow conversion of statue into woman permits pauses like this, for the utterance of lines of extraordinary beauty and intelligence. The chisel belongs to the stone, the breath to a living body; the Queen is between the two. Paulina resumes the role of conjurer:

> It is requir'd
> You do awake your faith. Then, all stand still.
> On; those that think it is unlawful business
> I am about, let them depart.
>
> (94–97)

> . . . her actions shall be holy, as
> You hear my spell is lawful.
>
> (104–5)

*"Mock" or "mock'd" occurs eight times in the play; Mamillius uses it when talking of women's makeup (II.i.14) and Leontes in V.iii.79, when he is about to kiss the statue despite its paint. The sea mocks the shouting of the drowning mariners, and the bear mocks Antigonus (III.iii.99, 101).

The idea of a dangerous sanctity is strong: *procul este, profani.* Music plays, as at so many awed moments in Shakespeare, and one thinks again of Marina and Pericles. "Come; / I'll fill your grave up," says Paulina to Hermione (100–1), and again we may think of Hermione as returning like Alcestis from the grave: "Bequeath to death your numbness" (102). And now the statue is fully a woman: "If this be magic, let it be an art / Lawful as eating" (110–11). The transformation has to be done not by simply pushing the plot along but by miracles of writing. The statue is now a queen, issuing from the hand of "great creating Nature," wrinkles and all. The purpose of art had been to assist its manifestation. All that is now needed is that she should speak, and she pronounces a blessing.

I have tried, without quoting the whole passage, to indicate how it is animated by an intense activity of mind; the sense of reverent awe that accompanies revelations which might have been merely theatrical and even cheap without these benefactions of sense. There is no attempt to escape theatricality; it is simply evaporated. The play is a winter's tale, like the one Mamillius tells his mother in the first act; a sad tale certainly, the onset of a long winter that ends in renovation, in the spring of Perdita and Florizel and the autumn of Leontes and Hermione. Vast poetic resources are evident in this great scene.

Some of its effect comes from the contrast between its language and the language of the rest of the play. It is familiar ground in that it needs different voices in its different parts. In this respect it has something of the versatility of *Hamlet,* though the tones of the first three acts are almost unrelievedly tragic. The language of Leontes's mad jealousy is as difficult as any in Shakespeare, but without the redundant involutions of *Cymbeline;* they are as decorous as the harshnesses of *Coriolanus.*

There is a moment of innocence at the outset, as Polixenes remembers his childhood friendship with Leontes; later they both "tripp'd" (I.ii.76), and what tripped them was sex. The chatter is unserious, but leads directly into the first mention of suspicion. Already, after Leontes's remark that Polixenes would not stay longer at his request, the tone grows a little hectic, in Hermione's joking thanks for a compliment:

> . . . cram 's with praise, and make 's
> As fat as tame things. One good deed dying tongueless
> Slaughters a thousand waiting upon that.
> Our praises are our wages. You may ride 's

With one soft kiss a thousand furlongs ere
With spur we heat an acre.

(91–96)

This is, one might say, Cymbelinian, the figuration as rough as the versification. Shortly afterwards she *"Gives her hand to Polixenes"* (108)—another conventional gesture to be misconstrued—and Leontes begins his mad muttering, "paddling palms and pinching fingers . . . making practic'd smiles" (115–16). He turns to Mamillius to make him as far as possible complicit, but here his unintelligibility has a purpose, for the boy will not understand it, and it is right that we have difficulty with it.

Affection! thy intention stabs the centre.
Thou dost make possible things not so held,
Communicat'st with dreams (how can this be?),
With what's unreal thou co-active art,
And fellow'st nothing. Then 'tis very credent
Thou mayst co-join with something, and thou dost
(And that beyond commission), and I find it
(And that to the infection of my brains
And hard'ning of my brows).

(138–46)

"Affection" in the language of the time means something like "amorous passion"; the Arden editor relevantly cites Romans 7:5: "the affections of sin wrought in us!"* "Intention" means something like "intensity." It is too weak to suppose "stabs" means merely "reaches," for it goes to the heart of the matter and wounds it. It corrupts the spirit with fantasies, with bad dreams, and attaches itself to impossibilities.† The sense seems to be that if "Affection" can do such things with fantasies, it will certainly "co-join" with realities—if with

***The Winter's Tale,* ed. J.H.P. Pafford (Arden edition, 1963), pp. 166–77. Pafford offers this paraphrase of the speech: "You make possible things normally held to be impossible just as dreams do [communicate = partake of the nature of, *O.E.D.* 5]. How can this be? Lust causes one to associate in the mind with persons who are purely imaginary, who do not exist at all, therefore it is very credible that the most unthinkable lustful association can take place between real people: and lust, you have brought about in this case, going beyond what is lawful—and I am the sufferer to such an extent that I am losing my senses and grow cuckold's horns."

†The Folio has a colon after "unreal," leaving the rest of the line to be taken with what follows; but the Folio's punctuation is not dependable.

nothing, then surely with something. That is what it is now doing, and why Leontes's brain is now diseased; he expects the appearance of the traditional symptom of cuckoldry, the growing of horns.

The next speech is Polixenes's "What means Sicilia?" (146), but it cannot mean that he has not followed Leontes's argument, as some critics suggest, only that Leontes's aspect and behaviour have changed as if he were indeed ill; the meaning is more like "Is there something wrong? Are you unwell?" Leontes is meant to be close to unintelligible; his unintelligibility is a strong indication of his disorder, and also a strong hint as to his behaviour in the near future, when he will be coactive with the unreal.

The next dialogue consists of uneasy reminiscences by both kings. Leontes sees himself in his young son—"unbreech'd" and with a muzzled (breeched) dagger—harmless, but with a potential of harm to come later. Polixenes commends his boy as a distraction from adult "Thoughts that would thick my blood" (153–71). The passage, ostensibly tender, has a kind of foreboding. When Polixenes and Hermione withdraw, Leontes gives way to his jealousy. The appropriate vocabulary is rich and horrible, as in *Othello:*

> How she holds up the neb! the bill to him!
> And arms her with the boldness of a wife
> To her allowing husband! Gone already!
> Inch-thick, knee-deep, o'er head and ears a fork'd one!
> Go play, boy, play. Thy mother plays, and I
> Play too, but so disgrac'd a part, whose issue
> Will hiss me to my grave: contempt and clamor
> Will be my knell. Go play, boy, play. There have been
> (Or I am much deceiv'd) cuckolds ere now,
> And many a man there is (even at this present,
> Now, while I speak this) holds his wife by th' arm,
> That little thinks she has been sluic'd in 's absence,
> And his pond fish'd by his next neighbor—by
> Sir Smile, his neighbor. Nay, there's comfort in't,
> Whiles other men have gates, and those gates open'd,
> As mine, against their will. Should all despair
> That have revolted wives, the tenth of mankind
> Would hang themselves. Physic for't there's none.
> It is a bawdy planet, that will strike
> Where 'tis predominant; and 'tis pow'rful—think it—

From east, west, north, and south. Be it concluded,
No barricado for a belly. Know't,
It will let in and out the enemy,
With bag and baggage. Many thousand on 's
Have the disease, and feel't not.

(183–207)

Shakespeare's associative late style is peculiarly well suited to disturbed mental states; the lexicon of jealousy is rich and foul, as we saw when Iago was exploiting it. Here the mouth, much loved except when used for sexual trespass, becomes, debasingly, "neb," a beak or snout, an animal part, a bill. The command to Mamillius that he should go and play now prompts sexual associations: "thy mother plays" (sexually, with the idea that he is a spectator, as at a pornographic display); and "playing" merges naturally with "acting," so he represents himself as having a part to play; but a "disgrac'd part" (unlike that of the rather exceptional "well-grac'd actor" of *Richard II,* V.ii.24).* At any rate, Leontes is not flattering himself by saying that he has a part to play, for to do so will bring him the hisses and contempt reserved for bad performances and cuckolded husbands.

The thought of cuckoldry brings him to the next self-inflicted grossness: his wife has been "sluic'd," a verb used in many contexts, though not often by Shakespeare; the unpleasant notion is of stopping up a conduit (like the sluices in *Venus and Adonis,* line 956). An alternative figure is that of the ingratiating neighbour feloniously fishing in one's pond.† Leontes now falls into the sort of rant used by Posthumus in *Cymbeline:* the sex of wives is a gate that can be opened by other men. For the despair into which such infidelity plunges the husband there is no cure. Lust strikes women like a planet.‡ That being so, there is no way of fortifying their bellies to keep out

*In *Coriolanus* there is: "Like a dull actor now / I have forgot my part, and I am out, / Even to a full disgrace" (V.iii.40–42). "Out" is a term for the condition of an actor who has forgotten his lines, and "disgrace" perhaps also has some theatrical sense. To Shakespeare's characters it is usually something of a disgrace to be thought of or compared to an actor; others who make the point include Macbeth ("a poor player, / That struts and frets his hour upon the stage" [V.v.24–25]), and the "unperfect actor" in Sonnet 23, where "unperfect" means not knowing his part. Hamlet may be a connoisseur of acting, but he is not an actor; only Polonius makes such a claim (III.ii.101).

†*Cymbeline,* I.iv.88–89: "but you know strange fowl light upon neighboring ponds." And in *Measure for Measure,* I.ii.90: Pompey's "fishing for trout in a peculiar river."

‡So Coriolanus "struck / Corioles like a planet" (II.ii.113–14) and Othello mentions a planet that "unwitted men" (II.iii.182). To be "planet-struck" was to fall under the influence of a planet in its hostile aspect, to be blasted, struck down with illness or madness. Here the planet is "bawdy" and of universally malign influence.

intruders. For a moment the image is military—the intruders come with bag and baggage (with, presumably, an allusion to genitals)—and then Leontes relapses into the well-worn figure of disease, suffered by unwitting cuckolds.

His agitation continues in his conversation with Camillo, his speech once again so tormented with allusion that the interlocutor cannot really make out the sense of what is being said. He gives full rein to his voyeurism. The prurient list of symptoms (I.ii.284–96) has an infected vitality, though it is Hermione he accuses of being infected. Camillo repeats this talk of disease when confiding Leontes's secret to Polixenes: "There is a sickness / Which puts some of us in distemper, but / I cannot name the disease, and it is caught / Of you that yet are well" (384–87). And Polixenes continues the allusion (398, 417–25). He flies with Camillo, and there is a powerful sense that what he flies from is a dreaded disease, suddenly infecting the court of Leontes. (So important in the play is this notion of dreadful infection that Leontes, greeting Florizel all those years later, asks the gods to "Purge all infection from our air whilest you / Do climate here!" [V.i.169–70].)

Mamillius says a sad tale's best for winter, perhaps a precognition of his own death and the fate of his mother, to whom alone he is willing to tell it. Leontes finds confirmation of his suspicions in the flight of Polixenes. Accursed and "pinch'd" by this knowledge but also "blest," he compares himself to a man who finds a spider in the bottom of a cup from which he has just drunk:

> There may be in the cup
> A spider steep'd, and one may drink; depart,
> And yet partake no venom (for his knowledge
> Is not infected), but if one present
> Th' abhorr'd ingredient to his eye, make known
> How he hath drunk, he cracks his gorge, his sides,
> With violent hefts. I have drunk, and seen the spider.
>
> (II.i.39–45)

This is a little allegory of sexual disgust; he is thinking again, as Othello did, that undiscovered adulteries may leave the husband calm, but when he finds them out, the notion of the good wine of his wife's favour becomes disgusting; again he introduces the idea of infection.

We note an extreme physical, nauseous violence in the lines, the tone once more of *Coriolanus,* of some of *Cymbeline,* and a dominant quality in the later verse. This tone reinforces the sense of Leontes's mad and utter conviction; his accusation of Hermione is all torrential violence, the sense barely flowing through the disjointed language. His speech at II.i.64ff., for instance, is surely a representation of a man furiously thinking, like the great speech of Aufidius in *Coriolanus,* with the difference that what is here recorded is *disordered* thought. Hermione's replies have, by contrast, a wounded stateliness. She tells him he "did mistake," but the idea is intolerable to him: his entire existence now seems dependent on the correctness of his belief:

> No; if I mistake
> In those foundations which I build upon,
> The centre is not big enough to bear
> A schoolboy's top.
>
> (100–3)

In its previous usage (I.ii.138) the "centre" seemed to refer to the heart, the seat of emotion; here it means the centre of the earth, his whole world. ("Top" might mean "head" or "cap"; more likely, though, a spinning top.) And he forbids anybody even to speak in Hermione's favour. His jealousy, like Othello's, lacks only "ocular proof," and here the text remembers that passage in the earlier play: "their familiarity / (Which was as gross as ever touch'd conjecture, / That lack'd sight only, nought for approbation / But only seeing . . ." (II.i.175–78).

Leontes careers onward to self-destruction, his language always tyrannical. Hermione stands trial with the sort of dignity that will be seen again in the trial of Katherine of Aragon in *Henry VIII.* The oracle is denied, but after the report of Hermione's death is, too late, believed. At this point Leontes has lost his son and his wife and sent his daughter into a hopeless exile. These first three acts are as fully tragic as those of *Measure for Measure,* although the important little "lighting scene," III.i, describing the reaction of the messengers Cleomines and Dion to the atmosphere of "Delphos," inserted before the Trial scene, creates an expectation that the oracle will ensure that the "issue" is "gracious" (III.i.22). But this expectation is of course falsified in the next scene, and the little episode proves to be ironic; by the time the oracle discloses "something rare" that "will rush to knowledge" (20–21), the show trial is over, Mamillius is dead, and the Queen is supposed to be so.

The opening acts are constructed with great assurance, and the characterisation is powerful, especially that of Paulina, who is given her own voice, and made to stand for female dignity and natural wisdom against male madness. But what impresses one most is the sheer turbulence of Leontes's verse. It is finally burnt out, as we can tell from the closing lines of III.ii ("Come, and lead me / To these sorrows" [242–43]). Now the tone must alter completely, in preparation for the great gap of time between Acts III and IV.

The child Perdita is rescued, but Antigonus is torn to pieces by a bear, a death witnessed by the Shepherd's son. The Shepherd, who has found the child, tells the young man, "Now bless thyself: thou met'st with things dying, I with things new-born" (III.iii.113–14), lines that are rightly taken to announce or predict the comic phase that follows, though a keen ear might hear an earlier promise of a comic outcome from the words of the oracle: "if that which is lost be not found" (III.ii.135–36); in romantic fiction babies abandoned in wildernesses do not die. But now the moment has come to signal a lapse of sixteen years before the business of recognition can begin.

Time, maker and unfolder of error, always changing yet always the same, agent of both change and perpetuity, like Spenser's Mutability, now wishes away sixteen years. This allegorical character is a refinement on Gower, the Chorus of *Pericles*. He introduces the name of Perdita, "now grown in grace / Equal with wond'ring" (IV.i.24–25)—another, though less beset, version of Marina. Obviously an altogether different language is now called for; we are among shepherds, and are to meet this wonderful girl. (She will be presented again in the next play as Miranda.) Nobility of birth will show through humble clothes and occupations. Perdita, a shepherd girl, must be so beautiful that, like both Marina and Miranda, she can be taken or mistaken for a goddess. These parts are almost impossible for modern actresses, for the audience is certain to note a discrepancy between the young woman they see before them and the amazed or reverent compliments she is paid.

Act IV.iii–iv, needed for balance and for contrast with the opening half of the play, is largely a prose entertainment with a fat part for Autolycus, the worst rogue imaginable in this rustic world. But the scenes between Florizel and Perdita, and theirs with the disguised Polixenes and Camillo, clearly call for a change of manner. The innocent sexuality of the Perdita-Florizel relationship is emphasised—the young Prince may fancy he is like Jupiter and Neptune visiting earthly women, but insists on a difference:

> Their transformations
> Were never for a piece of beauty rarer,
> Nor in a way so chaste, since my desires
> Run not before mine honor, nor my lusts
> Burn hotter than my faith.
>
> (IV.iv.31–35)

This emphasis on pre-nuptial chastity is repeated (50) and again by Leontes when the couple arrive in Sicily (V.i.230–31); the point is similarly insisted upon by Prospero in *The Tempest.* The semi-divine maiden must be chaste.

Her foster father reproaches her briskly for neglecting the guests—a fine speech in Shakespeare's busiest manner (IV.iv.55–70). Perdita responds with a set piece on flowers. This is not merely decorative, for it brings on the disagreement with Polixenes about "carnations and streak'd gillyvors" (82), hybrids she will not allow in her garden. They are unnatural because "There is an art which in their piedness shares / With great creating Nature" (87–88). She maintains that these flowers are bastards. Polixenes replies that she has made a philosophical error, for

> Yet Nature is made better by no mean
> But Nature makes that mean; so over that art
> Which you say adds to Nature, is an art
> That Nature makes. You see, sweet maid, we marry
> A gentler scion to the wildest stock,
> And make conceive a bark of baser kind
> By bud of nobler race. This is an art
> Which does mend Nature—change it rather; but
> The art itself is Nature.
>
> (89–97)

But Perdita does not change her opinion, and is given some celebrated and beautiful things to say about the flowers she approves of (103–8, 118–27). She draws from Florizel lines of equal virtuosity: "When you do dance, I wish you / A wave o' th' sea, that you might ever do / Nothing but that; move still, still so . . ." (140–42), where the rhythm mimics the rise and fall of a wave.

Dramatically the dialogue concerning art and nature is full of irony. Polixenes thinks of Perdita as "of baser kind," so he forbids Florizel, a bud of nobler race, to marry her, which seems contrary to the doctrine he has propounded. The conventions of romance ensure that the difficulty will be removed when Perdita turns out to be royal, a fact that also accounts for her beauty and her natural superiority to her circumstances, with which she nevertheless seems cheerfully to comply. It is the wearing of a special costume as mistress of the feast ("no shepherdess, but Flora" [IV.iv.2]) that brings out her true disposition. The text is now full of goddesses: Proserpina, Cytherea, Juno.

But there is more reason than this to include, at this point, a debate about art and nature. As I have already said, the debate is central to the moving of Hermione at the final moment of recognition. There is nothing new about the matter of the debate; one could argue on both sides of it, as Marvell does, taking Perdita's position in "The Mower Against Gardens," but still enjoying art in the gardens in his poem about Appleton House. On the whole, the gardener, representing art, is taken to be the agent of "great creating Nature." There is a predisposition to nobility in some seeds, which have to be nurtured. Gentle birth predisposes one to virtue, the strong bring forth the strong. Education is important, yet it can happen that a noble child, even if thrown into the wilderness at birth, will soon lose his or her barbarous ways and take proper rank. The theme is ancient, and when Shakespeare thought in romance terms it presented itself insistently to him. He was to return to it more explicitly in *The Tempest.* Meanwhile, in *The Winter's Tale,* we have an instance of philosophical romance that called forth his extraordinary linguistic powers, exhibited in all their variety from the onset of Leontes's jealousy until the moment when the statue moves and speaks—in one of the boldest and most beautiful scenes in Shakespeare.

THE TEMPEST

"The value of *The Tempest,*" said Henry James, "is, exquisitely, in its refinement of power, its renewed artistic freshness and roundness, its mark as of a distinction unequalled, on the whole . . . in any predecessor." He thought the story "a thing of naught," but the style, he believed, demonstrated "its last disciplined passion of curiosity."* James's essay expresses a not uncommon opinion as to the high merits of *The Tempest* (often regarded as the last play Shakespeare wrote, except for the works done in collaboration with John Fletcher), and it is unfortunate that James did not support his praise of its style with some close consideration of its language.

Despite the resemblances to the other Romances (which are responsible for the invention of Romance as a separate Shakespearian genre†), *The Tempest* is in some respects *sui generis.* It was probably written with the Blackfriars Theatre in mind, and it may be assumed that the King's Men performed it both there and at the Globe, but no proof of performance at either venue survives. However, it certainly was done at court (probably in the Banqueting House

*Introduction to *The Tempest,* first published in *The Complete Works of Shakespeare* (Renaissance edition, Vol. XVI, 1907); see *Henry James: Literary Criticism* (1984), pp. 1205–20.

†Edward Dowden (*Shakspere: His Mind and Art* [1875]) groups together *Pericles, Cymbeline, The Winter's Tale,* and *The Tempest* as "Romances," and seems to have been the first to give the genre this title.

in Whitehall) on Hallowmas night, 1 November 1611, when it was, if not a new, then still a recent play. It was performed again during the celebrations of the betrothal of King James's daughter Princess Elizabeth to the Elector Palatine during the winter of 1612–13.

The masque was probably in the text from the beginning, though some believe it was added for the royal betrothal (27 December 1612) or the wedding (14 February 1613). It is more suited to the first than to the second of these occasions, since it is an offering to Ferdinand and Miranda, who may be thought of as betrothed but emphatically not as on the brink of marriage.

But the idea that the masque or pseudo-masque* was written into the play for any special occasion is improbable. Other Blackfriars plays have masque-like elements, the King's Men occasionally took a humble part in court masques, and this entertainment may have been following a fashion appropriate to the more courtly pretentions of the indoor theatre. It contributes to the play's magical atmosphere and gives a distinctive quality to its structure. Its verse is different in style from that of the remainder of the play. Of course Shakespeare had long before used a contrasting "recessive" style for plays-within-plays, not only in *Hamlet* but in *Love's Labor's Lost* and *A Midsummer Night's Dream,* and the resort to not very impressive rhyming couplets in the midst of the "late" blank verse of *The Tempest* has no real bearing on the question as to whether the "masque" was there from the beginning. It is plausibly accommodated within the narrative and serves to slow down the movement towards the final scenes of recognition, reconciliation, and dynastic security.

To tell the story of *The Tempest* in the chronological order of its events—to extract what some call the *fabula* from the finished object—one would need first to describe the wicked plot that banished the scholarly Prospero and his daughter, Miranda, their voyage in a leaky boat, and their twelve-year sojourn on an island with two other inhabitants, a spirit and a "deformed slave." Years later, by good luck and with some help from the mage Prospero, the wicked conspirators involved in his overthrow are cast ashore on the island, where they are at the mercy of the ruler they wronged.

*Prospero has to interrupt the proceedings, since masques must end in dancing, in which the aristocratic audience took part. Stephen Orgel remarks, acceptably, that "the masque [in *The Tempest*] is not a court masque, it is a dramatic allusion to one, and it functions in the structure of the drama not as a separate interlude but as an integral part of the action." *The Tempest* (Oxford edition, 1987), pp. 43–44.

Dramatising this narrative straightforwardly ("and then . . . and then . . . and then . . ."), one would need to allow for a long gap, much like the one filled by Time as Chorus in *The Winter's Tale.* With *Pericles* and *The Winter's Tale* as well as more primitive romance plays as precedents, this could have been arranged easily enough.

However, Shakespeare preferred another solution. The play begins when the events of the *fabula* are near their end, with the ship buffeted by a storm and its occupants cast up on to the island. It then treats of the various confrontations between Prospero (with his assistants) and, on the other side, his brother and his associates. It is notorious that in this play Shakespeare, contrary to his usual custom, observed the classical unities of time and place. There is much insistence on the point that the time of the story is the same as the time of the action. And in a sense that entire action is concerned with recognition: the parties are brought together, the guilty are accused, purged, and reconciled—that, essentially, is what happens in the play. The storm and the other magical devices are instrumental in achieving this. It is as if *The Winter's Tale* should have begun when Florizel and Perdita arrive in Sicily. The whole matter of Leontes's jealousy, the flight of Polixenes, the saving of Perdita as a baby and her rustic education, the preservation of Hermione by Paulina, all these events would have had at this point to be explained and the narrative brought up to date.

The design of *The Tempest* is careful, and it would seem that Shakespeare really was attending to the rules for correct five-act construction as they were understood by more classically minded playwrights in his time. The first scene is a prologue; the exposition, or protasis, follows—all that occurred "in the dark backward and abysm of time" is recounted by the end of Act I; and the later act divisions reflect the business of what was called the epitasis, leading to the final catastrophe. The scheme is varied by the inclusion of the incomplete masque in IV.i, and despite the adherence to classical rule, the whole structure is highly original. The paradox is only apparent, for the rules were not intended to prevent originality; as Jonson pointed out, the ancients should be regarded as guides, not commanders. Nevertheless, the exposition—the inclusion of the past in the story of the present, taking the form of Prospero's account of what happened twelve years ago, and how things now stand—seems to have been a little awkward to negotiate, and the awkwardness shows in the language.

The prologue is extremely expert in the rendering of the storm and the reactions of the characters—and it was much admired by Coleridge—but the scene that follows, though neatly diversified by the appearances of Ariel and Caliban, is less so. Prospero explains why he has waited so long to tell Miranda this tale, and putting aside his magic robe (necessary gear, presumably, while he was magically arranging the tempest), he says, "The hour's now come" (I.ii.36) to do so. With some agitation and some bad-tempered admonitions to Miranda, of which the primary purpose is to prevent his having to deliver an unbroken monologue, he then describes the plot that overthrew him.

> Thy false uncle . . .
> Being once perfected how to grant suits,
> How to deny them, who t' advance, and who
> To trash for overtopping, new created
> The creatures that were mine, I say, or chang'd 'em,
> Or else new form'd 'em; having both the key
> Of officer and office, set all hearts i' th' state
> To what tune pleas'd his ear, that now he was
> The ivy which had hid my princely trunk,
> And suck'd my verdure out on't.
>
> (I.ii.77–87)

The general sense is not in dispute: acting as Prospero's deputy, Antonio, once he had learned his job, exercised his authority, granting or withholding favours, promoting some and checking overly ambitious officers, so that Prospero's dependants became his dependants, or perhaps changed them from one dependency to another, or, rather, remodelled them. He had the power of office and control over the administration, so that he called the tune for everybody; he was the ivy that enfeebled Prospero, the princely tree, sucking all his strength. All this is a single sentence, and the unwieldiness of a paraphrase arises from the repetitiveness of the original, the hurry and disconnection of its metaphors.

To "trash" is to restrain a hound; the figure is fleeting, and one wonders if some other sense of "trash" may not be lurking here; in Shakespeare the noun "trash" usually has a sense close to the modern one, and that is how Trinculo uses it in this play (IV.i.224). We remember Iago's triple use of the word in *Othello:* "this poor trash of Venice" (II.ii.303); "Who steals my purse steals trash" (III.iii.157). Shakespeare often invented verbs from nouns, for instance "godded" in *Coriolanus;* "he *words* me" in *Antony and Cleopatra;* and he might be doing something like that in this verbal usage of "trash." But the metaphor doesn't stay long enough to be clearly understood.

The creation of already created creatures (I.ii.81–82) gives a taut, compressed, anxious idea, but the effect is dissipated, no doubt in a further attempt to render Prospero's agitation, by the weaker synonyms "chang'd" and "form'd." The key (83) begins as a door key but immediately becomes a musical key, which enables Antonio to tune his dependants to suit his taste. (The synecdochic "hearts" reminds us of lines in *Antony and Cleopatra:* "The hearts / That spannell'd me at heels . . ." [IV.xii.20–21].*) The musical figure at once gives way to the figure of the trunk smothered in ivy, more usually an image of close friendship but here more accurately agricultural. We are well accustomed to such flurries of metaphor, but here the effect seems enfeebled like the tree, sacrificed to the representation of agitated speech; the long sentence with its complex grammar, its refusal of end-stopped lines, its relatively unimpressive, shifting figures, certainly achieves that, but at some cost to the auditor.

> He being thus lorded,
> Not only with what my revenue yielded,
> But what my power might else exact—like one
> Who having into truth, by telling of it,
> Made such a sinner of his memory
> To credit his own lie—he did believe
> He was indeed the Duke, out o' th' substitution,
> And executing th' outward face of royalty
> With all prerogative. Hence his ambition growing—
> Dost thou hear?
>
> (97–106)

The difficulty begins with "like one / Who having into truth . . ." By "into" we must understand "unto": who, by living a lie, had made his memory such a sinner against truth that he came to believe his own lie. But this is surely unnecessarily awkward, and the syntax of this long sentence is again a tribute more to Prospero's agitated state of mind than to any kind of expository clarity. The

*See above, p. 226.

speech breaks off without promise of a conclusion, with no vigour of metaphor, only repetitive statements concerning Antonio's perfidy and ambition.

What follows immediately is a metaphor, as if the lack of such had forced itself on the speaker's attention: "To have no screen between this part he play'd / And him he play'd it for, he needs will be / Absolute Milan" (107–9). The "screen" image is not clearly worked out. Prospero begins to say, "To have no screen between the office of duke and the title of duke" (where the screen is Prospero himself); but the sense is altered and the screen, standing between the dukedom and Prospero, is now Antonio. In the first use the screen is an impediment to Antonio's ambition; in the second it represents Antonio's function as regent, screening Prospero from the world. But the trouble such writing gives the auditor or reader is not well spent, and the puzzle hardly seems worth solving.

What can be said of this performance is that by abolishing the great gap in time between the early events and the arrival of Prospero's enemies on his island Shakespeare has forfeited immediacy; there is no vivid contrast between past and present; Prospero's angry account of his brother's treachery has little of the savage actuality of Leontes's sudden outburst, since the usurpation (except in so far as the murder plot of Antonio and Sebastian recapitulates it) belongs to the dark backward and abysm of time, not, terrifyingly, to the moment represented. Moreover, Prospero is entirely in control of events, and the play cannot convey, like *Pericles,* a sense that Chance or Providence is in charge of all the tragedy and loss, all the wanderings, that come to an end in recognition and forgiveness.

The account of Prospero and the baby Miranda in the "rotten carcass of a butt" introduces a romance quality to the verse; they cry conventionally to the sea that roars, sigh to the winds that sigh back. Gonzalo, in good romance style, has handsomely supplied their craft with "Rich garments, linens, stuffs, and necessaries" (164), and also with the magic books required for the present operation.

Miranda sleeps, and Ariel is the next interlocutor; he gives a brilliant account of his electrical feats during the storm and the safety of the ship and its passengers, now dispersed about the island. Ariel is expressly not human, and one of the achievements of the play is to have him observe human beings from a perspective that is fairy-like; knowing and partly understanding their behaviour but finding it strange, like Puck. The little picture of Ferdinand gives this idea immediately:

The King's son have I landed by himself,
Whom I left cooling of the air with sighs,
In an odd angle of the isle, and sitting,
His arms in this sad knot.

(221–24)

The small, sympathetic caricature is a sketch of a mourning human made by one who is merely familiar with the notion that humans feel sorrow and express it in their own ways. The oddness of the angle is reflected in the knot of the strange young man's folded arms; he is cooling the air with sighs like a Petrarchan lover, or like Miranda and her father sighing back to the wind in their little boat. Ariel's account of his journey for dew to "the still-vex'd Bermoothes" (229) has other values (it introduces the New World element so important in the play), but in its place it has an exotic, idiosyncratic charm; he is granted just the clear voice Prospero lacks, but is at once scolded as a bad servant, a "malignant thing" (257), reminded of his painful servitude to Sycorax, mother of Caliban, and threatened with a repetition of the travail from which Prospero had released him, to live pegged in the entrails of a tree.

Prospero is even less polite to Caliban. This character is very properly celebrated as one of Shakespeare's most remarkable inventions. For a master of language invents a character who needs to be taught language, who is willing to deal with the problems of one who acquires language without acquiring its social contexts of respect and privilege. Thersites, in *Troilus and Cressida,* calls Ajax "a very land-fish, languageless, a monster" (III.iii.263) because Ajax's vainglory has prevented him from making elementary discriminations of rank, and so forth. Words like these of Thersites are of course applied to Caliban, though he is a wild man, a man of the forest rather than a fish, and he has learned language, though his use of it is distinguished from that of his betters. His first speech illustrates his point that the profit he has from learning language is that he can curse, rather like that other outsider Coriolanus: "As wicked dew as e'er my mother brush'd / With raven's feather from unwholesome fen / Drop on you both! A south-west blow on ye, / And blister you all o'er!" (I.ii.321–24). But he can, as everybody knows, say a great deal in a very different key. What he lacks and always will is an understanding of the conditions that must prevail for the making of what the philosopher J. L. Austin called felicitous speech-acts.

His language is no more conformable with Prospero's than his attitude to sex suits Miranda. His complaint against the imperialistic pretensions of

Prospero has of late received a good deal of attention from critics, who as a rule have less to say about the skill with which the writing expresses a kind of *nativeness* that is, in the exoticism of its detail, as magical as the feats of Ariel.

Shakespeare borrowed much detail from the travellers who found that the "Bermudas," far from being "the most dangerous infortunate, and most forlorne place of the world" were "in truth the richest, healthfullest and pleasing land . . . [that] ever man set foot on."* The "Bermudas" were hard to get to, and one navigator, William Strachey, commanded a ship that was run on to the shore and wedged between two rocks; but once ashore the colonisers found the natives obliging and supplies ample. They claimed to have encountered very little in the way of fairies and devils.

However, the model for the typical New World native was the European wild man. How else could these exotic persons be visualised and understood? Since Alonso and his friends are on the way from Tunis to Naples, Caliban's island is presumably in the Mediterranean, and he is really the *homo selvaticus* of European tradition, with additional New World details. It is on this foundation that Shakespeare develops his unique character. His lust is as normal in savages who live outside the constraints of society as their knowledge of the food supply and their initial generosity. Prospero's attempts to make Caliban social by teaching him language and allowing him to live in the same cell as Miranda must fail. As Miranda rather forcefully puts it, "I endow'd thy purposes / With words that made them known. But thy vild race / (Though thou didst learn) had that in't which good natures / Could not abide to be with," to which Caliban's famous reply is "You taught me language, and my profit on't / Is, I know how to curse" (I.ii.357–64). Not the least offensive characteristic of colonialism was the assumption that the "Indian" had not a language but a brutish gabble.† Compelled to speak the language of civilization, to him another prison, all he can do is curse.

The idiolect that Shakespeare devised for Caliban has such depth and novelty that his representation of the peremptoriness, arrogance, and ill temper of Prospero seems shallow by comparison. Ariel is another wonder, a spirit who makes the carrying out of his orders an arcane, beautifully inhuman task. He

*From Sylvester Jourdain's *A Discovery of the Bermudas* (1610). The sentiment echoes William Strachey's *True Reportory of the Wracke,* which was written in 1610 though not published till 1625. It seems probable that Shakespeare saw it in manuscript.

†For some interesting reflections on this subject, see Stephen Greenblatt, *Learning to Curse* (1990), pp. 1–39.

leads in Ferdinand, and between his music and exotic songs ("Come unto these yellow sands" [375] and "Full fadom five" [397]), Ferdinand, now encountered for the first time, has his perfect speech, a blend of mourning and music that modern readers can hardly not associate with Eliot and *The Waste Land:*

> Where should this music be? I' th' air, or th' earth?
> It sounds no more; and sure it waits upon
> Some god o' th' island. Sitting on a bank,
> Weeping again the King my father's wrack,
> This music crept by me upon the waters,
> Allaying both their fury and my passion
> With its sweet air . . .
>
> (388–94)

The beauty of this depends much on the unexpected verb "crept"—it is as if the music came over the calmed water like a sea mist and had the same slow effect on the young man's grief. There follows Ariel's eery second song, in which the deep water transforms the supposedly dead king into coral and pearl. The conversion of eyes into pearls has just that touch of inhuman perception one associates with Ariel, and the speech of Ferdinand is drawn into this remoteness, the words of a young human with his arms in a sad knot. The meaningless refrains of landward, farmyard noises give way to the fainter ding-dong of the sea nymphs' knell, like the distant clang of a buoy.

The song absorbs Ferdinand, and it is at this point Miranda is first permitted to see him. "The fringed curtains of thine eye advance, / And say what thou seest yond," says Prospero. "What, is't a spirit?" asks Miranda (409–10). These words of Prospero's were condemned by Pope and Arbuthnot as "a piece of the grossest bombast," and Coleridge admitted that if they simply meant "Look what is coming yonder" they might be thought "to border on the ridiculous," but he defends them as appropriate to the moment when Miranda, still in a kind of dream, is invited to look at something absolutely new and extraordinary, which she will take for a spirit. The solemnity of Prospero's language is therefore, he says, "completely in character, recollecting his preternatural capacity, in which the most familiar objects in nature present themselves in a mysterious point of view."* This is brilliantly said; another way of putting it would be to say that the new, hieratic tone used by

*The Lectures of 1808 (Ninth Lecture, reported by J. P. Collier).

Prospero is appropriate to this moment of magical discovery, the display of a princess's future husband, a masque-like moment in a play that has several such. Assured of Ferdinand's humanity, Miranda still wants to call him "A thing divine" (419), and Ferdinand greets her with equal solemnity: "Most sure, the goddess / On whom these airs attend!" (422–23). Each of the Romance heroines is mistaken for a goddess, in a tradition that goes back at least to Virgil,* who was himself remembering a passage in the *Odyssey.* The Virgilian lines were often imitated in Renaissance literature, but Shakespeare, who drew on the *Aeneid* more than once in this play, was looking directly at Virgil.

Prospero welcomes the success of his contrivance but characteristically treats Ferdinand "ungently" (445), explaining that he thinks "too light winning" would make "the prize light" (452–53). So he calls Ferdinand a traitor, threatens him with base imprisonment, and strikes him motionless when he tries to resist, meanwhile simulating a just fury. Ferdinand is again spellbound ("My spirits, as in a dream, are all bound up" [487]).

The splendour of this first act proceeds from the language of Ariel and Ferdinand, not from Prospero, although he arranged the whole thing. Act II introduces a different and less amiable group. Gonzalo is making the best of their plight while Antonio and Sebastian sneer at him. The prose rhythm of their dialogue is in complete contrast to the verse we have just heard, with its alternations of anger and trance. Only at line 107, as Alonso interrupts them to talk of his bereavement, does verse return, and once again with a touch of that new-minted maritime dialect: "what strange fish / Hath made his meal on thee?" (113–14). He wins no sympathy from Sebastian: "The fault's your own" (136).

Gonzalo attempts consolation with his fantasy of a utopian commonwealth, in a speech celebrated as evidence that Shakespeare knew his Montaigne. Gonzalo is dreaming of a just society, an ideal commonwealth such as might be found among virtuous, uncorrupted natural men, a fantasy associated with "soft" primitivism as against the "hard" variety that regarded the state of nature as solitary, poor, nasty, brutish, and short. He is providing easy targets for the cynical comments of Antonio and Sebastian; they sneer at him, but he keeps them out of mischief, and it is when Gonzalo falls asleep that they are free to plot murder.

*Aeneas meets his mother, Venus: *o, quam te memorem, virgo? namque haud tibi voltus / mortalis, nec vox hominem sonat: o dea certe!* (Maiden, by what name should I call thee? for thy face is not mortal, and thy voice does not sound human. Surely you are a goddess.)

Coleridge was probably the first to point out that at this point the verse is reminiscent of *Macbeth:*

ANT. Th' occasion speaks thee, and
My strong imagination sees a crown
Dropping upon thy head.
SEB. What? art thou waking?
ANT. Do you not hear me speak?
SEB. I do, and surely
It is a sleepy language, and thou speak'st
Out of thy sleep. What is it thou didst say?
This is a strange repose, to be asleep
With eyes wide open—standing, speaking, moving—
And yet so fast asleep.
ANT. Noble Sebastian,
Thou let'st thy fortune sleep—die, rather; wink'st
Whiles thou art waking.

(II.i.207–17)

Here murderous ambition is indeed *Macbeth*-like, but the repetition of "sleep" (as if Gonzalo's nap prompted it) casts a distinctive shadow over the whole; the language is sleepy, on the border of sleep and waking ("wink'st" means "you keep your eyes shut"). It lacks the intensity of the Macbeths as they plan the killing of Duncan, but the conspirators grow alert and the tone of the verse alters, with an effect like that of slowly waking from a dream: Ferdinand is dead; who is the next heir? Claribel, she who is stranded in Tunis, "she that from Naples / Can have no note . . . till new-born chins / Be rough and razorable" (247–50):

she that from whom
We all were sea-swallow'd, though some cast again
(And that by destiny) to perform an act
Whereof what's past is prologue, what to come
In yours and my discharge.

(250–54)

Now they are actors in a play; they have survived the wreck, as if to fulfil a duty prescribed by the destiny that saved them. The script is written, the prologue spoken, all they need now do is to play their prescribed parts. Destiny is the playwright; the plot was prepared long ago. This rapid working out of the theatrical analogy is good mature Shakespeare; and it stirs in one's mind the deep-seated parallel between the notion of destiny and the role of the author who plans ahead and writes parts appropriate to his cast. Sebastian is persuaded to imitate the conscienceless Antonio and kill his brother; the attempt is forestalled by Ariel. The entire plot is no more than a dreamlike interlude, an episode, indeed, in Prospero's plot; it lasts just as long as Gonzalo's brief sleep, shaken off at Ariel's orders.

The tormented Caliban is introduced to Trinculo and Stephano, with much comic business (II.ii); the serious point is Caliban's willingness to serve them, expressed in verse and with a sure sense of the peculiar mixed resources available: crabs, pig-nuts, jays and "marmazets," filberts and "scamels," whatever they are. He celebrates admission to this new, drunken company with a drunken song of illusory freedom, followed, after his exit, by Ferdinand, doing the Caliban-like work of bearing logs; he has not transported many when Miranda enters and there is a scene of pure love, evidence that Prospero's plot is going well.

Ferdinand has the advantage in experience, for Miranda has never seen a man except her father and Ferdinand, and the point is touchingly made ("How features are abroad / I am skilless of" [III.i.52–53]); she is inexperienced but not naïve, educated but more candid than another young woman might be:

> . . . but by my modesty
> (The jewel in my dower), I would not wish
> Any companion in the world but you;
> Nor can imagination form a shape,
> Besides yourself, to like of.
>
> (III.i.53–57)

She emphasises her chastity, as her father would wish, but declares her love and her inability even to fantasise a lover more desirable. Ferdinand replies in kind; Prospero, secretly looking on, approves.

The scene in which Ariel interrupts Caliban and his new masters is just a series of music-hall jokes until Caliban comments on Ariel's music. The famous speech may look back to an ancient idea, that even beasts, the less than human, can be moved by music, but even so it surprises us; such sympathy as we are encouraged to feel for Caliban has depended on our resenting

Prospero's bullying and his evident exploitation of him as servant. Now Caliban responds to music as good men are supposed to do who have it in their souls. Stephano lacks it, reflecting only that he will have his music for nothing in his brave new kingdom, but Caliban speaks of it as magical, and as a promise, given in a dream, of harmony:

> Be not afeard, the isle is full of noises,
> Sounds, and sweet airs, that give delight and hurt not.
> Sometimes a thousand twangling instruments
> Will hum about mine ears; and sometimes voices,
> That if I then had wak'd after long sleep,
> Will make me sleep again, and then in dreaming,
> The clouds methought would open, and show riches
> Ready to drop upon me, that when I wak'd
> I cried to dream again.
>
> (III.ii.135–43)

He has learned language for other reasons than to curse. The pleasing sounds happen often enough, and some are especially remembered; hence the switches of tense: the sounds give delight, the instruments "will hum" (meaning that it is their custom to do so, it happens often); but then he recalls a particular instance when he was put to sleep, dreamed again, woke again, and cried to have the dream again. Sleeping, dreaming, waking, sleeping: the rhythm is of a child's rhyme, and the "riches" are of another world, a richer world than Prospero's.

Music has a different function in the scene of the banquet (III.iii). Spirits, gentler than humans, provide it, accompanied by *"Solemn and strange music."* The King's party interprets the show as kindly, but it isn't; "Praise in departing" (39), says Prospero aside, looking forward to the sequel. Ariel appears as a harpy, accompanied by thunder and lightning, and *"with a quaint device the banquet vanishes."** The sinners are confronted with themselves, and Ariel spells this out:

*This magically disappearing feast derives from the *Aeneid,* iii.225–28:

> *at subitae horrifico lapsu de montibus adsunt*
> *Harpyiae et magnis quatiunt clangoribus alas,*
> *diripiuntque dapes contactuque omnia foedant*
> *immundo . . .*

(But suddenly, descending horribly from the mountains, the Harpies are upon us, with loud clamours they shake their wings and tear apart the feast, fouling every dish with their unclean touch.)

You are three men of sin, whom Destiny,
That hath to instrument this lower world
And what is in't, the never-surfeited sea
Hath caus'd to belch up you . . .

(III.iii.53–56)

That Destiny has the lower world as its instrument is proper not only to romance but to the ethic that animates it; here it uses the sea, but, as Ariel goes on to explain, "The pow'rs, delaying (not forgetting), have / Incens'd the seas and shores—yea, all the creatures, / Against your peace" (73–75). The show is a call to repentance issued in the severest possible language. The immediate effect on Alonso is to drive him crazy with guilt, and he runs off to the seaside to join his supposedly drowned son:

O, it is monstrous! monstrous!
Methought the billows spoke, and told me of it;
The winds did sing it to me, and the thunder,
That deep and dreadful organ-pipe, pronounc'd
The name of Prosper; it did base my trespass.
Therefore my son i' th' ooze is bedded; and
I'll seek him deeper than e'er plummet sounded,
And with him there lie mudded.

(95–102)

The force of this tremendous passage derives from a combination of Ariel's music and his summoning of all the "instruments" of destiny as witnesses to guilt and agents of punishment. Alonso's speech takes the form of a kind of world-music, the speech of the sea caught up in the singing of the wind, the thunder providing the deep and terrifying bass, the whole a chorus of condemnation. Thus confronted with his guilt, Alonso seeks what seems the only possible relief, to join the son he believes drowned as a consequence of his sin. Antonio and Sebastian are defiant, but as Gonzalo sees, they are also desperate. And there Act III ends.

Ferdinand's sufferings, though Prospero calls them austere, are brief enough. Now released from servitude, he has only to undertake to respect Miranda's virginity until they are married. The masque follows, interrupted (as somehow it must be) by Prospero's remembering he still has to deal with the conspiracy of Caliban and Stephano.

The disappearance of the dancers *"to a strange, hollow, and confused noise"* (IV.i.138) gives rise to the famous speech "Our revels now are ended" (148ff.). A passage may be too well known to be well known, and this one is inevitably mixed up with speculations about Shakespeare's farewell to the stage. It restates the old topic of life, our world, as a dream, often hinted at in the play that has just ended. And the idea of comparing plays and actors to the dissolving pageant of dreams is ancient. There is much sleeping in this play (Miranda, Gonzalo, Caliban) and to suggest that life is a dream, that we "are such stuff as dreams are made on" and that our "little life is rounded with a sleep," is not to make a dashing new metaphor; however, the word is "rounded," not "ended," as if the whole course of life and death were a single entity; or perhaps, as Stephen Orgel proposes, "rounded" means "surrounded" ("our little life . . . being a brief awakening from an eternal sleep").* Certainly the very existence of plays, pageants, actors can induce in Shakespeare reflections of this sort.

But Prospero still needs to act in the other sense, to bring the play he is in to a close. Ariel gives a lively account of the tricks he has played on Stephano and his companions: they follow him "As they smelt music" (178), and they are now hunted by spirits *"in shape of dogs and hounds"* (254), a fate befitting their status. Now, at the end of Act IV, Prospero can say, "At this hour / Lies at my mercy all mine enemies" (262–63). His "project," as he calls it—as if he were an alchemist—is gathering to a head (V.i.1); the play, like the project, can now reach its end.

Prospero rather sourly declares his determination to forgive: prompted by Ariel's remark that he would pity Prospero's enemies "were he human," the mage states, "The rarer action is / In virtue than in vengeance" (V.i.27–28) (again a not uncommon position, here given rather gnomic utterance).

Having said farewell to anger, he says farewell also to magic. His second most celebrated speech is a renunciation of the powers he has used in bringing on the climax of this action. "Ye elves of hills, brooks, standing lakes, and groves" (33ff.) is a splendid set piece that owes a great deal to a speech of Medea in Ovid's *Metamorphoses* (vii.197–209). Ovid was always Shakespeare's favourite classical author, and here he looks to the Latin as well as to Arthur Golding's translation of 1567. Medea is a sorceress as well as an infanticide. The magic that Prospero abjures is "rough," and is said to include raising the

*See *The Tempest* (Oxford edition), p. 181.

dead. What is to follow is not a loftier magic but the resumption of mortal humanity: the breaking of the staff, the drowning of the book. The resumption of his formal clothing as Duke of Milan will ensure that he will be no longer a mage, only a duke.

One last demand for heavenly music finds Alonso and his friends within a magic circle, charmed, tranced; as the charm dissolves, Prospero addresses them in turn. Ariel celebrates his imminent freedom and is sent to look after the mariners, asleep in their ship. (Once more we have sleepers, people in trances; the play will not let us forget sleep, dreams, trances.) Prospero's forgiveness of his brother is notoriously not very gracious ("For you, most wicked sir, whom to call brother / Would even infect my mouth, I do forgive / Thy rankest fault" [130–32]). Firmly in control, he toys with Alonso, claiming to have lost a daughter as Alonso has lost a son, whereupon the lovers are discovered playing chess (another of the "discoveries" that punctuate this play). It is rightly thought Shakespearian that Sebastian should be given the exclamation "A most high miracle!" (177) and Ferdinand, the lucky lover, the key lines of the piece: "Though the seas threaten, they are merciful; / I have curs'd them without cause" (178–79).

Now, as the details of recognition are registered, Miranda makes her celebrated remark: "O wonder! / How many goodly creatures are there here! / How beauteous mankind is! O brave new world / That has such people in't!" (181–84) and Prospero his disillusioned reply: "'Tis new to thee." Miranda's lines have depth; she can see what her father has learned not to see. The comparison she has in mind is with Caliban and possibly her father; she does not know that the beauteous are likely also to be corrupt. The remorse of Alonso and the rejoicing of Gonzalo set the tone for these recognitions; as Gonzalo says they are divinely appointed (201–4). After so much practice Shakespeare knew how to achieve the right rapt tone for these conclusions: "O, rejoice / Beyond a common joy, and set it down / With gold on lasting pillars" (206–8).

The sailors arrive to be included, waking from their deep sleep to find their ship in wonderful shape, though they are immediately entranced and in another dream. The thieving drunks are then produced. Sycorax is mentioned as a witch having much the same powers as Prospero, described in the same passage of Ovid concerning Medea. As to her son, "this thing of darkness I / Acknowledge mine," says Prospero (275–76). He had made the mistake of offering nurture to one on whose nature it would never stick, civility and language to one incapable of receiving it. The play has hinted qualifications to this, but Caliban now says he has learned something and will "seek for grace."

The Epilogue—one of ten of Shakespeare's that survive—is a conventional appeal for applause. There is no good reason to believe that this example of the genre is dedicated to personal allegory. Prospero says he is now an actor without a part, a magician without magic; the spell he is under is a spell of disapproval and can be broken only by applause, which he prays the audience to provide. The Epilogue is neatly tied to the themes and language of the play—charms, spells, enchantment, bands, a project, a ship, an act of forgiveness. It is delivered by an ex-magician who, having renounced his powers, can only with the help of the audience get back to Naples (unlikely, here, to be a figurative version of Stratford).

A "disciplined passion of curiosity," said Henry James, and to think about the style of *The Tempest* is to have some sense of his meaning. After the awkward moments of the exposition, its linguistic discipline is extraordinary. Of course there are passages where the business is to carry forward narrative and no spectacular effects are called for. But the irruptions of Ariel, for whom, as for Caliban, a new dramatic language had to be invented; the pervasiveness of music; the quiet verbal insistence on dream, on spirit, on sea give *The Tempest* qualities that are in the end beyond description, and have for so long made it an object of something like veneration. Attempts to provide it with a close relationship to the author's life are a mark of that respect; and so, one hopes, are the readings that exaggerate the play's relevance to Jacobean colonialism. Of course it cannot be said that neither of these relationships exists, only that they are secondary to the beautiful object itself.

HENRY VIII *and* THE TWO NOBLE KINSMEN

The argument about the authorship of *Henry VIII* is a century and a half old and shows no sign of settlement. That it was included in the First Folio gives some colour to the view that it is Shakespeare's alone, but it is not a decisive consideration, and the weight of evidence, nowadays often very technical, is in favour of joint authorship by Shakespeare and John Fletcher, with perhaps some help from Francis Beaumont. The play is securely dated 1613, and the Globe burned down during a performance on 9 June 1613, when the play was still new.

The Two Noble Kinsmen was not included in the Folio and was first published in a quarto of 1634. The title page ascribes it to "William Shakespeare and John Fletcher." It has been argued that Shakespeare wrote it alone, but the evidence for collaboration is strong, though agreement about the exact limits of Shakespeare's share is hard to achieve.* However, one can feel reasonably confident that certain scenes in either play are by Shakespeare, whoever wrote the rest of them; and of those scenes one has to say that they often have the faults characteristic of the latest Shakespeare, and have them to a degree probably not matched in his earlier work.

*For up-to-date discussions of the possibilities and the difficulties in determining authorship and shares in these plays, see *Henry VIII,* ed. John Margeson (New Cambridge edition, 1990), pp. 4–14, and *The Two Noble Kinsmen,* ed. Lois Potter (Arden edition, 1997), pp. 24–34.

Henry VIII, or, to give it its alternative title, *All Is True,* displays, in the parts of it that seem certainly to be Shakespeare's, what the Oxford editors call "grammatical muscularity."* It is an episodic history play, beginning with the fall of the Duke of Buckingham as contrived by Cardinal Wolsey; the King's divorce and his preference for Anne Bullen over his first wife, Katherine; Wolsey's disgrace; the coronation of Anne and the birth of her daughter, Elizabeth; the King's promotion of Thomas Cranmer and the new favourite's escape from a plot to overthrow him; and, finally, the baptism of Elizabeth, with a prophecy of her glorious future.

These events are enacted with notable energy and strong characterisation. Shakespeare's earlier history plays ended with the accession of Henry VII, but this one, in describing the reign of his son, was presenting to an audience all of whom had lived under Elizabeth I—dead only ten years or so—an account of the circumstances of her birth. Her very existence was a defiance of Rome, and her long reign, though full of religious conflict, saw the end of the Marian Catholic persecutions and the establishment of the Church of England. The early part of the reign of James I was marked by a revival of interest in the dead Queen's achievements; she had presided over the establishment of England as an imperial power and won a victory over the Pope, now seen as Antichrist. King Henry VIII's divorce was a happy one (though not for Katherine), in that it made possible the birth of this incomparable Queen.

King James liked to be thought a peace-maker, and he wanted peace with Spain, the great Catholic enemy; so the Spanish Katherine is treated tenderly, with much attention to the sadness of her fate.† The King's theological scruples concerning the legality of his marriage to the widow of his brother are given their place, but so is his imperious passion for Anne. Above all, the play is a vindication of Protestantism, and its conception is plausibly related to the marriage celebration, in February 1613, of James's daughter Elizabeth to the

*Wells and Taylor, *A Textual Companion,* p. 134. The editors also believe that Heminge and Condell, and everybody else until they came along, gave the play the false title by which most people still know it; they prefer *All Is True.*

†See Frances Yates, *Shakespeare's Last Plays: A New Approach* (1975), and other historical readings reported in the Cambridge edition, pp. 26–32. A good brief account of the unusual liberties the play takes with the historical events as described by Holinshed is by Herschel Baker in *The Riverside Shakespeare,* p. 1023; a longer discussion is by Bullough, in *Narrative and Dramatic Sources of Shakespeare,* Vol. IV (1962), pp. 443–48.

Protestant Elector of Bohemia. It would seem that at the time of its writing the play had a more acute historical and political interest than any of the earlier history plays.

The opening passages are beyond doubt Shakespearian. Norfolk's description of the ceremonies at the Field of the Cloth of Gold may bring to mind some passages of *Antony and Cleopatra,* and certainly do not lack "muscularity":

> Men might say
> Till this time pomp was single, but now married
> To one above itself. Each following day
> Became the next day's master, till the last
> Made former wonders its. To-day the French,
> All clinquant, all in gold, like heathen gods,
> Shone down the English; and, to-morrow, they
> Made Britain India: every man that stood
> Show'd like a mine. Their dwarfish pages were
> As cherubins, all gilt; the madams too,
> Not us'd to toil, did almost sweat to bear
> The pride upon them, that their very labor
> Was to them as a painting. Now this masque
> Was cried incomparable; and th' ensuing night
> Made it a fool and beggar.
>
> (I.i.14–28)

Norfolk is an enemy of Wolsey, who "set the body and limbs / Of this great sport together" (46–47), and a touch of irony contributes to his excess, but the verse has that tortured, involuted quality I have noted elsewhere. The idea is of pomp marrying pomp and being the stronger for it, or, as Johnson put it, "Pomp is only married to pomp, but the new pomp is greater than the old." He calls the passage "a noisy periphrase."* One single pomp seems to be greater than the other, its nationality not specified (and presumably changing from day to day). The complexity of this idea seems much beyond its value; nothing much is gained by the introduction of the notion that one day marries another "above itself," and little by adding that "Each following day / Became

**Johnson on Shakespeare,* p. 634.

the next day's master" (where "next" means "the one before" and the culminating point is that the last day owned all the others). The awkward terminal possessive reinforces the sense that nothing above the ordinary is being said, though it seems to cultivate an appearance of meeting exceptional lexical and metaphorical demands.

The point about the gilded pages and sweating ladies is better made and amusing. But Norfolk continues in the knotty vein, so that as one reads one is always pausing (as audiences cannot) to work out what he is saying and to wonder why he is doing it so obscurely:

> As I belong to worship and affect
> In honor honesty, the tract of ev'ry thing
> Would by a good discourser lose some life,
> Which action's self was tongue to.
>
> (39–42)

These lines mean that he is prepared to swear that even an expert raconteur could not, in his description of it, equal the thing itself as it was. The personification of action, the redundant affirmation of his honour and honesty, the affected "tract"—all this is typical of the muscle-bound contortions of the late Shakespeare's language. The remainder of the opening scene carries a load of explanation and is more business-like, though the style is heavily parenthetical, as if, even in simple exposition, there was always some qualification or second thought one had better not leave unsaid.

The fine second scene contains the Queen's protest against Wolsey and the King's response to the accuser of Buckingham, strongly written though occasionally obscure. Before Buckingham's trial there is comment on new fashions, and a prime example of what this play offers more than any other, spectacle—the feast given by Wolsey, and the masque.

The opening of Act II is the first scene in which the tone and quality of the verse are distinctly different. Its centrepiece is the farewell speech of Buckingham, which, from its opening lines, announces the change of key:

> All good people,
> You that thus far have come to pity me,
> Hear what I say, and then go home and lose me.
> I have this day receiv'd a traitor's judgment,
> And by that name must die; yet, heaven bear witness,

And if I have a conscience, let it sink me,
Even as the axe falls, if I be not faithful!

(55–61)

The characteristic feminine endings, giving each line a sort of dying fall at its end, are already established, their elegiac quality contrasted with the rough "masculine" force of that opening scene (or of *Coriolanus* or indeed of Prospero's expository speeches in *The Tempest*). This is a manner normally associated with Fletcher, though I suppose it would not have been beyond Shakespeare to achieve, if he wanted, a softly elegiac tone, such as is required here and in the later scenes of Wolsey's disgrace. The transition from one manner to the other is particularly marked in III.ii, where Shakespeare is commonly credited with the first 203 lines, the remainder being left to Fletcher. The scene describes the King's reaction to the discovery that Wolsey has been lavishly lining his pockets as well as working secretly against his master's matrimonial plans. It is mostly lively and effective narrative. Not knowing that the King has been given written evidence of his treachery, Wolsey meditates, aside, against the presumption of Anne Bullen and her friends:

The late Queen's gentlewoman? a knight's daughter?
To be her mistress' mistress? the Queen's queen?
This candle burns not clear, 'tis I must snuff it,
Then out it goes. What though I know her virtuous
And well deserving? yet I know her for
A spleeny Lutheran, and not wholesome to
Our cause, that she should lie i' th' bosom of
Our hard-rul'd king. Again, there is sprung up
An heretic, an arch-one, Cranmer; one
Hath crawled into the favor of the King,
And is his oracle.

(94–104)

This is serviceable Shakespeare of the late period, not the kind of excited meditation we find in Aufidius or Prospero but a persuasive representation of thoughts turned over in the mind. The run-ons between lines 98 and 99, and more particularly from 99 to 100 and from 100 to 101, almost give the effect of prose divided as verse, of a marked, easy informality. All four lines, 98–101, end in prepositions, which hardly permit more than the slightest pause.

Yet Wolsey's manner is described by Norfolk (111–19) as agitated ("In most strange postures / We have seen him set himself" [118–19]). The King, having in his hand the evidence of Wolsey's earthly ambition, declines to believe these contortions have religious causes; he accosts him ironically and teases him into extravagant expression of allegiance and devotion before thrusting at him the papers that prove his guilt: "Read o'er this, / And after, this, and then to breakfast with / What appetite you have" (201–3).

This passage of dialogue, well managed, tinged with royal ironies, getting its business done, is again marked with weak endings and run-on lines, though it is rarely as self-involved as the verse of the act's opening scene. At its end the stage clears, and Wolsey soliloquises, now in a very different tone. He sees from the papers that his personal wealth has been made known to the King, and that his dealings with Rome in the matter of the King's marriage are also uncovered. And here, at line 222, the tone of valediction, the elegy for one's own greatness, is re-established:

Nay then, farewell!
I have touch'd the highest point of all my greatness,
And, from that full meridian of my glory,
I haste now to my setting. I shall fall
Like a bright exhalation in the evening,
And no man see me more.

(222–27)

The figure, though fine, is simply expounded, not self-involved; his career has been like a meteor, supposed to be caused by an escape of terrestrial gases that burn up when they reach the sphere of fire (perhaps with allusion to his rise from humble birth, so resented by the noblemen at court). Wolsey is now allowed a dignified resistance to the demands of his exultant enemies. After their altercation the stage is again cleared and a sort of aria, akin to Buckingham's, brings Wolsey to the end of his remarkable career: "Farewell? a long farewell to all my greatness!" (351).

In the simplicity of language in this celebrated speech, in the slow working out of its figures, it bears a stronger resemblance to the meditations of Henry VI than to the Machiavellian contortions of much verse in *Henry VIII*. There is the slowly evolved imagery of promise and failure—tender leaves of hope, full-blown honours, nipping frost, the death of the hopeful plant (352–58)—then the image of boys swimming on bladders, out of their depth, at "the mercy / Of a rude stream" (363–64). A general reflection on fallen greatness brings the speech to a close. The reprise at the end of the scene is for the benefit of Cromwell: "Cromwell, I charge thee, fling away ambition! / By that sin fell the angels" (440–41).

With the falls of Buckingham and Cromwell and the blessed demise of the Queen (heralded by a masque-like heavenly vision [IV.ii]) the play has depicted the fated falls of the great rather in the manner of the old "tragedies" such as *A Mirror for Magistrates,* in which the ghosts of noble personages return to recount their falls. The twist to this plot lies in the treatment of Cranmer, who by the King's grace survives the plot against him; he survives to christen the Princess Elizabeth and reform the liturgy (there is here no hint of his ultimate fate at the hands of Henry's successor, Mary). In the play the last days of Katherine are contemporary with the coronation of the new Queen, with more opportunities for theatrical display.

The voice of the opening scene of Act I is heard again at the beginning of Act V; muscularity characterises the words even of the Old Lady who comes to announce the birth of the Princess. But the play ends with Cranmer's long encomium of the child and his prophecy of her greatness. This speech (V.iv.14–55) is not surprisingly thought by some to lay it on too thick as a compliment to the Virgin Queen Elizabeth and also to James:

. . . as when
The bird of wonder dies, the maiden phoenix,
Her ashes new create another heir
As great in admiration as herself,
So shall she leave her blessedness to one
(When heaven shall call her from this cloud of darkness)
Who from the sacred ashes of her honor
Shall star-like rise as great in fame as she was,
And so stand fix'd.

(39–47)

The effect is of a sermon preached before the monarch by his archbishop, and properly so; Cranmer, as we know, was a master of style and of occasion. The speech is full of appropriately biblical references and has a quasi-liturgical grandeur, which is after all in character.

Henry VIII is an odd play, very skilful. The character of the King is strongly drawn, the pathos and dignity of Katherine is understandably celebrated, the farewells of Buckingham and Wolsey can please a crowd. There are valuable tensions in the structure: between the King's conscience and his desires, between the two Queens (Anne represented as innocent and without ambition; Katherine as regal, abused, and unhappy). And the contrasts between the moods of the verse, whether or not the differences arise from differences in authorship, reflect that structural tension. But in so far as Shakespeare was involved, he was writing with muscularity but also, it is possible to think, carelessly, writing far too many of those passages censured by Dr. Johnson—as if he had no more time to bestow upon them. If anybody was going to sort them out it would not be himself; the job was left to his careworn editors.

The Two Noble Kinsmen breaks the association of Shakespeare with the original Globe Theatre; it may have been performed in the new one, opened in June 1614, but it was probably performed at the Blackfriars. It must have been liked, since it is known to have been played in 1619, and the Quarto edition was published as late as 1634. As with *Henry VIII,* the question of authorship and shares remains contested, but it seems that in general Shakespeare is to be credited with Act I and the first scene of Acts II, III, and V, and the last two scenes.

Charles Lamb may have overstated the contrasts, but his comparison between the manner of Fletcher and that of Shakespeare has some justice: "[Fletcher's] ideas move slow; his versification, though sweet, is tedious; it stops every moment; he lays line upon line, making up one after the other, adding image to image so deliberately that we see where they join: Shakespeare mingles everything, he runs line into line, embarrasses sentences and metaphors; before one idea has burst its shell, another is hatched out and clamorous for disclosure."*

The terms of the comparison may be too favourable to Shakespeare: *The Two Noble Kinsmen* is a romance, light in texture and sometimes rather silly, and the style preferred by Lamb seems unsuited to it. A recent editor† suggests that at this stage of his working life, almost at its end, Shakespeare was somewhat under the influence of Donne, who had the habit, as Coleridge put it, of wreathing iron pokers into true love knots. It has been argued, defen-

*Quoted in Hallett Smith's Introduction in *The Riverside Shakespeare,* p. 1690.

†*The Two Noble Kinsmen,* ed. Lois Potter (Arden edition 1997), pp. 108–9.

sively, that "the age often found in incomprehensibility a positive virtue."* But Donne was not writing for a theatre audience.

The speeches of the Three Queens at the beginning of the play have a right to be impassioned, as they communicate their desire to bury their husbands, but they tend to be complicated in expression:

O, my petition was
Set down in ice, which by hot grief uncandied
Melts into drops; so sorrow wanting form
Is press'd with deeper matter.

(I.i.106–9)

She means that in her earlier plea she had spoken too coldly; now her grief has melted the ice and she weeps. So far so good; Shakespeare more than once thought of ice as candy, as we have seen in *Antony and Cleopatra.* But what follows is very obscure and, if puzzled out, adds little to the sentiment; it seems to offer the generalisation that sorrow is harder to bear if it cannot find a form of expression. This Third Queen is particularly hard to understand:

There, through my tears,
Like wrinkled pebbles in a glassy stream,
You may behold 'em. Lady, lady, alack!
He that will all the treasure know o' th' earth
Must know the centre too; he that will fish
For my least minnow, let him lead his line
To catch one at my heart.

(111–17)

What are to be beheld are presumably "eyes"; but "'em" has no plural antecedent. The remainder of the statement is presumably meant to suggest the depth of her grief by comparing it to the centre of the earth, and by saying that to fish for it you would need to weight the line. There are more examples of unprofitable complexity in this play.† Here Arcite addresses his friend and enemy Palamon in V.i:

*Stephen Orgel, quoted in ibid., p. 109.
†See I.ii.93–98, I.iii.26–33.

I am in labor
To push your name, your ancient love, our kindred,
Out of my memory; and i' th' self-same place
To seat something I would confound. So hoist we
The sails that must these vessels port even where
The heavenly limiter pleases.

(25–30)

The verb "port" and the noun "limiter"* give the expression of this perfectly understandable idea connotations more obscure and mysterious than its occasion seems to require. The general idea is expressed by a confusion of the figure of labour pains, the figure of ships sailing in different directions, and the idea that he wants to put in the place of his friend Palamon an enemy of the same name. But even this last notion is not clear, for he presumably does not want the enemy only in his memory.

Arcite's speech to his knights (V.i.34ff.) contains lines that have baffled commentators, lines of which an audience would deserve congratulations if they caught the general drift. Some compensation may be found in the fineness of his address to Mars, with its odd reminiscence of *Macbeth:*

Thou mighty one, that with thy power hast turn'd
Green Neptune into purple, [whose approach]
Comets prewarn, whose havoc in vast field
Unearthed skulls proclaim, whose breath blows down
The teeming Ceres' foison, who dost pluck
With hand armipotent from forth blue clouds
The mason'd turrets, that both mak'st and break'st
The stony girths of cities: me thy pupil,
Youngest follower of thy drum, instruct this day
With military skill, that to thy laud
I may advance my streamer, and by thee
Be styl'd the lord o' th' day.

(V.i.49–60)

The incantatory, almost liturgical purpose of the speech limits the scope of involution; there is no doubling back, but a cumulative celebration of the

*The word in earlier English usually meant "a friar licensed to beg within certain limits" *(O.E.D.)*, but, though obviously rare, it could be used in a broader sense.

destructive power of war; the battlefields are strewn with unburied corpses, the ruined harvests, the cities besieged and destroyed; and finally there is apt petition for "military skill," and the dedication of success to the praise of the god. The strange words—"armipotent," "laud," and "streamer" [pennon]—are all slightly out of the common way yet within reasonable intellectual compass; "the lord o' th' day" gives the sense to a festive combat or tourney, which, despite its homicidal purpose, this joust amounts to. The passage is indebted to Arcite's prayer to Mars in Chaucer's *The Knight's Tale,* but it is grander and has it own rapt quality.

Since she is the sister of the military Hippolyta, Emily, the reason for the fight between the kinsmen, is perhaps entitled on occasion to speak with the masculine persuasive force of Shakespeare:

> Half-sights saw
> That Arcite was no babe. God's lid, his richness
> And costliness of spirit look'd through him, it could
> No more be hid in him than fire in flax,
> Than humble banks can go to law with waters
> That drift-winds force to raging.
>
> (V.iii.95–100)

Emily's oath ("God's [eye]lid") has surprised the commentators, and might seem to fall under the ban of the Act of 1606, but the terms in which she praises Arcite are even more striking. "Costliness," a redundant reinforcement to "richness," is odd, as it applies to his spirit, not his fine duelling clothes; the notion of a fine spirit looking through a person's body is now more familiar from some famous lines of Donne, written and published at just this time.* Emily, having expressed this idea, finds two similes to reinforce it: the fire in the flax and, more remote, the impossibility that riverbanks can go to law against flood tides. This last comparison is bizarre enough without the added difficulty that the rush of water is due to "drift winds." Editors plausibly guess that the word "drift" means "driving"; indeed, it is hard to see what else it could mean, but the usage is apparently unique; and considering Shakespeare's ease in converting nouns to verbs, it

*"We understood / Her by her sight; her pure and eloquent blood / Spoke in her cheeks, and so distinctly wrought / That one might almost say, her body thought." *Of the Progress of the Soul* (1612), lines 243–46.

may be worth while occasionally to consider that the effect, though undoubtedly striking and "muscular," is sometimes merely distracting. "Waters / That drift winds force to raging" might be defended on the ground that the language itself is being driven and forced, in imitation of flood water in spate; but in the end the inability of the banks to do anything about it has hardly any relation to the original idea, that Arcite's noble spirit "look'd through him."

Sometimes it seems that Shakespeare, in these latter years, is simply defying his audience, not caring to have them as fellows in understanding. One finds editors reduced to saying, "The idea is clear . . . but it is hard to make grammatical sense out of the lines."* It is a price we have to pay. Consider this:

> Here we are,
> And here the graces of our youths must wither
> Like a too-timely spring. Here age must find us,
> And which is heaviest, Palamon, unmarried.
> The sweet embraces of a loving wife,
> Loaden with kisses, arm'd with thousand Cupids,
> Shall never clasp our necks; no issue know us;
> No figures of ourselves shall we ev'r see
> To glad our age, and like young eagles teach 'em
> Boldly to gaze against bright arms, and say,
> "Remember what your fathers were, and conquer!"
>
> (II.ii.26–36)

This is the soft, explicit Fletcher, admirably skilful with his dying falls and his willingness to spell everything out. Presumably the managers of the King's Men could have made him a collaborator with Shakespeare, fifteen years his senior, and the author who, for fifteen years, had so astonishingly enlarged the drama and educated its audience. It must have been a strenuous experience for everybody involved. But now those who could afford it might relax at the Blackfriars to the tunes of Fletcher. Shakespeare sounds still as if the work of transformation was not done, that the testing of the audience (and himself) must go on. Did he overestimate their endurance, and ours; did he perhaps even exaggerate his own?

*Arden edition, at I.iii.72–74.

APPENDIX

Thirty-six of Shakespeare's plays were collected in the 1623 Folio (F, or, to distinguish it from later editions, F1). (*Pericles* and *The Two Noble Kinsmen,* later accepted into the canon, were not included.) Of the thirty-six, eighteen had not been printed previously. The remainder had appeared earlier in cheap quarto (Q) versions. Some of these, called "Bad Quartos," were unauthorized; others, published with the consent of Shakespeare's company, are called "Good Quartos."

Bad Quartos, mostly based on memorial reconstructions by actors, were condemned by the editors Heminge and Condell in their Preface to the Folio as "stolen and surreptitious copies, maimed and deformed by the frauds and stealths of injurious impostors." Good Quartos, based on copy held in the playhouse, obviously have greater relevance to the business of determining the text, though there are occasions when the Bad ones need to be looked at. For example, the Bad Quarto of *Hamlet* (Q1, 1603) has some interesting features, though it naturally lacks the authority of the Good Quarto (Q2, 1604–5) and the Folio text (F, 1623).

The relations between Quarto and Folio texts are sometimes extremely complicated. Editors of *Hamlet,* for instance, still have to make the difficult choice between Q2 and F, which differ quite substantially, as the basis of their texts; and they cannot quite ignore Q1.

The nature and quality of the copy that reached the printer varied considerably. No autograph copy of a Shakespeare play has survived, and details of the journey from the playwright's desk to the printing house often remain obscure, despite the ingenuity of scholars. "Foul papers" was the accepted term for what the author first wrote; usually somebody then made a fair copy to serve as the basis of the theatrical prompt-book, which had to be licensed by a court official, the Master of the Revels. Changes of various kinds could occur all along the line—in the transcripts, by order of the Master of the Revels, by the prompter, occasionally by the author himself, or someone else, revising the text. The printer's copy might consist of foul papers, a fair copy, a prompt-book, a scribal copy of that book, or, in illicit quartos, a botched-up version based on actors' memories. For some Folio plays it seems that the printer had as copy a printed Quarto with manuscript corrections or supplemented by manuscript material (a prompt-book, perhaps).

This is a dangerously simplified account of matters that are still keenly disputed, but it may serve for the present purposes. I have used some of the terms defined here when there are considerable differences between extant versions of such plays as *Hamlet, Othello* and *King Lear,* for it proved impossible to write about the language of the plays without taking some account of these variations.

ACKNOWLEDGEMENTS

During the writing of this book I was helped, in fair weather and foul, and beyond all reasonable expectation, by two friends, Anthony Holden and Ursula Owen. I hope they will think it just and pleasant to share the dedication.

My learned friend Edward Tayler of Columbia read the manuscript, and his generous annotations gave me a good idea of how fine his own Shakespeare book would be if he would only write it. Elisabeth Sifton, old friend and unrivalled editor, tried to ensure that I wrote decently and kept in mind my promise to address intelligent readers rather than specialists. I am grateful to all the above, and offer the usual assurance that they are entirely blameless.

INDEX

Note: Works are by Shakespeare unless otherwise identified.